FACES OF MUHAMMAD

Faces of Muhammad

WESTERN PERCEPTIONS OF THE
PROPHET OF ISLAM FROM THE
MIDDLE AGES TO TODAY

{≈≈W≈≈}

John V. Tolan

PRINCETON UNIVERSITY PRESS
PRINCETON & OXFORD

Published by Princeton University Press
41 William Street, Princeton, New Jersey 08540
6 Oxford Street, Woodstock, Oxfordshire OX20 1TR

press.princeton.edu

Library of Congress Control Number: 2019935406
ISBN: 978-0-691-16706-0

British Library Cataloging-in-Publication Data is available

Editorial: Fred Appel and Thalia Leaf
Production Editorial: Karen Carter
Jacket Design: Layla Mac Rory
Jacket Art: Shutterstock
Production: Jacqueline Poirier
Publicity: Tayler Lord and Kathryn Stevens
Copyeditor: Dawn Hall

This book has been composed in Miller

Printed on acid-free paper. ∞

Printed in the United States of America

10 9 8 7 6 5 4 3 2 1

To my teachers,
especially Irene Harney, Steve Bruemmer, Mark Hilgendorf,
Jim Kearny, John Stephens, and Bernie McGinn
and Rob Bartlett.

خُذِ الْعَفْوَ وَأْمُرْ بِالْعُرْافِ وَأَعْرِضْ عَنِ الْجَاهِلِينَ

*Take what is given freely, enjoin what is good,
and turn away from the ignorant.*

—QUR'ĀN 7:199

CONTENTS

ACKNOWLEDGMENTS

THIS BOOK IS THE FRUIT of a career working on the history of how European Christians have understood Islam and how they have made sense of its rival claims to the heritage of Abraham. More immediately, it is the result of a proposal by Fred Appel of Princeton University Press who saw the need for a scholarly overview of the history of European perceptions of the prophet of Islam. My thanks to Fred for his encouragement and for accompanying this project to completion.

I received generous assistance from the Kulturwissenschaftliches Kolleg at the University of Konstanz, where I had the honor and pleasure of serving as a research fellow from January to June of 2016, allowing me precious uninterrupted time for reading and research along the banks of the Rhine. My warm thanks to the extremely helpful staff, in particular Fred Girod, Christina Thoma, Daniela Göpfrich, and Carolin Schulz. Special thanks also to Dorothea Weltecke for inviting me to the Kolleg.

I have presented parts of this book in various seminars and conferences in Europe, North America, and Iran: in particular at the conference "Crossing Boundaries, Creating Images: In Search of the Prophet Muhammad in Literary and Visual Traditions" at the Kunsthistorisches Institut, Florence (2009); at the colloquium "Representations of Muhammad" at the University of Edinburgh (2015); at the conference "Mimetic Theory and Islam" at the University of Innsbruck (2016); at the workshop "The Prophet Muhammad in the Eyes of Europeans" at the University of Isfahan (2016); at the symposium "The Location of Europe: Shared and Divided Memories in the Global Age" at Schloss Herrenhausen, Hannover (2016); at the seminar "Logiques d'Empire" at the Université Jean Jaurès, Toulouse (2017); and at the symposium "Processes of Entanglement and Disentanglement" at the University of Münster (2017). Many thanks to those who participated in these events and prodded me to explore these issues in greater precision and depth and in particular to those who invited me: Daniel Baloup, Wolfram Drews, Etienne François,

Tony Gorman, Christiane Gruber, Asghar Montazerolghaem, Wolfgang Palaver, Thomas Serrier, and Avinoam Shalem.

Thanks to Ashley Miller for information on Louis Bouquet's painting of Muhammad and to Megan Holmes for help in tracking down images. Thanks to Alberto Saviello for help and advice concerning several images. Thanks to Ann Watt for precious biographical information concerning her father, Montgomery Watt. Special thanks to those who read and offered corrections and commentaries to earlier versions of one or more of the chapters of this book: Dominique Avon, Ruchama Johnston-Bloom, Nabil Matar, and Karen Spierling. And above all to those who read through the whole manuscript and gave valuable feedback: Andrea Celli, Ana Echevarria, Ziad Elmarsafy, Christiane Gruber, Suleiman Mourad, and Amy Remensnyder.

FACES OF MUHAMMAD

Introduction

ON OCTOBER 2, 1808, Johann Wolfgang von Goethe and Napoleon Bonaparte met in Erfurt. The two men discussed politics and chatted about literature. When Napoleon learned that Goethe had translated Voltaire's play *Mahomet, ou le fanatisme* into German, he declared that it was not a good play, that it painted an unworthy portrait of a world conqueror, a great man who had changed the course of history.[1] In this discussion, Napoleon and Goethe talked about Muhammad, or perhaps better said, about "Mahomet," the fictitious scoundrel that Voltaire made into the epitome of fanaticism (in order to attack the Catholic Church), the charismatic leader and military genius who served as a role model for Napoleon; for Goethe he would become, in subsequent writings, the archetypal prophet, a figure that allowed him to explore the interstices between prophet and poet. For these three men, as for many other Europeans, "Mahomet" is not merely a distant historical character, prophet of a foreign religion, he is a figure whose story and whose living legacy are a constant source of curiosity, worry, astonishment, and admiration.

Not all European writers on Muhammad show him the admiration and respect that we find in Bonaparte and Goethe, of course. Much of what is written about him is hostile. It would have been easy for me to compile a chronicle of that hostility, a catalog of disdain, fear, and insult from the earliest Christian polemical texts against Islam to the shrill declarations of politicians like Geert Wilders, parliamentarian of the Partij voor de Vrijheid (Dutch extreme right) who, to discredit Islam, attacks its prophet, whom he calls a terrorist, a pedophile, and psychopath.[2] The 2005 controversy over the cartoons of Muhammad published in the Danish newspaper *Jyllands-Posten* illustrate the potentially explosive nature of Western views of the Muslim prophet, as do the killing of cartoonists of *Charlie Hebdo* in January 2015. Tinged by the history of European colonialism and orientalism and by terrorism that claims Islam as its justification, the controversy has provoked a flood of polemics and violence.

Muhammad has always been at the center of European discourse on Islam. For medieval crusade chroniclers, he was either a golden idol that the "Saracens" adored or a shrewd heresiarch who had worked false miracles to seduce the Arabs away from Christianity; both these depictions made him the root of Saracen error and implicitly justified the crusade to wrest the Holy Land from Saracen control. Such contentious images, forged in the middle ages, proved tenacious; in slightly modified forms, they provided the dominant European discourse on the prophet through the seventeenth century. In the nineteenth and twentieth centuries, variants of the image of Muhammad as an "impostor" have been used to justify European colonialism in Muslim lands and to encourage the work of Christian missionaries. This hostility toward Islam and its prophet is an important part of the story that will be told in these pages, but it is only a part. Muhammad occupies a crucial and ambivalent place in the European imagination; he figures as the embodiment of Islam, alternatively provoking fear, loathing, fascination, or admiration, but rarely indifference.

Indeed, the figure of Muhammad and the text of the Qur'ān could inspire interest and esteem, particularly from those who criticized the power of the Church in European society or who deviated from its accepted dogmas. Sixteenth-century Unitarian Miguel Servet mined the Qur'ān for arguments against the doctrine of the Trinity; condemned by the Catholic inquisition, he escaped only to be burned at the stake in Calvin's Geneva. In the midst of bloody confessional wars that were tearing Europe apart, some looked to the toleration of religious diversity grounded in the Qur'ān and practiced by the Ottomans as a model Europeans should follow. Various authors of the seventeenth and eighteenth centuries, in England, France, and elsewhere, portrayed Muhammad as a reformer who abolished the privileges of a corrupt and superstitious clergy, showed tolerance to Jews and Christians, and reestablished the true spirit of monotheism. In the eighteenth and nineteenth centuries, he is increasingly portrayed as a "great man," a sort of Arab national hero, bringing law, religion, and glory to his people. Many of these authors are interested less in Islam and its prophet per se than in reading in Muhammad's story lessons that they could apply to their own preoccupations and predicaments.

This book is not about Muhammad, prophet of Islam, but about "Mahomet," the figure imagined and brought to life by non-Muslim European authors between the twelfth and twenty-first centuries. This is why, throughout this book, I distinguish between "Muhammad" (which I use both for the historical person and for the figure portrayed in Muslim traditions) and the various spellings or deformations of his name found in European languages, which I have reproduced verbatim: Machomet, Mathome, Mafometus, Mouamed, Mahoma, and above all Mahomet. This book, examines the changing faces of Mahomet, the many facets of Western perceptions of the prophet of Islam.

If we are to appreciate the construction of a "European Mahomet," we must have some idea about the archetype, the seventh-century Arab Muhammad. Here the historian faces the same problem as with other great religious leaders: it is difficult, often impossible, to distinguish historical fact from pious legend, biography from hagiography. Did the biblical patriarchs even exist? Or are they merely mythical figures? Historians have expressed doubt about the existence of Moses, David, and others.[3] Jesus, like Muhammad, is a historical figure; we know when and where Jesus and Muhammad lived and what their followers believe about them. The four gospels provide a narrative of Jesus's life and death, which (despite some differences) gives a relatively coherent picture of who Jesus was and what he preached. Yet the Gospels were written between forty and seventy years after Jesus's death. They reflect not only what the authors remember about Jesus but also the social, political, and religious upheavals of the young Christian community. How can the historian use the Gospels to understand Jesus and the movement he founded? Is it possible to sift through layers of devotion and mythmaking to find a kernel of historical truth? This is the issue that nineteenth-century European scholars grappled with in their quest for the historical Jesus.[4] Their scholarship provoked controversy, of course, among some European Christians. It is still a problem for historians today seeking to understand Jesus and the beginnings of Christianity. It is impossible to avoid the Gospels, for without them we can know virtually nothing about Jesus. Yet by what criteria can one distinguish historical fact from pious legend?

The historian seeking to understand Muhammad faces similar problems; if anything, his or her task is more daunting. As Maxime Rodinson warned in 1957, "A biography of Mohammed limited only to absolutely unquestionable facts could amount to no more than a few dry pages."[5] The Gospels provide a narration of Jesus's life; the Qur'ān offers nothing of the sort for Muhammad. The dating and composition of the Qur'ān have been objects of scholarly debate, but recent scholarship has more or less confirmed important aspects of the traditional Muslim version: written copies of various suras (chapters) of the Qur'ān existed during Muhammad's lifetime. ʿUthmān, the third caliph (644–56), ordered the compilation of what became the standard, definitive edition of the Muslim holy text.[6] The Qur'ānic text was established by about twenty years after the death of Muhammad, at a time when many of the prophet's companions were still alive. While, as we shall see, many non-Muslim European authors see "Mahomet" as the author of the Qur'ān, for Muslims it is the word of God revealed through Muhammad. God speaks in the first person, frequently addressing Muhammad as *you* in the singular and Muhammad's audience as *you* in the plural. As the word of God directed through Muhammad to his Arab listeners, there is no need for the Qur'ān to narrate the life of Muhammad. Muhammad is mentioned by name four times in the Qur'ān, which affirms that he is the "Messenger of God" (rasul Allah). The Qur'ān refers to his preaching in Mecca, the hostility of many of the Meccan pagans to his teaching, his flight to Medina, some of his marriages, and his political and military struggles as ruler of the Muslim community.

Yet many of the events narrated or alluded to in the Qur'ān can only be understood through the context of later traditions, chiefly the hadiths, sayings attributed to Muhammad or his followers, thousands of which circulated orally during the first two Islamic centuries. It is in the ninth century, during the Abbasid caliphate, that Muslim scholars began to seriously study these hadiths, collecting them and classifying them as *sahīh* (authentic), *hasan* (good; i.e., theologically sound but not necessarily authentic), and *da'īf* (weak). These scholars, such as Muhammad al-Bukhari (810–870) and Muslim ibn al-Hajjaj (817–875), based their judgments notably on the reliability of the chain of transmission (*isnād*). In order to be authentic, a hadith must have a clear chain of transmission from Muhammad to one of his companions, to another trustworthy source and so forth, down to the informant of the compiler; the content of the hadith, and its compatibility to evolving Muslim doctrine, was also important in ascertaining its authenticity. Yet the compilers themselves acknowledged the difficulty of their task, at a distance of two centuries, to distinguish authentic hadiths among the thousands of spurious ones in circulation. The historian who tries to avoid or ignore hadiths will have little to go on to construct the biography of Muhammad and the early community of his followers. Yet the hadiths as preserved by the compilers of the ninth century reflect in many cases the consensus of Abbasid Baghdad, a very different place from seventh-century Mecca or Medina.

The other major source on the life of Muhammad, closely related to the hadiths, is the *Sīrat Rasūl Allāh* (*Life of the Messenger of God*), originally written by Ibn Ishaq (704–768) but preserved only in the version of Ibn Hisham (d. 833). Here one can read in detail (Ibn Hisham's text is over seven hundred pages long in Alfred Guillaume's English translation) about Muhammad's life and career. Ibn Hisham offers a pious biography containing many elements that explain in detail, and in chronological order, events only alluded to in the Qur'ān. Other passages contradict the Qur'ān; for example, at various places in the Qur'ān, skeptical Meccan pagans demand that Muhammad produce miracles to prove the truth of his preaching. The

Qur'ān responds, "Is it not enough of a miracle that we sent down to you this book?" (Q 29:51). Yet during the first two centuries following Muhammad's death, as Muslims praised their prophet to often skeptical Christians, Jews, and others, they attributed to him a series of miracles similar to those attributed to holy men in pre-Muslim texts. Ibn Hisham relates many of these stories: how angels cut open the chest of the boy Muhammad and purified his heart; how at the bidding of skeptical Meccans the prophet split the moon in two; how he visited heaven and hell in the company of the Archangel Gabriel, and many other miraculous stories. We also find inconsistencies in the texts relating Muhammad's last days: his illness, death, burial, and the succession of Abu Bakr as the first caliph. There are variant, indeed contradictory, accounts in the traditional sources, leading to uncertainty even in the basic questions of the date and place of his death.[7] Hence for the historian the problem of discerning the "historical Muhammad," of searching for kernels of historical truth in the *Sīra* and the vast collections of hadiths, is at least as difficult as the search for the historical Jesus.

These traditional sources nevertheless largely agree on the principal events in Muhammad's life. Born in the Hashimite clan of Mecca's ruling Quraysh tribe, Muhammad was an orphan—his father died before he was born and his mother when he was a young boy. He was brought up by his paternal uncle, Abū Tālib, and participated in his uncle's business, accompanying his caravans to Syria. On one of these trips, a Christian hermit, Bahīrā, recognized the young Muhammad as a prophet predicted in Christian scripture. At the age of twenty-five, Muhammad married Khadīja, a Meccan widow for whom he had worked. At the age of about forty, around 610, Muhammad began to retire to the cave of Hira, in the mountains near Mecca, to meditate. It is here that he received the first revelations of the Qur'ān from the Archangel Gabriel, informing him that God had chosen him as a messenger. He continued to receive these revelations, which he shared first with Khadīja and a close circle of family and friends, and eventually began to preach publicly in Mecca.

The essential message of God's revelation to Muhammad, as preserved in the Qur'ān, is that God is one, that he is the creator of the world and of man, and that it is sacrilegious to worship other divinities beside him or in his place. Muhammad called on his listeners to acknowledge God's unity, to reject the cult of idols, and to live righteously, giving alms to the poor and showing justice and compassion. To those who heeded his words, God promised the delights of heaven; to those who refused to listen, the agonies of hellfire. His message provoked hostility from Mecca's religious and social elite, though Abū Ṭālib protected his nephew. Some of Muhammad's followers took refuge across the Red Sea in the Christian kingdom of Abyssinia. When both Khadīja and Abū Ṭālib died, Muhammad's situation became more precarious and he decided to leave Mecca.

It is in 622 that Muhammad made his *hijra* (flight or immigration), a momentous event that marks the year 1 of the Muslim calendar. He went to the town of Yathrib, about 350 kilometers north of Mecca, which subsequently came to be known as the "City of the Prophet," *Madinat al-Nabi*, or simply Medina. Muhammad had been in contact with the people of the city, who agreed to make him their leader. The hijra thus marks a key transformation in Muhammad's life and mission, as he became a charismatic political and military leader as well as a religious and legal authority. Although here is not the place to relate the political and military history of the Medinan community in detail, Muhammad and his associates fought and defeated pagan rivals in Arabia, Jewish tribes in Medina, and finally imposed defeat on Mecca's Quraysh. The Qur'ānic suras from the Medina period allude to many of these struggles; they also provide legal guidance for the community of believers in Medina on topics including prayer, purity, marriage, and inheritance.

By about 630, Muhammad was the dominant spiritual, political, and military force in the Arabian Peninsula. He and his followers marched on Mecca in 630; the city surrendered without a fight, and Muhammad and his troops went to the Ka'ba and destroyed the idols there, purifying the sanctuary that, according to the Qur'ān, had originally been built by Abraham and his son Ishmael, the oldest temple to the One God. He returned to Medina, capital of his expanding empire. He would come back to Mecca in 631 and 632 to perform the rites of pilgrimage. Muhammad became ill in 632 and died in Medina in the month of June, his head in the lap of his wife Aisha. This narrative, based largely on the Sira, has been accepted by most people, Muslim and non-Muslim, who have tried to sketch the prophet's biography, though it bears repeating that it is difficult if not impossible to separate historically true elements from later pious accretions.

What is clear is that during the two centuries following Muhammad's death, Islam emerged as a religion linked to but clearly distinguished from Judaism and Christianity. Muslim caliphs of the Umayyad (661–750) and Abbasid (750–1258) dynasties ruled over an immense empire in which the majority was non-Muslim, prompting the caliphs and the ulama (religious/intellectual elite) in their entourage to clearly distinguish Islam both theologically and juridically. Muhammad's role was seen as central to this self-definition: the *shahada*, or Muslim credo, first attested during the Umayyad period, affirms "there is no God but God, and Muhammad is the prophet of God." The belief in Muhammad's stature as prophet became the essential element that distinguishes Muslims from non-Muslims.[8]

Muhammad has always been for Muslims not only a prophet who announced God's word but also a role model. Muslim perceptions of him have varied immensely over time and have led to divergent portraits: a Sufi might see him as a model mystic; a ruler might see him as a sacred king; a pious Muslim as a model to follow in everything from how to pray, to how to greet one's neighbor, to how to brush one's teeth. His very name means "the praised one," and he is variously "praised as a divinely sent apostle, eschatological messiah, political revolutionary, statesman and community leader, military strategist and commander, arbiter of disputes, dispenser of justice, or quintessential mystic."[9] The history of these rich diverse Muslim traditions about Muhammad has been chronicled and analyzed by a number of scholars, most recently Christiane Gruber.[10] For non-Muslim Europeans and Americans, Muhammad has been the object of everything from indifference, fear, or hostility to curiosity and admiration. My goal in this book is to offer an overview of these "Western" views of Muhammad.

One might fairly ask, in today's globalized world, what "Western" means. Too often, "Muslim" and "Western," or "Muslim" and "European," are presented as self-evident, mutually exclusive terms. Yet of course many Europeans are Muslim and have been so ever since the forces of Tāriq ibn Ziyād crossed the straights of Gibraltar in 711. Muslims were present in Spain and Sicily for centuries. Beginning in the fourteenth century, the Ottoman Empire expanded into the Balkans and central Europe; some of the ex-Ottoman territories in Europe have significant (in some cases majority) Muslim populations today: Bosnia, Albania, Kosovo. Perhaps rather than "Western" I should speak of "non-Muslim European and American perceptions of the prophet of Islam." Moreover, "Islam" and "Muslim" can be misleading as well, as the terms refer either to a religion or to a culture and civilization—and often to a confusion of the two. For this reason, historian Marshall Hodgson coined the term "Islamdom" to speak of Islamic civilization, and as a corresponding adjective used "Islamicate." Yet his terminology has not spread beyond a small group of scholars. In a similar vein, Montgomery Watt preferred to use the term "Eur-America" instead of "West."[11]

The terminology is difficult because these categories are both overlapping and in constant flux. Common fallacy opposes the categories of "Europe" and "Islam," even in scholarly circles. For Tomoko Masuzawa, "the European idea of Islam was curiously monolithic and, for the most part, consistently negative."[12] In fact, as we will see in this book, European ideas on Islam were anything but monolithic, and many of them have been quite positive. Until the nineteenth century, one could distinguish between traditional Muslim discourse about the prophet Muhammad and the writings of non-Muslim Europeans and Americans (which ranged from polemical to scholarly). Yet in the nineteenth century, many Muslim colonial subjects of the French and British empires read and reacted to European scholarship about Islam. Much scholarship about Islam in the twentieth and twenty-first centuries has been written by European and American Muslims (some of them immigrants or descendants of immigrants, others converts to Islam).[13]

Nor can we speak of "Christian" perceptions of Islam, for two reasons. First, European Catholic and Protestant Christianity are merely two branches of a world religion including Syriac, Coptic, Greek, Armenian, Ethiopic, and a host of other churches. Many of these latter, "Eastern," churches have a rich history of long and close contact with and knowledge of Islam. The story of their various perceptions of Islam and its prophet is a fascinating one, but it lies outside the ambit of this study (though I will at times refer to the works of Christians writing in Greek and Arabic, to the extent that they are influential in Western Europe).[14] Second, many of the Europeans whose writings we will be looking at did not define themselves as Christian, but as Jewish, Deist, or atheist. With these caveats in mind, in the nine chapters that follow, I will attempt to trace the history of European perceptions of the prophet of Islam.

In chapter one, we will see that some Europeans, from the twelfth century to the seventeenth and beyond, portray Islam as a cult of idols and imagine that "Mahomet" is one of their chief gods. A number of the chroniclers who described the capture of Jerusalem by the troops of the First Crusade cast their enemies in the familiar and despised guise of pagan idolaters. The imagined devotions of these "Saracen" enemies echoed the rites of the pagans of ancient Greece and Rome, but paradoxically also resembled the cult of Christian saints. Crusade chroniclers and epic poets like the author of the *Chanson de Roland* narrate wars between Christian knights and Saracen pagans. The victory of righteous Christian crusaders offers proof of the efficacy of Christ and his saints and of the impotence of the Saracen idol Mahomet.

Of course those who knew much of anything about Islam knew that it was monotheistic and that Muhammad was the Saracens' prophet, not their god. As we will see in chapter two, various medieval authors portray "Mahomet" as a wholly human founder of a new, deviant version of Christianity, a heresy. Through preaching, magic tricks, and false miracles, this charlatan hoodwinked the naive and lustful Arabs into taking him for a prophet and making him their leader. As the "Saracens" had taken over much of the formerly Christian Roman Empire, produced a rich and thriving culture, and consistently defeated crusader armies, these authors sought to comfort their readers that Christians were nevertheless favored by God, and that Mahomet had proffered nothing more than a crude caricature of true religion, which appealed to the Saracens because it gave them license to indulge in violent conquest and sexual debauchery.

One would expect a more nuanced approach from Christians in Spain, where Islam was present from the arrival of the troops of Tāriq ibn Ziyād in 711 to the expulsion of the Moriscos in the seventeenth century. Indeed, as we will see in chapter three, it was in thirteenth-century Spain that scholars like Archbishop of Toledo Rodrigo Jimenez de Rada studied Muslim sources on the life of Muhammad. Yet they did so largely to bolster their controversial image of Muhammad as a false prophet and rebel against legitimate political authority. In the fifteenth century, various Spanish and other European authors used this image of the prophet to argue for new crusades against Muslims in Nasrid Granada and the Ottoman Empire. Following the conquest of Granada in 1492, there was increasing pressure on Muslims to convert to Christianity; forced conversions created a large population of Moriscos, nominal Catholics, many of whom continued to practice Islam in secret or developed hybrid practices and beliefs. In this context, sixteenth-century Moriscos forged apocryphal texts that purported to be from the early Church, and which sought to confer legitimacy on their religious beliefs and practices.

At the same time, north of the Pyrenees, Europe's confessional landscape was undergoing tremendous upheaval, provoked both by the Protestant Reformation and by the Ottoman conquest of much of southeastern and central Europe. In order to understand these changes, various Christian authors tried to define the differences and similarities between Catholicism, Protestantism, and Islam, as we will see in chapter four. In order to denigrate Luther or Calvin, Catholic writers affirmed that they were worse than Mahomet, often highlighting similarities (iconoclasm, sexual license). Protestant polemicists responded in kind, asserting that the pope was worse than Mahomet, that "Mahometanism" and "Papism" were two great heresies concocted by the devil. In this inter-Christian strife and anxiety in the face of Ottoman conquests, a number of European intellectuals took an interest in the Qur'ān. In 1543, Theodor Bibliander published the first printed Qur'ān, the twelfth-century Latin translation by Robert of Ketton, accompanied by an anthology of texts about Islam, including a preface by Martin Luther who explained that there was no better way to combat the Turk than to expose the "lies and fables of Machomet."

The study of the Qur'ān was often undertaken in order to combat Islam, yet increasingly Christian writers mined it for arguments to use against other Christians. For some Protestants, Mahomet's success was made possible by the corruption of Christianity: the cult of the saints, relics, and the power of the clergy. Unitarians such as Miguel Servet went further, making Mahomet into a true reformer who rightfully rejected the absurd doctrine of the Trinity and who preached the unity of the true God. The prophet of Islam could even be mobilized for inter-Catholic doctrinal disputes; he is cited as an authority testifying to the doctrine of the Immaculate Conception, and as such we find him painted, proudly holding the Qur'ān, in altarpieces in central Europe between the sixteenth and eighteenth centuries. While most of what is written about the prophet in European languages continues to be negative, more positive assessments begin to be voiced.

England, too, experienced political and religious turmoil in the seventeenth century, and the prophet of Islam was drawn into English debates (as we shall see in chapter five). The first English translation of the Qur'ān was published in 1649, the same year that saw the beheading of King Charles I and the establishment of the commonwealth. The preface to this translation relates the life of Mahomet, making him into a crafty, cynical rebel against legitimate power and a destroyer of long-established social hierarchies, suggesting a parallel with Oliver Cromwell. Indeed, for royalists Cromwell was a new Mahomet. While some republicans rejected this parallel, at least one embraced it enthusiastically: Henry Stubbe, whose *Originall & Progress of Mahometanism* (1671) describes the Muslim prophet as a great reformer who fought the superstition and illegitimate power of Christian clergy and sought to return to a pure, unsullied monotheism. Stubbe's Mahomet is a religious reformer, beloved and admired ruler, and sage legislator. Stubbe becomes the first European non-Muslim to present the prophet in such glowing terms. He is followed by others, in particular English Unitarians and Deists of the late seventeenth century. Anglican scholars defended their Church from such criticism; Humphrey Prideaux, a fellow student with Stubbe at Oxford, in 1697 published his *The True Nature of Imposture Fully Display'd in the Life of Mahomet*, in order to show that Mahomet was an impostor and to defend Christianity. Yet increasingly, anticlerical writers such as Irish Deist John Toland portrayed Mahomet as a visionary anticlerical religious reformer, the better to smash the pretensions of the Church of England's priestly aristocracy.

In eighteenth-century France, Mahomet was similarly instru-mentalized to attack the prerogatives of the Catholic Church, as we will see in chapter six. Some painted him as an impostor in order to associate his imposture or fanaticism with that of Christians, nota-bly in the *Treatise of the Three Impostors* (1719) and in Voltaire's play *Le fanatisme, ou Mahomet le prophète* (1741). Yet others follow the lead of Stubbe and Toland to make Mahomet into a reformer who eradicates superstition and combats the power of the clergy. This is how Henri de Boulainvilliers paints the prophet in his *Vie de Ma-homed* (1730), and how George Sale presents him in the "prelimi-nary discourse" to his English translation of the Qur'ān (1734). Vol-taire, thanks in part to his reading of Sale, depicts Mahomet as a reformer and great statesman in his *Essai sur les mœurs*. Indeed, by the end of the century, writers such as English Whig Edward Gibbon see him as a "great man," charismatic leader, and legislator to the Arab nation.

Napoleon Bonaparte, as we have seen, was an admirer of Mu-hammad. Indeed, as we will see in chapter seven, for Bonaparte the prophet was something of a role model: stirring orator, brilliant general, sage statesman. Nineteenth-century romantics, from Goethe to Carlyle and Lamartine, place both Muhammad and Bonaparte in their pantheon of great men who have changed the course of history. A great man cannot be an impostor, he is neces-sarily sincere, affirms Carlyle; many other nineteenth-century ro-mantics would agree. Muhammad's sincerity and deep spiritual values are reflected in his humble lifestyle and simple generosity, which won him the love and admiration of his people. For these authors, Muhammad believed in the divine origins of his inspira-tion; Lamartine gives a psychological portrait of a genius and mystic convinced that his visions come from God. For many of these ro-mantic authors, Muhammad's spirituality shines even more when seen from an increasingly materialistic, skeptical Europe.

Things looked a bit different for nineteenth-century European Jews, as we shall see in chapter eight. Some of the century's finest scholars of the Qur'ān and hadiths were German and Hungarian Jews. Abraham Geiger was one of the leaders of the reform move-ment that sought to modernize Judaism by simplifying its ritual and making it more amenable to European society. He was also a scholar of Judaism, Christianity, and Islam. Geiger presented Mohammed as a brilliant reformer who had learned his monotheism from Talmudic scholars and who subsequently adapted it to his Arab audience. Geiger's Mohammed was in essence a Jewish reformer (as was Jesus): not strictly a Jew, to be sure, but nonetheless a better Jew than Geiger's Orthodox Jewish critics. Other Jewish scholars (in particular, Gustav Weil and Ignác Goldziher) embraced and refined this image of the Muslim prophet as a model for Jewish reform.

A number of European authors of the twentieth century, in the context of decolonization and increasing calls for interreligious and intercultural dialogue, argued that Christians should recognize Muhammad as prophet (as we shall see in the ninth and final chapter). In the twentieth century, the figure of the prophet is at the heart of a controversy that animates the Catholic Church concerning the universality of the Christian message and the attitude to be adopted toward the adherents of other faiths. If the issues were different from those of earlier periods, perhaps the essence remains the salvific role of the Christian religion: are only Christians (or only Catholic or Protestants) destined to Paradise, or is it imaginable that others can be saved? Louis Massignon, professor at the Collège de France, was a brilliant Arabist and a devout Catholic. At the same time, he showed a fascination and respect for Islam, especially its mystical currents. For Massignon, Muhammad was a genuine leader, inspired by God, who preached the truth and brought his people to the worship of one supreme God. But if not a false prophet, he nevertheless failed to reach the ultimate truth of Christianity. Subsequently, the Swiss Catholic theologian Hans Küng has developed in detail a theological argument for the recognition of the Prophet Muhammad by the Catholic Church.

Montgomery Watt, scholar of Islam and Anglican priest, was committed to ecumenical dialogue and struggled to find ways to eliminate (or at least reduce) doctrinal barriers to that dialogue. For him (as for Massignon and Küng), Christian recognition of the prophetic role of Muhammad was crucial. For Massignon and his disciple Giulio Basetti-Sani, Islam was positive and could lead to salvation, but it was imperfect because it did not recognize Christ as God and savior; their vision is what Küng classified as inclusive, "conquest by hugging." Küng and Watt try to go further, though each reaches his own limits. Küng remains grounded in the Catholic

Church and, though he confers more legitimacy than Massignon on non-Christian religions, in the end the recognition of Jesus Christ as God and savior remains the highest truth. Watt seems ready to go further still, at times imagining that one new world religion will emerge from a sort of fusion by emulation of the best elements of current religions, and that Islam has as good a claim, or better, than Christianity for providing the basis for that new world religion. For all of these twentieth-century Christian authors, Islam and Muhammad offer a positive, creative challenge to Christianity, an opportunity to rethink its claims to universalism and its relations with the wider world.

The portrayals of the prophet Muhammad that I address in this book represent only a sampling of the rich and varied portraits that European authors and artists have sketched of the prophet of Islam. What should be clear to anyone who reads this book is that European images of Islam and of the prophet Muhammad are anything but monolithic and are far from being invariably hostile. Yet that is how they are often perceived. In part this stems from trends over the last several decades' scholarship (particularly in English) in what has come to be called "postcolonial studies," in the wake of Edward Said's *Orientalism*, published in 1978. Said chronicles the ideological implications of representations of the Orient in nineteenth- and twentieth-century British and French culture. Orientalism as discourse, for Said, is the ideological counterpart to the political and military realities of British and French Empires in the Near East: Orientalism provides justification for empire. Said has had a profound impact on the field, not least because he emphasized how scholarship is not immune to the political and social pressures of the surrounding society, and how through deliberate distortion or unconscious bias scholarship can support or reinforce the colonial project.[15]

Said and other more recent scholars in postcolonial studies have helped us understand how institutions (including those devoted to teaching and research) can conceive and construct colonialist discourses and how the broader culture (including literature and the arts) can justify and even celebrate these discourses. Some of the writings about Islam and Muhammad that we will examine in this book indeed correspond to this schema; the supposed foibles of the prophet are used to explain the weaknesses and shortcomings of modern Muslims who need the tutelage of the French or the British. Yet to focus solely on these aspects of European discourse on Islam is to miss the ambivalence and nuance this book seeks to highlight. For Humberto Garcia, Said's schema is based on a "Whig fallacy" according to which, for example, radical Protestant writers and Deists of the seventeenth and eighteenth centuries are little more than precursors to the secular reformers of the nineteenth and twentieth centuries.[16] As a result, Said and others ignore the religious nature of much of these authors' work, or they reduce it to a kind of code for the political. For these authors, "Orientalism" defined Islam as religious and hence atavistic, enforcing a Western superiority and justifying Western domination. This makes them incapable of appreciating the complexity of European responses to Islam, in particular, for Garcia, what he calls "Islamic Republicanism": using primitive Islam, the community that Muhammad founded in Medina, as a model for a rightly ordered society and for proper relations between Church and State. It also makes them incapable of understanding the frank admiration that many European romantics had for Muslim spirituality and for the prophet Muhammad.

Restoring the variety, ambivalence, and complexity of European views of Muhammad and Islam is one of my principal goals in this book. For over a thousand years, Europeans have been writing, thinking, talking, and arguing about the prophet of Islam. Much of what they have to say is negative, but much is ambivalent or praiseful. Muhammad is seen as a brilliant general, a sincere reformer, an inspired mystic, a sage legislator. An apt example of the ambivalence that many Europeans felt toward the Muslim prophet is seen in a watercolor by Eugène Delacroix (fig. 1), a study for a painting in the library of the Palais Bourbon, the seat of the French National Assembly in Paris (though he did not in fact include it in the paintings that adorn the wall of the library).

Muhammad sits on a step, his elbow propped on the pedestal of a column, in a position that suggests either sleep or contemplation. Delacroix has not painted his facial features, so we do not know

FIGURE 1. Eugène Delacroix (1798–1863), *Étude pour Mahomet et son ange.*
Drawing with watercolor, nineteenth century. Paris, Musée du Louvre (RF 10017).
© RMN-Grand Palais (musée du Louvre) / Gérard Blot

whether his eyes are open or closed. Above him, in the upper right of the image, we see an angel descending toward him as if to make a revelation. The angel takes the form of a woman, with no wings, rather than the austere male figure of a winged Gabriel seen in the Muslim iconographical tradition. Is Muhammad receiving a revelation from an angel? Is he waking or dreaming? Is he inspired or deluded? Delacroix, whose travels in France's new colonies and protectorates in North Africa provided the inspiration of many of his works, presents a romantic, orientalist view of Muhammad in all its rich ambiguity. Delacroix's large, energetic brush strokes resist a tidy composition, a technique that echoes the dynamism with which Europeans forged images of Muhammad over the centuries. His subject not only fails to show his face, defying attempts to limit and define him, he also partakes of an angelic world (or is it a dream world?) that bursts in from beyond the neat confines of the paper. An apposite image of the European struggle to comprehend and appreciate the prophet of Islam.

CHAPTER ONE

Mahomet the Idol

RICHARD JOHNSON'S *FAMOUS HISTORIE of the Seaven Champions of Christendom* (1596) was "perhaps the pinnacle of the Anglophone reimagining of the Romance tradition."[1] One of its heroes, a thoroughly English Saint George, goes off to Egypt, where he finds a dragon ready to devour Sabra, daughter of King Ptolomie. He slays the dragon and is ready to take his prize, Sabra, but "the Trecherous Almidor the blacke King of Moroco" is in love with her and tries to kill our champion, first by setting an ambush of a dozen Egyptian knights (whom George makes short work of), then by trying to poison him during the victory celebrations at Ptolomie's court (Sabra foils Almidor's plan). She later declares her love for the English knight: "thy body is more precious to myne eyes than Kingdomes in my heart."[2] In response, George says:

> I am a Christian, thou a Pagan: I honour God in heauen, thou earthly shadowes below: therefore if thou wilt obtaine my loue and liking, thou must forsake thy Mahomet, and bee christned in our Christian faith. With al my soule (answered the Egiptian Lady) will I forsake my country Gods, & for thy loue become a Christian.[3]

Yet Almidor has overheard their vows; boiling with jealousy, he denounces them to Ptolomie, warning him that his daughter is planning to "forsake her God and beleeue as the Christians doo, and likewise shee intendes to flye from her native Countrie." "Now by my Mahomet, Apollo and Termagaunt, three Gods we Egiptians commonly adore (sayde the King) this damned Christian shal not gaine the conquest of my daughters loue." Since the rules of hospitality prevent the king from murdering his guest in Egypt, he has him sent off to Persia to be killed. George arrives at the Soldan's court on a great feast day when the Persians are sacrificing to their gods. Our George is a good Anglican, so "this vnchristian Procession so mooued the impatience of the English Champion, that he tooke the ensignes and streamers whereon the Persian Gods were pictured, and trampled them under hys feete: whereupon the Pagans presently fled to the Soldan for succor, and shewed him how a straunge Knight had despised their Mahomet and trampled their banners in the dust."[4] George is taken to the Soldan, who swears "by Mahomet, Apollo, and Termigaunt" to have him put to death for his blasphemies; he has him thrown to two particularly hungry lions. But when the first lion charges our Christian knight, he reaches into his throat and pulls out his heart; he similarly dispatches the second. The soldan has George thrown into prison, where for seven years he feeds only "upon rats and mice, with other creeping wormes which he caught in the dungeon."[5]

George subsequently escapes and goes to Hungary, where he defeats his nemesis Almidor and condemns him to death, to be boiled in a vat of molten lead. Yet, since "mercy harboreth in a Christian hart," George offers a pardon to the Moorish king, under certain conditions:

> First that thou wilt forsake theyr false Gods Termagaunt, Mahomet and Apollo, which be but the vayne imaginations of man, and believe in our true and euer-living God, vnder whose banner we Christians haue taken in hande this long warre: Secondly thou shalt giue commandment, that all thy barbarous Nations be christened in the faith of Christ: Thirdly and lastly, that thy three Kingdomes of Barbary, Moroco & India, sweare true alleagance to all Christian Kings, and neuer to beare Armes, but in the true quarrel of Christ and his annoynted nations.[6]

But Albimor refuses, saying he would die a hundred deaths before forsaking his gods, and he is tossed in the vat, which provokes much rejoicing and the massive conversion of the remaining pagans; all the ceremonious rites of Mahomet were trodden underfoot, the poet crows.

Johnson has dreamed up what one might call an Anglican crusade. The good Saint George, who abhors images and idols, delights in their destruction and in the conversion of the idolaters to the True Faith. Note the three conditions that George tries to impose on Almidor: abandonment of false Gods, conversion en masse of all his subjects, and political subjugation to Christian (presumably European) kings. In 1584, Queen Elizabeth I had granted Sir Walter Raleigh a charter for the colonization of Virginia; in 1600 (four years after the publication of Johnson's *Seven Champions*), Elizabeth granted a charter to the East India Company. George's heroics tell us something about how some Englishmen, at least, fantasized about these new colonial adventures: one slays heathen champions, one converts the masses, and (all in a good day's work) one obtains immense riches and the love of a beautiful princess.

Gentle reader, you may be surprised to find the author of an enormously popular sixteenth-century English romance portraying "Mahomet" as an idol worshipped by the "pagan" masses. Didn't Europeans know better? Didn't they know that Muslims were strict monotheists who rejected the use of images (much less idols)? Indeed, many Europeans did know better; as early as the eighth century in Constantinople, the ninth century in Spain, and the twelfth century elsewhere in Europe, Christian writers acknowledged that the "Saracens" were monotheists, often casting them as adepts of a deviant, heretical version of Christianity. But at the same time other authors, writing in Latin, French, and other European languages, preferred to portray them in the familiar and despised guise of pagan idolaters. This caricature remains popular into the nineteenth century, as the numerous editions of Johnson's *Seven Champions* shows, and is found in popular festivals in the twentieth and twenty-first centuries. This caricature is all the more puzzling when we bear in mind that it was often Muslims who accused Christians of idolatrous belief and practice: worshipping a Trinity that denied the essential unity of God; venerating a pantheon of saints; genuflecting before statues, relics, and painted images. Yet in spite of this, many Christian Europeans chose to portray Islam as a debauched form of pagan idolatry. Or perhaps rather because of this; perhaps Christian authors project onto Saracens anxieties about their own problematic relations with sacred images.

In any case, this caricature of Saracens worshiping a pantheon of idols, with Mahomet (or Mahon, Mahound, and such) as their chief god, is vividly expressed in the twelfth century by poets, chroniclers, and hagiographers. Even Peter, Abbot of Cluny, who commissioned the first translation of the Qur'ān in the 1140s, hesitated; should the Saracens be considered "pagans" (*ethnici* or *pagani*) or heretics?[7] From his Christian point of view, how was he to understand Islam? There was no question, for Peter or other Christian theologians, of creating a new box, of seeing Islam as a religion apart from these essential categories. Saracens were not Jews, it seemed, though they followed some aspects of Jewish law (practicing circumcision and eschewing pork); they were certainly not proper Christians, as they rejected essential Church doctrines such as the Trinity and the Incarnation. Those who knew a little about Islam tended to see it as a heretical, deviant variation of Christianity, as we will see in chapter two. But many of those who knew nothing about Islam (and some who no doubt knew better) preferred to portray it in the colorful and despicable guise of paganism, making Mahomet the Saracens' chief god.[8]

The Formation of the Image of Saracen Idolatry

Writers like Peter of Cluny, in seeking to understand the world around them, naturally reached for the authoritative books on their bookshelves: the Bible of course, but also the writings of the fathers of the early Church. Their exegetical works served as aids to understanding scripture; their historical works helped understand God's scheme for sacred history; their apologetical and polemical works helped understand the many ways in which the Devil led men and women into error and damnation. Hence Latin writers of the Middle Ages who wished to know who the "Saracens" were turned to Jerome (347–420), who had indeed written about them.

For Jerome, the "Saracens" are the same as the "Ishmaelites," descendants of the biblical Ishmael. Genesis tells how when Sarah was unable to become pregnant, she told her husband Abraham to have a child with her Egyptian slave, Hagar, who bore him Ishmael. Sarah later became pregnant and gave birth to Isaac; she subsequently had Abraham expel Hagar and Ishmael from their home. Several passages in Genesis offer the key, for Jerome, to understanding the descendants of Ishmael. In Genesis 16:11–12, the Angel of the Lord comes to Hagar in the desert and announces, "Behold,

thou art with child and shalt bear a son, and shalt call his name
Ishmael; because the Lord hath heard thy affliction. And he will be
a wild man; his hand will be against every man, and every man's
hand against him; and he shall dwell in the presence of all his brethren." Jerome, writing a commentary to Genesis at the turn of the
fifth century, explains this prediction thus: "Now it means that his
descendants would dwell in the desert, and refers to the Saracens
who wander with no fixed abode and often invade all the nations
who border on the desert; and they are attacked by all."[9] These Saracens are desert marauders, enemies of civilization, and their wild-
ness and hostility are permanent hereditary attributes that God assigned to Ismael and his descendants.

Moreover, these people, who should properly be called Ishmaelites after their common ancestor or Hagarenes after his mother the
slave Hagar, "now call themselves Saracens, falsely usurping the
name of Sarah, thus appearing to be born of a free lady."[10] They are
pagans who worship Venus (goddess of love and morning star). Jerome had read about the Saracens in Eusebius of Caesaria's fourth-
century world chronicle, which he had translated into Latin. It was
Eusebius who first identified the Saracens (Σαρακηνοί, a term previously used by Greek geographers to designate one of the peoples or
tribes of Arabia) with the biblical descendants of Ishmael. In other
works, Jerome describes the devastation wrought by Saracen raiders
on Christian monasteries in the desert. He offers a vivid description
of how one monk, Malchus, was captured by a pack of half-naked
camel-riding Saracens and reduced to slavery, forced to eat the Saracen diet of uncooked meat and camel milk.

Later Christians, schooled in the Latin works of the Church fathers, if and when they wanted to understand who the "Saracens"
were, would naturally reach for Jerome. They would learn that they
are the descendants of Ishmael, "wild men" who ride camels and
who attack and pillage innocent Christians. They fraudulently call
themselves "Saracens," vainly attempting to claim that they are descended from Abraham's legitimate wife, Sarah, rather than from
the slave Hagar; this charge is to be repeated by innumerable European authors in the Middle Ages and beyond, though of course no
Arab or Muslim ever called himself a "Saracen" or traced his lineage
to Sarah. And Jerome portrays the Saracens as idolaters devoted to

Venus. Of course he does not mention Muhammad, since he died 150 years before Muhammad was born. But later Christian writers follow Jerome's authoritative texts, and when they hear Muhammad's name often imagine that he must be one of their gods.

Bede (ca. 673–735), monk at the Northumbrian monastery of Jarrow, had heard of the conquests of the Saracens in North Africa and Spain. To understand these events, and to comprehend how they might fit into God's plan for human history, Bede quite naturally reached for the books in his monastic library, in particular Genesis and Jerome's commentary on Genesis. When Bede wrote his own commentary to Genesis, he recopied, word for word, Jerome's explanation that Ishmael's offspring are the Saracens "who are attacked by all." He then added this to what he found in Jerome: "But this was long ago. Now, however, [Ishmael's] hand is against all men, and all men's hands are against him, to such an extent that the Saracens hold the whole breadth of Africa in their sway, and they also hold the greatest part of Asia and some part of Europe, hateful and hostile to all."[11] Bede has brought Jerome up to date, briefly mentioning the sweeping "Saracen" conquests of the last several decades. He does not mention the name of Muhammad.

In a Europe continually ravaged by war and invasions, the Saracens were one among a number of non-Christian interlopers. Christian European writers showed little curiosity about the religion of these invaders, be they Huns, Saracens, Vikings, or Magyars. They all seemed to be part of the terrible tribulations through which God was putting His people; none provoked (it seems) the slightest suggestion that its religious beliefs and practices could be worth investigating—much less imbued with the slightest legitimacy. At one point in his commentary on the Acts of the Apostles, Bede repeats Jerome's assertion that the Saracens were devotees of Venus.[12] But he shows little interest in their religious beliefs and probably had never heard the name of Muhammad. Indeed, this seems to be the case of many Latin authors who wrote about the Saracens, with the notable exception of those from Spain, who had firsthand knowledge of Islam (as we will see in chapters two and three). When northern Europeans of the eleventh and twelfth centuries did hear the name of the Muslim prophet, they often imagined that this "Mahomet" must be the Saracens' god.

Jesus contra Mahomet: Saracen Idolaters
as the Enemies of the Crusaders

It is in the context of the celebration of the victory of the First Crusade, in which Christian European soldiers captured Jerusalem in July 1099, that we find a number of authors, writing in both Latin and French, depicting the idolatry of the "Saracens." Raoul de Caen, in the preface to his *Gesta Tancredi* (written between 1121 and 1131), which narrates the exploits of crusader champion Tancred de Hauteville, says that his subject is "that joyous pilgrimage, that glorious labor that restored to us our inheritance, that is our mother Jerusalem. That pilgrimage extinguished idolatry and restored the faith."[13] Raoul glorifies (and exaggerates) Tancred's military achievements during and after the First Crusade. He describes how, as the Holy City was captured, Tancred battled like a lion, surpassing the exploits of Ajax, Hector, and Achilles. He fought his way to the holy of holies, the Templum Domini, Temple of the Lord: the name given by crusader chroniclers to the Dome of the Rock. He forced open the doors, and there found, seated on a high throne "a cast image, made from silver . . . so heavy that six men with strong arms could barely lift it. . . . It was an image of Mahummet, entirely covered with gems, purple cloth and shining with gold."[14] The temple of Solomon has become the center of the cult of Mahummet; Raoul provides a vivid image of the "blasphemies" that different crusader chroniclers attribute to the Saracens. Tancred, first thinking the statue might be one of Mars or Apollo, finally realizes that it is Mahummet, whom he also calls Antichrist. His attributes are those of power and wealth (crown of gold, gems, royal purple) contrasted to those of Christ (crown of thorns, cross, nails). These attributes are necessary to distinguish the (real) devotion shown to statues of Christ from the (imagined) idolatry of the devotees of Mahummet, suggesting that the line between devotion and idolatry is thin. The destruction of this profane image, intruder in the Temple of the Lord, provides a dramatic, vindictive climax to the First Crusade. Other chroniclers recount more or less the same story; for Fulcher of Chartres this idolatrous worship of Mahomet had polluted the temple.[15]

Needless to say, crusaders never encountered idols of "Mahummet" in the Dome of the Rock or anywhere else. This fiction, repeated by a number of crusade chroniclers, provides a vivid justificatory image, showing how the crusaders "extinguished idolatry and restored the faith." These authors, clerics schooled in Latin, who had read the descriptions of pagan cults in their school books (often composed of extracts from Virgil, Ovid, and others) and who had read of the destruction of these idols by the Apostles and saints of the early church, naturally enough imagined their adversaries, the enemies of "God's army," in the familiar and despised guise of paganism. The name of the prophet, deformed in various ways (Mahomet, Mamet, Mahound . . .) they assumed, must be the name of one of the gods of the "Saracens."

The anonymous author of the *Chanson d'Antioche*, a French epic describing the First Crusade through the conquest of Antioch, presents the crusade as a sort of vengeance for the crucifixion. The epic opens with Christ himself, speaking to the good thief crucified at his side, predicting the eventual arrival of the crusaders: A "new people," he foretells, the Franks, will avenge the crucifixion, liberate the Holy Land, and extirpate paganism.

> "My friend," said Our Lord, "be assured that a new race will come from over the sea to avenge the death of their Father. Not a single pagan will remain between here and the East: The Franks will liberate the whole land. The soul of every man who is taken and killed on this journey will receive My salvation."[16]

The paganism of the Saracens is a key element in the theological justification of the crusade: the pagans killed Jesus, and the crusaders will wreak vengeance on the pagans for the murder of their "father."

The *Chanson* gives a vivid picture of Saracen idolatry, along with a glowing account of their idols' destruction, heralding the imminent demise of paganism. The center of the pagan cult, for the *Chanson d'Antioche*, is Mahomes, an idol held in midair by magnets.[17] A defeated Saracen general, Sansadoines, strikes the idol, knocking it down and breaking it after it has shown itself powerless to secure victory for its devotees. The pagan enemy himself realizes the powerlessness of his idols and destroys them with his own hand. One thirteenth-century manuscript illustrates this scene (fig. 2).

FIGURE 2. Sansadoines destroys the idol of Mahomet. *Chanson d'Antioche*, Bibliothèque Nationale de France, MS Français 786, f 186v (late thirteenth century). © BNF

Within the very name of Mahomet, in the large initial M, we see, on the left, the crowned Saracen king and his men in prayer. At the right we see the object of their prayer, a standing golden idol of a naked human figure atop a column; behind it stand two men, one with his arm raised to strike the idol. Curiously, the scene on the left could be one of Christian worship: the crowned king and his men look European in features and dress; they kneel and hold their hands in prayer as do Christians. Hence it is not the form of their devotion that is foreign or erroneous but the object, as we see clearly on the right. The nakedness of the idol recalls the statues of classical Greek and Roman paganism, and perhaps serves also to differentiate the idol from the statues of saints that could occupy the same spot in a scene of Christian worship. The artist gives a vivid portrayal of Saracen worship to their idol at the dramatic moment in which Sansadoine's raised arm is poised topple it. The image has been damaged: while the Saracen worshippers on the left are still clearly visible, some of the paint has been scratched off the representation of the golden idol. This may well have been deliberate— one or more readers may have wished to insult and damage this pagan idol by scratching at its paint.[18]

The poet then has Sansadoine predict to the Saracens that they will be defeated by the Christians who will "smash down the walls and palisades of Mieque [Mecca]; they will drag Mahomet down from the pedestal where he resides and seize the two candelabra that sit there, which they will carry off to their Sepulchre where their god rose from the dead."[19] At the end of the poem the crusader Godfrey of Bouillon vows to go to "Mahomet's shrine in Mieque," to seize the two candelabra, and to place them in front of the Holy Sepulchre in Jerusalem.[20] The conquest of Mieque, the Saracens' cultic center, will mark the ultimate defeat of paganism.

The *Chanson d'Antioche* describes, in vivid detail, an embassy to Miecque, which is ruled over by three brothers; hymns are sung to the golden idol Mahomés as the "Apostle Caliph of Bauda" (presumably Baghdad) presides over a grand "parlement." Mahomés is brought in on the back of an elephant; a silken canopy protects him from the sun. He is accompanied by a hundred musicians. The Saracens, through enchantment, have caused a demon, Sathanas, to inhabit the idol of Mahomés, which now speaks to them. "Christians who believe in God," says Sathanas/Mahomés, "misguided race that they are, have no right to these lands; they have seized them wrongfully. Let God keep his Heaven; the earth is in my fiefdom."[21] The "Califes de Bauda" then announces a "rich pardon that Mahons will give us" a sort of inversion of the indulgences that Pope Urban II had granted to the crusaders: the Caliph says that Mahons will allow every man who fights the Christians to have twenty or thirty wives, or as many as he wishes. Those who die in battle will take to the gates of heaven two gold bezants in one hand and a rock in the other; with the bezants they can buy their way into heaven, or if that fails, with the rock they can force their way in.[22] Again an inversion or parody, this time of the hope of martyrdom proffered to the

Christian crusader. The pagan enemy, it seems, is a deformed mirror image of the righteous crusader, devoted to the Devil rather than God, granted indulgences by the Caliph of Baghdad/Mecca rather than the pope, hoping to buy or fight his way into heaven.

The pagan adversaries are themselves made to acknowledge—both before and after the conflict—the inevitability of their defeat at the hands of the Christians. Sansadoines, as we saw, predicts that the Christians will take Mecca. Later in the poem, his fears are confirmed by a dream, which he narrates to Curbaran (a figure based on Kurbuqa, the Atabeg of Mosul, who led an army against the crusaders at Antioch in 1098): he stands before Antioch and sees, pouring out of the city, "leopards, boars, snakes, bears, and dragons all about to devour our people."[23] Solimans, one of Curbaran's men, retorts that Mahons is very powerful and would never let this happen to his people. Curbaran is warned but heeds not the warnings and is subsequently routed in battle; he himself, as he sees his defeat, calls one last time on Mahomet, this time to curse and threaten him:

> Alas, lord Mahmet! I have always loved you and served and honored you with all my might. If ever I get back to my own land, I shall have you burned and the ash cast to the winds, or I shall have you trampled underfoot by horses.[24]

Once again, Christian victory over paganism culminates in the pagan leader's rejection and destruction (even if, as here, only threatened) of his idols. In the *Conquête de Jérusalem*, a continuation of the *Chanson d'Antioche*, the caliph himself decapitates the idol Mahon.[25] And, as we have seen, some of the *Chanson*'s readers continued this work of destruction by scratching away at the painted images of Mahomet's idol.

Mahomet the idol provides a tangible and satisfying focus for the righteous Christian knight, as we have seen in this sampling of twelfth-century Latin and French texts concerning the First Crusade. Christian victory will result in the idol of Mahomet tumbling down, whether smashed by the Christian knight (as we see with Tancred in Raoul de Caen's twelfth-century chronicle or Saint George in Richard Johnson's sixteenth-century romance) or by the defeated Saracen enemy.

Mahumet among the Saracen Idols
of the Chanson de Roland

At about the same time as these crusade chroniclers imagined Mahomet as the idol of their Saracen enemies, an anonymous French poet put into writing the *Chanson de Roland*, the founding text of what was to become one of the major genres of medieval literature, the *chansons de geste*.[26] The earliest written text survives in one manuscript, currently at Oxford, dating from the mid-twelfth century, though there is some evidence of oral transmission of the poem during the second half of the eleventh century. The epic as preserved in the Oxford manuscript portrays Saracen idolatry in very similar ways as the *Chanson d'Antioche*: the "pagans" worship a triad of idols: Mahumet, Apollin, and Tervagant, a sort of anti-Christian Trinity. Yet while *Antioche* was grounded in the recent events in the Holy Land, *Roland* situates the dramatic conflict at the edges of Charlemagne's empire, in Spain.

In the opening lines, the poet sets the stage:

> King Charles, our great Emperor,
> Has been in Spain for seven long years.
> He has conquered that haughty land right to the sea,
> No fortress can resist him.
> No wall, no city, remains to be smashed,
> Except Saragossa, which is on a mountaintop.
> King Marsilie, who does not love God, defends it,
> He serves Mahumet and prays to Apollin:
> He cannot prevent misfortune from befalling him there. (vv. 1–9)

Charlemagne, with his long flowing beard, at the ripe old age of two hundred, is at the point of his culminating victory over Saracen Spain. Only Saragossa remains in the hands of Marsilie, devotee of "Mahumet" and "Apollin." Marsilie, afraid of losing his kingdom, plots with the treacherous Ganelon (Charlemagne's brother-in-law); Marsilie offers lavish gifts to Charlemagne: bears, lions, camels, mules laden with gold. He promises that he will come to the emperor's court at Aix, convert to Christianity, and become Charles's vassal. After some debate in the camp of the "Franks," this offer is accepted, and the Frankish army abandons the siege and heads home. Marsilie then leads his troops out to attack the Frankish rear guard, which is captained by Charlemagne's nephew Roland; the ensuing battle is the heart of the poem. The outnumbered Frankish knights, led by Roland, fight valiantly, and Roland cuts off Marsilie's hand in single combat. Roland finally blows his horn (*olifant*) to call back Charlemagne before dying. When Charlemagne and his troops get to the scene of the battle, they find only the dead bodies of their comrades. An epic battle ensues between the Franks and the Saracens, whose forces have been augmented by the arrival of fresh troops led by Baligant, *Amiralz* of Babylon. Charlemagne and Baligant face off in single battle; when Baligant injures the emperor with a mighty blow, the Archangel Gabriel intervenes, because "God does not wish him to be killed or vanquished" (3609): Charlemagne splits Baligant's head with his sword, spilling out his brain. The pagan army scatters and flees. The Christian warriors take Saragossa, where they smash with hammers the idols they find in the "*sinagoges*" and "*mahumeries*" (3661–65).

The Frankish champions are larger-than-life heroes; the enemy is portrayed in equal and contrasting color: Baligant is older than Virgil or Homer (2614–16): "God! What a knight," the poet exclaims, "if only he were Christian!" (3164). He leads an army recruited from the entire non-Christian world, from pagan eastern Europe to Persia to Africa. His troops include monstrous semihumans: the Micenes have large heads and spines on their back; the soldiers from Occian have skin as hard as steel armor; those from Malprose are giants (3214–64). The Saracen army includes such figures as "Siglorel, the sorcerer who was once in Hell: Jupiter led him there by sorcery" (1390–92) and Chernuble de Munigre, who comes from a land inhabited by demons, where the sun never shines and rain never falls (979–83). When Archbishop Turpin sees Abisme, "black as pitch," approach carrying a banner with a dragon on it, he proclaims: "This Saracen seems quite heretical to me; it would be much better if I were to kill him" (1484–85). And what reader or listener would not feel righteous pleasure when Roland kills Valdebrun, who had once taken Jerusalem through treachery, sacked Solomon's temple, and murdered the Patriarch at the baptismal fonts? (1566–68).

The religion of these Saracen enemies, as in the roughly contemporary crusade chronicles and epics, is a form of pagan idolatry. The pagans swear by their gods, in particular Mahumet:

> The Amiralz swears as solemnly as he can
> By the power and body of Mahumet (3232–33)

They invoke them in battle:

> The Amiralz calls upon Apolin
> And Tervagan and Mahumet also:
> "My lord gods, I have served you very long,
> I shall make all your graven images pure gold." (3490–93)

While this Saracen idolatry in many ways evokes the pagan past of Greece and Rome, a much closer and more troubling comparison is to the Christian cult of saints, whose statues, sometimes arrayed in gold and gems, grace Christian churches. In the *Chanson*, the Frankish knights frequently call on the saints: Denis, Mary, Peter, Michael. Indeed, the Saracen knight Turgis tells Marsilie, "Do not be dismayed! Mahumet is worth more than Saint Peter of Rome. If you serve him, we shall be left in possession of the field" (920–22). In this Saracen world that is the inversion or mirror image of the Frankish world, the gods seem to play the role of the Christians' saints, more than the Christian God.

The Saracens also, it seems, have their scriptures, a book of Mahum's laws:

> Marsilies had a book brought forward:
> It was the law of Mahum and Tervagan. (610–11)

They worship idols and images of Mahumet. In Saragossa, as the Saracen troops prepare to go off to battle, the idol of Mahumet is hoisted onto the highest tower of the ramparts, where the pagans pray to it and worship it (852–54). When Baligant goes forth into battle, he is preceded by his standard, which sports images of a dragon and of Tervagan, Mahum, and Apolin (3266–68). The poet uses the forms "Mahum" and "Mahumet" interchangeably, his choice dictated principally by the needs of poetic meter.

The difference between the pagan gods and the Christian saints is perhaps above all their efficacy. "Pagans are wrong and Christians are right," proclaims Roland as he rides into battle (1015). It is on the battlefield that this is to be proven. We have seen that Turgis tells Marsilie that Mahumet is worth more than Saint Peter, but of course he is to be proven wrong. Those who invoke Mahumet as they go into battle are defeated. This is seen repeatedly in the *Chanson*, for example when Roland lops off the head of Marsilie's son, and the pagans cry out, "Help us, Mahum! Gods, avenge us on Charles" (1906–7). Mahum proves powerless to help them. In another passage, it is Roland himself who says to Chernuble, whom he has just sliced in two: "You'll never receive any aid from Mahumet" (1336). It is the fall of the "standard of Mahumet," the ensign sporting the image of the god, that symbolically marks the defeat of the Saracen army and that leads Baligant to realize that he is in error:

> Baligant sees his pennon fall
> And Mahumet's standard brought low;
> The Amiralz begins to realize
> That he is wrong and Charlemagne is right. (3551–54)

This realization neatly brings the epic to a dramatic climax. Roland engaged battle declaring Christians are right and pagans wrong; now at last their great Amiralz realizes it himself. The rest of the action—Baligant's death, the rout of the Saracen army, and the destruction of the idols in Saragossa—is now a foregone conclusion.

The final destruction of the Saracen idols of Saragossa by the Christian knights is foreshadowed by a first destruction by the Saragossa Saracens themselves. When Marsilie returns from battle wounded, his right hand chopped off by Roland, twenty thousand of his men curse Charles and "fair France" before venting their rage on their gods:

> They run to an idol of Apolin in a crypt,
> They rail at it, they abuse it in vile fashion:
> "Oh, evil god, why do you cover us with such shame?
> Why have you allowed this king of ours to be brought to ruin?
> You pay out poor wages to anyone who serves you well!"
> Then they tear away the idol's scepter and its crown.
> They tie it by the hands to a column,
> They topple it to the ground at their feet,
> They beat it and smash it to pieces with big sticks.
> They snatch Tervagan's carbuncle,
> Throw the Mahumet into a ditch,
> And pigs and dogs bite and trample it. (2580–91)

The Saracens punish the gods who have failed to protect their king, a tacit recognition of their powerlessness. Some of these punishments inflicted on the idols (stripping off the regal attributes, tying it to a column) are those one might inflict on a human enemy, signaling the ambiguous relationship between the idols and the gods they are supposed to represent.[27] This also echoes, perhaps, contemporary Christian rituals of humiliation of the saints, where saints' images or relics are symbolically "punished" to incite them to answer the demands of their devotees.[28] Apolin is in a "crypt," which seems more fitting for a saint's relics than for a pagan idol. The particular punishments inflicted on Mahumet, being trampled on and bitten by dogs and pigs, echo contemporary stories of the false prophet Mahumet whose corpse is allegedly attacked by dogs or pigs in hostile legends we will examine in chapter two.

The Queen of Saragossa, Bramimonde, recognizes the impotence of the Saracen gods. Baligant sends two messengers who arrive in Saragossa shortly after the scene of the destruction of the idols. They greet the queen by saying, "May Mahumet, who has us in his power, and Tervagan and Apollin, our lord, save the king and protect the queen" (2711–13). Bramimonde shoots back:

> What rubbish I hear!
> Those gods of ours have given up the fight.
> At Roncevaux they did us a colossal bad turn,
> They allowed our knights to get killed.
> They failed my lord in battle,
> He lost his right hand, he no longer has it,
> Mighty Count Roland severed it from him.
> Charles will have all Spain in his power. (2714–21)

Queen Bramimonde also gives the poem's last evocation of the name of Mahum, calling in vain on his help one final time. Charlemagne has slain Baligant, the Christian troops are charging toward Saragossa, and the queen cries out "Help us, Mahum!" (3641). Bramimonde herself then surrenders the citadel to Charlemagne, who has over a hundred thousand pagans baptized by force. Charlemagne makes an exception for the queen, who is taken captive to France, where she is to be converted "by love" (3674).[29]

Saracen religion in the *Chanson de Roland* and in subsequent *chansons de geste* contributes to the paradoxical portrayal of the enemy as both inexorably other and uncannily familiar. "Pagans are wrong" because they place their confidence in the wrong deities, but their devotion to those deities at times looks very much like Christian devotion to the saints. While some Christians doubted the efficacy and appropriateness of the cult of saints and the use of images, *Roland* redirects that anxiety; idolatry and devotion to the saints may be superficially similar, but their radical difference is proven in the field of battle. Those devoted to God and His saints (Peter, Denis, Mary) vanquish the devotees of Mahomet, Apollin, and Tervagant.

Mahowndes and Mahounds in Medieval Letters

This confrontation, association, and distinction between Christian cult of the saints and Saracen idolatry plays a key role in many of the liturgical dramas of the thirteenth and fourteenth centuries, in French, English, and other languages. Many of these plays were hagiographical; they dramatized the power of saints, at times by pitting them against malefic forces—in some cases "Saracen" idols.

In Jean Bodel's *Jeu de Saint Nicolas*, first performed in December 1200, the main protagonists are less the nameless humans (Christian and Saracen) than the statue of Saint Nicolas who is opposed by the "mahommet" (idol) of Tervagan; the deformed name of the prophet of Islam has become a common noun designating an idol.[30] In a blending of the exotic and the ridiculous, the (nameless) King of the Saracens leads an army recruited from mythic lands such as Orkenie, "from beyond Grey Wallengue, where dogs crap gold" (vv. 362–63), Oliferne, a burning land replete with precious gems (368–72), or "beyond the Dry Tree," where people use millstones as coins (373–76). The king is particularly devoted to his idol of Tervagan, which he covers with gold (136). The king asks Tervagan to show him who will win the upcoming battle with the Christians: "If I must win, laugh; if I must lose, cry" (181–82); enigmatic, the demon-inhabited idol cries and laughs simultaneously, signifying that the Saracen king will win the battle but lose his Saracen faith. Contrary to the *chanson de gestes* or the *chanson de croisades*, which culminated in glorious Christian triumphs, here the Saracen military victory is complete, the only Christian survivor being a nameless wise man ("Preudome") captured while praying to his icon of Saint Nicolas, which the Saracens mistake for a "mahommet." Yet Nicolas produces a miracle for the king: he appears in a dream to three robbers who have stolen the royal treasure and frightens them into bringing it back. The king acknowledges the power of the saint and converts, along with all his men. He orders his seneschal to expel the idol of Tervagan from the "sinagoge"; before destroying the idol, the seneschal addresses these words to it, reminding his audience of the idol's prophecy at the beginning of the play:

> Tervagan, you will in time see the fulfillment of your prophecy
> When you laughed and cried
> In your pain.
> What lies you tell me!
> Down with you! You have no right to be up there!
> We do not care a whit for you! (1522–27)

As the idol comes crashing down on the stage, the audience's devotion to Saint Nicolas is vindicated; he proves himself more powerful than the "mahommets" of the Saracens.

Another type of medieval drama was the "mystery play," narrating the events around the passion of Christ. In the fourteenth- and fifteenth-century English mystery plays, Saracen idolatry serves as a foil to Christian piety. In the York cycle of mystery plays, the pharaoh is a devotee of Mahownde pitted against Moses, follower of the True God.[31] This opposition typologically prefigures the whole spiritual conflict that these plays seek to dramatize: a continual struggle between the followers of Christ and the satanically inspired devotees of Mahownde. In the Chester cycle, a pagan named Balaam predicts that the incarnation of Christ will lead to the destruction of the "mawmets"; the pagan king Balak responds, "Mahound giue the mischance!"[32] In a parallel prophecy, angels announce that when the infant Christ flees into Egypt, the "mahumetis" will fall.[33] Herod subsequently introduces himself as "prince of Purgatorre ... and cheff capten of hell ... Reysemelyng the fauer of thatt most myght Mahownd; From Jubytor be desent and cosyn to the grett God."[34] Herod and the other villains of the drama claim an eclectic (and often deliberately comic) allegiance to Saracen idols, classical

Roman deities, and the forces of hell. The devils worship Mahound, as do the Jews (especially the Pharisees); it is the scheming of Jewish devotees of Mahound that leads to Christ's crucifixion.[35] In the Chester cycle, King Herod calls on his God "Mahounde full of might!"[36] In the Townley mystery cycle, Pontius Pilate is a Jewish devotee of Mahowne who calls on "Sir Lucifer" and hails his soldiers as descendants of Cain.[37] The soldiers who torture Christ mock him in the name of Mahowne and ridicule his pretensions to be savior of mankind; the soldiers express doubts about Christian doctrine that the audience is not allowed. The sharp dichotomy between the forces of good and evil served its didactic and doctrinal purpose; doubt about Christian doctrine could only come from demonic inspiration. Those who rejected Christianity—Jews, Saracens, and pagans—are united in their diabolical hostility toward Christ and his followers.

As we have seen in Jean Bodel's *Jeu de Saint Nicolas*, "mahommet" became in medieval French a common noun designating an idol: the Saracens in Bodel's play worship not an image of the god Mahomet, but a "mahommet" of their god Tervagant.[38] In both French and English, this word, in various forms (mahon, mahum, mahun, mahoun, makemet, mahounde, mahowne, and so on) becomes a standard term to designate idols: those worshipped by ancient Greeks and Romans, the gods of Vikings or other northern heathens, or the purported gods of the Saracens.[39] For example, Lazamon, a twelfth-century English monk, has pre-Christian Saxons worshipping "maumets." A Middle English biblical commentary on Isaiah says that Baal was the principal "maumet" of the Babylonians.[40]

In depictions of biblical-era Jews who lapsed into idolatry we see them worshipping "mahomets." One prominent example is in a thirteenth-century stained glass window in the Sainte Chapelle in Paris. In a series of scenes narrating the life of the Prophet Isaiah, he reprimands Jews for worshipping an idol of gold (fig. 3; cf. Isaiah 40–48).

The prophet, standing, holds up his finger in reprobation as two men kneel before a golden statue of a standing naked youth, placed in a gothic niche. Two names are written in white on a black background: that of Isaiah at the top of the scene and, at the very bottom, "Mahomet." As in the illumination in the manuscript of the *Chanson*

FIGURE 3. The Prophet Isaiah chastises two Jews worshipping a "Mahomet." Stained glass
window in the Sainte Chapelle, Paris (1242–1248). © akg-images / Hervé Champollion

d'Antioche, the "Mahomet's" nudity distinguishes it from an image
of a saint and is the only element that makes clear that this is idolatrous worship rather than proper Christian worship. The Isaiah
cycle was part of the rich iconographic program in stained glass
executed between 1242 and 1248, commissioned by King Louis IX
to grace the Sainte Chapelle, the new home for the crown of thorns,
which he had purchased in 1239.[41] In Saint Louis's France, wayward
biblical Jews are portrayed worshipping a "Mahomet" (fig. 3).

Other images depict Jewish idol worship, in particular the worship of the golden calf in the Sinai desert, at times identifying the
idols as "mahum" or "mahmet." The Hereford map, a large and very
detailed world map composed in England about 1300, depicts a
horned Moses at the top of Mount Sinai receiving the "tablets of the
testament" from the hand of God reaching out of a cloud. Directly
underneath, a group of Jews (identified as such, "Iudei") kneel in
prayer before the golden calf, which seems to be defecating onto its

FIGURE 4. The flight into Egypt, from the Holkham picture bible
(early fourteenth century). British Library Add. 47682, f.15.
England, circa 1320–1330. © akg-images / British Library

pedestal. The idol is labeled "mahum."[42] Similarly, we find idols
called "maumez" in the Holkham picture bible, a lavish manuscript
produced in England, probably in the 1320s, with full-page illustrations of scenes from the Old and New Testaments. The page devoted
to the flight into Egypt shows Mary with the baby Jesus in her arms,
riding on a donkey that Joseph is leading by a rope (fig. 4). They
have just passed under an arch, and in front of them is a pedestal
from which two idols are toppling. The apocryphal gospel of Matthew had related how, when the holy family entered into a temple
in Hermopolis, the 365 idols there all toppled to the ground and
shattered. This scene becomes standard in iconography of the flight
into Egypt, although usually no more than one or (as here) two idols
are portrayed.[43] Here the idols, far from being stiff statues that shat-
ter, are portrayed as demons, with horns and goatlike feet, bearing
red shields. The one on the left is toppling off his pedestal, while the
one on the right seems to be bowing down before Jesus. The accompanying text, in French, says that "les maumez" fell down through
the power of the son of Mary.

English monk Ranulph Higden penned his *Polychronicon*, a world chronicle, in the fourteenth century. For Ranulph, "Machometus" is a false prophet, not a god; he follows the standard polemical narration of his life that we will examine in chapter two. At one point, he says that as a youth Machometus had shown devotion to the cult of idols, in particular to Venus. John of Trevisa, in his 1387 translation of the *Polychronicon*, writes, "he worschipped mawmetrie."[44] When Machometus subsequently preached his new law, he prohibited the pagans from practicing idolatry ("paganis idolatriam inhibens"), or, for Trevisa "forbeed þe paynyms mametrie."[45] Trevisa perhaps did not recognize that the common noun, *mawmetrie*, which he used to translate the Latin *idolatria*, was derived from the name of the person Machometus, whose life he was narrating. Trevisa's translation, subsequently published by William Caxton in 1480, is one of the books that will provide the English reader with a very different image of the prophet of Islam than the image we have seen in this chapter, a vitriolic vision of Muhammad as a trickster and false prophet, which we will examine in chapter two. Yet ironically, it at the same time preserves "mawmetrie" as the common noun to designate idolatry. The stereotype of Saracen idolatry still was alive and kicking, it seems.

The comicall history of Alphonsus, King of Aragon (1599) is probably the first play written by the popular English playwright Robert Greene.[46] It portrays the struggles of its eponymous hero (perhaps very loosely modeled on King Alfonso V of Aragon, r. 1416–58) to recover his kingdom. Alphonsus's rival and nemesis, Belinus, takes refuge in Constantinople, where the (fictive) Sultan Amurack pledges to help him. Alphonsus ends up defeating the Ottoman armies, marrying Amurack's daughter, and thus obtaining the vast Ottoman Empire. In this comic fantasy, the Ottoman sultan and his subjects are cast in the stereotypical role of Saracen idolaters. Amurack repeatedly invokes his god, the "mighty Mahomet" (acts III and IV, passim). The fourth act opens at a "temple of Mahomet," presided over by two priests; the stage directions indicate, "let there be a brazen Head set in the middle of the place behind the Stage, out of the which cast flames of fire, drums rumble within." The "brazen head" is an idol of Mahomet, to whom the priests pray and who answers them. Mahomet orders Amurack to take his troops to Naples and conquer the kingdom of Aragon. As they set off, Belinus chirps, "and since we have God Mahound on our side, the victory must needs to us betide" (IV.1.86–87). When, at the end of act IV, Amurack learns that Belinus has been slain and his army routed, he does what is expected of a defeated Saracen monarch: he curses and threatens Mahomet.

> What news is this? And is Belinus slain?
> Is this the Crown which Mahomet did say . . .
> He should with triumph wear upon his head?
> Is this the honor which that cursed god
> Did prophesy should happen to them all?
> Oh Daedalus, and wert thou now alive
> To fasten wings upon high Amurack,
> Mahound should know, and that for certainty,
> That Turkish Kings can brook no injury. (IV.3.49–57)

He subsequently threatens:

> For Amurack doth mean this very day
> Proud Mahomet with weapons to assay. (IV.3.72–3)

This image of idolatrous worship of Mahomet is alive and well, it seems, on the English stage five centuries after its first formulation by French poets and Latin chroniclers. Not that the image was meant to be taken seriously; this is after all a "comicall history," a light fantasy of easy Christian conquest of a rival empire that in fact, as Greene's audience was painfully aware, was the major military power in the eastern Mediterranean and central Europe. The image of Turkish idolatry is not common on the English stage, though we do find it elsewhere, for example in Robert Dahorne's *A Christian Turn'd Turke* (1611), where a "Mahomet's head" is part of the paraphernalia that accompanies a Christian's conversion to Islam.[47] And it is just three years before Greene's *Alphonsus*, as we have seen, that Richard Johnson published his *Famous Historie of the Seaven Champions of Christendom*, which was to assure a long life to the stereotype of Saracen idolatry.

Even a nineteenth-century French historian of the crusades continued to reiterate the medieval legend of the idol of Mahomet. Antoine Caillaud, in his *Tableau des croisades pour la Terre Sainte*

FIGURE 5. Tancred destroys the idol of Mahomet in Jerusalem. Antoine Caillot, *Tableau des croisades pour la conquete de la terre-sainte* (Paris, 1843), frontispiece. D.R.

(1818), describes how, as the crusaders captured Jerusalem in 1099, Tancred de Hauteville had his men destroy the statue of Mahomet that they had found in "the great mosque."[48] He includes a frontispiece (fig. 5) showing the statue at the moment of its destruction: Mahomet holds a sword in one hand and a book in the other. This statue is a fusion (or perhaps, more properly, confusion) of the polemical stereotypes of Mahomet as idol and as false prophet whose attributes are the sword and the "Alcoran," as we will see in numerous modern European representations of the prophet.

The idols of Mahomet live on into the twentieth century in the festivals of small towns in Spain, many of which involve annual ritual reenactments of the reconquest of the town from the Muslims. In a number of these *fiestas* of "Moors and Christians," a squadron of local inhabitants dressed up as *Moros* take over a mock citadel and set up a "Mahoma"—a dressed-up effigy—on the walls. In the mock siege that follows, the Christian troops take over the citadel and destroy the *Mahoma*. In some of the *fiestas*, the *Mahoma*, filled with fireworks, explodes in a spectacular (and somewhat dangerous) pyrotechnic finale. In the second half of the twentieth century, many of the towns, in a post-Vatican-II spirit of ecumenism, banished *Mahoma* from these festivities as an embarrassing travesty of Islam.[49] Yet eight centuries after the *Chanson de Roland* describes the Saracens of Saragossa toppling the idol Mahomet into a ditch, eight centuries after Raoul de Caen imagines Tancred destroying a gilded idol of Mahomet in the Temple of Solomon, Valencian villagers reenact this imaginary idol destruction as a central part of their dramatization of the *reconquista*.

Yet despite this persistence of these Saracen idols in the European imagination, European authors more often imagined Muhammad in the guise of a deviant Christian, a wily trickster and heretic who led the Arabs astray. It is to this image that we now turn.

CHAPTER TWO

Trickster and Heresiarch

IN 1409, LAURENT DE PREMIERFAIT, humanist at the court of French king Charles VI, sat down to revise and expand his translation of Giovanni Boccaccio's *De casibus virorum illustrium* (The fate of famous men).[1] At one point Boccaccio had mentioned the Byzantine emperor Heraclius (r. 610–41) and added that during his reign the "seducer Mahumeth" usurped the name of prophet and issued deadly laws.[2] When he first translated *De casibus* in 1400, Laurent de Premierfait simply translated this brief sentence about the "false prophet."[3] Nine years later, he decided to include a biographical sketch of "the disloyal traitor Machomet," whom he calls a "false, lying prophet and magician."[4]

Machumet, Laurent tells us, was born to plebian parents in "Meca," where he worshipped idols as his family had before him. He became a merchant and traveled with his camels to Egypt and Judea, where he spoke with Jews and Christians, learning from them parts of the Old and New Testaments. He traveled to the province of Corozan, where he sold spices and other goods to the powerful and rich lady "Cadige," who marveled at him. Machomet was an enchanter and sorcerer, and he was thus able to convince "this powerful and noble woman" that he was "the Messiah, that is the son of God that the Jews awaited." Machomet and Cadige were married and his reputation spread, attracting Jews and Saracens from far and wide. Machomet, realizing he could not become king of Corozan, feigned to be a prophet. At this point he was joined by a "very famous priest," exiled in the Orient with his followers because the

FIGURE 6. Mahomet preaching with a dove on his shoulder; a bull brings the Qur'ān on his horns. Illustration ca. 1409–25, in Laurent de Premierfait, *Des cas des nobles hommes et femmes*, drawn by the "Master of Rohan." Paris, BNF MS Français 226, f. 243 (XVe s.). © BNF

pope had opposed him. On the advice of this priest, Machomet trained a dove to eat grains of wheat out of his ear; when the astounded people saw the dove landing on his shoulder and putting its beak in the false prophet's ear, he explained to them that this was the Holy Spirit coming to speak to him as he had to John the Baptist. Through this trick, he hoodwinked "simple, rustic people" who flocked to him in great numbers.

Machomet goaded his followers on to war: the Arabs conquered large swathes of Persia and of Heraclius's empire. God, in order to show people the true nature of "the traitor Machomet," struck him with epilepsy; Cadige was "very perturbed." But Machomet was not so easily foiled; he explained that the Archangel Gabriel had come to speak to him, and that he fell down because he was awed by the brightness emanating from the celestial face of the angel. Machomet and the priest wrote laws mixing their own novelties with items gleaned from the Old and New Testaments; the book they wrote is the "vile and undignified Alcoran." He then placed this book on the horns of a bull that he had trained to eat from his hand. One day as he preached to the people, the bull suddenly appeared with the book attached to its horns; it was hailed as a divine messenger and the book revered as the word of God. Machomet also revealed jars of milk and honey that he had hidden in the desert, but which he presents as gifts sent down by God. Laurent concludes by saying that Machomet then died and went straight to hell. His "stinking corpse" was placed in an iron casket that was taken to a temple in Meca that had magnets in the ceiling. He says that he read all this in book 24 of Vincent of Beauvais's *Miroir historiale* (*Mirror of History*, the medieval French translation of Vincent's thirteenth-century encyclopedic chronicle, the *Speculum historiale*).

Some of the manuscripts of Laurent's work are lavishly illustrated, and several contain portraits of Machomet. One artist, often identified as the Master of Rohan, has painted a scene showing a turbaned Machomet preaching from a pulpit with a dove perched on his shoulder, its beak in his ear (fig. 6). In front of the pulpit, the bull walks in, with the "Alcoran" between his horns. On the left, five people listen attentively, looking at Machomet: two women and three men, sporting visibly oriental headgear (turbans and "Turkish" hats). Other manuscripts have similar images.[5]

These manuscript paintings, along with Laurent's brief biographical notice, give a good idea of how various fifteenth- and sixteenth-century writers and artists portrayed the life of Muhammad. We have seen that Laurent cites thirteenth-century encyclopedist Vincent de Beauvais, who himself had compiled his life of the prophet from diverse (and contradictory) Latin texts of the twelfth century. Vincent's Latin text was a medieval best seller, with hundreds of manuscripts in Latin and translations in French and Dutch. Laurent de Premierfait's text also became widely known, with fifty-seven French manuscripts. Benedictine monk John Lydgate translated Laurent's text into English verse sometime between 1410 and 1450; there are some thirty-four extant fifteenth-century manuscripts.[6] Printed editions of both the French prose text (by Antoine Vérard in Paris) and the Lydgate English verse version (by William Caxton in London) appeared in 1494.

Here we have, then, a hostile version of the life of Muhammad, forged essentially in the twelfth century, based to a certain extent on earlier Latin and Greek polemical texts. Details vary, as we will see: some authors add episodes not given in Laurent's brief text or narrate slightly different versions of events in the life of the false prophet. But by and large, they agree in the general narrative: the Muslim prophet is presented as a charlatan and sorcerer who feigns prophecy in order to marry a rich and powerful woman and to become leader of the Arabs. His Alcoran is a hodgepodge of Old and New Testament laws along with new measures that are all the more popular because they are easier to follow; many authors insist on the sexual debauchery supposedly authorized by this new law. The sorcerer Mahomet passes off his tricks as miracles, hoodwinking the naive Arabs who flock to him. The Christian reader could rest assured that the "Saracen error" that had seduced a large part of the planet's population was the crass invention of a vile man. This caricature was colorful and appealing and it encountered great success among those Europeans who knew nothing about Islam. For these authors, Mahomet was not a golden idol based on the gods of Greek and Roman antiquity, he was a debauched swindler and heretic, modeled after false holy men and heresiarchs from Arius to more recent preachers who had challenged the Church. The writers who forged these polemical biographies were preoccupied with the spread of heresy, of dissent concerning the doctrines and the authority of the Church, in an age when issues of reform and heresy sharply divided the Church and European society. Hence their caricatural portraits of Muhammad reflected their own worries about potential charlatans, false reformers, and heretics, rather than curiosity about Islam or its prophet.

Other Christian authors knew more about Islam and tried to come up with more sophisticated (though not necessarily less hostile) ways to understand and portray Islam and its prophet. Those living under Muslim rule, from Iraq to Andalus (Muslim Spain), sought to discourage their coreligionaries from converting to Islam by presenting it as a tissue of lies; while their image of the prophet is negative, it is often closer to the Muslim sources than is the unrecognizable caricature of Laurent de Premierfait. Beginning in the twelfth century, Latin theologians attempted to refute what they portrayed as the "Saracen" heresy; in the thirteenth and fourteenth centuries, mendicant friars learned Arabic and studied the Qur'ān, the better to combat the "Saracen heresy" in a largely futile attempt to obtain converts to Christianity. They aggressively (mis)read Muslim sources (and depended on earlier Arab Christian sources) to present Muhammad as a heresiarch. Indeed, heresy—deviant versions of Christianity that rejected the authority of the Church—was a major preoccupation of many of the twelfth- and thirteenth-century churchmen who wrote about Mahomet. Making the prophet of Islam into yet another heresiarch served to explain away the successes of Islam and the challenges it posed to a triumphalist Christian vision of history and at the same time permitted these authors to denigrate heretics closer to home by associating them with the charlatan Mahomet.[7]

From the twelfth century well into the sixteenth, the perception of Muhammad that dominates in Europe is that of a heresiarch and false prophet. In this chapter, we will look at one example of a formative text of the twelfth century, from the crusade chronicle of Guibert de Nogent and then see how the legend is reworked by fifteenth-century authors such as Laurent de Premierfait and John Lydgate. We will also see how this view of Muhammad as a heretic proffering false miracles was shared even by those few Latin writers who studied the Qur'ān, had it translated into Latin, and attempted to forge Christian theological responses to Islam.

The Twelfth-Century Legend: Guibert of Nogent

In 1109, Guibert, abbot of the Norman monastery of Nogent sous Coucy, penned his chronicle of the First Crusade, *Deeds of God through the Franks* (*Dei gesta per Francos*), glorifying and justifying the exploits of the knights who captured Jerusalem in 1099. Guibert had no firsthand knowledge of the crusade or of Islam. But he had come across a chronicle of the crusade written by one of the participants (the anonymous *Gesta Francorum et aliorum Hierosolimitanorum*, "The deeds of the Franks and the others who went to Jerusalem"). Guibert found that the text was poorly written and failed to communicate the importance of the momentous events it relates. So he undertook to rewrite it, in proper order and in elegant Latin. He also set out to explain the meaning of the events and their place in God's plan of history. For it was not simply a story of the "Deeds of the Franks," but it was God working through His army, it was more properly the *Deeds of God through the Franks*. He sought to explain why the Europeans (or "Franks") had to go east, to Christ's birthplace, to restore his native city to him.[8] Guibert contrasts the valor and religious zeal of the Franks with the moral turpitude of the Orient, nest of heresies from the time of Arius onward.

Guibert places a brief life of Muhammad near the beginning of his *Dei gesta per Francos*, as a part of a narration of the history of Jerusalem and of oriental Christendom from the time of Constantine to the moment the crusaders set out for Jerusalem. After the glorious foundation of the basilica of Jerusalem by Helen, mother of Constantine, the East slides slowly but surely into heretical error. Orientals, Guibert explains, are clever, flighty intellectuals whose brilliant circumlocutions carry them off into heresy, contrasted implicitly to the stodgy, earthbound, authority-respecting Latins. Is it any wonder, Guibert continues, that virtually all the heresiarchs were Orientals, from Mani and Arius forward? These Orientals continue to defend their errors through reasoning (*ratiocinatio*): the use of leavened bread in the Eucharist, the lack of proper deference to the pope, clerical marriage and Trinitarian errors regarding the procession of the Holy Spirit. It is because of these errors, Guibert affirms, that God allowed the eastern empire to fall to the Arab invaders.[9] It is at this point that Guibert narrates Muhammad's biography, placing him in a dual role: as divine scourge sent to punish the heretical eastern Christians and the latest and worst of a long line of Oriental heresiarchs.

It is as the worst of these eastern heretics, then, that Guibert presents the man he calls "Mathomus," who led the Orientals "away from belief in the Son and the Holy Spirit. He taught them to acknowledge only the person of the Father as the single, creating God, and he said that Jesus was entirely human. To sum up his teachings, having decreed circumcision, he gave them free rein for every kind of shameful behavior." Guibert acknowledges that he found no reliable texts about "Mathomus" and his life, so has repeated what he has heard: "to discuss whether these things are true or false is useless, since we are considering only the nature of this new teacher, whose reputation for great crimes continues to spread. One may safely speak ill of a man whose malignity transcends and surpasses whatever evil can be said about him."[10] Guibert is aware that Saracens "contrary to what some say, do not believe that he [Muhammad] is their god, but a just man and their patron, through whom divine laws were transmitted."[11] Guibert looked for a theological refutation of Muhammad's doctrine among the writings of the Church fathers; he found none, which led him to believe that "Mathomus" lived after the fathers wrote. Guibert would prefer to speak of Mathomus from the security of patristic authority, but, lacking that, must merely recount what the common people say about him. Much of what he says about the prophet he probably gleaned from his reading of the Theophanes the Confessor, a Byzantine monk and aristocrat who inserted a brief, polemical sketch of "Μουάμεδ" (Mouamed) in his *Chronographia*, a chronicle of world history (ca. 815), which was subsequently translated (ca. 875) into Latin by papal librarian Anastasius.[12] Guibert takes Theophanes's narrative and livens it up by making "Mathomus" into a colorful scoundrel whose acolytes provide a satisfying enemy for the Frankish knights. Guibert is one of several early twelfth-century Latin authors to portray Muhammad in this way.[13]

We have seen that Laurent de Premierfait gives his Machomet a Christian sidekick, a priest who has fallen out with the pope and who is clearly seeking revenge. The ultimate model for this deviant Christian is Bahira, the Christian monk who (according to various hadiths) recognized in the young Muhammad the future prophet, and whom hostile eastern Christians made into an Arian or Nestorian heretic who had schooled Muhammad in doctrinal perversion; later Christian writers often refer to him as Sergius. Like Laurent, Guibert does not name him, though he relates his story in much greater detail.[14] Guibert explains that the patriarch of Alexandria died and that there was much disagreement over who should succeed him. Finally, a nearby hermit with a reputation for sanctity was chosen. Yet as men of the Church got to know the hermit they realized that he was a heretic and rescinded their choice. "Scorned, torn apart by bitter grief, since he had been unable to reach what he had striven for, like Arius, [the hermit] began to think carefully how to take vengeance by spreading the poison of false belief, to undermine Catholic teaching everywhere." It is at this point that the "ancient

Enemy," the Devil himself, came along and told the hermit to look for the young "Mathomus" and to ally himself with him. Muslim sources tell of Muhammad's first marriage (at the age of twenty-five) with the widow Khadīja (forty at the time).[15] Laurent de Premierfait calls her Cadige; Guibert does not give her name, presenting her merely as "a certain very rich woman [who] had recently become a widow." The hermit persuaded the woman to marry Mathomus, convincing her that he was a prophet; "and the formerly wretched Mathomus, surrounded by brilliant riches, was lifted, perhaps to his own great stupefaction, to unhoped-for power."

Theophanes claimed that Mouamed had had an epileptic seizure, and at this Khadīja became distressed; he soothed her by telling her, "I keep seeing a vision of a certain angel called Gabriel, and being unable to bear his sight, I faint and fall down."[16] Laurent de Premierfait made his epilepsy into divine punishment for his blasphemy. Guibert turns it into a sexually transmitted disease: "since the vessel of a single bed frequently received their sexual exchanges, the famous prophet contracted the disease of epilepsy." Terrified, the woman went to the hermit and berated him for having urged her to marry an epileptic.[17] The hermit shot back "you are foolish for ascribing harm to what is a source of light and glory. Don't you know, blind woman, that whenever God glides into the minds of the prophets, the whole bodily frame is shaken, because the weakness of the flesh can scarcely bear the visitation of divine majesty?" In her "womanly flightiness," she believed the hermit and revered her husband as a true prophet. Mathomus's fame spread and acolytes flocked from afar. He ordered his devotees to fast for three days and to pray that God reveal a new law to them, "from an unexpected hand." Mathomus, with the help of the hermit, had written his law in a book that he now tied to the horns of a cow. Theophanes does not relate this story, which seems to be a twelfth-century invention; other twelfth-century authors say it was a bull (as does Laurent Premierfait).[18] Here is how Guibert tells it:

> Meanwhile, he had a cow, whom he himself had trained to follow him, so that whenever she heard his voice or saw him, almost no force could prevent her from rushing to him with unbearable eagerness. He tied the book he had written to the horns of the animal, and hid her in the tent

in which he himself lived. On the third day he climbed a high platform above all the people he had called together, and began to declaim to the people in a booming voice. When, as I just said, the sound of his words reached the cow's ears, she immediately ran from the tent, which was nearby, and, with the book fastened on her horns, made her way eagerly through the middle of the assembled people to the feet of the speaker, as though to congratulate him. Everyone was amazed, and the book was quickly removed and read to the breathless people, who happily accepted the license permitted by its foul law. What more? The miracle of the offered book was greeted with applause over and over again. As though sent from the sky, the new license for random copulation was propagated everywhere, and the more the supply of permitted filth increased, the more the grace of a God who permitted more lenient times, without any mention of turpitude, was preached. All of Christian morality was condemned by a thousand reproofs, and whatever examples of goodness and strength the Gospel offered were called cruel and harsh. But what the cow had delivered was considered universal liberty, the only one recommended by God. Neither the antiquity of Moses nor the more recent Catholic teachings had any authority. Everything which had existed before the law, under the law, under grace, was marked as implacably wrong.[19]

Guibert does not relate some of the other legends that Laurent de Premierfait would subsequently include in his narrative: the dove that eats from the false prophet's ear, or the hidden pots of milk and honey, though other twelfth-century authors indeed relate these tales.[20] The cow revelation suffices, for Guibert, all the more as the law the cow reveals panders to the perverse sexuality of these Oriental people. Theophanes had denounced Mouamed for promising his followers a heaven replete with sensual delights. Guibert goes a step further in imagining that sexual license is the essence of the new law and the base of its appeal to a sensuous people. Guibert, of course, is a monk under a vow of celibacy; when he denounces religious enemies (be they Jews, Cathar heretics, or here, Muslims), he often attributes to them perverse sexual practices.[21]

A scoundrel and heresiarch deserves an ignominious death. Guibert relates that one day, Mathomus fell into an epileptic fit and "was devoured by pigs, so that nothing could be found but his heels."[22] Mathomus's heels, for Guibert, become the supreme relics of Islam; attacking false relics (in general, closer to home) was one of Guibert's favorite pastimes.[23] The story is supposed to explain why Saracens do not eat pork.[24]

Guibert's Mathomus is a colorful scoundrel. This well-crafted portrait serves its purpose well, signaling as it does that Orientals, subject to the ill effects of the sun and the air, are prone to heresy and enslaved to the pleasures of the flesh. The ideological point is clear: the conquests of God's army, of valorous and pure Christians from the West, are justified and necessary, against the Saracen followers of Mathomus and against the weak and perfidious Greeks. Guibert uses the image of the flighty and sensual Oriental to affirm the right—indeed the duty—of the vigorous stolid European to appropriate his lands and to rule over him.

Guibert asserts that the Saracens worship the relics of their prophet; Gautier de Compiègne, a twelfth-century Latin poet, describes this worship in vivid terms:

> And his people, believing that his spirit to the stars
> had passed, dared not submit his body to the earth.
> They established therefore an ark of admirable workmanship:
> In this they placed him as best they could.
> For, as is told, [the ark] seems to hang
> With Machomus' members lying inside
> So that without any support it hangs in the air,
> And without any chains holding it from above.
> And if you ask them by what artifice it does not fall,
> They erroneously repute it to Machomus' powers.
> But in fact it is covered in iron,
> Placed in the center of a square building
> Made out of magnetic rock, on all four sides
> The measurements are the same inside and out.
> By nature it attracts the iron to itself equally
> So that it is unable to fall in any direction.[25]

Through a final posthumous phony miracle, Muhammad dupes the naive Saracens into revering him. Gautier places the tomb in *Mecha*, an appropriate name since Muhammad was an adulterer

(*Mechus*); others, Gautier tells us, place his tomb in Babel, also appropriate since Muhammad's effrontery matched that of the builders of the tower of Babel (verses 1077–86). This imagined cultic center of the Saracen world, the floating tomb of Muhammad at Babel/Mecca, is a sort of mirror image of the crusaders' Jerusalem, an anti-Jerusalem; just as Christian pilgrims journey to Christ's tomb in Jerusalem, Saracen pilgrims flock to the floating tomb of their false prophet and god. It is also meant to explain the power and attraction of Islam to the numerous Saracens.[26]

Learned Assault on the Prophet: From Petrus Alfonsi to the Dominicans

Guibert in 1109 noted the lack of reliable information and sound theological refutation of Islam; the following year, Petrus Alfonsi purported to provide exactly that; based on his knowledge of Arabic and his familiarity with Arabic Christian polemics against Islam, he inserted a brief refutation of Islam into his *Dialogues against the Jews* (*Dialogi contra Iudaeos*). His polemic soon became one of the most widely read Latin theological texts on Islam. One of its readers was Abbot Peter of Cluny, who in 1142–43 traveled to Spain, where he commissioned a Latin translation of the Qur'ān; he subsequently wrote two treatises of learned polemics against Islam, in which he branded Muhammad as a heresiarch.

Petrus Alfonsi was born Moses, a Jew from al-Andalus (Muslim Spain). He was schooled in Hebrew and Arabic; his writings show familiarity with the Talmud, with texts of Arabic astronomy, medicine, and philosophy, and with the Arabic literary traditions. Moses converted to Christianity and was baptized on June 29, 1106, in the cathedral (and former mosque) of Huesca, capital of the Pyrenean kingdom of Aragon. He explains that he took the name Petrus (Peter) in honor of Saint Peter and Alfonsi in honor of his godfather, King Alfonso I of Aragon. Four years later, in 1110, he wrote his *Dialogues against the Jews*, because, he says, Jews accused him of having abandoned his former faith out of contempt for God's law, misunderstanding of the prophets, and lust for worldly gain. The *Dialogues* are his response to these accusers; he seeks to "destroy their objections with reason and authority." Alfonsi explains that he has given the name Moses to the Jewish debater because that was his own name as a Jew; he gives the Christian debater his new name, Peter. The twelve *Dialogues* fall into three parts: in the first, an attack on Judaism (*Dialogues* I–IV), Peter "proves" to Moses that Judaism is no longer valid, that Jews "obey the law only in part, and that part is not pleasing to God." Much of his argument turns on rationally and scientifically based attacks on the Talmud. He then launches into an attack on Islam (*Dialogue* V), in which he presents Muhammad as a fraud and a pseudoprophet, and Muslim rituals (such as ablutions, fasting, and pilgrimage) as sullied by their supposed pagan origins. In the final section (*Dialogues* VI–XII), Peter attempts to prove the basic doctrines of Christianity to Moses, or at least to show how they do not contradict either reason or the Old Testament. By the end of the exchange in the *Dialogues*, Moses is convinced and tamely converts to Christianity.[27]

Alfonsi is Andalusian; it is natural for his *Dialogues against the Jews* to contain a chapter directed against Islam, otherwise, his defense of Christianity would be incomplete. Since Peter is attempting to convince the Jew Moses (not a Muslim) of the weaknesses of Islam, his arguments are less developed than those of his anti-Jewish polemic. This, combined with the fact that a Christian need not have the respect for the Qur'ān that he has for the Torah, gives his rejection of Islam a different flavor than his anti-Jewish arguments. For Alfonsi it is enough to impugn the morals of Muhammad, the pagan origins of the cult of Mecca, and the questionable textual transmission of the Qur'ān, to prove that Islam is based on falsehood. This attack on Islam is nevertheless better informed and more thorough than anything previously written in Latin. Unlike the other Latin (or French) writers whose work we have examined, Alfonsi knew Arabic and had lived among Muslims. He was also familiar with apologetical works written by Arab Christians.

In fact, Alfonsi bases his anti-Muslim chapter almost entirely on a tenth-century Arabic Christian work, the *Risālat al-Kindī*. This text purports to be an exchange of letters, in Arabic, between two prominent members of the 'Abbasid court: a Muslim (unnamed in the text, but whom a later tradition identified as 'Abd Allah al-Hāshimī), presents Islam to a Nestorian Christian friend (traditionally referred to 'Abd al-Masih al-Kindī), and invites him to convert;

in reply, al-Kindī presents a long, detailed refutation of Islam and defense of Christianity and invites al-Hāshimī to convert. In fact, both letters were probably written by one Christian author: the letter ascribed to al-Hāshimī presents Islamic doctrine in an unconvincing way and makes only feeble attacks on Christianity; he is there to lend an air of authenticity to the refutation, a fictitious Muslim witness to a Christian theological triumph. This "Muslim" devotes more space to the praise of Christian monks than to the defense of Islam.[28]

The *Risālat al-Kindī* is both polemical and apologetical: it attacks Muslim doctrine and provides a defense of key Christian doctrines that would be distasteful to Muslims. The author shows a good knowledge of Islam and of the Qur'ān; the Muslim's letter presents Abraham as the first Muslim; the Christian retorts by saying that Muhammad himself said that *he* was the first Muslim and provides a citation from the Qur'ān to prove it.[29] He defends the Trinity while affirming God's unity; far be it from a true Christian to say "God is the third of three."[30] Does not God, in the Bible, refer to himself in the plural?[31] God has many attributes, he asserts, two of which are eternal: life and knowledge. Life corresponds to Christ (λογὸς, *kalima*), knowledge to the Holy Spirit (πνεῦμα, *rūh*); thus the Trinity can be proven from a reflection on God's nature.[32]

The Christian next launches a concerted attack against Muhammad in order to prove that he was no prophet.[33] He recounts Muhammad's biography in as acerbic and derogatory fashion as possible, showing all the while a good knowledge of the Qur'ān and early Muslim historiography. He notes that Muhammad had first been an idolater and had enriched himself through trade and through his marriage with Khadīja. Wishing to rule over his tribe, he decided to pretend to be a prophet; his companions, gullible nomads who knew nothing of the signs of prophecy, believed him. He and his followers enriched themselves through war and pillaging. These acts, for the Christian writer, are enough to prove that Muhammad was not a prophet; the failures of some of the expeditions (especially the defeat at the battle of Uhud, where he was injured) even more so: a true prophet would have foreseen (and avoided) defeat.

This Christian monk is particularly shocked by Muhammad's sexual life, which he attacks with zeal. Muhammad himself, he says, claimed to have the sexual powers of forty men. He presents a catalog of Muhammad's fifteen wives, dwelling on the scandals surrounding Zaynab (divorced wife of Muhammad's adopted son Zayd) and 'Ā'isha (whom the Qur'ān defended from accusations of adultery).[34] Did not the Apostle Paul proclaim that "he that is unmarried cares for the things that belong to the Lord, how he may please the Lord: But he that is married cares for the things that are of the world, how he may please his wife" (1 Corinthians 7:32–33)? Is this not even more true of a man with fifteen wives, a man, moreover, constantly involved in planning war? "How could he, with this continual and permanent preoccupation, find the time to fast, pray, worship God, meditate and contemplate eternal things and those things appropriate to prophets? I am certain that no prophet was as attached to the pleasures of this world as was your master."[35]

In much of this, the Christian author compares (explicitly or implicitly) Muhammad with Jesus: Christ shunning sex and worldly power, Muhammad eagerly pursuing both; Christ prophesying true things, Muhammad failing to foresee his defeats in battle; Christ producing miracles, Muhammad none. He carries this contrast into his description of Muhammad's death. Muhammad, he says, ordered that his companions not bury him after his death, for angels would come within three days to carry his body up to heaven. At his death, his disciples did as he had ordered: "after they had waited for three days, his odor changed and their hopes of his being taken up to heaven disappeared. Disappointed by his illusory promises and realizing that he had lied, they buried him."[36]

This Arabic Christian polemical work was probably composed in tenth-century Iraq. As often in works of polemics and apologetics, the author writes not for members of the rival religion (here, Muslims) but for his own (Christians). He seeks to assure them that they follow the true religion and to discourage them from converting to Islam by presenting it as a degraded, heretical version of Christianity. Attacking Muhammad as the founder of this "heresy" was a fundamental part of this strategy, for this polemicist and for others living as dhimmis (tolerated and protected minorities) under Muslim rule.

The *Risālat al-Kindī* was widely known among Arabic-speaking Christians from Iraq to al-Andalus, and it provided Petrus Alfonsi with ready-made arguments to denigrate Muhammad and to justify Alfonsi's own rejection of Islam in favor of Christianity. Alfonsi has his former Jewish self, Moses, open the fifth *Dialogue* by asking Peter, "I wonder why, when you abandoned your paternal faith, you chose the faith of the Christians rather than the faith of the Saracens, with whom you were always associated and raised."[37] Moses goes on to summarize the tenets of Islam. Islamic law, he says, is a mandate to serve the delights of this life. The Muslims' faith is rooted in reason. They are clean, washing themselves before entering a mosque. They worship one God whose prophet is "Machomet." They fast once a year, for the whole month of Ramadan. They travel as pilgrims to Mecca, which they claim was once home to Adam, Abraham, Ishmael, and Muhammad. They attack and subject enemies of their faith, making them either convert or remain subject to them. They follow the same dietary restrictions as the Jews. They practice polygamy. Their legal tradition preserves much of Mosaic law. They shun wine. The paradise that they promise is a lush garden where trees drop ripe fruit, milk and wine are served in silver chalices, and a harem of beautiful virgins awaits each of the faithful. Peter responds that Machomet himself could not have done a better job of summarizing the rudiments of Islam.

Peter then launches his attack on Islam and its prophet. Machomet, he says, was an orphan and a pagan. He seduced and married an older widow for her money. Out of pride, he wished to become king of the Arabs, but feared his fellow tribesmen, who were stronger than he. So he pretended to be a prophet. He was educated by a Jacobite heretic named Sergius (who had been condemned by a council of Antioch) and by two Jewish heretics named Abdias and Chabalahabar. He performed no miracles, as the Qur'ān itself admits. He led a life of iniquity, "rejoicing in theft and rapaciousness, and so burning so much with the fire of lust that he did not blush to befoul another man's bed in adultery, just as if the Lord were commanding it."[38] He seduced Zanab (Zaynab), wife of his disciple Zed (Zayd), and when caught said that the angel Gabriel had commanded his adultery. He was defeated in the battle of Uhud and had his teeth broken, a sure sign that God's favor was not with him.

Ritual ablutions are useless, Peter continues; Muslims confuse corporeal cleanliness with spiritual purity. These rites, he says, are a survival of the cult of Venus in pre-Islamic Arabia. Muslims fast during the day in the month of Ramadan, but this only leads them to more perverse gluttony and lechery at night. They ignore the true purposes of fasting, which are to control the vices of the flesh and induce penance. There is no authority for the belief that Mecca was the home of Adam and Abraham, Peter says. Indeed, he says, before Machomet "preached the law, this house was full of idols."[39] Machomet incorporated the idol of Saturn into the wall of the house and buried that of Mercury, placing on top of it a large stone that the Saracen pilgrims kiss. Alfonsi stops short of calling Muslims pagans, but he implies that their monotheism is sullied by the vestiges of these pagan rites.

Cupidity, not faith, inspired the conquests of Machomet and his followers, Peter continues. "If anyone wishes to convert someone else, he should not do this with violence, but diligently and sweetly, just as Machomet himself attested in his Alcoran," says Peter, citing a string of Qur'ānic injunctions (lifted from the *Risālat al-Kindī*) against the use of compulsion or violence in religion.[40] By their warlike behavior, the Saracens thus break their own laws. The Alcoran was composed not by Machomet but by his disciples after his death; hence, one cannot know how much of it reflects the beliefs of Machomet.

Islam's marriage laws legalize adultery, Peter affirms. Machomet loved women greatly and was extremely lustful, and—as he himself admitted—the lust of forty men was in him. And particularly, since the Arabs were very lustful, he satisfied their will, so that they might believe. For the same reason he promised his followers carnal pleasures in paradise. Since the soul and the four elements that made up the body will be separated from each other, pleasures of the body will be impossible in the next life.

Peter then relates the following story, which combines a legend about Muhammad's death with an account of the origins of Shiite Islam:

After his death, they all wanted to abandon his law. For he himself had said that on the third day his body would be raised up to heaven. When they knew that he was a deceiver realized that this was a lie and saw that his cadaver stank, with the body unburied the greater part [of his followers] departed. Haly ('Alī), however, the son of Abytharius (Abū Tālib), one of Machomet's ten companions, obtained the kingdom after his death. He preached flatteringly and cleverly admonished the people to believe, and told them that they did not properly understand Machomet's expression. "Machomet did not say that he would be raised up to heaven before burial, nor while people watched. Indeed, he said that after the burial of his body the angels would bear off to heaven, with none being aware of it. Therefore, because they did not bury him immediately, certainly he began to stink, in order that they might bury him right away." Therefore, by this argument he held the people a while in their earlier error.[41]

Peter goes on to give a rather garbled account of how 'Alī's sons, Hasan and Husayn, became disillusioned with Machomet and his law and began to drink and abandoned his law in part. Alfonsi has adapted the story of Machomet's failed resurrection from the *Risālat al-Kindī*: Muhammad's supposed claim that his body would be taken to heaven after three days clearly reflects a Christian belief that he is a false Christ, or anti-Christ.[42] Alfonsi has a fairly accurate knowledge of the names of 'Alī, Hasan, and Husayn, and a vague sense that they and their followers have "cast down the law." His choice of wording shows that he sees the Shiites from a Sunni perspective, as is natural for an Andalusian; he seems to have only a vague idea of how Shiism differs from Sunnism. Alfonsi, like many polemicists, views existence of doctrinal division in a rival religion as a proof of its error.

Alfonsi wraps up his attack on Islam by noting that Muslims deny that Christ was crucified and died, whereas Christians and Jews agree at least on this. While Alfonsi never denies Islam's essential monotheism, he insinuates that it is compromised by vestiges of its pagan past, by its birth out of Christian and Jewish heresies, and by the immorality of its founder, Muhammad. Alfonsi's text was to become an important source of information on Islam for the Latin west. There are seventy-nine extant medieval manuscripts of the *Dialogues*, which quickly became one of the most widely read Latin texts on Islam; several medieval scribes copied only the anti-Islamic chapter of the *Dialogues*. Latin writers on Islam in the twelfth and thirteenth centuries cited him prominently, and his biography of Muhammad was copied into two thirteenth-century best sellers, James of Voragine's *Legenda aurea* and (as we have seen) Vincent de Beauvais's *Speculum historiale*.[43]

One of Alfonsi's readers was Peter, abbot of the rich and influential Burgundian monastery of Cluny, who in 1142–43 traveled to Spain, where he commissioned a Latin translation of the Qur'ān from English scholar Robert of Ketton. He also had other Arabic texts about Islam translated into Latin, including the *Risālat al-Kindī*.[44] The corpus of texts commissioned by Peter is introduced by two works of the abbot himself: a letter and the *Summa haeresis Sarracenorum*, in which Peter summarizes the contents of his anthology of translated texts and lays out the main lines of his argument against Islam.[45] The principle focus of the *Summa* is an hostile biography of Muhammad. The only source of information that he explicitly cites on Muhammad's life is Anastasius Bibliothecarius's Latin translation of Theophanes's *Chronographia*. Peter fills in Anastasius's account with information gleaned from Latin translation of the *Risālat al-Kindī* and from Petrus Alfonsi's *Dialogi*. Peter gives a clear sense of where the prophet and his followers fit in the history of error: the devil works behind and through Muhammad, leading a third of the world's population into error. Mixing good and evil, sublime and ridiculous, Muhammad created a monstrous cult, similar to the animal Horace described with a human head, a horse's neck, and feathers. Peter sees three great adversaries whom the devil uses to lead Christians astray: Arius, Muhammad, and Antichrist.

The *Summa haeresis Saracenorum* seeks to furnish the basis of a polemical vision of Islam by giving the principle elements of the "detestable life" of Muhammad, a base-born man and a clever manipulator of ignorant Arabs. Peter denounces the errors of Muhammad's teaching concerning the Trinity, concerning Christ (in particular his refusal to accept the incarnation), and in his conception of heaven as a place of eternal lust. This polemical tract seeks to show (as the title indicates) that Islam represents the sum of all the heresies previously known to Christendom. The oldest manuscript uniting these anti-Islamic works contains a caricature of "Mahumeth": the head of a bearded man on the body of a fish, perhaps suggesting a monstrous, siren-like creature who leads men astray. It is the earliest European caricature of the prophet.[46] Of these works commissioned by Peter of Cluny, Robert of Ketton's Qur'ān translation and Peter of Toledo's Latin translation of the *Risālat al-Kindī* were widely read and copied and were subsequently diffused in print when Theodor Buchman (Bibliander) published them in Basel in 1543 (as we will see in chapter four). Peter of Cluny's own texts on Islam were seldom read or copied.

Shortly after 1300, Riccoldo da Montecroce, a Florentine Dominican, composed his *Contra legem sarracenorum*, a refutation of the Qur'ān. Riccoldo had traveled to Baghdad in about 1288, confident that he could debate with Muslims and convert them to Christianity. In his various writings, he describes how he marveled at Baghdad's wealth and beauty and at the learning and piety of its Muslims. He learned Arabic and read the Qur'ān but soon realized that he would make little progress converting Muslims, who were confident that they held the truth and that God had granted them victory over the Christian "Franks." Riccoldo saw European captives brought through Baghdad bound for slave markets after the Mamluk capture of Acre, last mainland stronghold of the crusader states, in 1291.[47]

Riccoldo is awed by the opulence of Baghdad, distraught by the fall of Acre, in frank admiration of the piety and learning of the Muslim scholars he met. In his *Five Letters on the Fall of Acre*, Riccoldo recounts the doubt and perplexity he experienced: is it true, as the "Saracens" say, that God prefers them? That Abraham, Moses, Mary, Jesus, and the Apostles were all "Saracens"? As he studied the Qur'ān, he was shocked at these ideas, which for him were blasphemies uttered by Mahomet, author of the Alcoran. What troubled him most was that such blasphemies were left unpunished. In one of his letters, he addresses the following prayer to Jesus:

> I beg you, read what he says about you, your mother, and your apostles. As you know, frequently when reading the Qur'ān in Arabic with a heart full of utter grief and impatience, I have placed the book open on your

altar before your image and that of your most holy mother and said, "read, read what Mahomet says!" And it seemed to me that you did not want to read.[48]

While Riccoldo has a better knowledge of the Qur'ān than any previous Latin polemicist against Islam, he presents Islam in the *Contra legem sarracenorum* essentially in the same way as Peter of Cluny had 150 years earlier: as the sum of all heresies. He explains that Christians have experienced three waves of persecution: that of the Jews and pagans in the first centuries of the Church, followed by that of the heretics. Muhammad is part of the third wave of persecutors. "During the reign of Heraclius there arose a diabolical man, first-born of Satan, a lustful man dedicated to obscene deeds, by the name of Mahomet, who, through his [Satan's] advice and help, composed a false and nefarious law, as if from the mouth of God. He called this law Alcoran, which means anthology of the precepts of God. This Mahomet was the greatest persecutor of the Church that there ever was or shall be."[49]

Riccoldo offers a more detailed and systematic treatise on the Qur'ān than anything previously available in Latin. He outlines what he sees as its "principal errors": the rejection of the essential Christian doctrines of the Trinity, Incarnation, Crucifixion, and Resurrection. He laboriously compares Qur'ānic doctrine to earlier Christian heresies such as Nestorianism, Jacobitism, Arianism. He reproaches the Qur'ān for being confusing, contradictory, unorganized, violent—in a word *irrational*. While Muslims claim that the beauty of the Qur'ān's Arabic proves its divine origins, Riccoldo affirms the contrary: the Qur'ān is in verse, when everybody knows that God speaks to prophets clearly, *in prose*.[50] He derides the Muslim legends of the *isrā'* (Muhammad's night journey from Mecca to Jerusalem) and *mi'rāj* (his ascension into heaven).[51]

The real author of the Alcoran, Riccoldo affirms, is the devil. When Emperor Heraclius defeated the Persians and destroyed their golden and silver idols, the devil realized he could no longer defend polytheism, nor could he fight the growing recognition of the Old and New Testaments. Instead, he decided to create a new law (*lex*) composed of elements from both Mosaic and Gospel laws in order to lead the world astray. And Satan found his man: "a certain diabolical man by the name of Mahomet, idolatrous in religion, impoverished of any fortune, arrogant in spirit and a very famous sorcerer." Despite Riccoldo's knowledge of the Qur'ān and familiarity with Muslim scholars, he falls back on the hostile legends fabricated by earlier Christian polemicists. He tells of Mahomet's marriage to a rich widow and his promotion to "prince of thieves" who longed to become king of the Arabs. He was struck by epilepsy but passed his fits off as the consequences of his conversations with an angel. As he was illiterate, he surrounded himself with heretical Jews and Christians: Riccoldo here gives a list of names, the most important of which was a Jacobite named Baheyra. "Mahomet composed a sort of law, taking from his associates some elements of the Old Testament and some of the New Testament, but the people did not yet have the Alcoran." Indeed, Riccoldo says, when Mahomet died the text of the Alcoran had not yet been established, and this subsequently became a cause of disagreement and conflict. From his reading of Qur'ānic commentaries and his discussions with Muslim intellectuals in Baghdad, he has become acquainted with different versions of how the Qur'ān was composed after Muhammad's death. Here he uses these stories to attempt to discredit the Muslim holy book. Following the lead of Petrus Alfonsi, he also refers to divisions within Islam that he links to the question of the establishment of the Qur'ānic text: "Some indeed follow Mahomet, and they are many; and some follow Haali ('Alī), and they are fewer and less evil, and they say that Machomet usurped through tyranny the authority which was Haali's. Then there arose against both of these groups some Saracens who were learned in philosophy, and they began to read the books of Aristotle and Plato, and they began to despise all the sects of the Saracens and this Alchoran."[52]

Riccoldo is less interested in narrating Mahomet's biography than are other Christian polemicists; his target is the Qur'ān, and he relates Mahomet's life in brief snippets, principally to cast aspersions on the revelation and compilation of the Qur'ān. A fourteenth-century reader of Riccoldo's treatise would find little that would dispel the polemical legendary texts concerning the prophet, and much that would confirm it: his cynical marriage to a wealthy widow, his epileptic fits, his dependency on heretical Jewish and Christian advisors. Riccoldo's learned assault on the Qur'ān would be very influential over the coming centuries, as we will see in chapter four. In 1543, Theodore Bibliander publishes alongside Robert of Ketton's translation of the Qur'ān and the Latin translation of the *Risālat al-Kindī*; in the same year, Martin Luther publishes his own translation of Riccoldo's tract. Riccoldo's vision of Muhammad and the Qur'ān will shape how European intellectuals of the following centuries conceive of the prophet of Islam.

Before 1288 and after his return from the east about 1300, Riccoldo was friar in the Dominican convent of Santa Maria Novella. There he may well have met a poet who frequented the convent's library, Dante Alighieri; indeed, Riccoldo may have been an important source of Dante's knowledge of Islam.[53] Dante was banished from Florence in 1302; over the course of the following decades he produced his magnum opus, the *Divine Comedy*. When Dante and Virgil approach the infernal city of Dis (*Inferno* VIII:70), they see mosques red with fire marking the entrance. It is in the ninth pouch of the eighth circle of Dante's hell, among "sowers of schism and scandal," that we meet "Maometto." Maometto has been sliced down the middle by a demon bearing an enormous sword: his entrails hang down and he pulls open his own chest; ahead of him walks 'Alī, whose head is split open. As often with Dante, the torments of hell are symbolically appropriate to the crimes punished: here the "schismatic" Maometto is punished for having split Christian unity by himself being split; 'Alī (seen here above all as the instigator of Shiism) further split Islam into two, meriting a similar punishment. It is as schismatics (and not heretics) that Maometto and 'Alī are punished, emphasizing the divisions that they inflicted on Christian unity. The splitting open of the prophet's chest echoes the Muslim legends of the angels who opened the young Muhammad's chest to purify his heart. A number of manuscripts of the *Commedia* have illuminations showing the punishments inflicted on Maometto and Ali.[54] Fourteenth- and fifteenth-century commentators on the *Commedia* explained Dante's treatment of Maometto by evoking the legendary biography of the trickster and heresiarch found in writers from Guibert of Nogent to Laurent de Premierfait.

Mahomet the Scoundrel and Impostor in Late Medieval and Early Modern European Culture

It is this colorful, despicable villain Mahomet that will become a stock figure in European culture in the fifteenth and sixteenth centuries. John Lydgate, sometime between 1410 and 1450, penned a rhymed verse rendition of Laurent de Premierfait's *Des cas des nobles hommes et femmes*, in which he devotes 112 lines to the life of "Machomeete."[55] Lydgate follows Premierfait in insisting on the base lineage of Machomeete ("of low kynreede," 55). He became a merchant and traveled with his camels:

> Fals and double, sotil in his deuises;
> To Iewes & Cristene sondry tymes sent,
> Lerned the Olde and Newe Testament. (61–63)
> False and double, subtle in his tricks
> To Jews and Christians he was often sent
> He learned the Old and the New Testaments

Lydgate relates his marriage to "Cardigan," his claims to be the Messiah, his epileptic fits dismissed as the effects of his dialogues with Gabriel. And we find the standard miracles:

> On his shuldres wer ofte tymes seyn,
> Whan he to folkis shewed his presence,
> Milk whit dowes, which that piked greyn
> Out of hi eris; affermyng in sentence
> Thei cam be grace of goostli influence
> Hym to visite, to shewe and specifie
> He was the prophete that called was Messie. (92–98)
> On his shoulders were often seen
> When he showed himself before the people
> Milk white doves, which picked grain
> Out of his ears; he swore to them
> That they came by grace of the Holy Ghost
> To visit him, to show and indicate
> That he was the prophet that was called Messiah

FIGURE 7. Machomeete preaching, with doves at his ears. Lydgate, *Fall of Princes*, London BL Harley 1766, f. 223. © akg-images / British Library

In one manuscript copied around 1450, an artist (fig. 7) shows Machomeete preaching with a dove at each ear, to an attentive and rather astonished audience.[56]

Lydgate seems to garble Premierfait's next two false miracles, the pots of milk and honey hidden in the desert and the Alcoran tied to the horns of a bull; he has the pots of milk and honey hanging from the bull's horns. "A clerk of his, called Sergius" wrote down Machomeete's law and miracles; Lydgate then relates his first victories over

Heraclius. Machomeete was lecherous and had an image of Venus set up, making her day (Friday) the holy day of the "Sarsyns." He forbade wine to his people, but he imbibed excessively, which in the end is his undoing:

> Lik a glotoun deied in dronkenesse,
> Bi excesse of mykil drynkyng wyn,
> Fill in a podel, deuoured among swyn.
> This was the eende of false Machomeete,
> For al his crafftis of nigromancie,
> The funeral fyn of this seudo prophete,
> Dronklew of kynde, called hymsilf Messie,
> Whom Sarsyns so gretli magnefie. (152–59)

This scene, too, has been graphically rendered by the illuminator of British Library Harley MS 1766, who shows two sows devouring the fallen Machomeete (fig. 8).

Lydgate ends his narration with Machomeete's death; his source, Laurent de Premierfait, had gone on to relate the false prophet's burial in an iron coffin held aloft by magnets. This legend proved popular through the Middle Ages and well beyond.[57] Various written accounts by supposed travelers and pilgrims describe the floating coffin. Dominican Felix Fabri, describing his pilgrimage to Jerusalem in the 1480s, relates that he was unable to see the interior of the Dome of the Rock mosque in Jerusalem since entry to non-Muslims was forbidden. He tells us that "in the whole of this temple there is nothing whatever save only on the north side there is a likeness a raised marble tomb, representing the sepulcher of Mahomet at Mecca, which they so greatly revere that they worship its likeness in all mosques."[58] He then explains:

> The Saracens, therefore, journey to Mecca, not only to fulfil the commandment of Mahomet, but many go that they may see Mahomet's coffin hung in the air without rope or chain, albeit by natural causes. The people, cheated by this trick, think that this body is thus raised up because of his holiness, and so the besotted people are confirmed in the error.[59]

Christians went in Pilgrimage to Jerusalem to visit Christ's tomb; many of them assumed that Muslims went to Mecca to see Ma-

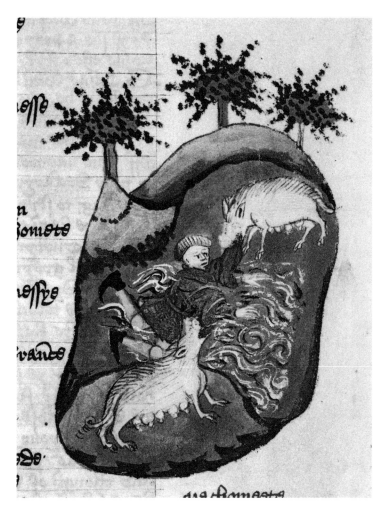

FIGURE 8. Machomeete killed by swine. Lygdate, *Fall of Princes*,
London BL Harley 1766, f. 224. © akg-images / British Library

homet's tomb. The floating coffin at Mecca even becomes a standard
feature of world maps. In the Catalan Atlas (ca. 1375) we see a turbaned Saracen kneeling before the city of "Mecha," with the floating
coffin in the middle (fig. 9). The text above explains that the Saracens go to Mecha to visit the tomb of their prophet.

Lopo Homem, a sixteenth-century Portuguese cartographer,
produced a lavishly illustrated world atlas in 1519, with the collabo-
ration of painter Gregorio Lopes (fig. 10).[60] Twenty-one years after

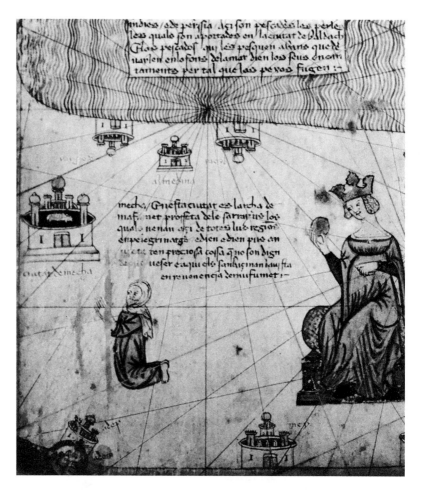

FIGURE 9. Saracen praying before Mahomet's floating tomb in Mecca. Catalan
Atlas (1375), Paris, BNF, MS Esp. 30. © akg-images / De Agostini Picture Library

Vasco de Gama's first voyage to India, Homem and Lopes map the
subcontinent; figure 10 is the double page devoted to India and the
Indian Ocean with, to the left, the Arabian Peninsula. The sea teems
with Portuguese caravels; on land, the artist has indicated key natural features (rivers, mountains) and a series of walled cities. With a
strong emphasis on the exotic, the artist portrays the trees, animals,
and human inhabitants of these lands. To illustrate the city of
"Mecha" (Mecca), the artist has painted a temple; four square col-
umns hold up a vaulted roof crowned by a small dome. A closer look

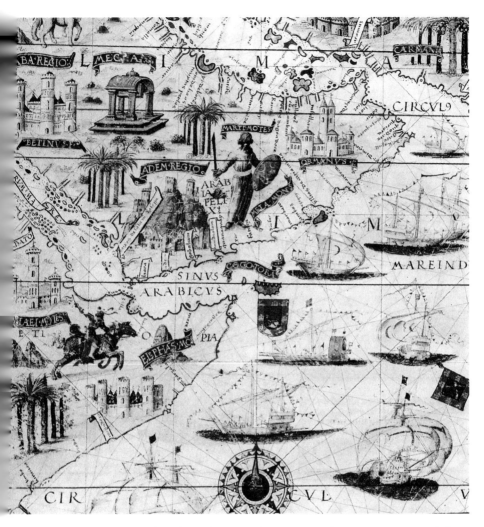

FIGURE 10. Lopo Homem, Miller Atlas, Lisbon, 1519 (BnF Cartes et plans, GE DD 683 RES f. 3), India, The Indian Ocean and Arabia. © akg-images / De Agostini Picture Library / J. E. Bulloz

shows that an oblong box is suspended from the ceiling of the structure. Mahomet's floating coffin again represents Islam's holy city and occupies a key place in the imagined geography of sixteenth-century Portugal.

We saw at the end of chapter one how the legend of Mahomet as idol persisted until the nineteenth century. The polemical legends we have encountered in this chapter (epilepsy, the trained dove and bull, the floating coffin, and so on) prove even more tenacious. Various elements could be referred to casually, by those who showed no particular interest in Islam, with the assurance that others would be familiar with them. In the context of the English civil war and the ideological controversies it engendered, various authors portray either Cromwell or Charles I as a new Mahomet.[61] Mary Wollstonecraft, in her *Vindication of the Rights of Woman* (1792), says that "women appear to be suspended by destiny, according to the vulgar tale of Mahomet's coffin."[62] She recognizes the tale as "vulgar" but apparently feels that it is well-known enough for use as a metaphor. And Alexander Eckhardt found the image of Muhammad's floating coffin still in use in the late nineteenth and early twentieth century, in both Hungary and Sicily.[63]

And we find it in sixteenth-century Iberia, not only in Lopo Homem's world atlas, but also in several Spanish dramas, whose authors preferred to import slanderous legend from northern Europe than to base their critique of the prophet of Islam on the centuries of engagement with Islam in Spain. It is to this, to the use of the biography of Muhammad to marginalize and finally exclude Muslims from Christian Spain's body politic, that we now turn.

CHAPTER THREE

Pseudoprophet of the Moors

IT WAS THE DAY after Christmas, 1462, in the city of Jaén, not far from the border of the Muslim emirate of Granada. The ruler of the city, Constable Don Miguel Lucas de Iranzo, had organized a show of jousting, a mock battle with two hundred combatants. He had half of them dress up *en habito morisco* (in Moorish dress), complete with fake beards. The "Moors" arrived in solemn procession:

> And they brought before them their prophet Mahomad, of the house of Mecca, with the Alcoran and the books of his law, in great pomp, riding a richly caparisoned mule. Above his head was lavish canopy held aloft on poles by four faqis. And behind him came the king of Morocco, richly attired, and with him noble knights, accompanied by trumpets and drums.[1]

The knight impersonating the king of Morocco presented a letter addressed to Don Miguel that was read aloud. He saluted the valorous constable and complained that his military exploits in the kingdom of Granada had terrorized its inhabitants, and that the king's uncle, king of Grenada, had complained to him. "Seeing that our Mahomad thus forgets us and your God thus helps you," he says, he has come to observe the Christian law and to propose a battle between the Moroccan knights and the Christian knights. "If here, as in war, your God helps you prevail, then our prophet Mahomad and the books of our law which I have brought with me will be renounced by myself and by my renegade Moors. And I and they henceforth will submit to your will and order, and will become your vassals, and will receive your Christianity in the river where we shall be baptized." Three hours of jousting in the packed square ended with the predictable result: the king of Morocco comes before the constable and proclaims that "your God helps you, whence we must believe that your law is better than ours. And since it is so, my Moors and I renounce it and its Alcoran, and our prophet Mahomad." The Moors' books were tossed to the ground and trampled. Then they made a raucous procession (with blaring trumpets and shouts) to the Church of the Madelena, where they tossed "Mahomad" into a fountain and poured a bucket of water over the head of the king of Morocco.

Satisfying fun for the inhabitants of Jaén, allowed to fantasize, during the Christmas festivities, that the military victories of their constable could provoke the conversion of the king of Morocco. The renouncement of the prophet "Mahomad" and his "Alcoran" comes not through preaching or theological dispute, but through the force of arms. The victory of Christian troops provides proof that their God is more powerful than Mahomad, and hence that the Christian law is superior to that of the Alcoran. The false prophet Mahomad provides an ideological justification of the subjection of Muslim Spaniards to Christian Castilian rule. Where Guibert de Nogent used the polemical biography of the prophet to justify the conquests of the First Crusade, this chronicler does the opposite: he justifies the rejection of the prophet and his law by the defeat that Christians impose on Muslims.

Various Christian Iberian authors between the thirteenth and sixteenth centuries narrate the life of Muhammad. Some jurists and chroniclers denigrate the Muslim prophet in order to justify the conquest of Muslim territory and the submission of Muslim subjects to the power of Christian kings. Missionaries and theologians proffer arguments meant to convince Muslims of the truth of Christianity; for many this means denouncing the Muslim prophet as a fraud. Yet others wrote to discourage Christians from converting to Islam; in border regions where either captivity or emigration could take Christians into Muslim territories, some Christian writers tried to inoculate them against apostasy by painting Islam as a depraved heresy—and often by vilifying the prophet.

The years 1492 to 1609, from the conquest of Granada to the expulsion of the Moriscos, saw the extinction of the Muslim community in the Iberian Peninsula. Moriscos (converts from Islam to Christianity and their descendants) of the late sixteenth century forged texts meant to reconcile Christianity and Islam; one of these texts, the Gospel of Barnabas, had Jesus announce the coming of the "Messiah" Muhammad. This Morisco Muhammad is a subversive apologist for Islam in a context of denigration and persecution of what was left of Iberian Islam. Yet in the wake of the Moriscos' expulsion, as Spain became a land of one people, one faith, and one language, some Spanish authors preferred to import into the peninsula the polemical legends we examined in chapter two.

Rodrigo Jiménez de Rada and Mark of Toledo

Christian writers needed to come to terms with Muhammad and place him in God's plan of history, a history in which error may win for a time, but in which true (Christian) religion will always triumph. We have seen this in polemical and apologetic works (such as those of Petrus Alfonsi and Peter of Cluny) and in chronicles— crusade chronicles such as that of Guibert de Nogent or universal chronicles such as Theophanes's.

Rodrigo Jiménez de Rada was archbishop of Toledo (1208–47) and close advisor to Castilian kings Alfonso VIII (r. 1158–1214) and Fernando III (r. 1217–52). Rodrigo actively preached crusade against the Almohad dynasty that dominated al-Andalus and much of North Africa; he participated in the battle of Las Navas de Tolosa, in which Alfonso VIII and his allies routed the Almohads, initiating what Spanish historians have called the "gran reconquista," which led to Fernando III's conquest of Cordova (1236) and Seville (1248).[2] Soon after his arrival in Toledo, Rodrigo commissioned Mark, deacon of the cathedral of Toledo, to translate the Qur'ān into Latin. Mark completed the translation in June 1210, two years before Las Navas de Tolosa, when the Almohad presence was still a serious threat.

It is in this context that Mark presents his translation as part of the intellectual and spiritual arsenal that Christians must deploy to affirm their control over their polluted sanctuaries and to drag the Saracens back into the Christian fold. In the preface to his translation of the Qur'ān, Mark presents a brief hostile biography of "Mafometus," a skilled magician who through his travels learned the rudiments of both Judaism and Christianity and urged his people to abandon their idolatry and worship the Unique God.[3] Hesitating between Judaism and Christianity, he decided that the law of the Gospel was too difficult, since it enjoined love of one's enemy and spurning the pleasures of the flesh. He opted for Judaism yet realized that the Jews were everywhere despised because they killed Jesus Christ. For this reason, he proclaimed that Jesus had not really been killed and he promulgated a new law, the Alcoran, mixing Jewish law, Christian law, and his own fancy. In order to foist this law on the Arabs, he called them together outside of the city of "Mecha" (which in Latin, Mark reminds the reader, means adultery), feigned an epileptic seizure, and announced to the assembled masses that Gabriel had revealed a new law to him. Mark goes on to give a fairly accurate catalog of Qur'ānic doctrine on the unity of God, the virgin birth, the role of Jesus as prophet, the rites of prayer and ablution, fasting, and pilgrimage. Mark affirms that Mafometus established himself as a prophet and messenger of God reigning over his people as had David and Solomon.

Having forged his new law, "in which he speaks as one who is delirious," Mafometus "like a magician seduced barbarous peoples through fantastic delusions," and his Saracens through war subdued the world, oppressing Christians from the north to the Mediterranean and from India to the west—to Spain, where "once many priests swore holy allegiance to God, now evil men give supplication to the execrable Mafometus, and the churches which were consecrated by the hands of bishops have now become profane temples." Mark presents the conversion of churches into mosques as a profanation or pollution; the reconquest of these places by Christian rulers, who will have them duly purified and reconsecrated by bishops, is implicitly legitimate.

Opposing the Saracens in Spain is Rodrigo Jiménez de Rada, archbishop of Toledo. Mark tells how the good archbishop was moved to tears by seeing the Saracen oppression of his archdiocese; where priests once performed mass in honor of Christ, now the name of the "pseudoprophet" is invoked. In the towers of the churches where bells once rang, now "profane proclamations [the call of the muezzin] deafen the ears of the faithful." Rodrigo, deploring this state of affairs, making his tears his arms, urged Mark to translate the book containing the Saracens' "sacrilegious decrees and strange precepts." The point of this translation is to allow those among the orthodox who are not permitted to use arms to combat the precepts of Muslim law; in this way they can refute the "detestable decrees" of Mafometus and in so doing, "not a few Saracens may be dragged to the Catholic faith." The language here is one of force and coercion; the intellectual combat permitted through Mark's translation of the Qur'ān is complementary to that carried out by Christian armies. By forcibly reclaiming the Spanish churches converted into mosques, Christian princes banish the muezzin and reinstate the church bells; Christ's name, and not Mafometus's, is to be invoked. Moreover, knowledge of the Qur'ān will provide churchmen with the intellectual weaponry needed to defeat Islamic doctrine and drag the Saracens back to the faith.

Rodrigo himself offers a similar biography of "Mahomat" in his *Historia Arabum* (*History of the Arabs*), employing, he says, "their" sources; he indeed uses Mark's translation of the Qur'ān along with hadiths and the traditions concerning the *mi'rāj* (*Celestial voyage of Muhammad*), though he also uses the works of Christian chroniclers.[4] His purpose is to show the reader "how, through false revelation the sly man Mahomat from his heart crafted a pestilential virus." Rodrigo's presentation of Muhammad is much more detailed than Mark's and more faithful to Muslim sources. Yet the essential image is the same: a pseudoprophet who concocted bogus revelations in order to obtain power. Rodrigo stresses the *political* illegitimacy of the rule of the prophet and his followers: the Muslim conquests constitute a "rebellion" against Roman power. This clearly sets the scene for the remainder of the *Historia Arabum*, which is principally devoted to the Muslim rulers of Spain; they, like Mahomat before them, were usurpers who have taken Spain by force from its legitimate Gothic rulers.

This vision of history, legitimizing the Christian (re)conquest of Spain, is clearly laid out in Rodrigo's *De rebus Hispaniae*, completed between 1243 and 1246. He describes the progressive conquest by

Castilian monarchs as a restoration of Christian and Gothic rule, town by town. He describes, for example, how Córdoba, "the noble city, was purged of the filth of Mahomet."[5] King Fernando III transformed the main mosque into a cathedral; the filth (*spurcicia*) of Machomet was cleansed with holy water. Atop the minaret "where the name of the perfidious one used to be invoked," were placed a crucifix and the royal standard: Christ and the king replace Machomet.[6]

The vilification of Muhammad plays an important role in justifying Christian kings' wars of conquest against Muslims. It also is crucial in explaining the inferior legal status they will seek to impose on defeated Muslims who come under their rule, as we see in the *Siete partidas*, the law code composed under the direction of Fernando's son, Alfonso X "the Wise" (r. 1252–84).[7] For Alfonso X the Muslim religion is an "insult to God"; the "proof" of this is that "Mahomat" did not show the "extraordinary sanctity" necessary to prove he was a prophet. This is the "foolish belief" of the Moors, a belief that, just like the "obstinacy" of the Jews, condemns them to a subordinate role in Christian society. Legal apparatus restrictions attempt to prevent the "pollution" of Christians by Muslims or Jews and to facilitate their peaceful and voluntary conversion to Christianity. Moors may not have mosques in Christian towns and should not practice their sacrifices in front of Christians. Their mosques are royal property, and hence the king may do of them what he wishes; implicitly, this includes the right to have them converted into churches or on the contrary to reserve some of them for continued use as mosques. Muslims coming from other kingdoms to the royal court are protected. Muslims have a right to live and practice their religion, but this freedom of religion is constrained much as that of the dhimmi in Muslim lands, allied to an inferior social status. The Muslim (or Jew) may not own Christian slaves; he may not bear witness against a Christian except in treason cases. In sum, in Castile, as elsewhere in Spain, Sicily, or the crusader states of the Latin East, Muslims (like Jews) are legally inferior and subordinate members of Christian society, just as in contemporary Muslim societies, dhimmis (principally Christians and Jews) were protected and inferior members of Muslim society. Alfonso invokes the figure of Muhammad to explain and justify their special legal status.

Alfonso X earned his sobriquet "el Sabio" (the Wise) largely through his patronage of scholars, artists, poets, and musicians. The king oversaw the production of a vast library of Eastern and Western scholarship in Castilian. Some of the sumptuous miniatures in these works strikingly depict him as the king of all three religions: he is playing chess with a Muslim subject; listening to music with Christian and Muslim musicians; or, book in hand, directing his staff of Christian, Jewish, and Muslim scholars. The king ordered the translation from the Arabic of several scientific and practical works: treatises in astronomy and astrology, divination, hunting, and chess. For centuries, his *Alfonsine Tables* remained the standard reference for European astronomers. He also was interested in the polemical confrontation with Islam; he had a Spanish translation of the Qur'ān produced (that translation is now lost) and had Abraham of Toledo produce, in 1264, a Spanish account of the night voyage of Muhammad, based on Arabic sources, which Bonaventure of Siena subsequently adapted into a Latin version with his own comments, as the *Liber Scalae Machometi* (*Book of Machomet's Ladder*). The work proved popular; it was translated into French and may have served as an inspiration for Dante's *Commedia*.[8]

It is not clear what text Abraham of Toledo translated from Arabic; there was by the thirteenth century an abundant literature in Arabic concerning the prophet's *isrā* (night journey from Mecca to Jerusalem) and *mi'rāj* (ascension into heaven).[9] These texts relate that one night the Archangel Gabriel came to Muhammad in Mecca, and brought Buraq, a winged steed who carried him to *al-masjid al-aqsā*, the "farthest sanctuary," in Jerusalem. In the second part of the journey, the *mi'rāj* (literally "ladder"), Buraq bore him aloft to visit the seven circles of heaven, where he spoke with the earlier prophets such as Abraham, Moses, John the Baptist, and Jesus; eventually he is brought before the divine presence. Some versions of the *mi'rāj* have God tell Muhammad that Muslims must pray fifty times per day; however, Moses told Muhammad that it was very difficult for the people and urged Muhammad to bargain for a reduction, until finally it was reduced to five times per day. In Bonaventure of Siena's translation, "Machometus" himself is the narrator, recounting his adventures in the first person. Muslim theologians looked on such traditions as pious legends that encouraged devotion, but they certainly did not see them as canonical texts. Yet for Bonaventure of Siena and those who read his *Liber scalae*, Muhammad himself was the author. Hence many of them assume that it carried the same authority with Muslims as did the Qur'ān itself. For Juan Gil de Zamora, tutor to Alfonso X's son, Sancho IV, the *Liber scalae* was "the second book of Mahoma."[10] It will be a frequent object of attack by Christian polemicists over the following centuries.

Alfonso el Sabio's vision of the place of Muslims in Castilian society is seen not only in his law texts, but also in his chronicles. The king seems to have closely supervised the creation of the *Estoria de España*. Most of the text (or, of that part of it that was actually composed under Alfonso) deals with Roman and Visigothic history. Alfonso apparently meant it to strengthen his claim to the imperial crown. The *Estoria*'s vision of history justifies Alfonso's supremacy as Gothic king and Roman emperor; its objective is to trace the history of Spain "from Noah's time to our own."[11] It narrates the different dynasties that ruled Spain: Greeks, Carthaginians, Romans, Vandals, Visigoths, and Arabs. Only two of these groups are legitimate: the Romans and the Visigoths; Alfonso, king and emperor, is legitimate successor to both. The others are illegitimate interlopers—in particular the invaders from Africa, Carthaginians and Moors.

The *Estoria de España* paints Mahomat as a heresiarch. The compilers bring together different sources, including the chronicles of Rodrigo Jiménez de Rada. This leads to the multiplication of narratives and of persons: the young Mahomat works for one of his relatives, a woman named Hadaya; several chapters later, "Queen Cadiga" falls in love with him; the compilers did not realize that these two women were one and the same.[12] The *Estoria* recounts Mahomat's preaching, his epilepsy (and his explanation that it was the effect of his rapturous exchanges with the Archangel Gabriel), his multiple marriages (or rather his "adultery" and "fornication"). Yet the *Estoria* is relatively free of many of the legendary polemical elements we saw in chapter two (doves and bulls); on the contrary, we find elements from Muslim tradition (via Rodrigo's *Historia Arabum*): the story of angels purifying his heart, his role in solving the dispute among the Meccans as to who should lift the black stone into place when the Kaaba was renovated, the story the *mi'rāj*, taken from the *Liber scalae*.

Yet when recounting the prophet's death, Alfonso deliberately rejects Rodrigo's account in favor of the more flamboyant (and far less reliable) legend from another thirteenth-century chronicler, Lucas de Tuy. According to this account Machomet had predicted that he would resurrect on the third day after his death and that, when he failed to do so, his corpse was desecrated by dogs. Various stories about Muhammad's death had circulated among Muslims and Christians in the first centuries of Islam. Among Muslims, these stories framed debates about the nature of the prophet as wholly human (and hence subject to death and decay) or exceptional (hence a body miraculously preserved and sweet smelling). Some Christian authors crafted polemical versions of these legends to make Muhammad into a false messiah whose rotting corpse is proof of his mendacity.[13] Such polemical legends circulated among Christians in Spain in the ninth century; we find them in the "Istoria de Mahomet," which is subsequently taken up by Christian chroniclers, including Lucas de Tuy.[14] Mahomat is not only a false prophet but also an anti-Christ, someone who claimed to be the Messiah and who claimed he would resurrect. His rotting, desecrated corpse was supposedly evidence that he was *not* on God's side.

Alfonso (or rather the compilers of the *Estoria de España*) preferred Lucas's hostile legend to Rodrigo's more sober account. Rodrigo had focused on the implicit contrast between Mahomat and Jesus: Christ, shunning sex and worldly power; Mahomat, eagerly pursuing both. Alfonso wanted to carry this contrast further, to their deaths: Christ's, supreme sacrifice and glorious victory; Mahomat's, the death of an anti-Christ, complete with a failed resurrection and a rotting, dog-defiled corpse. The death story, gleaned from Lucas, made dramatic and theological sense. It also made sense in the broader sweep of Alfonso's narrative, in which he describes the various groups that had ruled Spain. He privileges two groups, the Romans and the Goths: their rule is legitimate, is celebrated. Alfonso sees himself, of course, as the incarnation of both: Roman emperor and Gothic king. The Arabs, by contrast, he portrays as interlopers, never as legitimate rulers. Just as Alfonso glorifies the origins of Roman and Gothic rule, he must denigrate the origins of Arab rule.

What better way than by presenting their prophet and first statesman as a liar, scoundrel, and anti-Christ?

Pedro Pascual

The Castilian, Aragonese, and Portuguese conquests of the thirteenth century, and the subsequent collapse of the Almohad Caliphate, left the Nasrid kingdom of Granada as the only Muslim state on
the peninsula. The Nasrid emirs did their best to survive, at times
allying themselves with Castile (and often paying monetary tribute
to its kings), at times with the Marinids of Morocco. While the kingdom's borders changed little between the middle of the thirteenth
century and the middle of the fifteenth, there were periods of low-
level warfare and raiding: Castilian attacks on the Granada border-
lands or Granadan raids against the kingdom of Valencia or south-
ern Castile. In 1298, Muslim troops of the Nasrid King Muhammad
II of Granada attacked Jaén, a Castilian town just about twenty-five
kilometers north of the Granadan frontier. They allegedly attacked
a convent of Santa Clara, where several nuns chose death rather
than captivity.[15]

In the same raid, the Granadan troops captured the town's
bishop, Pedro Pascual, who remained a prisoner in Granada until
his death, two years later. While in prison, Pedro looked on as many
fellow Christian captives converted to Islam; in an attempt to discourage this apostasy, he composed an anti-Islamic tract in Castilian, *Sobre la seta Mahometana*. So, at least, is what the author of the
tract affirms in the prologue; a number of fourteenth-century anti-
Jewish and anti-Muslim texts were attributed to Pedro, and it is
unclear which (if any) of them the bishop actually wrote. But even
if *Sobre la seta* was not written by Pedro himself, it was clearly composed in the fourteenth century by people who had known the
bishop and shared his concerns about the dangers of Christians converting to Islam.[16] For our purposes, what is particularly interesting
is that the tract includes a hostile description of the life and teachings of "Mahomat," a standard practice of anti-Muslim polemic.
What is unusual, however, is that the author (we will call him Pedro)
gives Mahomat's biography *twice*: first, he explains, according to
Muslim sources, then according to Christian sources.[17]

The first of these two biographical sections shows Pedro's knowledge of Arabic and his familiarity with Muslim sources, which he cites in Arabic, transliterated into Latin letters. He explains his method in the following way: "I translated into romance the history of Mahomat as I found it written in our books. Beyond what is found in this history, I wrote some things that certain Moors told me as they attempted to praise their law, and [others] that I found written in the books of the Moors.[18] In addition to his frequent citation of the Qur'ān, hadith ("Alhadiz"), and the *Liber scalae*, he cites the *Risālat al-Kindī*. He also claims to have read (or at least to know about) Muslim works of polemic, but this knowledge seems limited. "And when I hear what some Moors say in their disputations, the praises of Jesus Christ that Mahomat pronounced bother them, because he clearly said them against the Moors."[19] This is clearly not a sentiment he would find in any Muslim polemic against Christianity.

When Pedro does present material from actual Muslim sources, he often interjects polemic into his narration. When he remarks that Muhammad was born at "Meca," he reminds his readers that "Meca" is Latin for adultery.[20] He berates "Adiga" (Khadīja) for believing that Mahomat had seen the Archangel Gabriel; don't you know, Pedro asks her, that men lie?[21] Mahomat invented his visions of heaven, Pedro says, to stir his troops into battle; that God is not on the Muslims' side is made clear when one thousand Christian troops defeat two thousand Moors, as we see in the exploits of Alfonso VI and the Cid.[22] Pedro issues the standard enumeration and disapprobation of Mahomat's multiple marriages and in several places condemns him for being a diviner and interpreter of dreams.[23] He describes contradictions or errors from the Qur'ān and hadith.[24]

Even in this section, supposedly on the Muslim version of the life of the prophet, Pedro incorporates material both from the *Risālat al-Kindī* and the polemical Latin biographies. He claims, for example, that the Christian Sergio—and his false miracle of finding water in the desert—are found in the Muslim sources.[25] In his section on "how Mahomat died according to the books of the Moors," he says (following earlier Christian polemics) that Mahomat tried to baptize himself on his deathbed, and that he had declared that either he would ascend alive to heaven or his body would be taken

up by angels.[26] Pedro has nevertheless produced a biography that—
while invariably hostile to the prophet—is still largely based on
Muslim sources.

Very different is Pedro's life of the prophet according to, as he
puts it, "those Christians who saw Mahomat and struggled to know
the truth concerning his beginnings and his end."[27] The young Mahomat, Pedro tells us, is the protégé of a heretical Christian monk,
from whom he learns the arts of necromancy and astrology. Mahomat becomes king of the Arabs by defeating a bull he has raised (but
which the people believe to be sent by God); he passes himself off
as prophet by having a trained dove eat in his ear and claiming that
it is the Holy Spirit; he has another bull deliver the Qur'ān on its
horns.[28] The most fantastic and vicious element in this Christian
caricature of Mahomat is the account of his death. As Mahomat goes
off to sleep with a beautiful Jewess who dares not refuse him, her
family ambushes him, kills him, and has his cadaver cut up and
devoured by pigs—all but one foot, which they dress in myrrh and
sweet-smelling unguents. When his companions come looking for
him, the woman claims that angels took Mahomat from her bed and
that she held on to his foot, which came off in the subsequent tug of
war. She gave them the foot and told them to venerate it; the tomb
of Mahomat's foot, established in "a place with no fruit," becomes
the object of the Moors' pilgrimage.[29] Clearly aware of the outra-
geousness of this tale, Pedro here inserts a disclaimer. I do not know,
he says, if these stories are in fact true, but I found them in Latin
and was asked to translate them, so I did. Anyway, he says, "it seems
that the aforementioned writing is true."[30] In other words, Pedro
refuses to choose between the Muslim and Christian biographies of
Muhammad but hints that the Christian sources, by "those Christians *who saw* Muhammad and struggled to know the truth" are
more reliable.

Why does Pedro Pascual seem to prefer his dubious Christian
sources to his impeccable Muslim ones? Pedro knew Arabic and
Hebrew; he composed polemics against both Judaism and Islam (if
these works are indeed by the same author). Yet his goals are very
different from, for example, Dominican Riccoldo da Montecroce.
These authors wrote in Latin for a highly educated cadre of missionary friars. Pedro Pascual wrote in the vernacular—Valencian and

Castilian—for a less educated audience to whom he presented edifying religious stories and clearly defined boundaries between true religion and error. If Riccoldo has dreams of converting Muslims, Pedro Pascual in apprehension watches Christians converting to Islam; his *Sobre la seta Mahometana* is an attempt to stem that tide of conversion. It is defensive where Riccoldo's work was offensive. Pedro tells his readers that his book contains "the material with which you can defend yourself against the enemies of our law."[31]

This is why Pedro can include—and indeed prefer—the Christian polemical legends about Muhammad's life and death. While such material would only be ridiculed by the Muslims whom Dominican missionaries wished to convert, it proves useful to explain and vilify Islam to Pedro's "amigos," to whom he addresses his tract by recommending that they read it rather than "fables of romances of love or other vanities," which is apparently their more usual fare.[32] That Pedro knows what he is doing is clear in the organization of his tract. He intends his first chapter (which includes the dual biography of Muhammad) to discredit Islam in the eyes of his Christian readers. In chapters two to sixteen, by contrast, the beleaguered Christian can find arguments in support of the Trinity, the cult of images, noncircumcision, the Eucharist, the incarnation and divinity of Christ, and so on; in short, for the basic Christian doctrines and practices that Muslims find most shocking or perplexing. He at times tells his readers which specific arguments they can use against Muslims. Significantly, it is only innocuous, defensive arguments that he urges on his flock, not offensive attacks on Islam or its prophet. Pedro's strange double biography of Muhammad makes sense; he needs to give his readers an idea of what Muslims say about Muhammad yet to inspire in them so much contempt for Islam that they are ready to prefer death to apostasy.

Crusading against Moor and Turk in the Fifteenth Century

Not quite two centuries passed between the day Granadan troops raided Jaén in 1298, capturing its bishop, and January 2, 1492, when the last sultan of Granada, Abu 'Abdallah Muhammad XII (known to the Castilians as Boabdil), surrendered the city to Queen Isabel of Castile and her husband Fernando II of Aragon. During these two centuries, the Nasrid emirs alternated between low-level warfare and uneasy truces with their neighbors. Over the course of the fifteenth century, various Christian writers in Spain called for renewed crusading efforts in Granada and North Africa. The Marinid dynasty in Morocco, which had been a constant menace in the fourteenth century (they had captured the port city Algeciras in the south of the peninsula in 1329 and held onto it for fifteen years), was collapsing, and Granada itself was significantly weakened. The Portuguese had seized the Moroccan port of Ceuta in 1415, and Aragonese and Castilians did not want to be left out. Moreover, conquest could help counter the more distant but quite real threat of the Ottoman Empire, which was pushing into southeastern Europe, captured Constantinople in 1453, and was expanding its influence in the western Mediterranean.

The years from 1451 to 1461 saw a significant number of texts about Islam and the Ottoman menace as prelates debated the merits of crusade and mission; a number of these texts were written by churchmen who had met at the councils of Basel (1432) and Ferrara/Florence (1437). They all agreed on the urgency of the issue but differed in their assessment of the problem and in their prescriptions for a solution. Their views on these topics were colored by their preoccupations during the councils, which strove for the unity of Christendom by attempting to put an end to the papal schism and to reconcile the Catholic Church and various eastern churches; Christian unity was all the more necessary in face of the Ottoman threat.

Jean Germain, bishop of Châlons and advisor to Duke Philip the Good of Burgundy, was a fervent advocate of crusade. In his *Débat du Chrestien et du Sarrazin* (1451), dedicated to the duke, he affirms that the Turk is everywhere victorious in the Mediterranean, preventing Christian commerce with the East and enticing Christians to apostatize, to adopt the "law of that vile and dishonest Mahomet" in order to be able to indulge in carnal pleasure. There is an urgent need to wage a double war against the "Saracens": by the sword, as Philip had undertaken to do, and by the pen, as Jean undertook to do. He in fact does little more than compile earlier Latin polemical works (in particular Petrus Alfonsi, and the Latin translation of the

Risālat al-Kindī). The novelty of Jean's work is that he makes this material available for the first time in French.[33]

Two other friends who had met at Basel and together studied the Qur'ān, Nicholas of Cusa and Juan de Segovia, came up with a quite different approach. Twenty years after their meeting, Nicholas wrote his *De Pace Fidei* (1453), a fictitious dialogue in which representatives of different religious traditions discuss faith. Nicholas emphasizes the unity of belief and purpose among the sages. Their faith and religion are one, under a diversity of rites (*una religio in rituum varietate*), and the capacity to understand this unity and to respect the diversity has the potential to lead to a greater understanding of God and the achievement of peace among people of different religions. In this irenic dialogue, Muhammad is mentioned only once, in very neutral terms, as one whom the Arabs believe has transmitted divine commandments. Dialogue between representatives of different faiths can lead to unity, for Nicholas. Peaceful discussion can allow unity of faith among diversity of practice not only among Christians (Eastern and Western) but also with Muslims.[34]

Juan de Segovia also promoted peaceful dialogue as the appropriate response to Islam. Juan was in the Savoyard monastery of Aiton when he received word of the fall of Constantinople in 1453. In 1453–54, he wrote to both Nicholas of Cusa and Jean Germain suggesting a scheme of organized debates between Christian and Muslim intellectuals to rationally persuade Muslims of the truth of Christianity. Nicholas responded warmly to the idea; Jean Germain was skeptical, thinking crusade was still the best option. Juan's idea (to which he frequently alluded in his different letters, without ever systematically spelling it out), was to send a delegation of Christian leaders to speak with Muslim leaders about the faith; he never specified exactly who should be involved. The goal was to respond with peaceful Christian dialogue instead of violence and to dispel Muslims' misconceptions about Christianity (that the Trinity contradicts monotheism, for example). The conciliar strategy, which had eventually found peaceful solutions to differences with heretics (Hussites) and schismatics (Eastern Christians), could, he hoped, bring peace between Muslims and Christians in the short term and Muslims' conversion to Christianity in the long term.[35]

Juan sought to engage with Islam, its beliefs and texts; his strategy was very different from that of Cusa's *De Pace Fidei*.[36] He wanted to study the Qur'ān, yet he was unsatisfied with Robert of Ketton's Latin translation. So in 1455 he convinced the *faqīh* of his native Segovia, Içe de Gebir, to come to Aiton for four months and help him produce a new translation. Juan describes how Içe copied out the Arabic text of the Qur'ān in one column, then composed a Castilian translation in a parallel column. Içe became Juan's Arabic teacher as they studied the text together and discussed its interpretation and translation. Içe then returned to Segovia and Juan wrote in a third column his own Latin translation from the Spanish.[37] At the same time he was working with Içe on the Qur'ān, he was composing his own tract on how to argue against Muslims, *De gladio divini Spiritus in corda mittendo Sarracenorum* (On thrusting the sword of the Holy Spirit into the hearts of the Saracens). The violence in the title is metaphorical; it is not the sword of steel, which Mahumet and his followers wield, that will give victory to Christians, but the sword of the Holy Spirit, which is to say the word of God.

Indeed, Juan's opposition to crusade is based to no small extent on the opposition between Christ's message and method and those of Mahumet. *De gladio divini Spiritus* shows a good knowledge of the Qur'ān, as one would expect given that Juan was at the same time working closely with Içe on the translation. Yet when it came to understanding the prophet of Islam and narrating his life, Juan turned not to the *faqīh* of Segovia working by his side, but to the *Speculum Historiale* of Vincent de Beauvais, which (as we have seen) proffers many of the polemical legends we examined in chapter two. In his chapter on the "life and deeds of Mahumet," Juan repeatedly cites Vincent by name.[38] He relates that the young Mahumet was a merchant who traveled with his camels and learned about the Old and New Testaments from Jews and Christians of Syria, Egypt, and Palestine. He seduced and married "Lady Cadiga" and by means of "incantations" convinced the Saracens that he was the Messiah. Juan says that Mahumet was frequently stricken by epileptic fits and claimed that they were the result of his visits from Gabriel. He relates the stories of the bogus miracles of the dove, the bull with the book on its horns, the pots of milk and honey hidden in the desert. He notes that he found no trace of these stories in the

Qur'ān, yet he relates them nonetheless.[39] Juan asserts that other common Christian accusations against the prophet, such as his use of violence and his sexual appetite, are confirmed by reading the Qur'ān. Juan also takes from Vincent the story of how Mahumet had predicted he would resurrect on the third day after his death and how his disciples, unable to bear the stench of his corpse, finally "buried him ignominiously." Juan here is checking the standard European account of the prophet's life, which he read in the *Speculum historiale*, against the text of the Qur'ān. Like Pedro Pascual, he provides both Muslim and Christian versions of Muhammad's biography. But while Pedro privileges the hostile Christian legends in order to discourage Christians from apostasy, Juan is more ambivalent, neither approving nor dismissing them. Juan's ostensible goal is to convert the Saracens to the Christian faith by pointing out the errors of the Qur'ān and explaining Christian doctrines such as the Trinity and Incarnation in order to answer Muslim objections to them. Despite his intimate familiarity with the Qur'ān and his close and friendly working relationship with Içe de Gebir, his works reflect a quite traditional hostility toward Muhammad and Islam. Pope Pius II praised Juan for having "unraveled [the Qur'ān's] stupidities with reasons and arguments as well-founded as they were realistic."[40]

Cardinal Juan de Torquemada composed his *Contra principales errores perfidi Machometi* in 1459.[41] A Dominican from a family of *conversos* (converts from Judaism), he had also took part in the Council of Basel. He participated in the election of Aeneas Silvius Piccolomini, who became Pope Pius II in 1458; Pius had long been a staunch advocate of crusade. Torquemada's tract, dedicated to the new pope, could only encourage him in this project. In this long and verbose diatribe, Juan de Torquemada seeks to identify Machomet with the Beast from the Earth (Revelation 13:11) and structures his tract accordingly in order to prove the identification point by point. Yet there is little new in the content and nothing that betrays contact with real Muslims; he reiterates the standard legends of the trained dove and of the false prophet's failed resurrection, without any of the circumspection shown by Juan de Segovia. Pius in 1461 wrote a letter to Ottoman Sultan Mehmed II urging him to convert to Christianity; he relies on Torquemada for his understanding of Islam.

Despite polite (and somewhat perfunctory) praise of the sultan and his wisdom, the pope presents the Muslim prophet as a charlatan who proffers a creed justifying violence and debauchery.[42]

Nicholas of Cusa read Juan de Torquemada's treatise. He was familiar with the anti-Muslim polemics of Riccoldo da Montecroce, Thomas Aquinas, and others. What he proposes is something different, a *Sifting of the Alkoran* (*Cribratio Alkorani*, 1461) in order to identify nuggets of truth and wisdom. His approach is essentially positive; he differs from many of his predecessors and contemporaries in his efforts to find a *pia interpretatio* ("pious interpretation") of the prophet's intentions and of Muslim doctrines and practices. Nicholas judges that, where the Qur'ān differs from the Bible, it was the result of Mahumetus's ignorance of Christ, not of his hostility. Thus, the Qur'ān's rejection of the Trinity is best understood as a refusal of polytheism and idolatry, and Mahumet did not teach the crucifixion and resurrection of Christ because he felt it would compromise his attempts to lead idolatrous Arabs to strict monotheism.[43] In other words, Mahumet, who himself understood the truth, revealed only as much of it as he felt would be effective in abolishing idolatry and establishing monotheism.

In a similar way, Nicholas gives pious interpretations of other Qur'ānic passages that contradict Christian doctrine. If Mahumet denies that Christ died crucified, it is because he wishes to glorify Christ in the eyes of uncultured Arabs who would see death by crucifixion as shameful. Nicholas also excused Mahumet for promising sensual delights in heaven, arguing that such descriptions are to be understood metaphorically, and that the wise among the Saracens indeed do so.[44] On these key points, Nicholas stresses Mahumet's good intentions, affirming that he was doing what he thought was necessary to bring the Arabs away from idolatry and to monotheism.

Nicholas is in this way the first Latin Christian author to see the prophet's life and mission as positive. This is not to say that he shows no hostility toward Mahumet. On the contrary, he sees the errors of the Qur'ān as the product of the influence of Mahumet's frequenting Jews and Nestorian Christians and accuses him of pandering to his own lust and ambition: "Mahumet sought not the glory of God and the salvation of men but rather his own glory."[45] Yet we see for the first time a Latin Christian author recognizing in the Muslim prophet not merely a divine scourge sent to punish Christians but a partially (if imperfectly) inspired leader whom God used to spread monotheism and abolish idolatry.

Nicholas's novel approach to the Qur'ān provoked interest among European scholars, as we see from the testimony of the five extant fifteenth-century manuscripts of the *Cribratio* and five printed editions between 1488 and 1565. In particular, his work is printed in 1543 by Theodor Bibliander alongside Robert of Ketton's Latin Qur'ān and other texts on Islam, one of the most important Latin humanist volumes on Islam, as we shall see in chapter four. The work of Nicholas and many of the medieval authors we have examined will be essential tools for sixteenth-century authors who write about Islam in the context of the Ottoman expansion into Europe and the wars of religion between Catholics and Protestants.

Juan Andrés

In 1515 Juan Andrés, a convert from Islam to Catholicism, published his *Confusión o confutación de la secta Mahomética y del Alcorán* in Valencia.[46] The confessional landscape of the Iberian Peninsula was very different from what it had been in the mid-fifteenth century. Queen Isabel of Castile and King Fernando of Aragon conquered Granada in 1492 and expelled the Jews from their kingdoms in the same year. In 1502, Muslims of Castile were forced to choose between conversion and exile; in 1525, the same measures were imposed on Muslims of the Crown of Aragon. Just as forced conversion of Jews had produced *conversos* whose real religious affiliation provoked suspicion among both Jews and Christians, the 1502 and 1525 edicts produced a large population of Moriscos, formerly Muslim subjects nominally converted to Christianity, who were suspected of practicing Islam in secret.[47] It is in order to convince this Morisco population of the truth of Christianity, it seems, that Juan wrote his tract, though it also may be an implicit ploy to assure readers of the earnestness of his own conversion.

In the introduction to this tract, Juan says that he was born in Jativa and that his father, Abdalla, "alfaqí" (*faqīh*) of the town, instructed him in the "Muhammadan sect." At his father's death, he became *faqīh* of Jativa. On August 15, 1487, he was in Valencia, where he met Dominican Friar Juan Marqués, who convinced him that the Muhammadan sect was "bad and perverse" and that the "holy Law of Christ" was the only means to salvation. He was baptized, took the name Juan Andrés, and entered the orders.

> From being a *faqīh* and slave of Lucifer I became a priest and minister of Christ. I began, like St. Paul, to preach and expound the opposite of what I before had falsely believed and professed, and with the help of the high Lord I first converted in this Kingdom of Valencia and finally brought to salvation many souls of Moorish infidels who were bound, lost, to hell and the power of Lucifer.[48]

He says that King Fernando of Aragon and Queen Isabel of Castile subsequently sent him to newly conquered Granada, where he preached to and converted many Moors. He later undertook, at the behest of Martín García, Bishop of Barcelona and Inquisitor of Aragon, a translation into Aragonese of "the whole law of the Moors, that is the Alcoran with its glosses and the seven books of the Sunna."[49]

We know little more about Juan Andrés beyond what he himself says in the *Confusión*, and we have no way of knowing how much of what he says there is true, though none of it is implausible; his knowledge of Islamic sources, and his lack of recourse to traditional Christian polemical saws, make it quite possible that his tract was written by a former *faqīh*. Various historians have argued over whether he existed at all, and if so how much of this brief autobiography may be true. Ryan Szpiech has stressed that this authorial autobiography, in the *Confusión* as in other texts written by converts (real or imaginary), plays a key rhetorical role; the author's knowledge of his former "sect," its rites and its key sources is affirmed to lend authority to his work, while the narration of his passage to the true religion confirms, for his readers, the superiority of his new adopted religion. The comparison with Paul is a standard topos for converts from Judaism to Christianity. It is more surprising for a convert from Islam, in particular for a tract purportedly addressed to Moors, as Muslim traditions vilify Paul as the deformer and perverter of God's revelation to Jesus. By rehabilitating Paul (even suggesting that Qur'ānic exegetes wrote favorably of him), Juan is countering a traditional Muslim objection to Christianity.[50]

Juan Andrés decided to write his *Confusión* in order, he says, to collect the "fabulous fictions, jokes, inventions, bestialities, stupidities, craziness, absurdities, filthiness, impossibilities, lies and contradictions that Mahoma, in order to dupe simple people, scattered throughout the various books of his sect, principally the Alcoran."[51] Juan's first chapter is a brief biography of Mahoma. As we would expect from a former *faqīh*, he abstains from the denigratory legends of many Christian biographers: no doves or bulls, no epileptic fits, no failed resurrection or desecrated corpse. Instead, he sticks to Muslim sources, which he reads with a hostile eye in order to discredit Muhammad and Islam through association with pre-Muslim pagan rites.[52]

He begins by tracing Mahoma's genealogy from Ishmael, insisting that he came from a long line of pagan idolaters. This he contrasts to the glorious lineage of Jesus. Moreover, Mahoma himself had worshipped idols in Mecca before his calling as a prophet. He relates in particular the story of the black stone of Mecca, which Mahoma and the other Meccan idolaters had kissed. Once he had become prophet, Mahoma ordered that the stone be preserved in the sanctuary at Mecca and that the Moors continue to kiss it as before. The other rites of the pilgrimage, as well as the Ramadan fast, also contain vestiges of pre-Islamic idolatry, Juan asserts (104–7). Moreover, while he was still in Medina, Mahoma changed the direction of prayer from Jerusalem to Mecca, even though the temple there was still full of idols; Juan insinuates that this implies that Mahoma and his companions were all practicing idolatry during the five years between the change of the *qibla* and the cleansing of the Ka'ba of idols in 630. He implies that Muslim ritual remains sullied by its pagan origins.

Throughout his work, Juan cites passages from the Qur'ān and the Sunna in transliterated Arabic, then gives the Spanish translation of the passage. He frequently addresses his hypothetical adversary, a "Moro," asking him what reply he has to Juan's argument.[53] At one point he says to his "Moor," "you are a *faqīh* and a man of letters, and you have read all of the Alcoran and its glossators . . . and seven hundred books that the Moors have in their law or sect"

(184). It is unclear whether he has someone specific in mind or even if, like Petrus Alfonsi four centuries earlier, he imagines his interlocutor as his former, "infidel," self. In any case, the "Moro" never responds. In several cases, he asserts "the only response you can make is to be silent," and the ultimate response, he hopes, is to be the conversion of the Moor to Christianity.[54]

Juan insists on the lubricity of Mahoma: his many wives and concubines, in particular his scandalous marriage to Zaynab (164–66), his marriage to the nine-year-old Aisha, the promise of houris in heaven. He contrasts this with the purity and virginity of Jesus (173–74). He describes the banquet that, according to tradition, awaits each of the blessed, then the beautiful houri who will come to him and enfold him in a sweet embrace that will last fifty years. What, he asks, will these men's wives be doing during those fifty years? "I say that their glory will turn into grief and sorrow . . . these wives will be left alone and disconsolate like widows."[55] He mocks the "fables" of Mahoma, from Qur'ānic stories about biblical figures (such as Solomon) to the legends of the prophet's celestial journey.

Juan also cites Qur'ānic verses in which Meccan enemies of Muhammad mocked him and alleged that the prophet's revelations had been in fact composed by two slaves, Christian swordsmen (*espaderos*), who knew many stories from the bible, which they told him (114). He uses Muslim traditions concerning the compilation of the Qur'ān to affirm that Mahoma himself never ordered the Qur'ān to be compiled, that he announced revelations in Mecca and in Medina over a period of many years (and that the Qur'ān did not descend in one night, as some traditions affirmed). He describes the compilation of the Qur'ān during the caliphate of ʿUthmān (126–28). "The Alcoran is nothing more than old stories put into rhyme by Mahoma" (204). Similarly, the six books of Sunna or hadiths were compiled long after the death of Muhammad at the order of the caliphs of Damascus, who then had all unauthorized collections tossed into a river. The Moors subsequently split up into four schools (the madhabs), which, Juan insinuates, show that they cannot agree about their own doctrine (131–32).

Some argue that the military and political successes of the Moors attest to the truth of their doctrine. Juan responds with a chapter countering this argument. The Moors of Mahoma's age, he says, were ignorant idolaters. Mahoma was thus able to seduce them into his sect, concocting a law mixing elements of Jewish and Christian law with Arab superstitions. He then prohibited disputations with Jews and Christians in order to assure that the Moors would be unable to learn the truth (218–21). Juan also devotes a chapter to the Qur'ānic passages that are in harmony with Christian belief concerning the purity and sinlessness of the Virgin Mary, Jesus as Messiah, the virgin birth, the revelation of the Gospels. Such verses should lead Moors to Christian truth, he affirms. In the closing sentence, he cites a Qur'ānic passage affirming that Jesus is the Messiah, son of Mary and spirit and messenger of God, and concludes in these words, "you, Moor, can know that you should declare that Jesus Christ is God and Man."[56]

Juan's *Confusión* became something of a best seller, especially in Italian (there were no fewer than six printed editions in the sixteenth century), but also in French (1574), Dutch (1580), German (1598 and 1685), Latin (1595, 1600, and 1656), and English (1656).[57] It was perhaps one of the two most important books on Islam published in sixteenth-century Christian Europe, the other being Theodore Bibliander's 1543 edition of Robert of Ketton's twelfth-century translation of the Qur'ān (as we will see in chapter four). It offered a view of Muhammad and the Qur'ān that, while of course remaining very hostile, was nevertheless based on Muslim sources, thus permitting access to knowledge about Muslim doctrine and practice.

A Morisco Muhammad

In fifteenth- and early sixteenth-century Spain, the Pauline transformation of Juan Andrés from *faqīh* to priest and missionary (whether accurate autobiography or pious fiction) is representative of broader social trends: increasing pressure on Mudejars (Muslims living in Christian Spain) of the fifteenth century to convert; the conquest of Granada in 1492; the edict of February 12, 1502, which sought the mass conversion of the remaining Muslims. The crown had established the royal Inquisition in 1480 to eradicate what they perceived as vestiges of Judaism among *conversos*, converts from Judaism and their descendants. In the sixteenth century, particularly from about 1525 on, the Inquisition was used in a similar way to eradicate the vestiges of Islamic practice among the Moriscos. The fear of "contamination" of the "Old Christians" by "New Christian" converts from Judaism and Islam was pervasive, leading notably to measures restricting New Christians' access to prominent places in the Church and the royal administration (even though these measures were unevenly applied and descendants of Jews and Muslims often managed to obtain or buy certificates of "pure blood"). Paradoxically, this situation also led to new hybrid forms of spirituality, such as the movement of the Alumbrados (Illuminists), such as Isabel de la Cruz (of Jewish origin), who promoted the doctrine of universal salvation: all people, Christian or not, would be saved through Jesus's sacrifice of himself. Isabel's follower, Juan de Castillo, affirmed that God revealed this truth to "Mahoma," who taught that all would be saved.[58]

In 1588, workers in Granada who were demolishing a minaret in the former great mosque to make way for the new cathedral made a startling discovery: a small chest containing bones, a piece of veil, and a parchment.[59] The parchment contained texts in Latin, Arabic, and Spanish, including a prophecy by Saint John, purported to come from a group of first-century Christians living in Granada; the veil was from the Virgin Mary and the bones belonged to early Christian saints. Initial enthusiasm gave way to skepticism; after all, Christians of the first century did not write in Spanish, a language that did not yet exist. Seven years later, in 1595, lead plaques with Arabic and Latin inscriptions were found in caves in the mountains near Granada, accompanied by ashes and bones said to be those of martyrs put to death under Nero, including a certain Cecilius, who had been mentioned in the parchment found in 1588. One text, *The Essence of the Gospel* (*Haqīqat al-indjīl*) was supposedly revealed to the Virgin Mary by the Archangel Gabriel. It prophesized that a humble person of Arab origin would explain the text during a great gathering and that this would lead to the conversion of the whole world to the true faith, marking the imminence of the end of time. This and other texts, subsequently shown to be forgeries by sixteenth-century Moriscos, played on the ambiguity of the Moriscos' status as officially Christian but in some cases continuing to practice Islam in secret. Jesus is referred to in Qur'ānic terms as messiah and spirit of God (*rūh Allah*). The syncretic and ambiguous nature of the texts allowed Christians to think that the prophecies foretold the conversion of Muslims to Christianity and Muslims to think that it announced the conversion of Christians to Islam. Perhaps above all it glorified the role of the Moriscos themselves, whose often-syncretic practices precariously poised them between Christianity and Islam. Or perhaps subversive is a better term than syncretic; Leonard Harvey described it as a "project to enter, penetrate, and subvert Christianity," to transform Christianity, through false revelations, into something more palatable to converts from Islam.[60] It is a project that had some initial successes, as local Granadan church officials celebrated the discoveries: what bishop would not like to think that his diocese had been graced with relics and texts from early Christians close to the Apostles?

Similar motives probably underlie the apocryphal Gospel of Barnabas, purportedly the narrative account of Jesus's life by one of his disciples, Barnabas, but probably composed by Moriscos; the oldest extant version, in Italian, may have been written in Istanbul around 1600.[61] The text makes Paul into the chief culprit for the corruption of Jesus's message by calling him the son of God, rejecting circumcision, and allowing his followers to eat ritually impure food. Barnabas, the narrative voice in this long (222-chapter) gospel, gives a vision of Jesus's life and mission that curiously mixes Christian and Muslim perspectives.

We find the Qur'ānic assertion that Jesus had never claimed to be the son of God. At one point, the apostle Philip remarks that the prophet Isaiah wrote that God is our father; how is it then that God has no sons? Jesus responds that the prophets wrote in parables, and that this should in no way be understood literally. He adds that where the ancient prophets often spoke "darkly," "after me shall come the Splendour of all the prophets and holy ones, and shall shed light upon the darkness of all that the prophets have said, because he is the messenger of God."[62] Although Jesus does not name Muhammad here, he does in other passages.[63]

Jesus relates to his disciples the creation of Adam and clearly inscribes the sacred mission of Muhammad ("Machometo") into the divine plan. The first thing that Adam sees is "a writing that shone like the sun, which said: 'There is only one God, and Machometo is the messenger of God.' "[64] God explains to Adam that he is the first man created, and that "Machometo" "is your son, who shall come into the world many years hence, and shall be my messenger, for whom I have created all things; who shall give light to the world when he shall come; whose soul was set in a celestial splendour sixty thousand years before I made anything." When Adam and Eve are expelled from Eden, he turns back to see the shahada once again, this time inscribed on the gate of the garden from which he is now banished. Weeping, he prays, "May it be pleasing to God, O my son [referring to Machometo], that thou come quickly and draw us out of misery."[65]

Jesus reveals to his disciple Barnabas "great secrets":

> I tell thee that if I had not been called God I should have been carried into paradise when I shall depart from the world, whereas now I shall not go thither until the judgement. Now thou seest if I have cause to weep. Know, Barnabas, that for this I must have great persecution and shall be sold by one of my disciples for thirty pieces of money. Whereupon I am sure that he who shall sell me shall be slain in my name for that God shall take me up from the earth, and shall change the appearance of the traitor so that everyone shall believe him to be me; nevertheless, when he dieth an evil death, I shall abide in that dishonour for a long time in the world. But when Machometo shall come, the sacred messenger of God, that infamy shall be taken away.[66]

This passage condenses a number of traditional Muslim critiques of Christianity. First, Jesus affirms (as he does in the Qur'ān) that he has never claimed to be God or son of God. What's more, he asserts that he is not to die on the cross, but Judas will die in his place, as punishment for his treachery. But it will seem to everyone that is Jesus who has died, to Jesus's "dishonor." Only when Machometo comes and announces the truth will this dishonor be lifted from his name.

These passages and many others reflect a Muslim understanding of Jesus and his place in divine history. If Nicholas of Cusa "sifted" the Qur'ān to find confirmation of Christian doctrine, here the author of the Gospel of Barnabas seems to be sifting the Gospel to find confirmation of Muslim Christology. Yet other passages depart from standard Muslim doctrine, conferring on Muhammad the title of

Messiah that the Qur'ān reserved for Jesus and giving him a role in the last judgment generally accorded to Jesus in Muslim tradition.[67] Jesus announces to Herod's priest the coming of the Messiah and says that his name will be Machometo; the assembled crowd responds, "O Machometo, come quickly for the salvation of the world!"[68] What are we to make of this story, which has little to do with standard Muslim doctrine? It is true that *al-Masīh* (the Messiah) was one of the attributes that Muslim authors gave to Muhammad, and that a number of Muslim traditions have Jesus announce the coming of Muhammad (often associated with the Paraclete). But here the author goes further in denying Jesus the title of Messiah or indeed any role beyond the essential function of announcing the coming of the prophet Muhammad.

While there are similarities between the Gospel of Barnabas and the various texts of the Sacromonte lead tablets, there are also important differences. For the authors of the lead tablets, Jesus was the Messiah, and Muhammad was never mentioned by name. The positive role given to the Arabs is highlighted by the prophecies, but they remain ostensibly Christian texts, deftly avoiding areas of doctrinal conflict between Christianity and Islam. The Gospel of Barnabas explicitly rejects and refutes key Christian doctrines such as the Trinity and Incarnation. If these are projects to subvert and transform Iberian Christianity, they of course fail; if anything, they contribute to doubts about the Moriscos' orthodoxy, leading to the expulsion of the Moriscos from Spain between 1609 and 1615. It is north of the Pyrenees, a century after that expulsion, that Irish skeptic John Toland will use the Gospel of Barnabas to call into question the privileges of the Church and the doctrines on which its privileges are based (as we will see in chapter five). In fueling the Enlightenment critique of Christianity, the Moriscos would have an unexpected revenge.

Meanwhile, seventeenth-century Spain had become a purely Catholic country at pains to expunge remaining traces of Judaism and Islam. Having forcibly converted its Muslims in 1502, then expelled their descendants in 1609, Spain is now ready to replace the Morisco Muhammad with the charlatan and false prophet of northern European legend. This "Mahoma" becomes a colorful and detestable figure on the Spanish stage, particularly in the 1642 drama

Vida y muerte del falso profeta Mahoma.[69] The author deploys many of the legends we examined in chapter two, adding new elements that paint the false prophet in even more sinister colors. In the opening scene, Mahoma is walking through the desert, carrying in his arms the frail, elderly Abdimanoples. He explains to the old man that he is in love with his wife and plans to marry her: "I love Cadiga . . . And through your death, I will obtain her beauty and your wealth."[70] Deaf to the old man's outraged protests, he tosses him off a cliff. The heretical Christian monk Sergio then convinces Cadiga to marry Mahoma. Sergio and Mahoma plot together: "If Jesus was a lamb, I'll be a wolf," proclaims Mahoma, "pretending to be a prophet, I will preach my new sect."[71] When Mahoma tires of Cadiga, he has her killed and marries a bevy of young beauties. We find the stories of the trained dove, the bull with the "Alcoran" on its horns, the false prophet's death by poisoning and the stench of his cadaver, and his sepulcher made from magnetic stone. In a land that had seen nine centuries of Islam, we now find the crudest of the polemical legends about the prophet, who becomes the stage incarnation of deceit and fraud. Not content merely to proffer the standard medieval polemical fare, the author invents new crimes attributed to the false prophet: the murder of the aged Abdimanoples and of his own wife Cadiga.

Ironically, Spain was importing this northern European caricature of Islam precisely at the moment when some northern European authors were publishing learned anti-Muslim polemics based on material from Spain, such as Robert of Ketton's translation of the Qur'ān and Juan Andrés's *Confusión o confutación de la secta mahomética y del Alcorán.* These authors used their study of Islam to fuel their polemics against rival Christians, as the Protestant reformation divided Europe.

Prophet of the Turks

THE OTTOMAN EXPANSION into central Europe colored European responses to Islam during the sixteenth and seventeenth centuries. Intra-Christian conflicts, between Catholics and Protestants and at times between factions within Catholicism or Protestantism, also affected the ways in which Christian Europeans perceived Muslims. While many continued to portray Muhammad as heresiarch, a false prophet, and an impostor, it is often to contrast him with deviant Christians, who are cast as worse. In an almanac published in Paris in 1687, we find an image of "the impostor Mahomet" in hell alongside the "seducer Calvin" (fig. 11). Both preached heretical doctrine to their followers, who now, furious at finding themselves condemned to hell, turn in violence on their leaders. On the right, a Protestant "heretic" tugs on Calvin's beard and confronts him with an open book of his writings as, behind him, another prepares to hit him over the head with a stick. On the right, the Pacha of Buda (Ottoman governor of what is now Budapest) tramples on the open Qur'ān and threatens the false prophet with his sword. In the center, a demon looks on gleefully. Protestant disputants in a similar fashion branded "papists" as similar to or worse than "Turks."

A very different image of Muhammad is found in a number of paintings relating to the Immaculate Conception, such as that of Michele Luposignoli.[1] This doctrine, according to which the Virgin Mary was conceived without sin, was the object of considerable

FIGURE 11. L'imposteur Mahomet et le séducteur Calvin, *Almanach pour l'an de grace*, 1687. Bibliothèque nationale de France, Paris, France. © BNF

debate within the Catholic Church from the twelfth century to the nineteenth, and only became official doctrine of the Church in 1854. Here we see the Virgin portrayed in a classroom, surrounded by doctors of the Church holding scrolls representing their writings in favor of this doctrine. One might be surprised to see, at the bottom right, Mahomet, bearing a scroll with the text: "There are none of those from Adam that Satan does not hold, except Mary and her son. Mahomet in the book of the Coran."[2] Luposignoli and others mobilize Mahomet and the Coran to bolster the arguments of those promoting the doctrine of the Immaculate Conception. Mahomet becomes a positive figure, worthy to be portrayed in a painting of the Virgin surrounded by her learned devotees, a painting moreover meant to adorn the altar of a church.

In the sixteenth and seventeenth centuries, the figure of the prophet Muhammad challenged, on a number of levels, the certainties of Europeans embroiled in religious and civil strife. In this chapter, we will look at how Catholics and Protestants used the prophet as a rhetorical tool in their polemics against Christian adversaries and how the study of Islam, in particular the Qur'ān, served to feed these polemics. This resulted in a relativization of Islam's "otherness," as it came to be seen as in many ways closer to true Christianity than other, deviant forms of Christianity. Some Christians used their study of the Qur'ān to attack one of the central doctrines of Christianity, the Trinity; for these Unitarians or Socinians, such as Miguel Servet, Mahomet was a reformer who taught the unity of God and fought Trinitarian error. Despite (or perhaps because of) this reassessment of the Islamic prophet, others reaffirmed traditional legends of Mahomet as trickster and impostor. We will see how various translators and commentators of the Qur'ān, as well as chroniclers who narrated the life of Muhammad and the history of the Ottoman Empire, reaffirm the traditional view of Islam and its prophet, incorporating into their written works (and in the printed images that often accompanied them) not only recent erudition but also time-worn legends denigrating Mahomet. Finally, we will look at how the prophet came to be a witness for the Catholic doctrine of the Immaculate Conception and found his way onto the altars of Catholic churches.

We will be concentrating principally on German- and French-speaking Europe, and in particular on how the social, intellectual, political, and military upheavals caused by the Reformation and the wars of religion influenced the way the prophet of Islam was perceived. While on the whole the polemical attitude remains dominant, it is increasingly mitigated by considerations closer to home. Islam and its prophet are used as a measuring stick of error; Catholics (or Protestants) are said to be worse than Mahomet. Qur'ānic scholarship is deployed to combat error (of Muslims and of rival Christians), but it also raises troubling questions. The polemical edifice begins to crack, and in the cracks other ways of understanding Islam and its prophet begin to appear.

European Wars of Religion and the Turkish Prophet Mahomet

On September 25, 1396, Ottoman Sultan Bayezid I inflicted a crushing defeat on an army of crusaders at the battle of Nicopolis, marking another significant advance in the Ottoman conquest of the Balkans. Among the captives taken in the battle was a sixteen-year-old boy, Hans Schiltberger, who was reduced to slavery and became a page in the sultan's entourage. When Bayezid himself was routed by Timur in 1402, Schiltberger was subjected to a new master. He eventually escaped and returned to Istanbul and then to Germany, where he wrote an account of his travels. He describes Muslim belief and ritual without resorting to polemic. In his narration of the life of Muhammad, he relates the Bahīra legend with a new twist: the unnamed Armenian monk sees the Meccan caravan approaching and notes that there is a cloud hovering over the head of the young Machmet; this is consistent with Muslim legend, for which it shows God's special favor to the prophet by shading him from the harsh sun. But Schiltberger makes it into a *black* cloud, symbolizing the havoc that Machmet is to wreak on Christendom. The Armenian monk recognizes the youth as one predicted to be a scourge to Christians; his reign is destined to end after a thousand years. Schiltberger affirms that Muslims chide Christians for not respecting the law of their gospels, and that they acknowledge that this is the sole reason that God allows Muslims to triumph over Christians.[3]

Schiltberger sought to reassure his German readers: Christianity would triumph over Islam; the Turkish conquests would cease as soon as Christians began to respect the laws of their own faith. Yet such facile assurances must have rung hollow to Europeans who faced not only the continuing advances of the Ottoman troops but also, in the centuries that were to follow, increasing religious division at home as Europe descended into a war of religions. Plagued by violence and religious strife at home, Europeans looked to the Ottoman Empire not only as a threatening military power but also as a model of political unity and stability and of tolerance for religious diversity. European Christian writers, Protestant and Catholic, saw the Turk as a double threat, who could both conquer and seduce unwary European Christians.

Martin Luther's assessment of Muslims (or "Turks," as he invariably calls them) is based on his apocalyptical sense of history, in which the pope is the principal ally of Antichrist. In 1518, in defense of his ninety-five theses, Luther affirmed that the Turk served as "the lash and rod of God"; those who seek to fight the Turk rather than combating their own iniquities oppose God's will.[4] God is punishing Christians for their sins, notably those of the corrupt church; the way to stop the Turkish threat is not to muster armies, but to make penance. Luther develops this theme in greater detail in 1528, when, in the aftermath of Suleiman the Magnificent's annexation of much of Hungary, there was a real risk of large swaths of the German lands falling under Ottoman dominion. While Luther acknowledges that the emperor has the right and duty to defend his empire against the Turk, he affirms in his *On War against the Turk* (1529) that the most effective means of protection remain repentance and prayer in order to "take the rod out of God's hand."[5] Luther's message is the same in his *Appeal for Prayer against the Turk* of 1541: "The Turk, you see, is our 'schoolmaster.' He has to discipline and teach us to fear God and to pray. Otherwise we will do what we have been doing—rot in sin and complacency."[6] Just as the Israelites refused to listen to their prophets and needed to be whipped by the king of Babylon, so do Christians need the chastisement of the Turk.

Beyond assigning to the "Turk" the role of scourge or schoolmaster, Luther struggled to understand the place of Islam in God's plan; he sought out material on the rites and beliefs of the Muslims and on their attitudes toward Christians. One of his principal sources was a veritable best seller in the fifteenth and sixteenth centuries: George of Hungary's *Book on the Rites and Customs of the Turks*. Like Hans Schiltberger forty-two years earlier, George was taken captive in 1438, at the age of sixteen, and taken to Istanbul, from which he managed to escape twenty years later. His treatise provides a vivid description of the social and religious life of the Ottoman capital. Luther himself wrote a Latin preface to the 1530 reedition of George's treatise, in which he pays particular attention to the meticulousness with which Muslims practice their rites:

The religion of the Turks or Mahomet is far more splendid in ceremonies ... than ours, even including that of the religious or all the clerics.

The modesty and simplicity of their food, clothing, dwellings, and everything else, as well as the fasts, prayers, and common gatherings of the people . . . are nowhere seen among us—or rather it is impossible for our people to be persuaded to them. Furthermore, which of our monks, be it a Carthusian . . . or a Benedictine, is not put to shame by the miraculous and wondrous abstinence and discipline among their religious? Our religious are mere shadows when compared to them, and our people clearly profane when compared to theirs. Not even true Christians, not Christ himself, not the apostles or prophets ever exhibited so great a display. This is the reason why many persons so easily depart from faith in Christ for Mahomet and adhere to it so tenaciously. I sincerely believe that no papist, monk, cleric, or their equal in faith would be able to remain in their faith if they should spend three days among the Turks.[7]

In other words, the Turks are better Catholics than the papists themselves; convinced that their merit is reflected in their works, they excel in charity, fasting, devotion and prayer. Proof, for Luther, that Catholics are doomed, just like the Turks, for placing their hope in ceremonies, indulgences, fasting, and the like, rather than in faith. As often, Islam interests Luther as a means to attack "Papism": both are based the vain belief that works (ascetic practice, scrupulous respect of rites, and such) can save them. As he says in his *Appeal for Prayer against the Turks*: "the Pope's devil . . . is bigger than the Turk's devil."[8] For Luther, the pious Turk can be used to bash (literally and figuratively) the dissolute papist. This passage also shows that Luther recognizes the appeal of Islam: not only do many abandon Christ in favor of "Mahomet"; they cling tenaciously to their new faith.

Luther sought to counter those Germans who admired Muslims for their piety and justice and who would prefer the sultan's dominion to oppression at the hands of their compatriots. "Some praise the Turk's government because he allows everyone to believe what he will so long as *he* [the sultan] remains the temporal lord."[9] "Since now," he writes in 1530, "we have the Turk and his religion at our very doorstep, our people must be warned lest, either moved by the splendour of the Turkish religion and the external appearance of their customs, or offended by the meagre display of our own faith or the deformity of our customs, they deny their Christ and follow

Mahomet."[10] This fear pervades Luther's writings on Islam, fear not merely of conquest of the German lands by the Ottoman armies, but—what was of course much worse for Luther—of the attraction that Turkish culture and Muslim religion could exercise on the sultan's German subjects, leading them to convert to Islam, or rather, as Luther puts it, to apostatize, to "become Turks." Luther clearly is on the defensive; he recognizes that the Qur'ān's rejection of the divinity of Christ is "extraordinarily pleasing to reason."[11] For Luther, the religion of the Turks is the cult of the Devil, and the Turk's army is the Devil's army. Some authors rehashed the standard polemical biography of the prophet: Heinrich Knaust, who had met Luther in Wittenburg in 1537, in 1542 produced a brief life of "Machomet"; he reiterates the standard tales of the dove eating out of the false prophet's ear, his preaching as far as Spain, and his ignominious death.[12]

Yet given the urgency of the Turkish military threat and the real appeal of Islam, Luther could not content himself with crude caricatures of the prophet. He sought, starting in the 1520s, to learn more about Islam. He turned, quite naturally, to the works of medieval scholars and polemicists who had confronted Islam between the twelfth and the early fourteenth centuries. In the 1520s, he came across a Latin manuscript of Riccoldo da Montecroce's *Contra legem Saracenorum*. In 1542, the Basel city council jailed two publishers who wanted to print, in Latin, a collection of texts about Islam including Robert of Ketton's twelfth-century Latin translation of the Qur'ān and Riccoldo's *Contra legem*. The city fathers proclaimed that it was dangerous to publish the "fables and heresies" of the Qur'ān. Luther intervened to help the editor Theodor Bibliander convince the council that the Qur'ān should be printed since there was no better way to combat the Turks than to permit everyone to see for themselves Machomet's "lies and fables." Bibliander's edition of Robert of Ketton's Qur'ān was published the following year, with a preface by Luther. The year 1542 was when Luther published his own German translation of Riccoldo's *Contra legem Saracenorum*. In his preface to his translation, he affirms that those who believe in the Alcoran cannot truly be human:

> If the Turks or Saracens seriously believe such a book of Mahmet— the Alcoran—they are not worthy to be called men since they have

been robbed of common human reason. They have become stones and blocks.[13]

Luther gives a free and loose translation of Riccoldo's work, not hesitating to inject expressions of his outrage. While he had earlier acknowledged that reason could seem to legitimate the Qur'ān's rejection of Christ's divinity, here he takes a quite different approach: in response to Qur'ān 6:101 ("How could it be that He [God] should have a child without there ever having been a mate for Him"), he lambasts "Mahmet" for his obsession with the flesh, which makes him unable to understand the spiritual: "Oh how over-powered in the flesh of women Mahmet is. In all his thoughts, words, deeds, he cannot speak or do anything apart from this lust. It must always be flesh, flesh, flesh."[14] "Women," he says, "are Mahmet's God, heart, and eternal life."[15]

The Turk was, of course, neither Luther's sole nor his principal foe. He wrote against numerous adversaries, from reformers who had broken with him to humanists who disagreed with him to Jews who refused to be convinced by him. But his main adversaries remained the "Papists." He produced a tremendous output of controversial texts aimed at his numerous enemies; these tracts showed learning and eloquence, but often also intransigence, violence, and vulgarity.[16] While the Turk needed to be combated with sword and pen, he could also be a useful foil against the greater enemy, the Papists. Luther peppers his polemics against different adversaries with references to the Turk. Those Christians who reject the doctrine of the Trinity are Turks and apostates.[17] Luther works into his translation of Riccoldo's work his own anti-Catholic diatribes; to cite one example:

> [The Pope] has certainly initiated so many wars, murder, bloodshed amongst the kings, has robbed, stolen, plundered, and unrelentingly thrashed so much land and so many people, and has also conducted himself with such arrogance over all the kings, and most blasphemously under the name of Christ. Mahmet appears before the world as a pure saint in comparison with him.[18]

Mahmet is a "saint" of course only in comparison with the pope. Yet Luther introduces a note of relativism that marks an important change in European discourse on Muhammad and Islam. In a divided, sectarian Europe, Islam begins to be perceived as one "sect" among many, never of course anywhere near as legitimate as "true" Christianity, but often presented (if primarily for rhetorical purposes) as better than rival Christian sects. As Luther affirms in his *War Sermon against the Turk*, "The Turk fills heaven with Christians by murdering their bodies, but the pope does what he can to fill hell with Christians through his blasphemous teachings."[19]

Other Protestants made similar comparisons. For Calvin, the religion of the pope and that of Mahomet have the same origin: "wicked additions" to scripture. Instead of being content with the Bible, they add other sources to the law.[20] Calvin presents Mahomet as a "seducer and sorcerer" ("seducteur et sorcier").[21] Mahometans, like papists, cite centuries of tradition to assert their legitimacy, but in both cases, their authority is usurped.[22] For Thomas Drant, archdeacon of Lewes, in 1570, Muhammad and the pope both err in defending works as justification.[23]

Catholics shot back with similar comparisons. Just as Mahomet once did, so Luther is now doing, affirms Thomas More in his *Dialogue concerning Heresies* (1529). Lutheran clergymen taking wives is reminiscent of Mahomet's polygamy; the two schismatics show their true natures in encouraging the lustful desires of their followers; both incite violent revolt against proper religious and civil authorities. Luther, by marrying a nun and encouraging others to similarly break their vows of celibacy, is worse than Machomet and his polygamy. Other than that, the two heretics are similar: they denigrate the saints and the sacraments; they advocate violence against the Church. Luther is doing now what Machomet once did, he affirms.[24] Other Catholic writers, such as sixteenth-century chronicler Johannes Sleidanus, similarly compare Luther's authorization of clerical marriage with Mahomet's permission of polygamy.[25]

Guillaume Postel brought to his polemics an impressive knowledge of Arabic and of Islam. Postel learned Arabic in Tunis and Istanbul, and in 1538 he became the first professor of Arabic at the Collège Royal in Paris (the future Collège de France). He was familiar with Nicholas of Cusa's *Sifting of the Qur'ān* and with Bibliander's edition of the Latin Qur'ān.[26] Expert in Hebrew and Arabic, promoter of a new Christian Kabbala, Postel remained a fervent defender of the Catholic Church against Lutheran heretics, or (as he called them) "cenevangelists." In 1543, he published in Paris an anti-Lutheran tract titled *A Book on the Agreement between the Qur'ān, or the Law of Mahomet, and the Evangelicals.*[27] Postel makes a list of twenty-eight similarities, in doctrine and in practice, between "Muhametans and Cenevangelists," then offers a refutation of each of them. Both groups teach that works are useless. Both deny the intervention of the saints and the use of images. Both undermine the clergy, reject the authority of the pope, and fight the true Church with the sword. Like the Jews and the Anabaptists, the Muhametans teach that sin can be washed away with water, which only encourages all kinds of lechery. While Postel identifies Muhamet with Antichrist, his real target is Luther, and the association of Lutheranism and Islam serves as a means to denigrate and discredit the Protestant movement. As the first waves of Protestant iconoclastic frenzy swept Europe, Postel defended Catholic practice by associating the new iconoclasm with Islam.

English Catholic William Rainolds published in 1597 his magnum opus, *Calvino-Tvrcismus*, a 1,222-page tract comparing the "sects" of Calvin and Mahomet.[28] It is a theological debate between a "Mahometan" and an Anglican, in which the Muslim eventually carries the day, showing that his faith is more rational than Protestantism. But above all, the two find much to agree about, since both heresies, according to Rainolds, teach predestination, denigrate the Trinity, reject the devotional use of images, and practice an idolatrous devotion to scripture. Calvin, he affirms, sought nothing better than to unseat the pope and replace him with the Ottoman sultan. Theologians like Rainolds found Islam useful as a foil to Protestantism; bad by definition, the "Mahometan" sect was superior to the Protestant heresy. Popular works such as the 1687 almanac depicting the "impostor Mahomet" and the "seducer Calvin" together in hell (which we examined in the beginning of this chapter) brought this same message to a broader public that was unlikely to read a 1,222-page Latin theological tract. In the same way, Protestant illustrators associated papists and Turks. An anonymous engraver of the seventeenth century drew a "tree of heresies" springing from the loins and heart of Satan, with leaves bearing the names of the principal Christian heresies of antiquity and the middle ages, crowned with the images of the pope and Mahumet (fig. 12).

These sixteenth-century polemicists, Protestant and Catholics, used comparison with Islam to discredit Christian adversaries in Europe: Catholics (or Protestants) were worse than "Turks." Yet at the same time such comparisons introduced a degree of relativism that could provoke discomfort. Some, following the lead of Nicholas of Cusa, portray the prophet of Islam as a reformer more than an impostor: an imperfect, flawed reformer, but a reformer nonetheless.

Swiss humanist Theodor Bibliander shows a profound ambivalence toward Islam and its prophet. In his *Ad nominis Christiani socios consultatio* (published in Latin in 1542, the same year in English as *A Godly Consultation*, and the same year as his Latin edition of the Qur'ān), Bibliander writes:

> Mahumet denounces the Jews' infidelity and affirms that Christ was conceived of the Holy Spirit and born of Mary a pure Virgin. And he called him the great prophet of God and the word and soul and spirit of God who shall come to judge the whole world. Nor would Mahumet seem in any way to be Christ's enemy or to seek to abolish his doctrine, but only to take upon himself to correct those things that were depraved. . . . Thus does Mahumetes' doctrine valiantly resist certain old heresies condemned by the word of God and judgement of the Catholic Church, such as the Anthropomorphites who held the opinion that God was compact and had the body and members of a man. In conclusion, he cuts the throat of heathen superstitions, utterly denying the plurality of gods. Nor will he grant any use of images in anyway in the practice of religion.[29]

For Bibliander, Mahumet denounced the Jews and affirmed the basic truths of Christianity: the Virgin birth, Christ as Word of God, the Holy Spirit. He eradicated idolatry and banned images; he combated heresy. He was in other words a preacher and reformer, in many ways analogous to the Protestants. For Luther, Mahomet was a stick with which to bash the papists; the Saracen prophet was by definition the epitome of error, and affirming that the pope was worse was good rhetorical warfare. Bibliander is doing something quite different, informed by his close and careful study of the Qur'ān.

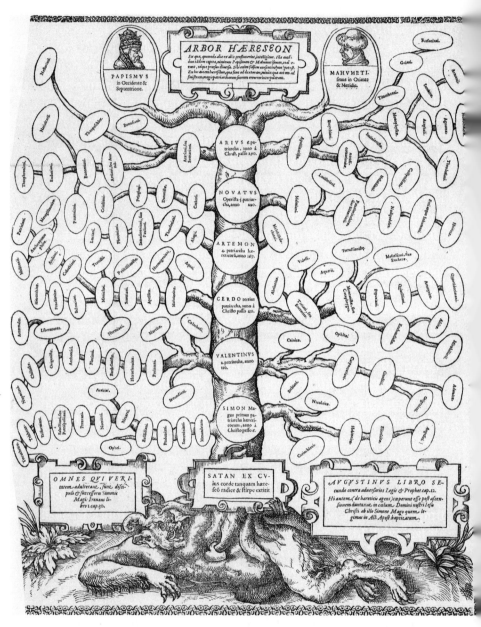

FIGURE 12. Tree of Heresies, ca. 1560, print, Amsterdam, Rijksmuseum FMH
435-F. http://hdl.handle.net/10934/RM0001.COLLECT.442616

His Mahomet seems a reformer and a visionary, yet one that must finally be rejected because he has not built on the foundation of scripture and does not recognize Christ as the basis for salvation. His religion is after all a "devilish plantation" destined to be uprooted by "the Spirit of Christ's mouth."[30]

When he narrates Mahomet's life, Bibliander chides his "detestable deeds," inspired by a mind that was "covetous, cruel, unrighteous, desirous, and very greedy of honor and dominion, prone and ready to all manner of foul and filthy pleasure." Luther denounced the pope and Muhammad; Bibliander finds a connection between the two. Rome was plagued by the tyranny of Popes Gregory I and Boniface III. The latter oppressed his bishops so much that he provoked contention among them. It is in this context that Muhammad is born and founds his own sect, which appears to be both the result of Roman factionalism and a divine punishment of it. Bibliander's version of the life of the prophet is in keeping with the scholarly polemics that he will publish with the Qur'ān, and he eschews on the whole polemical legends: no trained animals, no bogus miracles. This makes it all the more surprising to find, after the description of Mahomet's death (poisoning followed by wounds suffered in battle), the story of his floating tomb, held aloft by magnets. Bibliander assured his readers that God had long since struck it down with lightning, but that the Mahometans continue to flock to Mecca to pay homage to "the body of this stinking prophet," just as Catholics go to Compostela to venerate the relics of Saint James.

Mahomet, Unitarian Prophet?

While Bibliander framed his Qur'ān in order to defuse the potential troubling impact it could have on Christian orthodoxy, the possibilities opened by using the Qur'ān to critique Christianity became clear in the years following his publication of Robert of Ketton's translation. Miguel Servet (or Michael Servetus, 1511–1553) used his reading of Bibliander's Qur'ān to refute the doctrine of the Trinity.[31] An Aragonese humanist and polymath, Servet published on topics ranging from the circulation of blood in the lungs to geography and astrology. He also was interested in theology. He came to the conclusion early that the Trinity was an unfortunate innovation of the fourth-century Church councils, a doctrine that neither Jesus nor his apostles ever preached. Servet's first work, published at the age of twenty, was *On the Errors of the Trinity*. While his arguments are for the most part based on a close reading of biblical texts, he also cites Jewish and Muslim objections to the Trinity:

> How much this tradition of the Trinity has, alas! been a laughing-stock to the Mahometans, only God knows. The Jews also shrink from giving adherence to this fancy of ours, and laugh at our foolishness about the Trinity; and on account of its blasphemies they do not believe that this is the Messiah who was promised in their law. And not only Maho-metans and Hebrews, but the very beasts of the field, would make fun of us did they grasp our fantastical notion, for all the works of the Lord bless the one God. Hear also what Mahomet says; for more reliance is to be given to one truth which an enemy confesses than to a hundred lies on our side. For he says in his Alcoran that Christ was the greatest of the prophets, the spirit of God, the power of God, the breath of God, the very soul of God, the Word born of a perpetual virgin by God's breathing upon her; and that it is because of the wickedness of the Jews toward him that they are in their present wretchedness and misfortune. He says, moreover, that the Apostles and Evangelists and the first Chris-tians were the best of men, and wrote what is true, and did not hold the Trinity, or three Persons in the Divine Being, but men in later times added this.[32]

Jews and Muslims correctly chide and ridicule Christians for the creation of the absurd doctrine of the Trinity, which can inspire only mockery. As a result, Jews incorrectly conclude that Jesus was not their messiah and Muslims erroneously refuse to accept that he was the son of God. The Qur'ān, of which at this point Servet probably had only secondhand knowledge (perhaps via Nicholas of Cusa's *Cribratio*), offers a more correct assessment of Christ than do the Trinitarian theologians.

Servet subsequently came across a copy of Bibliander's Qur'ān and made extensive use of it in his *Christianismi Restitutio*, pub-lished in Vienne in 1553 as an expanded broadside against Trinitar-ian doctrine that was to provoke the ire of Catholic and Protestant authorities and would eventually cost him his life. He examined the principal biblical proof texts that Trinitarian theologians from

Augustine to Melanchthon and Calvin (whom he brands "sophists") had used to support the doctrine, in each case offering a refutation of their interpretations. "What," asks Servet, "shall we say about the Mahometans who disagree with us?"[33] He offers a selection of Qur'ānic passages denouncing and refuting the Trinity, gleaned from Bibliander's edition. The Qur'ān confirms and complements Servet's antitrinitarian arguments, notably showing how the Trinity was a blasphemous innovation of the early Church and quite alien to the teachings of Jesus and his apostles. Moreover, Muhammad's anti-trinitarianism prevented him from recognizing Jesus as the Son of God: "Because of the misguided teachings of the Trinitarians, he dissented from Christianity, which was truly an unfortunate tragedy for the world."[34] Catholic polemicists had charged that Luther and Calvin were as bad as or worse than Muhammad; Protestants had affirmed that the Papists were worse than the Turks. For Servet, Mahomet is better than all of them, Catholic or Protestant, because he is closer to the teaching of Christ; he is a reformer who preaches the unity of God. This does not mean that Servet approves of Islam; Mahomet's dissent from Christianity is a "tragedy," but a tragedy for which the responsibility lies with those who preached the absurd doctrines of the Trinity. Obviously it comes as no surprise, he says, if the Turks laugh at us more than at asses and mules, since we have been made like the horse and the mule, which have no intellect.[35] Turks and Jews may be far from the Truth, but not as far as Catholics and Protestants; neither in the Talmud nor in the Alcoran are such horrifying blasphemies found as the doctrine of the Trinity.[36]

Catholics and Protestants were partners in error, for Servet; Catholic and Protestant authorities collaborated in silencing him. Servet had been exchanging letters with Calvin for years, trying to convince him of the errors of the Trinity and provoking the reformer's ire. Shortly after the publication of *Christianismi Restitutio*, one of Calvin's associates wrote to the Catholic inquisitor of Vienne, who had Servet and his publisher arrested. Servet escaped from prison; the Inquisition condemned him as a heretic, burning him in effigy along with his book. He went to Geneva, it seems, in order to confront Calvin and to become a martyr for his Unitarian faith. He was arrested and put on trial before the Geneva city council. At one point in the proceedings, Calvin read out before the court a statement of the thirty-eight articles that he and the council found heretical in Servet's work. Servet, relishing the chance to reply, argued that his views were in harmony with those of church fathers Irenaeus and Tertullian and condemned Calvin as an agent of the devil; the council should put Calvin to death, not him, Servet charged. The council convicted him of heresy. He was burned at the stake on a pile of his books on October 27, 1553. The need to burn Servet and his book, it seems, was one of the few things that Genevan Protestants and a Catholic inquisitor could agree on.[37]

Despite the best efforts of Protestant and Catholic authorities to have the *Christianismi Restitutio* burned, it continued to be read by a small coterie of Unitarians. Two prominent Unitarians, Ferenc Dávid and Giorgio Biandrata, relied heavily on Servet for their own Unitarian tract, *De falsa et vera unius Dei Patris*, which they published in Alba Iulia, Transylvania, in 1568.[38] Ferenc Dávid had attended in the same year the Diet of Torda, where Hungarian King John II, vassal of Ottoman Sultan Suleiman the magnificent, had issued an edict of toleration allowing different preachers (Protestant, Catholic, and Unitarian) to preach their doctrines unmolested. Dávid and Biandrata affirm that the whole Orient has abandoned Christianity because of the doctrine of the Trinity, giving a string of Qur'ān citations against the doctrine. They have not only read Servet, they have themselves studied Bibliander's Qur'ān. Mahomet frequently thanks God for liberating him from the superstitions of the Christians, who adulate images in their churches and worship Mary in place of God. Jesus never taught that he was God, they affirm. It is because Christians have departed from the true faith that God has justly punished them.[39]

To Protestant and Catholic critics, the fact that Unitarians cited the Qur'ān and flourished in an Ottoman protectorate confirmed their worst fears. A century later, in 1660, Johann Heinrich Hottinger wrote: "those teachings that have been called from the abyss of the old anti-Trinitarians may pave a way for Islam within the boundaries of Europe." The "the Socinians" (Unitarians), he says, "are in fact even worse than Islam."[40] Hottinger, a Swiss Protestant theologian and scholar in Oriental languages, used his considerable erudition to attack the rival faiths of Catholicism and Islam. In his *Historia orientalis*, published in Zurich in 1660, Hottinger uses his meticulous study of the Qur'ān to understand the Christian East during the life of Muhammad. He depicts the Christian East as riven by doctrinal divisions and plagued with superstition; in this land of heresies, Islam is the newest and most perverse heresy. This allows him to attack seventeenth-century Catholicism (which he associates with the near-pagan devotions of seventh-century Eastern Christians) and to dismiss Islam. His Muhammad is a "cunning fox" who proposes "a new religion, which he cobbled together from the rites of all other religions, and the more it accommodated their carnality and sensuality the more applause it immediately received."[41] Hottinger particularly sought to fight Unitarians, expounding and refuting Qur'ānic passages on the unity of God as well as the works of Muslim exegetes. Yet in many ways (as Jan Loop notes), in so doing he opens "Pandora's box"; in seeking to refute European Socinians, he provides them (and other critics of Christianity) arguments that they will use against institutional Christianity. All the more so as one of Hottinger's principal critiques of Islam and Socianism is that they are too exclusively based on reason and reject doctrines of faith that seem irrational.[42] Hardly an argument likely to convince many of Hottinger's seventeenth- and eighteenth-century readers.

We find a similar association of Socianism and Islam by a French convert to Protestantism, Mathurin Veyssière La Croze, a former Benedictine monk, librarian of the Royal Library in Berlin, in his *Réflexions historiques et critiques sur le mahométisme et socinianisme* (1707). La Croze was worried that young intellectuals might be seduced by Unitarianism's apparent rationality, yet he affirmed that it was a faith that lacked substance and led its adepts into doubt and hesitation. Socinians do not stay in their faith: "Some of them embrace Spinosism, some Popery; others go over to Judaism or to Mahometanism, and very few of them return to the Orthodox [Protestant] Religion."[43] Yet for some, La Croze was too lenient with these heretics. Johann Heinrich Oelven denounced him as *Der turbanisierte Socinianer* (The Turban-Wearing Socinian). He attacked La Croze for praising the religious tolerance in Islam—and implicitly criticizing the European Christian society. For Oelven, such praise of Islam was dangerous.[44] The study of the Qur'ān, even when undertaken for the sake of refuting the errors of the Turks, raised uncomfortable questions about Christian doctrine. Islamic critiques of Christianity were being branded by Unitarians and, increasingly at the turn of the eighteenth century, by radical reformers and free-thinkers (or "Spinosists"), as we will see in chapters five and six.

Meanwhile, the Catholic nightmare of a Protestant-Ottoman alliance against the Habsburgs became reality in Hungary in the last quarter of the seventeenth century, with help and encouragement from the very Catholic King Louis XIV of France. The Peace of Westphalia of 1648 brought an end to the Thirty Years' War by, among other things, establishing the principle *cuius regio, eius religio*, by which Catholic or Protestant rulers could enforce religious conformity in their realms but would let dissidents emigrate. While this may have put an end to the "wars of religion" internationally, it left princes free to quell religious dissent and diversity at home. Habsburg Emperor Leopold I (r. 1658–1705) took measures to close Protestant churches and remove Protestants from positions in the army and administration. This was one of the main factors that provoked the Kuruc revolt in summer 1672, in which mostly Protestant rebels took over key fortresses in upper Hungary; Habsburg forces finally regained control in October 1672.[45] This led to more reprisals against Hungarian Protestants, most infamously the show trial of 1674 in Bratislava that sent hundreds of Protestant ministers to the slave galleys.[46] In 1678, a new war broke out as rebel Imre Thököly, in alliance with Ottoman Sultan Mehmed IV and French King Louis XIV, rallied disenfranchised Hungarian Protestants and carved out a principality in Upper Hungary: Mehmed recognized him as king in 1682 and offered protection to the new kingdom in return for an annual tribute of 40,000 tallers. Thököly and his troops accompanied the Ottoman forces that besieged Vienna in 1683. The success by the Habsburgs and their allies in repulsing this siege is often seen by historians as a watershed, marking the end of Ottoman expansion. The Treaty of Karlowitz in 1699 formalized the transfer of large parts of the western Ottoman domains (in Hungary and Bosnia) to Habsburg rule. Yet for European observers of the late seventeenth and early eighteenth centuries, it was not at all clear that the Turk was the "sick man" of Europe, and the specter of an alliance between Protestants and Turks continued to inspire fear.

All the more so as a French Hungarian revolt against the Habsburgs, led by Francis II Rákóczi, erupted between 1703 and 1711.

Sixteenth- and seventeenth-century Europeans could not be indifferent to Islam and its prophet. The danger of much of Europe falling under Ottoman dominion was quite real. The possibility that Europeans would be seduced by Ottoman opulence, by the relative peace that reigned among its numerous religious communities, by the simplicity and rationality of its doctrines, was ominous to both Protestants and Catholics. The intellectual tools they forged to fight this menace, such as Bibliander's Qur'ān, were being used against them by dissident Christians and risked weakening and dividing Christian Europe even further, or so it seemed to some. In this context, it is not surprising that many Christian Europeans preferred to avoid any real engagement with Islam and its fundamental texts and to take refuge in traditional medieval legends about the heresiarch and trickster Mahomet.

Fusing Qur'ān and Traditional Polemics in the Sixteenth Century

Bibliander's Qur'ān became an important source of information on Islam and Muhammad for generations of Europeans. Giovanni Battista Castrodardo translated Bibliander's Latin version into Italian in 1547; Salomon Schweigger translated the Italian translation into German (1616); Schweigger's text was published in Dutch translation in 1641. Some of these vernacular translators attempted to frame the Qur'ān in ways that could explain the religion of the "Turks" to their readers in simpler, less academic terms than Bibliander employed. They frequently added prefaces or introductions narrating the life of Muhammad, often integrating elements from medieval polemics. And some of the translations were accompanied by prints illustrating key episodes from Muhammad's life. Authors of chronicles fused the Qur'ān and traditional polemics in their presentations of the "Turkish prophet."

Castrodardo's Italian translation of Bibliander's Qur'ān was published by Andrea Arrivabene in Venice in 1547.[47] Arrivabene prefaced the work with a dedicatory letter to Gabriel de Luetz, French ambassador to the Ottoman Empire. The perspective of a French-Venetian-Ottoman alliance, in the interests of commerce and of opposition to the Habsburgs, perhaps explains the interest in the religion of the Turks, which Arrivabene describes in the long introductory essay, using a mixture of Venetian historiography, Morisco texts from Constantinople, Juan Andrés, and the texts from Bibliander's anthology. The intention is not purely polemical; on the contrary, Arrivabene seeks to provide his Italian readers with a readable guide to Islam and Ottoman society. Moreover, he works into his introductory material an anti-Habsburg, pro-Ottoman bias. Yet he does this with a certain ambiguity. He presents "the true history of Macometto, taken from the histories of Christians," in which he presents the prophet as a scheming heretic, inspired by a "diabolical spirit."[48] He stresses the desperate plight of Christians in Turkish lands, be they slaves or free. The closing words of the translation say that it has been offered with the goal of confusing the "diabolical spirit of Macometto, precursor of the Antichrist."

Castrodardo's and Arrivabene's book was widely read in Italy and elsewhere in Europe; as we have seen, it was translated to German (and thence to Dutch) in the seventeenth century. Amsterdam Jews subsequently translated it into Hebrew and Ladino. One of its readers was the miller Menocchio, who found in this Alcorano the story of Abraham destroying the idols, which he used to argue that Catholics should abolish the cult of relics. Menocchio was sent to his death for this and other heretical beliefs in 1599; no doubt his inquisitors saw this as proof of the dangers of reading heretical books like the Qur'ān. No wonder that the book had been put on the *Index Librorum Prohibitorum* in 1564, and that a number of its copies were seized and burned. Yet this did not prevent it from circulating widely and from being read and appreciated by intellectuals as diverse as Guillaume Postel, Joseph Scaliger, and Montesquieu. The Qur'ān could be painstakingly framed with polemical caveats, but this did not prevent readers from finding in Castrodardo's translation (as in Bibliander's text) arguments against the doctrines and practices of Catholic or Protestant Christianity.

Perhaps better to combat this dangerous use of Qur'ān and to counter admiration for the Turks and their religious tolerance, Johann Israel de Bry and Johann Theodor de Bry published, in 1597,

The Acts of Mechmet I Prince of the Saracens, offering a blend of the medieval scholarly and legendary traditions we examined in chapter two, supplemented by the first printed images of these scenes.[49] Their life of Mahomet (1–27) is followed by an account of the history of his successors (Arab, Mongol, and Turk) until 1596 (27–58) and then a series of prophecies concerning the end of Ottoman rule, ascribed to different people (including Emperors Severus and Leo VI). The final prophecy is attributed to Mahomet himself (94–96), who prophesied that his "law" (*lex Maumetana*) would disappear after one thousand years, which is to say in 1621, the authors explain. Their work is meant to reassure their readers (the Ottoman threat will disappear within twenty-five years) and to inspire in them a strong contempt for the "Mahometan law." The unacknowledged subtext is that their readers might well fear that the Ottoman threat is anything but on the wane and that they might feel that Ottoman Islam, with its recognition and toleration of diverse religious communities, should be admired rather than despised.

Hence the de Brys forge a hybrid life of Mahomet from elements gleaned in very different kinds of sources. They begin by narrating the story of Hagar and Ishmael, tracing the genealogy of Mahomet, then relating his birth. At age eight, his mother died and he was raised by his uncle Abutaliph, who had him educated in science, the occult, and in the scriptures of the Jews and Christians. The young Mahomet became a merchant and traveled to Egypt, where he met Jews and heretical Christians, in particular Sergius, who became his close associate. With Sergius's help, Mahomet "patched together" the Alcoran from pagan, Jewish, and Christian elements. This law authorizes fornication, adultery, and sodomy, the authors affirm; they give the names of a number of Mahomet's wives (citing "Alcorani Azoar 4.2") and describe the carnal delights that the Alcoran promises in heaven ("Azoar 4.5"). Clearly the authors have read Bibliander's Qur'ān, which they use as the basis of their quite hostile assessment of the "Mahometan law."

Yet in the following chapters, rather than using the intellectual arsenal provided by Bibliander (as had Arrivabene), they prefer to reiterate the polemical legends that we encountered in chapter two. They relate that the merchant Mahomet travels to the land of Cana and manages to trap in his "net" Queen Tagida, convincing her that he is the Messiah. His fame spreads, and he becomes duke and prince of the region. He travels through Africa and to Spain; the devil warns him that Saint Isidore is coming to confront him, and he flees back to Africa. He then foments a revolution against the Roman Empire of Heraclius. Africa and Syria come under his sway, and he is crowned king in Damascus. Here the de Brys have inserted an image showing, in the background, fierce battles on land and on sea and, in the foreground, Mahomet being crowned, surrounded by Ottoman-looking Janissaries. This Mahomet is a Saracen king in Ottoman Turkish guise, as we see from the way he and his associates dress.[50]

But God punishes Mahomet, striking him with epilepsy. The authors seem to fear that their readers might have a hard time believing this slanderous tale; they insist that the "most serious and excellent authors" confirm this. Tagida is consternated, but when Mahomet recovers, he stands up and says "don't cry, dearest wife," explaining that he was simply speaking with the Archangel Gabriel. The epileptic fit receives an illustration as well: Mahomet has tumbled, his arms flailing and his legs in the air; his crown has fallen to the ground. His courtiers show their consternation in theatrical gestures. In the foreground is the Queen "Tagida," who also sports a crown over her veil. The setting, as Ulrike Ilg notes, seems closer to a Renaissance Italian city than to Mecca (or for that matter Constantinople); the probable artist, Jean-Jacques Boissard, was familiar with Venice and its architecture.

The authors then devote a chapter to Mahomet's "tricks" (praestigiae), relating the legends of the dove who eats from his ear, the bull with the book on his horns, and the pots of milk and honey hidden in the desert. The dove and bull scene are each illustrated; both show Muhammad before an exclusively male throng in Turkish garb, in a public square where an obelisk in the background suggests the hippodrome of Constantinople, underlining the fact that "Mechmet" is the "prophet of the Turks." In both scenes, the members of the audience show their astonishment with large gestures of their arms as they look either at Mahomet or at each other.

In the scene with the bull, we see the animal twice: in the background advancing toward Mahomet, then in the center of the composition, next to him. The illustration of these bogus miracles provided an easy means to ridicule Mahomet and his "law" as well as the Turks who follow it. In recounting the story of the bull, the authors proclaim "O blindness! O immense stupidity of the people!" The following chapter offers a list of fourteen principal errors contained in the Alcoran, from the rejection of the Trinity and of Christ's incarnation, crucifixion, and resurrection to practices such as polygamy and ritual ablution. For a number of these doctrinal errors, the authors cite parallels with other heretics, from Manichaeans to Anabaptists. Here they are guided by their reading of the Qur'ān and by anti-Qur'ānic polemics such as Riccoldo da Montecroce's *Contra sectam*. They then mock the "vanities and fables" regarding Mahomet, ridiculing stories from the Qur'ān and traditions, and in particular the story of the mi'rāj.

Finally, they related the "pernicious fall and the tragic death of Mahomet." Mahomet, poisoned by one of his disciples, falls into an epileptic fit that lasts fourteen days, making him writhe and foam, and finally dies miserably. In the illustration of his death we see, in a room in his palace, Mahomet, wearing turban and crown, tumbling to the ground from his chair. A woman seems to be moving away from him, holding a vase or cup in her hand. While the text says that one of his male disciples poisoned him (*a quodam suorum discipulorum*), Muslim tradition says that it was a woman, Zaynab bint al-Harith, who put poison into a shoulder of lamb and served it to Muhammad. Did the artist have knowledge (perhaps partial or garbled) of this tradition? Moreover, in the background, in a courtyard, the artist places Mahomet lying on the ground (already dead?), with two dogs biting him and a third following behind. At the left, a turbaned man runs toward Mahomet, his arms flailing, either to show his distress, to attempt to drive off the dogs, or both. We have seen that various medieval legends have Mahomet devoured by dogs or (more often) pigs. Yet the authors say not a word of this; again, the artist seems to be integrating elements from the standard polemical biographies of Mahomet that he had read elsewhere.

Since he had announced that he would be resurrected on the third day, the text continues, his followers stood by his corpse. Seeing after twelve days that the cadaver stank, they put it in an iron coffin and took it to a temple in Mecca, where thanks to magnets it remained suspended in the air. This was done, they explain, so that the blind and simple people would take this as an irrefutable proof that Mahomet's doctrine was true. And an illustration shows the sanctuary with a group of Turks in reverence below the floating coffin (fig. 13). The false prophet's tomb is in fact an Ottoman tomb, complete with a cenotaph topped with a turban and concentric lamps.

The Turks visit his tomb "religiously," the authors affirm. Or at least they did until 1470. In that year, a great thunderbolt, a "celestial fire," fell from heaven and destroyed the tomb, leaving only ruins. The story of the floating coffin, first found in twelfth-century Latin texts such as Embrico of Mainz's Vita Mahometi, remained common until the eighteenth or nineteenth century. Here we find a satisfying and reassuring tale (from the authors' point of view) of its destruction: just as God struck down Mahomet with epilepsy, so he now has destroyed his tomb, foreshadowing the imminent destruction of his law. The de Brys are not the first to report the destruction of Mahomet's sanctuary at Mecca; in the thirteenth century, English chronicler Matthew Paris wrote that fire from heaven had fallen on the "temple of Mahomet" and that then the ground opened up and swallowed the whole city of Mecca into the abyss.[51]

The de Brys' strange hybrid of the learned and the preposterous was in fact nothing unusual. Their woodcuts found their way onto the title page of the Dutch translation of the Castrodardo/Arrivabene/Schweigger Qur'ān in 1641. It is indeed common in the seventeenth century to "recycle" woodcuts, from one book to another. Here we find the exact reproductions of the de Brys' woodcuts showing Mahomet's epileptic fit, the miracles of the dove and bull, and his floating coffin. While Castrodardo and Arrivabene had avoided those hostile legends, they found their way surreptitiously back into the Dutch version of their text.

Such hostile images found their way into other European Qur'ān translations. André du Ryer published a French translation in 1647, despite opposition from Saint Vincent de Paul, spiritual advisor to the French queen, Anne of Austria (regent for her son Louis XIV). Jan Hendrick Glazemaker, who moved in freethinking circles and translated Descartes and Spinoza into Dutch, produced a Dutch translation of Ryer's Alcoran, first published in 1658, and republished frequently in the seventeenth century.[52] It was republished

FIGURE 13. Pilgrims in adoration before Mahomet's floating coffin; de Bry & de Bry, *Acta Mechmeti I. Saracenorum Principis*, p. 26. © Bayerische Staatsbibliothek

in 1696 by Timotheus ten Hoorn, an Amsterdam publisher, author of pornographic novels and purveyor of prohibited books (he got into trouble the following year for selling a book by Spinoza).[53] Ten Hoorn had engraver Caspar Luyken make a series of illustrations showing Muslims in different positions of prayer, with mosques in the background—images both instructive and no doubt of interest as exotica. He also includes one polemical saw, showing the false miracles of dove and bull (fig. 14).

Protestant theologian Johann Georg Pritius published a German translation as part of his 1699 tract on "The Constantinopolitan or Turkish Church-State" (a title that shows again the Protestant association of Muslim Constantinople and Catholic Rome), which contains, as usual, a polemical life of the prophet. The title page sports a mosque, and the frontispiece shows a turbaned Mahomet with the dove on his shoulder, his arm pointing to the Alcoran on a pulpit; the bull walking toward it on the other side. Beneath the Alcoran are a double-bladed sword and a blazing torch, promising destruction; above, a crescent moon is surrounded by dark foreboding clouds.[54]

Such examples could be multiplied ad nauseam. Scores of authors, now for the most part completely forgotten, similarly blended scholarship and slander to present their religious rivals, in this case Mahomet, as beneath all serious consideration. Their efforts to discredit Islam and its prophet are in some ways backhanded compliments, or at least acknowledgment of the troubling questions that Islam posed to sixteenth- and seventeenth-century European Christians. They attest to a vigorous propaganda campaign against the Ottomans, Islam, and the prophet, a propaganda campaign that was in many ways quite successful, but the text of the Qur'ān and information about Ottoman society also found more sympathetic readers.

Mahomet Testifies to the Immaculate Conception

We have seen how the prophet of Islam could be instrumentalized in polemics between Catholics, Protestants, and Unitarians. He was also mobilized in debates within the Catholic Church in a much more positive light: as one who testified to the truth of the doctrine of the Immaculate Conception. This belief, according to which the Virgin Mary was conceived without sin, became official doctrine of the Catholic Church only in 1854; it was hotly debated in the Middle Ages and the sixteenth and seventeenth centuries, opposed in particular by a number of Dominican theologians.[55] Muhammad became an unlikely ally of those seeking to promote the doctrine.[56]

A hadith related by traditionists Muhammad al-Bukhārī and Muslim ibn al-Hajjaj has the prophet affirm: "Satan touches every son of Adam on the day when his mother gives birth to him with the exception of Mary and her son."[57] In the context of the ninth-century Abassid caliphate where the two traditionists lived, this hadith

FIGURE 14. Dove and bull miracles, from 1696 Dutch translation of the
Qur'ān, engraving by Casper Luyken. © Utrecht University Library

served perhaps above all to emphasize the harmony that should reign among those who venerate Mary and her son, and the universalism of the message transmitted by the prophets Jesus and Muhammad. Five centuries later, Franciscan friar Marquard von Lindau cites this hadith in a pastoral text, the *De reparatione hominis*, in which he defends the Immaculate Conception; he also gives a string of citations from the "Alkoron" in praise of the Virgin.[58] Of course Marquard is wrong to think that Muhammad, the Qur'ān, or Muslim theology attested to Mary's Immaculate Conception. The whole basis of the doctrine is the original sin that corrupts the rest of humanity, an idea completely foreign to Islam. But it is easy to see how this well-read German friar coming across these passages would feel that they vindicated his position. Surely if "Machmet" and the "Alkoron" offer these praises of the Virgin's purity, Christian skeptics who doubt it gravely err.

Marquard makes the same argument at some length in German in the 1380s, in his *Dekalogerklärung* (Explanation of the Ten Commandments), an immensely popular pastoral text that was widely diffused throughout German-speaking Europe. He subsequently affirms in his commentary on the Gospel of John: "There is no sect of faith wherein there are not some who are not called to the faith of Christ but are chosen friends of God."[59] While Marquard does not go as far as calling Machmet a "chosen friend of God," he cites him as a respectable authority without any polemical caveats, suggesting that, at least in what concerns the respect accorded to the Virgin Mary, Machmet and his followers are better than some Catholic Christians—particularly the Franciscans' Dominican rivals, who (following their master Thomas Aquinas) rejected the doctrine of the Immaculate Conception.

Various fourteenth- and fifteenth-century authors follow Marquard and cite the hadith in support of the Immaculate Conception. Marquard cites, somewhat confusedly, "Alkoron" or "Albokon," the prior referring probably to the Qur'ān and the latter perhaps a deformation of the name of traditionist Bukhārī. Later authors often simply attribute the passage to the Qur'ān. Catalan Carmelite Francesc Martí in 1390 composed his *Compendium veritatis immaculatae conceptionis Virginis*, a massive tract in defense of the doctrine, in which he cites the same hadith but attributes it to sura 5 of the Qur'ān.[60] Various fifteenth- and sixteenth-century authors similarly invoke Mahomet as a "Saracen" or "pagan" authority in support of the doctrine, implicitly or explicitly affirming that if even Mahomet and the Saracens recognize the purity of the Virgin, good Christians should do so as well. Juan Andrés, whose *Confusión o confutación de la secta Mahomética y del Alcorán* we examined in chapter three, also affirmed that the Qur'ān affirms the purity of the Virgin and that Muslim exegetes conclude that the Virgin was exempt from diabolical temptation and original sin.[61]

Between the sixteenth and the eighteenth centuries, various painters offer visual depictions of Muhammad as defender of the Immaculate Conception. As we saw in the introduction to this chapter, Nikola Braličpainted a retable devoted to the Immaculate Conception in 1518, currently extant in a 1727 copy by Michele Luposignoli, *Disputa*. The Virgin appears twice in the painting: top center, in a niche with arms crossed, standing on a crescent moon, and bottom center, in a painting representing her breastfeeding Christ. She is surrounded by doctors of the Church who wield scrolls or books with their texts in favor of the doctrine. In the lower left-hand corner is Luther and, as we have seen, Muhammad is in the lower right-hand corner, with the hadith (attributed to the Qur'ān) on his scroll. Certainly, Luther and Muhammad are relegated to the bottom of the painting, placed in the margins of this group of saintly doctors, but are present as witnesses anyway, and as such they found their way onto this retable destined to be placed behind the altar of a church.

Other sixteenth-century painters similarly depict Muhammad as witness to Mary's Immaculate Conception: Francesco Signorelli in 1524 and Durante Nobili in 1546. This prominent, honorable place given to the prophet of Islam in retables meant to adorn church altars may have puzzled or vexed some. Luigi Primo Gentile, in any case, gives a drastically different rendition in 1663 (fig. 15). Gentile places around the Virgin a veritable army of saints, monks, nuns, theologians, popes, bishops, and cardinals. Muhammad and Luther are both present, but they lie supine at the very bottom of the composition, in a very ambiguous position—more defeated rivals than honored witnesses, though they still bear the writings that testify to the Virgin's purity.

FIGURE 15. Luigi Primo Gentile, *Triunfo dell'Immacolata* (1663), Santa Maria in Monserrato degli Spagnoli, Rome. © akg-images / Pirozzi

Yet on the whole, in these altarpieces, as in the texts promoting the doctrine of the Immaculate Conception, Muhammad (like Luther) does not serve as a foil; on the contrary, he is highlighted as a positive testimony to the purity of the Virgin. With, as a corollary, of course, that the Catholic who does not accept this doctrine is somehow worse than Muhammad and Luther. The prophet is a strategic challenge in the context of a very specific intra-Christian controversy. It is not that these writers and artists were more "tolerant" toward Islam or better disposed toward this prophet than others, but rather that evoking him as witness could be an effective rhetorical strategy in the context of a very specific controversy.

Where Medieval European Christian portrayals of Muhammad were almost invariably negative, casting him either as object of idolatrous worship or clever inventor of a diabolical heresy, in the sixteenth and seventeenth centuries there seemed to no longer be a unified front of opposition to Islam and its prophet. The prophet was a figure of contention among rival Christians, Protestants and Catholics, who insulted each other by claiming that their Christian opponents were worse than the Turks and the prophet Muhammad. Muhammad was a positive (if flawed) figure for a few of these reformers, and even more so for Unitarians like Miguel Servet and his followers, who gleaned in the Qur'ān arguments against the Trinity. The Turk controlled much of Europe and ruled an empire that inspired fear and admiration, repulsion and desire. Ottoman Istanbul was both an enemy capital and a bustling cosmopolitan city. The Ottoman emperors seemed to have found ways to tolerate religious diversity and peaceful coexistence that Europe, riven by religious strife, was unable to put into place. European writers traced much of this legacy back to the life and work of Muhammad himself. While for many Europeans in the seventeenth and eighteenth centuries Mahomet continued to be seen as a dangerous heresiarch, for others he became a model of religious reform and political revolution, as we will see in the next two chapters.

CHAPTER FIVE

Republican Revolutionary in Renaissance England

IN 1697, HUMPHREY PRIDEAUX, Anglican minister and Oxford-educated doctor of theology, published a work called *The True Nature of The Imposture Fully Display'd in the Life of Mahomet*. Prideaux casts a critical eye on many of the legendary elements concerning the prophet that had been popular in medieval and early modern polemical lives of Muhammad. Prideaux claims to present, in lieu of fables, the "true nature" of Mahomet's "imposture." His Mahomet is dominated by the twin passions of lust and ambition, which cause him to feign a religious vocation. Unable to produce miracles, Mahomet gains adherents through threats of violence and promises of a carnal paradise, well-adapted to the hot temperaments of the inhabitants of the "torrid zone." Prideaux is moved less by the desire to attack Islam than to defend Christianity—not from Muslims, but from Deists. In the opening passages of his tract, he lambasts Deists who affirm that Christianity is an imposture; his goal is to show them a true imposture, that of Mahomet and then to demonstrate (in a tract published in the same volume) that Christianity is no imposture, but the true religion.

Why would a conservative Anglican minister in 1697 feel that he needed to defend Christianity by attacking Muhammad as an impostor? Although Prideaux does not say so, he is responding to the claims of Henry Stubbe, who had presented the Muslim prophet as a reformer and visionary who proposed a renewed monotheistic revelation in a time when Jews and Christians, victims of bickering clerical elites, had strayed from their pristine monotheism. Stubbe produced a glowing portrait of the prophet of Islam, indeed the first wholly positive biography of Muhammad written by a European Christian. Stubbe and some of his English contemporaries saw England during and after the civil war as fragile and divided, burdened with a corrupt powerful clerical elite, its religious divisions exacerbated by official persecution. Travelers to the Ottoman Empire often described a thriving, prosperous state where subjects of different faiths and languages lived in harmony; shouldn't England follow this example? Stubbe goes further by looking for a model in the community formed by Muhammad himself. Prideaux, who along with Stubbe studied at Oxford under Arabic professor Edward Pococke, needed to respond to this affront to the Anglican Church.

From the capture of Constantinople in 1453 to the failure of the siege of Vienna in 1683, the Ottoman Empire loomed large in the British imagination. Of course, the English did not have to worry, as did Luther and other central Europeans, that their lands might soon be annexed to the empire. Yet thousands of Englishmen did end up captives in the empire or in the allied "Barbary" states of North Africa. In May 1626, there were reportedly three thousand British captives in Algiers and 1,500 in Salé (Morocco).[1] In the following decades, Barbary corsairs conducted raids along the coasts of Cornwall and Ireland; in 1627 Algiers corsairs raided as far as Iceland. For those living along exposed coasts as well as those venturing abroad on seaborne vessels, the threat of captivity was quite real. English monarchs responded with periodic punitive missions, but more often with ransoming expeditions. Returning captives and travelers wrote of their impressions of Algiers, Salé, or Constantinople. These portraits varied widely; some stressed the hardships of those deprived of their freedom, forced to work in often degrading and difficult conditions, denigrated (at times literally spit on) by Turks or Arabs who considered them inferior. Yet at the same time, many of these travelers were impressed by the sophistication and wealth they saw and expressed admiration at the tolerance shown to a confusing mix of Jewish, Christian, and Muslim communities speaking a Babel of languages. And travelers noted that some of the English and other Europeans who gained their freedom (or who came voluntarily) were happy to stay on and did quite well in the Ottoman army and administration. Indeed, the Ottomans and their Barbary allies seemed to offer more possibilities for advancement and enrichment than many European societies.

We saw in the previous chapter how for many Protestants of the sixteenth and seventeenth centuries, including Anglicans, Catholics were worse than Protestants. This could also be put in a positive formulation: Islam is close to true Christianity, Anglican Protestantism. As the threat of Spanish invasion of England loomed in the 1580s, Queen Elizabeth sought an alliance with the Ottomans and wrote to the Sultan Murad. The queen insisted on the concord between Protestant and Islamic religiosity; she, like Murad, rejected popish idolatry.[2] Francis Bacon reiterated this notion that the English and Turks were natural allies in the fight against Catholicism.[3]

Ambivalence was also felt by those who never strayed from England. While travelers reported that English converts to Islam, such as the pirate John Ward, were thriving in the Ottoman Empire, English playwrights wrote them into moralizing dramas that transformed them into diabolically inspired villains punished by a violent death.[4] Culturally, the Ottoman world also provoked unease, as it was a legendary land of wealth, sophistication, and opulence. The supposedly hedonistic culture of the Turk was denounced by those who feared its appeal to English men and women, including those who never left their island, but who could be enticed into consuming Ottoman wares: coffee, for example. In 1652, the first coffee house opened in London. Coffee quickly became popular, and some attributed semimiraculous properties to the drink. Edward Pococke, professor of Arabic at Oxford, in 1659 translated an Arabic treatise enumerating the health benefits of coffee. Yet others attacked this "Mahometan berry." An anonymous tract, *The Character of a Coffee-House* (1665) saw the popularity of the drink as a dark sign of the times, associated with Cromwell's rebellion and the publication of the first English translation of the Qur'ān:

When Coffee once was vended here,
The Alc'ron shortly did appear.[5]

As usual, Europeans' views of Islam and of Muhammad tend to reflect their own preoccupations close to home more than any real interest in or engagement with Muslim history. In England in the seventeenth century, we see fierce debates about Muhammad or the Qur'ān, which in fact are coded polemics about the English kings, the civil war, the role of the Anglican Church, and the place of radical Protestants in English society. As Humberto Garcia has shown, Muhammad and his primitive community of Muslims came to represent for some Englishmen (such as Stubbe) exemplary anticlerical radical republicans, a free society in which the power and privilege of the Church was abolished and religious freedom was granted to members of different faith communities. The fierce reactions of Prideaux and others, who upheld the traditional negative view of Mahomet, have as much or more to do with their abhorrence of republicanism as they do with their defense of Anglicanism (although clearly the two were closely linked for them). These debates then, must be examined against the backdrop of key events: the civil war, which culminated with the execution of Charles I in 1649 (the same year that saw the publication of the first English translation of the Qur'ān); the Restoration, which brought Charles II to the throne in 1660; the (unsuccessful) Rye House plot to assassinate Charles II and his brother James in 1683 (the same year as the failed Ottoman siege of Vienna); James II's Declaration of Indulgence in 1687 (granting freedom of worship to Catholics and dissident Protestants), the Glorious Revolution that deposed James the following year.

Cromwell as Mahomet: The English Alcoran (1649)

We have seen that the desire to publish a Latin translation of the Qur'ān landed its publisher in jail in Basel, and it took the vigorous intervention of Luther to free him and his associates and to allow the translation to go forward. This unease or ambivalence reflects the fear that publishing the "heretical errors" of Mahomet might entice some to embrace his heresy. Luther, as we have seen, countered that there was no better way to combat the Turk than to expose Mahomet's errors for all to see. Ambivalence and controversy were also to accompany the first English translation of the Qur'ān.

This translation (made not from the Arabic but from André du Ryer's French translation of 1647) was published in April 1649. The translator is not identified, but it is perhaps a young scholar named Thomas Ross.[6] A disgruntled soldier named Anthony Weldon, having caught wind of the publication, had petitioned Parliament in March to stop the publication. The authorities arrested the printer, Robert White, confiscated the printed copies, and held a hearing that eventually cleared all involved and authorized the publication.

In order to placate readers and to justify the translation, Alexander Ross, former royal chaplain, writes a brief "caveat" meant to reassure his readers that the publication of the Qur'ān in English was not dangerous. It is unclear whether the parliamentary commission requested this caveat from him or whether his relative Thomas Ross or others involved in the project deemed it prudent to have him lend his name to the project. In any case, as Matthew Dimmock has noted, Ross is "in the unenviable position of having to defend the publication of the Alcoran while at the same time needing to refute it absolutely."[7] He affirms that Mahomet's errors are no worse than those of heretical Protestants whose works one can find in any bookstall. His central justification for the translation of the Qur'ān is essentially the same as Luther's for the publication of the Latin translation in Basel a century earlier:

> We cannot do better service to our Countrymen, nor offer a greater affront to the *Mahometans*, than to bring out to the open view of all, the blind *Sampsons* of their *Alcoran*, which have mastered so many Nations, that we may laugh at it, of which even their own Wise Men are ashamed, and are sorry it should be translated into any other language: for they are unwilling that their grand Hypocrite should be unmasked, or that the Visard of his pretended holiness should be taken off, whose filthy nakedness must appear when he is devested.[8]

Thomas Ross wrote a preface, "the translator to the Christian Reader," in which he justified the publication of the Qur'ān while at the same time implicitly criticizing the new commonwealth authorities who had grilled him. "It may happily startle thee, to find him so to speak English, as if he had made some Conquest on the Nation; but thou wilt soon reject that fear, if thou consider that this his Alcoran, (the Ground-work of the Turkish Religion) hath been already translated into almost all Languages in Christendom, (at least, the most general, as the Latin, Italian, French, &c.) yet never gained any Proselyte, where the Sword, its most forcible, and strongest argument hath not prevailed."[9] There is no danger, he continues, that such a "rude" and "incongruous" text should seduce Englishmen any more than it has other Europeans. Why then would the Cromwellian authorities attempt to prevent its being published? Ross cannot of course criticize them openly, but he gives a good idea of what he thinks:

> (Christian Reader) though some, conscious of their own instability in Religion, and of theirs (too like Turks in this) whose prosperity and opinions they follow, were unwilling this should see the Press, yet am I confident, if thou hast been so true a votary to orthodox Religion, as to keep thy self untainted of their follies, this shall not hurt thee: And as for those of that Batch, having once abandoned the Sun of the Gospel, I believe they will wander as far into utter darkness, by following strange lights, as by this Ignis Fatuus of the Alcoran. Such as it is, I present to thee, having taken the pains only to translate it out of French, not doubting, though it hath been a poyson, that hath infected a very great, but most unsound part of the Universe, it may prove an Antidote, to confirm in thee the health of Christianity.[10]

Ross addressed those Christians who have a firm and healthy Christianity, in other words Anglicanism presented as "orthodox religion." Over and against these orthodox Christians is the "batch" of those who no longer follow the Gospel, whose behavior shows their "instability in religion": the Turks, but also the Cromwellians who have killed the king and attacked the Church.[11]

Thomas Ross hides his royalist critiques of Parliamentarism in his anti-Mahometan polemics. He gives a brief and vitriolic biography of "Mahomet," containing many items with which we are now familiar. He says that Mahomet was a "vicious Pagan," an orphan whose uncle, Abdal Mutalib, sold him to Ishmaelite slave traders. A wealthy merchant named Abdemonople bought him and had him drive his camel caravans to Syria, Egypt, and Persia. The heretic Sergius, secretary of Nestorius, fled to Arabia and was welcomed by Abdemonople. Abdemonople then died, and Mahomet through sorcery seduced his widow Ajissa and through marriage to her gained great fortune. At this point the heretical Sergius saw his chance:

> Sergius, as subtile, as malicious, observing his disposition, and withal, after some discourse concerning the two Religions, of both which he found him excellently ignorant, seeing it no difficulty to distill into him the poyson of his Heresie, easily perswaded him, That Jesus Christ was but Man simply, that for the merit of his vertues he was held as Deified: that the sufferings of his death were but humane inventions; that he was transported from this life to an immortal, and glorious, by another way than that of Death; That there is but one God, in one Person; so that the Faith of the Christians is vain, and invented, and that of the Iews too loose, and lean, through their own obstinacy. That the Arabians being a dull and ignorant people, inclining neither to the one nor the other, but all (as many as had been touched with the fame of his new sanctity) admiring his perfections; The Iews and Christians being likewise enemies to each other, and the Christians at variance among themselves; He might in that juncture of affairs, assume the title of a Prophet sent from God, to disabuse the one, and the other, and save the World by another Law.[12]

Mahomet ardently desires to be esteemed a prophet. He "retires to a solitary cave" and leaves Sergius to preach to the people, praising the new prophet. God, in mercy, sought to set Mahomet on the right path by striking him with "the falling sickness," but Mahomet "instead of repenting, made an advantage to promove his wicked design." He explained to his distraught wife "that being constrained frequently to converse with the Angel Gabriel, his frail body, unable to abide the splendor of his heavenly presence, fell into that distemper, and at the departure of the Divine Ambassador, recovered its former condition."[13] This provoked even greater esteem and reverence, and Mahomet then promulgates some chapters of his Alcoran, mixing elements from the Law of Moses, the Psalms of David, and the Gospel of Jesus Christ; part of the Alcoran is brought on the horns of an ox. Ross spares his readers the dove but incorporates other elements of earlier polemical lives, such as Mahomet's promise that he would rise from the dead after three days.

But what interests Ross most is Mahomet's project of political revolution under the guise of religious reform. Not content to be a prophet, he says, Mahomet schemes to become king. A feigned revelation, a learned heretical sidekick, and false miracles let Muhammad convince the Arabians that he is a prophet, all the more so as his Alcoran fits with their "loose humor" far better than the more "burdensome" law of the Christians; they can indulge in hedonistic pleasures in this life and look forward to even more and better ones in the next. Ross says that he managed thus to attract "a numerous, though vulgar party of the people." Just like Cromwell, Ross may be tempted to say (but of course does not). That the parliamentarians are the object of this portrait of Mahomet becomes even clearer in what follows. He had "under pretence of Reformation of Religion, gained many followers"; now "he resolved to yoak to it that other concomitant in popular disturbances, liberty, proclaiming it to be the will of God."[14] English revolutionaries invoked religious reformation (greater tolerance and curbing the wealth and influence of the Anglican Church) and of course asserted the liberty of the English people to their self-government. Mahomet does the same: he frees his slave Zeidi in the name of universal liberty.

> This bait, as it inhaunced his fame, so it added to his retinue; for as multitudes, affecting novelty, and a mutation of condition, daily added themselves to his party; so slaves from all parts of Arabia forsook their Masters, and fled to him as their Redeemer, and embraced his Law, as the means of their salvation. These through a fond conceit of his piety, ready to sacrifice their lives at his command, he divided into troops, and sent to rob the Caravans of Merchants that travelled through the deserts; and by this means, having added to his treasure by spoil; and his retinue daily encreasing by a multitude of Fugitives and Vagabonds, who by reason of this liberty, to act any villany, resorted to him; he at length took up thoughts of imploying them in the confirmation of his Law, which he knew to be the ready way to his establishment, in that power to which he aspired.[15]

In other words, Mahomet is a rabble-rouser and a revolutionary; he is Cromwell. He is the leader of a band of fugitives and vagabonds who delight in robbery and pillage and who glorify their actions through invoking liberty; a batch of dissolute villains who gleefully trample underfoot the doctrines of Orthodox Christianity and the prerogatives of the Church. Indeed, Mahomet is Cromwell, or perhaps Cromwell is Mahomet. Thomas Ross cannot say that, for his troubles would be much greater than those he already had with the Council of State. Indeed, he was arrested in 1654 on suspicion of treason (in an affair that has nothing to do with the Qur'ān translation) and subsequently released on bail; he later went to Cologne to join Charles II in exile.[16]

The famous tragedie of King Charles I basely butchered was published in May 1649, just four months after Charles's execution.[17] The anonymous author, in his prefatory poem dedicated to exiled monarch Charles II, laments the "Reformation dire, that kils our King," subverting and inverting discipline, law, and propriety. "Those Plebeians, who procure our ills Feed high, sleep soft, have Kingdomes at their cals. Strange revolution, O accurst mutation that appoints Coblers for to rule a Nation." These cobblers seem to be the moral equivalent of Mahomet's freed slaves in Ross's narrative. There is no need to dwell on the plot or the dialogue of this broadsheet; for our purposes we can focus on the following lines that Cromwell addresses to his collaborator Hugh Peter:

> Thou art that Load-stone, which shall draw my sense to any part of policy i'the Machiavilian world, we two (like Mahomet and his pliant Monke) will frame an English Alchoran, which shall be written with the self-same pensil great Draco grav'd his laws. (4)

Cromwell is a new Mahomet that is composing a new "Alchoran" with his sidekick Peter, identified both with the "pliant monk" (Sergius) and with the magnet or loadstone said to hold up Mahomet's coffin. From our point of view, the most striking aspect of this is the brief and offhand nature of the reference. The author assumes that his readers will be familiar with various aspects of the Mahomet legend that we examined in chapter two. Cromwell is Mahomet—he is also Machiavelli and Draco; this shows to what extent discourse on the prophet and his "Alcoran" was a standard part of the intellectual baggage of Englishmen in the mid-seventeenth century. Subsequent royalist writers also compared Cromwell to Mahomet.[18]

Lancelot Addison, for example, in his *First State of Mahumedism* (1678), says that Mahomet "so well managed his ambition and injustice, under the cloak of Religion, as never have any yet proved his Equal: the nearest and most exact Transcript of this great Imposter was the late Usurper."[19] Other royalists lambasted the government for permitting the publication of the "Turkish Alcoran," proof of their impiety (whereas for Thomas Ross their desire to censure it had shown them to be like the Turk).[20] For royalists, Cromwell and his "batch," like Mahomet and the Turks, insulted religion and sapped the foundations of good government.

Parliamentarians reacted in kind: John Milton affirmed that the royalists who tried to present the slain king as a martyr have

> stolen the pattern from Mecha, and to hang it in that ayrery Mahometan regality, supported by this their impostured Loadstone, whereby to present his sacred memory, in his Solitudes, to posterity, surely it may be suspected, they were not so exactly their Crafts-masters, or so much friends as foes, to Saint him before his time, and in such a shrine, as necessarily must render him to future times infamous an imparalelld dissembler, and a greater deceiver than Mahomet ever was.[21]

Cromwell is no Mahomet; on the contrary, the royalists are guilty of the same sleight of hand as the impostor and his loadstone. Milton's friend Andrew Marvell condemns Quakers and monarchists because of their opposition to Cromwell; he denounces their rantings as "prophecies fit to be Alcoraned."[22]

Mahomet, Republican Visionary: Henry Stubbe's Originall & Progress of Mahometanism (1671)

As comparisons with Muhammad were facilely bandied about by royalists and parliamentarians, Protestants and Catholics, Anglicans and dissidents, their polemical edge, it seemed, became blunted. In the quarrels over religious and political systems, Islam became one rival faith system among many, neither better nor worse than many of the Christian denominations; the religious toleration of the Ottoman Empire became for some Englishmen a model. Yet none of these authors presented the prophet Muhammad as a frankly positive figure.

None, that is, until Henry Stubbe (1632–1676) penned his *Originall & Progress of Mahometanism* in 1671.[23] Stubbe, a well-read physician, knew no Arabic and had never traveled to any Muslim country. Yet it is he who, for Nabil Matar, effected a "Copernican revolution in the Study of Islam."[24] Based on Arabic sources in translation (mostly in Latin), he undertook a complete reassessment of Muhammad's mission and life, vindicating him against earlier Christian polemicists. In England as elsewhere in Europe, the study of Arabic, and the translation of key texts, had taken root over the fifteenth and sixteenth centuries. Guillaume Postel (1510–1581) in Paris, Joseph Scaliger (1540–1609) in Leiden, Pococke (1604–1691) in Oxford, and others had breathed new life into the study of Arabic letters and Muslim history and had translated key texts. Stubbe particularly relies on Edward Pococke's *Specimen historiae Arabum* (1650), a Latin translation of the chronicle of Gregory Bar Hebraeus, a thirteenth-century Syriac bishop; he also uses Johann Heinrich Hottinger's *Historia orientalis*.[25] While some of these scholars depict Muslim doctrine and devotion in a relatively positive light, they all see it as inferior to Christianity. Not so Stubbe.

From the outset, it is clear that this portrait is to be nothing like earlier European Christian depictions of Muhammad, whom Stubbe presents as an "extraordinary person" with a "great soul." He has a "grave aspect wherein the awfulness of majesty seemed to be tempered with the admirable sweetness which at once imprinted in the beholders respect, reverence and love." "The Arabians compare him to the purest streams of some river gently gliding along, which arrest and delight the eyes of every approaching passenger."[26]

Far from corrupting or deforming Christianity, "Mahomet" tried to return to its purest expression. Stubbe traces the history of Judaism and early Christianity, accenting the doctrinal and institutional fractures and the pagan origins of much of Christian practice and doctrine. Baptism, for Stubbe, "comes from the pagan custom . . . of washing away expiatorily in rivers the most enormous sins."[27] Of pagan origin, too, are most of the Church's feast days, the titles proudly borne by the clergy, and the sacrament of the Lord's Supper. Jesus himself never claimed to be God, and indeed most early Christians, being Jews, did not consider him God; the idea is an adaptation from the pagan tradition of deifying great respected leaders.

The introduction of the doctrine of Jesus's divinity caused sharp divisions among the early Christians.[28] Nor were all the early Christians monotheists: the Egyptian Christians happily worshipped Serapis.[29] Constantine, he says, convoked two thousand bishops for the Nicene Council, but then excluded all but 318; the resulting canons and Nicene Creed in no way represent a consensus of Christians.[30] Stubbe describes the different factions of Christianity: Donatists, Novatians, Arians, Nestorians, Jacobites. The worst are "the Trinitarians, who I cannot but represent as enemies to all human learning."[31] Christianity, Stubbe affirms, had degenerated into a variety of paganism, devoted to the "three gods of the Trinity" and to a goddess, the Virgin Mary. The saints, and the devotions given to them, "differed little from that of the pagans to their heroes and lesser gods."[32] The only ones who seem untainted by paganism are the Syriac or "Judaizing Christians."

Into this world dominated by divided, corrupt Christianity and shaken by wars between Byzantium and Persia comes Mahomet. An orphan at the age of six, he is raised by his uncle Abutaleb, who takes him along on his business travels to Jerusalem and Damascus. Abutaleb saw to it that his nephew received an education and became familiar with the tenets of the different sects of Judaism and Christianity. Stubbe places in Syria his encounter with the rich widow Chadija, whom he marries and for whom he conducts business. Stubbe remarks that there is nothing ignoble about commerce for the Arabs, any more than for nobles of latter-day Venice or Genoa.[33] Mahomet travels to Egypt, throughout North Africa, and even crosses over to Spain, where his stay is cut short by Saint Isidore. "This voyage gave him an opportunity of seeing the weakness, the secret animosities, factions of the Christians, not only in Spain but Africa."[34] Chadija's cousin Warekeh teaches Mahomet to write, and he becomes well versed in scripture: "being asked how he attained to so refined a language, rather than discover the means he had used, he told them that he had learned it from the Angel Gabriel who had taught him the dialect of Ishmael himself."[35]

Mahomet grew in the esteem of his countrymen, who took him for a prophet. He preached simplicity, wore rough wool garments and slept on a simple mattress on the floor. Mahomet "frames his poems" in pure Arabic, praising God in his unity, calling on people to adore Him. Stubbe rejects the hostile Christian legends that made him an epileptic; on the contrary, the prophet is widely reputed to be "able to gratify forty women in one night, whereas nothing is more inconsistent with, or pernicious in, that disease than immoderate venery."[36] He preaches against the idols and provokes the hostility of some of the Meccans, but his uncle Abutaleb protects him. Shortly after his uncle dies at age eighty, in 622, Mahomet immigrates to Medina.

In Medina, "he erects a prophetical monarchy."[37] There "he wrote at sundry times the greatest part of his Alcoran."[38] Stubbe's Mahomet is a sagacious and just ruler, and he won the allegiance of the Medinans, then of neighboring tribes:

> They admired his poetry, perpetually sang them and thought it a great honor to their tribe and city to have so eminent a person reside among them. They were witnesses of this valor and piety and saw in his deportment and the doctrine he spread to be such as they needed, not fear oppression from his cruelty, extortion from his avarice, nor tyranny from his government. Tyranny consists not in the unlimitedness of power, but in the extravagant use of it.[39]

Stubbe relates how Mahomet rallied the Medinans and their allies to force the submission of Mecca and the rest of the Arabian Peninsula. "His followers became more fixed and endeared to him, and they who had embraced his religion out of fear persisted in it out of affection and conscience."[40] Stubbe was a friend and admirer of Thomas Hobbes, with whom he corresponded frequently; in the 1650s, Stubbe was at work on a Latin translation of Hobbes's *Leviathan*.[41] His Mahomet fits well the model of the benevolent monarch portrayed in the *Leviathan*, using the precepts of a simple, natural religion to enforce morality and uphold authority, without handing over power to a caste of grasping priests. Hobbes proposed a civic, natural religion devoted to the honor of the one God, in which vain disputations about his nature would be prohibited, since "volumes of disputation about the nature of God . . . tend not to His honour, but to the honour of our own wits and learning; and are nothing else but inconsiderate and vain abuses of His sacred name."[42] Stubbe's Mahomet is a Hobbesian monarch who returns to a simple form of natural monotheism in accordance with the religion of the primitive Christians.

This Mahomet is unrecognizable to those familiar with standard European Christian polemical biographies, which Stubbe dismisses and ridicules. Jerome and others affirm that the "Saracens" pretend to be the descendants of Sarah; on the contrary, they proudly acknowledge their descent from Hagar and Ishmael.[43] Muslims laugh at Christians who relate the ridiculous stories of the monk Sergius, of Mahomet training a pigeon to eat out of his ear or tying the Alcoran to the horns of a bull.[44] Mahomet's tomb in Medina is not "suspended in the air by loadstones."[45] The Muslim paradise is full of sensual delights, but how else are we to describe ineffable celestial pleasures than through imagining them as more intense forms of pleasures of this world?[46]

"Vulgar opinion" affirms that Mahomet propagated his doctrine by the sword and vowed to extirpate Christianity. Nothing could be further from the truth: "Mahomet did levy war in Arabia, but it was under the pretense of restoring an old religion, not to introduce a new one."[47] He and his successors used force to combat idolatry and to spread their empire, but never to compel Christians or Jews to relinquish their religion. This Stubbe contrasts to the Jewish kings of the Old Testament and to the practice of many Christian kings. He cites Omar's pact with the Christians of Jerusalem and contrasts it with the brutality showed by Spaniards to the Indians of America. Muslim rulers in Spain showed tolerance to "Mozarabick Christians." Citing Scaliger, he asserts that "the vulgar Greeks live in better condition under the Turk at present than they did under their own emperors when there were perpetual murders practiced on their princes and tyranny on their people."[48]

Other Christian authors had portrayed Arabia as a haven for heretical Christians and unorthodox Jews; for Stubbe "Arabia was the common receptacle for the persecuted Jews and Christians of all sorts and sects to retire unto."[49] In particular, there were the "Judaizing Christians," whom Stubbe presents as practicing a simple ascetic monotheism similar to that of the Essenes and far superior to the superstitions of the Trinitarians. It is this religion that Mahomet sought to restore. Stubbe offers particular praise for the five fundamental articles of the Mahometan religion (the five pillars of Islam).

Pilgrimage and fasting help train and hone the body and spirit of Muslims, preparing them for the rigor and hardships of military expeditions. The "Zacat" or alms prevented the accumulation of excessive wealth and the overindulgence in luxuries. The obligation to pray five times daily is equally conducive to sobriety and discipline.

"It were an endless task to descant upon the particular motives upon which depends the excellency of his laws," concludes Stubbe. Mahomet prudently chose to reject all of Christian scripture rather than to pick and choose among a confused and contradictory accumulation of texts issued from different sects. The Alcoran is wise and sober in its precepts, elegant in its language, simple in its message. None of the arguments that Christians habitually make against it stand up to scrutiny; all could be equally made against "our Bible." On the contrary, it compares favorably with "the Talmud and our ecclesiastical history, or the popish legends or the fables recorded in our Fathers and believed by the primitive Christians."[50] Stubbe's work is not merely an academic exercise in the history of religion, of course; it is a polemical work aimed at the Anglican Church and the monarchy. Like Mahomet, the king should strip the priests of their power and ban superstitious doctrine, returning to the simple, rational monotheism of the early Christians. He should also allow for the practice of diverse cults, just as the "Mahometans" do. Charles II should become a new Mahomet.

Stubbe's work circulated in manuscript; it would have been impossible to find a publisher in Britain, and the open diffusion of his ideas would perhaps have hurt the radical cause more than it would have helped it. But, as Nabil Matar has shown, in the second half of the seventeenth century a number of English Christians looked to Islam and the Qur'ān for positive proof of religious truths; in particular, for arguments to be used against Jews or atheists. The Puritan *Nova Solyma* affirms "Mahomet bore witness as against the Jews that Christ was that great prophet whom Moses foretold."[51] Presbyterian Richard Baxter and Anglican Isaac Barrow similarly affirm that the Qur'ān offers testimony to the truth of Christianity; the anonymous author of *The Atheist Unmasked* (1685) calls on "Mahometans and Jews who worship the creator" to help him refute the blasphemies of the atheists.[52]

In 1683, a group of radical Whigs hatched a failed scheme to assassinate Charles II, the "Rye House Plot." In the same year, the

Habsburgs and their allies repelled the forces besieging Vienna, the Ottomans, and their Hungarian allies. Some royalists saw the two events as closely related, proof that the radical Hungarian "Mahometan Protestants" led by Imre Thököly (known in England as "Count Teckely") were in alliance with the radical Whig Protestants, in a plot against the English monarchy and the Anglican Church. As far-fetched as such conspiracy theories may seem, they provided grist to the royalist propaganda mills, leading to shrill calls for the repression of non-Anglican "conventicles."[53] These fears were complicated and in many ways amplified by the accession of Catholic King James II at his brother Charles's death in 1685 and new monarch's subsequent proclamations of religious liberty in the kingdom. Laurence Addison, who in 1678 had used Mahomet to attack Whigs who had spread rumors of a "popish plot" against Protestantism, in 1687 remarketed him; the Catholic King James was a new impostor along the lines of Mahomet and Cromwell.[54] It was in part fears that James would bring England back into the fold of the Catholic Church that led to the Glorious Revolution of 1688, in which James's daughter Mary became Queen and her husband William of Orange king. On May 24, 1689, the new monarchs promulgated the Toleration Act, granting religious freedom to dissident Protestants, but not to Catholics, antitrinitarians, atheists—or Muslims.

In the same year, John Locke argued that England should tolerate the presence of, and grant full rights of citizenship to, not only dissenting Protestants but also to Jews, Catholics, and "Mahometans." He noted that in Constantinople a Calvinist or Armenian would be free to practice his religion and imagined that "the Turks meanwhile silently stand by and laugh to see with what inhuman cruelty Christians thus rage against Christians."[55] While Locke, unlike Stubbe and other Deists and Unitarians, offers no theological assessment of Islam or Muhammad, he clearly sees Islamic religious tolerance as a positive model for Anglican England.

Mahomet, Prophet of Unitarianism or Impostor?

In the wake of the toleration act, English Unitarians wrote pamphlets defending their beliefs as consistent with primitive Christianity; they of course published these pamphlets anonymously. Like earlier Unitarians such as Miguel Servet, they took antitrinitarian arguments from the Qur'ān and saw Muhammad as a Unitarian reformer. *The Naked Gospel* (1691), probably by Arthur Bury, asks rhetorically "whether Mahomet or the Christian doctors have more corrupted the Gospel?"[56] His charge against Christian Trinitarian theologians makes clear what the answer is for him. In the same year, *A letter of resolution concerning the doctrines of the Trinity and the Incarnation*, probably by Stephen Nye, presents Mahomet as closer to the truth of the Gospel than Trinitarian Christianity, in a passage that shows familiarity with Stubbe. Mahomet, he affirms, did not try to create a new religion, "but to restore the Belief of the Unity of God, which at the time was extirpated among the Eastern Christians, by the Doctrines of the Trinity and Incarnation." Muslims affirm that they are "the true Disciples of the Messias or Christ," while "Christians are Apostates from the most essential Parts of the Doctrine of the Messias; such as the Unity of God." God is to be worshipped without use of images. Muslims and Jews "are perpetually and without hope of regaining them, alienated from us, that they suppose the Trinity to be the Doctrine of all Christians; and from thence conclude, that modern Christianity is no better nor other than a sort of Paganism and Heathenism."[57] Nye (if this is indeed Nye) offers a ringing indictment of the Anglican Church and of Trinitarian doctrine. He takes care to put this criticism in the mouth of Mahomet and the Mahometans, whose beliefs he found by reading "divers Historians." He goes on to lament that those who are still pagan reject Christianity because "of the corrupt Doctrines against which we are arguing." He presents the "calamitous Instance" of the Tartars. In 1245, he says, Pope Innocent IV sent emissaries to Batu Khan, who received them honorably and listened carefully to their presentation of "the chief points of the Christian Faith, the Trinity, the Incarnation, the Transubstantiation, etc." (19). Batu thanked the emissaries politely and sent them on their way. Shortly afterward, the "Mahometans" sent an embassy to present "the more plausible sect of Mahomet." Batu and his whole kingdom went over to Mahometism. "These," writes Nye, "are the Damages sustained by Christianity, by occasion of these Doctrines" (19). Those who oppose and reject the doctrines of the Trinitarians—Mahometans and Unitarians—have reason on their side. "Till our Opposers can extinguish Reason and common Sense in Men; while there are any left who are not wholly Priest-ridden," he concludes, Unitarians can be confident that they will prevail. The Trinitarian ideas have prevailed in the Catholic and Anglican Churches, despite their irrationality, because they maintain the interests of the priesthood.

Republican and Unitarian praise of Muhammad provoked rebuke, in the form of the reaffirmation of the traditional Christian polemical view of the Muslim prophet. In 1697, as we have seen, Humphrey Prideaux published his *The True Nature of The Imposture Fully Display'd in the Life of Mahomet.*[58] Prideaux had studied with Pococke in Oxford; indeed, he may have had as a fellow student Henry Stubbe.[59] While it is uncertain that he had read Stubbe's *Originall & Progress of Mahometanism*, in many ways Prideaux's work reads as a reponse and rebuttal of Stubbe's work as well as to the more recent pamphlets by Unitarians. Like Stubbe, Prideaux casts a critical eye on much of the hostile legends concerning the prophet. He dismisses medieval tales of bogus miracles: stories of a bull bearing the Qur'ān on its horns, or a pigeon that Mahomet trained to eat grains from his ear in order to pretend it was the Holy Spirit. These stories are "idle fables not to be credited" (38). He similarly dispels what he identifies as other common misconceptions about the prophet: that Muslims expected him to resurrect ("totally an error," 102). When describing his burial beneath Aisha's bed, he remarks, "there he lyeth to this day, without iron coffin or loadstones to hang him in the Air, as the Stories which commonly go about him among Christians fabulously relate" (103). Hostile stories that seem less improbable to him, however, such as Mahomet's epilepsy, he includes without criticism. Prideaux claims to present, in lieu of fables, the "true nature" of Mahomet's "imposture."

> The whole of this imposture was a thing of extraordinary craft, carried on with all the cunning and caution imaginable. The framing of the *Alcoran* (wherein lay the main of the cheat) was all contrived at home in as secret a manner as possible, and nothing hazarded abroad, but the success of preaching it to the people. And in doing of this, no art or cunning was wanting to make it as effectual to the End design'd as possible: and therefore whatever stories are told of this matter, that are inconsistent with such a management, we may assure ourselves are

nothing else but fables foolishly invented by some zealous Christians to
blast the imposture, which needed no such means for its confutation.
(38–39)

He uses a number of medieval polemical texts, citing by name Theophanes, Riccoldo da Montecroce, and others; he has consulted Robert of Ketton's twelfth-century Latin translation of the Qur'ān and
the other works published by Bibliander. He also relies on more
recent works, including Pococke's 1650 edition and translation of
Bar Hebraeus's *Specimen historiae arabum* (which, as we have seen,
was also one of Stubbe's principal sources). Prideaux presents Mahomet as dominated by the twin passions of lust and ambition,
which cause him to feign a religious vocation. Unable to produce
miracles, the impostor gains adherents through threats of violence
and promises of a carnal paradise, well-adapted to the hot temperaments of the inhabitants of the "torrid zone." Prideaux seeks to
counter claims of Deists and Unitarians that Islam is closer to true
monotheistic Christianity than is Anglicanism. Mahomet is an impostor, not Christ. Neither Stubbe nor the Unitarian authors of the
1690s had presented Jesus as an impostor; on the contrary, they saw
Muhammad as a reformer who sought to restore Jesus's true monotheism. But in some freethinking circles, the charge that Jesus was
simply one of a line of impostors was indeed made, as we will see
with the publication in the early eighteenth century of the *Treatise
of the Three Impostors* (chapter six). Prideaux's tract became something of a best seller, going through numerous editions. In 1698, the
year after its publication in English, Dutch and French translations
were published in the Netherlands.[60]

Stubbe, followed by the Unitarians, saw in early Islam a purified
form of Christianity stripped of its pagan superstitions and its corrupt class of priests. In the early eighteenth century, the iconoclastic
Irish freethinker John Toland came across a manuscript in Italian
of the Gospel of Barnabas that, he affirmed, offered proof of this
close correspondence between pure primitive Christianity and early
Islam. Toland writes about his discovery in two works: *Christianisme judaique et mahometan*, which he sent in manuscript to Prince
Eugène de Savoie, and a longer, more cautiously argued tract in
English, *Nazarenus, or Jewish, Gentile, and Mahometan Christian-*

ity, published in 1718.[61] We have seen that the Gospel of Barnabas was most likely produced among sixteenth-century Moriscos in order to reconcile the practice of Islam with the supposed doctrines of early Christians. The text provides Toland with an opportunity to provide textual authority to many of the anticlerical arguments of radical republicans.

Toland recounts his discovery of the manuscript in Amsterdam and says he quickly realized that this was the Gospel that Mahomet had acknowledged. He affirms, moreover, that this is the Gospel observed by the earliest Christians, and that it provides "the Original plan of Christianity." The first Christians, whom he refers to as both Ebionites and Nazarenes, were Jews, who continued to observe Jewish law; they welcomed in their midst Gentiles who were only obliged to follow the law of Noah, not that of Moses. They followed the teachings of Jesus, the son of Joseph and Mary, on whom they conferred the title "Son of God" in a merely metaphorical sense, to indicate that he was a man of unusual and exemplary piety. Yet many of the Gentile converts to Christianity, he laments, "gave their bare names to Christ, but reserv'd their Idolatrous hearts for their native superstitions. These did almost wholly subvert True Christianity."[62] In their hatred of the Jews, the Gentile converts changed the date of Easter and sought to avoid frequenting Jews. In many respects, Toland's diatribe echoes that of Stubbe: both accuse early churchmen of corrupting primitive Christianity with pagan rites. Yet Toland couches this criticism in a much more cautious and learned garb, insisting that he is merely presenting the results of his philological research. And he takes a key step further than Stubbe; for Toland, the principal culprit is Paul. Toland offers a close critical reading of selected passages from Acts and the Pauline Epistles, exploiting in particular the conflicts and disagreements of Paul with Peter and Barnabas. Paul, he says, proffers a new Gospel to the uncircumcised, with a message very different from that of Jesus, creating a clear break from the primitive church founded by the Apostles, that of the Nazarenes. Without explicitly saying so, Toland has proffered a very Muslim vision of Paul as the chief corrupter of the message revealed by God to Jesus.

Unlike Stubbe, Toland does not offer a biography of "Mahomet," since that is not his chief concern. He mentions the prophet briefly, saying how "tis but very lately that we begun to be undeceiv'd about Mahomet's pigeon, his pretending to work miracles, and his tomb's being suspended in the air: pious frauds and fables, to which the Musulmans are utter strangers."[63] He credits this debunking of "vulgar errors" to recent scholars such as Adrian Reland and Humphrey Prideaux; in the latter case in particular, with deliberate irony, since Toland's prophet is a far cry from the impostor of Prideaux. His Mahomet has two functions: a witness to the authenticity of the Gospel of Barnabas as the expression of true unadulterated Christianity, and a civil and religious reformer who should serve as a model for contemporary European monarchs. Hence, he tells his reader, "you'll discover some of the fundamental doctrines of Mahometanism to have their rise, not from Sergius the Nestorian monk (a person who has hitherto serv'd for a world of fine purposes) but from the earliest monuments of the Christian religion."[64] Mahomet, he suggests, was a better Christian than Paul. "The Mahometans may not improperly be reckon'd and call'd a sort or sect of Christians"; hence, "they might with as much reason and safety be tolerated at London and Amsterdam, as the Christians of every kind are so at Constantinople and thro-out all Turkey."[65] He later asserts "the Mahometans may be as well allow'd Moschs in these parts of Europe, if they desire it, as any other Sectaries."[66]

Yet neither Muhammad nor the Muslims are Toland's main interest. By opposing Barnabas and Paul, Toland throws into question the validity of the whole scriptural basis of the Church and its doctrine. As he tells it, the Ebionites or Nazarenes were the true Christians and the Gospel of Barnabas corresponds to Jesus's teaching as well as or better than any of the four canonical Gospels. How serious is Toland? Does he really believe that the Gospel of Barnabas is authentic? Justin Champion has stressed how important it is to understand the ludic quality of *Nazarenus* (as of most of Toland's writing).[67] Indeed, the summary I have given is perhaps misleading, since it is far too clear, putting in the affirmative ideas that are suggested and couched in a language of scientific inquiry, of a historian's scrupulous respect for his sources, of a pious Christian's zeal for truth and reform. It is this allusive and elusive character of Toland's work that has led some historians to class him as a mocking atheist, others as a devout Deist. Champion sagely renounces any attempt to identify the "real" Toland behind the contrasting facets of the scholarly persona that he presents in his writing. At any rate, Toland defended himself from his numerous detractors by affirming that he never attacked religion but only "the superstitious practices and worldly usurpations with which it has been often deform'd."[68]

Toland skillfully cultivates his authorial persona in *Nazarenus*, but it is clear that beyond the scholarly issues at stake, he is presenting a polemical argument against the caste of priests who have taken control of the Church. Why did the Jews of Jesus's time reject him? "They were chiefly irritated against him by the influence of a rampant Priesthood, who, for their own profit and power, had openly and shamelessly perverted the Law of Moses."[69] The Jewish priests had corrupted Judaism, and Jesus came to restore it to its pure and simple message. Yet alas Jesus's message was also perverted by the Gentiles, "who, not enduring the reasonableness and simplicity of the same [true Christianity], brought into it by degrees the peculiar expressions and mysteries of Heathenism, the abstruse doctrines of their Philosophers, an insupportable pontifical Hierarchy, and even the altars, offrings, the sacred rites and ceremonies of their Priests."[70]

At the end of the first letter of the *Nazarenus*, Toland affirms, "what the Mahometans believe concerning Christ and his doctrine, were neither the inventions of Mahomet, nor yet of those Monks who are said to have assisted him in the framing of his Alcoran: but that they are as old as the time of the Apostles having been sentiments of whole sects or Churches."[71] Whether or not Toland believes in the authenticity of the Gospel of Barnabas, he uses the Morisco text to undermine fundamental Christian doctrine (notably the Trinity) and to deny the legitimacy of ecclesiastical (Catholic and Anglican) claims to authority. For the anonymous author of the Gospel, writing in vain to rescue the honor and dignity of the persecuted Moriscos, this would have been sweet revenge indeed.[72]

Between the mid-seventeenth and early eighteenth centuries, England was rocked by political and social upheaval. In this context, English intellectuals, Whig and Tory, Anglican, Presbyterian, Unitarian, and Deist, engaged in debates about the proper place of religion in society and the proper relations between Crown and Church. The republican program was to overthrow "Priestcraft": to take power out of the hands of the corrupt clerical elite, to expunge "papist" rites from the mass, to return to a simpler, purified form of Christianity. As Justin Champion has stressed, "For the Republican, the Anglican priest was an instrument of both irreligion and social tyranny. To overthrow priestcraft was to purify both religion and society."[73] Much of this debate was conducted in scholarly exchange over the history of the Church. On the rare occasions when Muhammad was mentioned (or more generally the "Mahometans" or the "Turks"), it was in negative terms; the Anglicans (or Unitarians, or Papists) might be worse than Mahomet, but the latter served principally as a rhetorical foil.

That all changed with Henry Stubbe. It became possible to argue (though in many cases still dangerous to openly affirm) that Mahomet was a better Christian than most, that he properly understood the relations between state power and clergy, that he had happily stripped power away from a corrupt and grasping clerical elite, and that he put into place a policy of toleration that was still practiced by the Ottomans and that should be imitated by enlightened European monarchs. Stubbe transformed the prophet of Islam into a republican revolutionary, and subsequent writers (Bury, Nye, Toland, and others) would confirm and elaborate upon this transformation. In the eighteenth century, several French intellectuals will use Muhammad in the same way to attack the preeminent place of the Catholic Church in France.

CHAPTER SIX

The Enlightenment Prophet

REFORMER AND LEGISLATOR

OVER THE COURSE of the seventeenth century, as we saw in chapter five, various Whig intellectuals came to see the prophet Mahomet as a model reformer, one who smashed "priestcraft," the grasping greed of a clerical class that built its power on the ignorance and superstition of the masses. Mahomet, far from establishing a new religion, offered a purified monotheism stripped of abstruse doctrines and idolatrous rites. He abolished the privileges of the clergy and reestablished a direct relationship between God and his believers. In all these things, reason was his supreme guide. This vision, most fully expressed by Stubbe and Toland, met fierce opposition from those who defended the privileges of Anglican Church, who reaffirmed the traditional view of Mahomet as a dangerous impostor and did not hesitate to paint their opponents as new Mahomets.

In the eighteenth century, Mahomet plays a similar role in France; opponents of the wealth and power of the Catholic Church present Mahomet's purified, anticlerical monotheism as an antidote to French ills. To be sure, in some freethinking circles Mahomet the impostor lives on. *Le traité des trois imposteurs* makes Moses and Jesus impostors along with him; Voltaire, in his *Le fanatisme, ou*

Mahomet le prophete: Tragédie, uses the stereotyped figure of the impostor to implicitly criticize fanaticism closer to home. But other eighteenth-century writers, working in both French and English, see the prophet as a salutary model. Georges Sale in the preface to his English translation of the Qur'ān, Comte Henri de Boulainvilliers in his biography of the prophet, or Voltaire in his *Essai sur l'histoire générale et sur les moeurs et l'esprit des nations.* Indeed, Mahomet came to represent one of the "great men" of world history. Edward Gibbon paints a vivid and laudatory portrait in his *History of the Decline and Fall of the Roman Empire.*

The Three Impostors

Le traité des trois imposteurs (*The Treatise of the Three Impostors*), first published in 1719, was an antireligious diatribe popular in freethinking circles in the eighteenth century.[1] Inspired by the works of Hobbes and Spinoza (and at times attributed to the latter), it presents revelation as a pious fiction invented and manipulated by priests and kings to reduce their subjects to cowed obedience. Protestant polemicists had often accused the "Papists" of having deformed the pure message of Christ; Unitarians had laid the blame on Constantine and the Council of Nicea, or even on Paul. *The Treatise of the Three Impostors* goes further: the blame lies with Moses, Jesus, and Mahomet.

The anonymous author lambasts the priests and rulers of ancient Greece and Rome, who took advantage of the credulity of their people to give their power a sacred aura and to create a cadre of rich and compliant priests. But the greatest scoundrels, for this author, are the founders of the three monotheistic religions. Moses, a magician trained in Egypt, fell out of favor with the pharaoh and fled Egypt after committing several murders. He then plotted revenge against the pharaoh, and through a series of stunts and magical tricks convinced the ignorant Hebrews to rise up against their Egyptian masters and to follow him through the desert. He was an "absolute despot . . . a trickster and impostor" (22). His final trick cost him his life; he threw himself off a high precipice in the desert, so that his body might never be found and that the people would think he had been spirited off to heaven. Jesus Christ was no better; he "got himself followed by some imbeciles whom he persuaded that the Holy Spirit was his Father; & his Mother a Virgin" (23). The author expresses admiration for his adroitness in hoodwinking the people through bogus miracles and for his cleverness in arguing with the Pharisees. "One can judge from all that we have said that Christianity, like all other religions is no more than a crudely woven imposture, whose success & progress would astonish even its inventors if they came back to the world" (31).

The author paints Mahomet in similar colors. This "new legislator," like his predecessor Moses, took the title of Prophet and foisted bogus miracles on an ignorant people. He was opposed by "Corais, a powerful Arab, jealous that a nobody had the audacity to deceive the people." Mahomet sweet-talks Corais into becoming his collaborator, and then finds a way to dispatch with him:

Mahomet persuaded him [Corais] to hide himself in the ditch of the Oracles. This was a well from which he spoke in order to make the People believe that the voice of God declared itself for Mahomet who was in the midst of his proselytes. Tricked by the caresses of this traitor, his associate went into the ditch to counterfeit the Oracle in his usual fashion; Mahomet passing by at the head of an infatuated multitude, a voice was heard which said: "I who am your God declare that I have I established Mahomet to be the Prophet of all the nations; it will be from him that you will learn my true law which the Jews & the Christians have adulterated." This man had been playing this role for a long time, but in the end he was rewarded with the greatest & the blackest ingratitude. In fact Mahomet hearing the voice which proclaimed him a divine man turning towards the people, commanded it in the name of this God who recognized him for his Prophet, to fill with stones this ditch, from which had issued so authentic a testimony in his favor, in memory of the stone which Jacob raised up to mark the place where God had appeared to him. Thus perished the wretch who had contributed to the elevation of Mahomet; it was on this pile of stones that the last of the most famous impostors established his law: this foundation is so solid & fixed in such a manner that after more than a thousand years of reigning one does not yet see any sign that it is on the point of being shaken.

Thus Mahomet raised himself up & was happier than Jesus, insofar as he saw before his death the progress of his law, which the son of

Mary was not able to do because of his poverty. He was even happier than Moses, who by an excess of ambition cast himself down a precipice to finish his days; Mahomet died in peace & with all his wishes gratified, he had moreover some certainty that his Doctrine would subsist after his death, having accommodated it to the genius of his sectaries, born & raised in ignorance; which an abler man might perhaps not have been able to do.[2]

Here the author shows little familiarity with serious scholarship on Islam or with the fables of doves and bulls. Instead, he invents a new scurrilous legend of his own, around the opposition between Mahomet and "Corais" (perhaps from Quraysh), presented both as a disciple and potential rival, whom Mahomet cynically eliminates. The anonymous author sketches a portrait of an impostor, similar to that drawn by other European authors from the twelfth century on. Indeed, what is new is that he has applied to the lives of Moses and Jesus the same techniques of denigration and misrepresentation of religious traditions that Christian European authors had used against Muhammad for centuries. The author's purpose is to denounce Christianity and above all what the English radicals of the seventeenth century had called "priestcraft": the crass manipulation of religion by a cadre of cynical, greedy clerics, who took advantage of the ignorance and gullibility of the people to obtain power and wealth. For Stubbe, Toland, and others, Mahomet was usefully seen as an anticlerical reformer who wisely abolished clerical privilege; hence, they argued against the traditional Christian polemical image of Mahomet the impostor. The author of *The Treatise of the Three Impostors* makes a much more radical attack on religion by dragging Moses and Jesus down to the status of impostors; the implication is that Judaism and Christianity do not represent true faith corrupted but are from the very beginning based on imposture.

An Anticlerical Hero

Henri, Count of Boulainvilliers (1658–1722), wrote a *Vie de Mahomed* that was published posthumously in 1730.[3] Boulainvilliers, a Normand nobleman, wrote works of history and politics defending the traditional rights of the aristocracy against the increasing absolutism of Louis XIV and exalting enlightened feudalism as the best form of government, deriving the rights of the aristocracy from the conquest of their supposed Frankish ancestors over the Gallo-romans. Yet Boulainvilliers cannot be reduced to a mere aristocratic reactionary; he showed a keen interest in astrology and in deism, frequenting some of the same intellectual circles as Toland. Like Toland, he came to see in Mahomed a model of religion free from "priestcraft"—in his case, the stultifying dominance of the French Catholic Church.

In his *Vie de Mahomed*, Boulainvilliers presents the prophet as a divinely inspired messenger whom God employed to confound the bickering oriental Christians, to liberate the Orient from the despotic rule of the Romans and Persians, and to spread the knowledge of the unity of God from India to Spain. "Since if the fortune of this personage was not the effect of natural means, the success could be only from God; whom the impious will accuse of having led half the world into an error, and destroy'd violently his own revelation."[4] Arguing against Prideaux, he scoffs at the hostile Christian legends around the prophet's supposed heretical Christian sidekick, denies that Muslim doctrine is irrational or that Muhammad is a coarse impostor. On the contrary, the prophet rejected all that was irrational and undesirable in Christianity as he found it: the cult of relics and icons, the grasping power of superstitious and avaricious monks and priests. Mahomed "seems to have adopted and embraced all that is most marvelous in Christianity itself. So that what he retrenched, relates obviously to those abuses alone, which it was impossible he should not condemn" (222).

What was Mahomed's view of Christianity? His profound devotion to the unity of God led him to reject the doctrines of the Trinity and the Incarnation. But what bothered him most was the corruption of the clergy.

Mahomed regarded the bishops, priests and secular clergy, chiefly as a political combination of men, united for the purpose of making religion subservient to their passions, their concupiscence, avarice, pride and dominion, and who had the secret of persuading the people that an implicit obedience to them was inseparable from what was due to God. Moreover he looked upon them as the real authors of an infinite number of disputes, which then divided the professors of Christianity; as the inventors of the superstitions of those times; in short, as false teachers who had labour'd to plunge all men into errour, according to their several conditions, ranks, and degrees of capacity.[5]

This is an attack against the French Catholic Church of the eighteenth century; Boulainvilliers puts his own criticisms into the mouth of the prophet. The clergy, lusting after power, riches, and glory, concoct schisms and superstitions the better to affirm and justify their power over a people they maintain in ignorance. His Mahomed is a reformer who abolished the power of the clergy in order to return to a direct relationship between God and His faithful. It is no surprise that this thinly veiled diatribe against the power and privilege of the Catholic Church was published in Amsterdam and London, rather than in Paris.

The 1731 Amsterdam edition has woodcut illustrations of various scenes from Mahomed's life: his prophesizing, the hijra, the building of the mosque in Medina, his military victories, his marriages, his death and burial. These illustrations give the impression once again of a "Turkish" prophet, as Mahomed and his followers are in Ottoman dress. The illustrator emphasizes the martial nature of Mahomed's leadership, as each image bristles with spears and swords wielded by the prophet and his followers. The image here (fig. 16) shows Mahomed victorious at Mecca, kneeling and holding a crescent-topped scepter in the midst of his army, as one of his men places a crown on top of his turban. In the foreground, his men destroy idols. Boulainvillier's Mahomet is above all an enemy of idolatry, a champion of uncorrupted monotheism.

Sale's Qur'ān

One of the subscribers to Boulainvilliers's *Vie de Mahomed* was Arabist George Sale, who in 1734 produced a new English translation of the Qur'ān that represented a landmark in the European study of Islam. It is the first translation of the Qur'ān in a European language not framed as a means to refute Islam or to "expose" the errors of the Turks. Sale prefaces his translation with a 187-page "preliminary discourse": a scholarly presentation of the life of Muhammad,

pag. 11.

FIGURE 16. Mahomet crowned king has idols destroyed everywhere.
Boulainvilliers, *Vie de Mahomed*, 2nd ed. (Amsterdam, 1731), p. 430. D.R.

the composition of the Qur'ān, an analysis of Qur'ānic doctrine, and a history of the emergence and expansion of Islam. Sale's work is remarkable in his careful use and citation of recent scholarship and polemics.[6] Indeed, Sale exhibits a considerable erudition and peppers his pages with footnotes citing the work of recent scholars: Pococke, Jean Gagnier, Toland, Reland, Ludovico Marracci, and others.

Sale is an enigmatic character about whom little is known. He apparently never left England, he never held an academic position, and it is unclear how he learned Arabic. He helped produce an Arabic translation of the New Testament for the Society for Promoting Christian Knowledge, an Anglican missionary organization. He also participated in the production of the immensely popular *Universal History, from the Earliest Account of Time*, though the volumes dealing with Arabic history were published after his death and are very different in spirit from his writings.[7] As Alexander Bevilacqua has shown, he is particularly indebted to the work of Ludovico Marracci, a Catholic cleric who learned Arabic from Maronites in Rome and who sought to study Arabic and Islam in an aim to convert Muslims to Christianity. Chair of Arabic at the University of Rome, La Sapienza (1656–99), Marracci translated the Bible into Arabic and exposed the Granadan lead tablets as a forgery. He then embarked on an annotated Latin translation of the Qur'ān, which he published in 1698.[8] The massive 850-page volume is in many ways a monument of European Qur'ān scholarship: Marracci provides the Arabic text for each sura, followed by his Latin translation, accompanied by notes and by extensive "refutations"; he bases his work on a large range of important Muslim commentaries on the Qur'ān, having access to the rich Arabic collection of the Vatican library. It is in his refutations that Marracci's missionary and polemical goal comes to the forefront. He carefully avoids basing his anti-Muslim arguments on the work of earlier Christian polemicists, wishing, as he says, "to fight the Alcoran with the Alcoran and to slaughter Mahomet with his own sword insofar as I am able."[9] Despite his care in using only Muslim sources, his perspective remains resolutely Catholic, and his arguments those likely to convince Catholics of the shocking or irrational nature of what he finds in the Qur'ān. Sale's perspective is very different, and though he uses Marracci extensively in his own translation, and accesses through Marracci many of the Muslim sources he consulted (Sale had no Vatican library at his disposal), in his judgments he sides most often with two recent scholars who had a much more positive view of Islam, Adrian Reland and Jean Gagnier.

Reland, son of a Protestant minister and professor of Oriental languages at the University of Utrecht, bristled at what he saw as Marracci's abuse of his Arabic erudition to present a hostile and biased vision of Islam. Reland set out to give a more balanced (if far briefer) account in his *De religione Mohammedica libri duo* (*Two books on the Mohammedan religion*, 1705).[10] The first of these two books is an Arabic treatise, a "short system of the Mohammedan theology," which he prints in Arabic with a facing Latin translation. It presents, from a Muslim point of view, the five pillars of Islam and basic Muslim doctrines concerning the unity of God, angels, scripture, prophets, and the last days. The second book is Reland's own exposition and refutation of thirty-nine erroneous beliefs and false accusations often made against Islam. Reland's book, which was published in the following decades in German, Dutch, French, and English translations, was a mine of information for Enlightenment readers with an interest in Islam. In the frontispiece of Reland's treatise, Muhammad appears in the dress and trappings of an Ottoman sultan; in the foreground, again, is an image of destruction of idols, whose heads roll at the bottom left of the image.

In his description of the rituals of the Mecca pilgrimage, and in particular the circular movement around the Ka'ba, Reland compares it to the rites that Numa Pompilius imposed on the Romans, citing Plutarch's life of Numa. Here and elsewhere, Reland uses comparisons with classical antiquity to valorize Islam both by associating it with the revered cultures of Greco-Roman antiquity and by removing it from a simple comparison with Christianity. Reland was not the first to compare Mahomet and Numa. Several Italian humanists of the sixteenth century had compared Numa's claims to have received laws from Egeria to Mahomet's assertion that the Qur'ān came from God. Jesuit Antonio Possevino, in 1593, explains that Numa subdued the Roman people through his fictive relations with Egeria, and his successor Tullus Hostilius then imposed this law through the force of arms; in the same way, Mahomet imposed his laws on the Arabs by referring to the Archangel Gabriel.[11] Sale, as we will see, uses this comparison central to vindicate Muhammad's role as lawgiver.

Jean Gagnier (ca. 1670–1740), French convert to Anglicanism, became professor of Arabic in Cambridge. Like Reland, Gagnier looks askance at Marracci's Catholic anti-Muslim polemics. He too seeks to offer as an antidote a Muslim Arabic account of the prophet's life, in this case an Arabic edition and Latin translation of passages of Abu al-Fida's *Concise Chronicle*, which makes an important Arabic source on the prophet available to European readers.[12] The translated passages focus in particular on Muhammad's night journey. Gagnier subsequently wrote a popular biography of the prophet in French, *La vie de Mahomet* (1732), which purports to present the "impostor" Mahomet not as he really was, but as orthodox Muslims believed him to be. He relies heavily on his own edition and translation of Abu al-Fida and hence emphasizes the fantastic: miracle stories and the night voyage.[13] If his vision of the prophet is more nuanced and less polemical than Marracci or Prideaux, Gagnier's Mahomet is still an impostor.

In his dedicatory letter to John Carteret, Sale presents Mohammed as a great lawgiver, linking him to prestigious lawgiver-kings of classical antiquity: "as Mohammed gave his Arabs the best religion he could, as well as the best laws, preferable, at least, to those of the ancient pagan lawgivers, I confess I cannot see why he deserves not equal respect, though not with Moses or Jesus Christ, whose laws came really from heaven, yet with Minos or Numa."[14]

Sale opens his "Preliminary discourse" with a description of Arabia at the time of Muhammad's birth. His pre-Muslim Arabs are a freedom-loving nation that had managed to preserve its liberty by repelling foreign invaders. Their love of eloquence raised poetry to a high art among them. Their traditional religion was essentially monotheistic, to which a number of idolatrous practices and minor deities had accrued. In all ways, they compare favorably to the decadent Roman and Persian empires:

> As these empires were weak and declining, so Arabia, at Mohammed's setting up, was strong and flourishing; having been peopled at the expense of the Grecian empire, whence the violent proceedings of the

domineering sects forced many to seek refuge in a free country, as Arabia then was, where they who could not enjoy tranquillity and their conscience at home, found a secure retreat. The Arabians were not only a populous nation, but unacquainted with the luxury and delicacies of the Greeks and Persians, and inured to hardships of all sorts; living in a most parsimonious manner, seldom eating any flesh, drinking no wine, and sitting on the ground. Their political government was also such as favoured the designs of Mohammed ; for the division and independency of their tribes were so necessary to the first propagation of his religion, and the foundation of his power, that it would have been scarce possible for him to have effected either, had the Arabs been united in one society. But when they had embraced his religion, the consequent union of their tribes was no less necessary and conducive to their future conquests and grandeur.[15]

Here he is very much in continuity with Stubbe, Toland, and Boulainvilliers; the political degeneracy of the two world empires combined with the religious corruption of Christianity provide the opportunity for Mohammed and his freedom-loving Arabs. In Sale's lengthy narration of the life of "Mohammed," he frequently cites Abulfeda (with references to Gagnier's Latin translation), Prideaux, and Boulainvilliers, offering numerous correctives and criticisms of Prideaux and Boulainvilliers. He in particular rejects Prideaux's assertion that Mohammed made the Arabs "exchange their idolatry for another religion altogether as bad." On the contrary, "his original design of bringing the pagan Arabs to the knowledge of the true God, was certainly noble, and highly to be commended."[16] He similarly rejects or attenuates other standard tropes in Christian polemics: Mohammed's authorization of polygamy was nothing scandalous, but in accordance with previous and contemporary Jewish and Arab practice. As to the idea that Islam was propagated by the sword, he retorts, citing Machiavelli, that "all the armed prophets have succeeded, and the unarmed ones have failed. Moses, Cyrus, Theseus, and Romulus would not have been able to establish the observance of their institutions for any length of time, had they not been armed."[17] In this passage full of ambiguity, he cites Moses and Mohammed alongside Theseus and Romulus as statesmen and generals who imposed their new legal and political order by the sword.

He remarks dryly that it is generally accepted principal that one may use force to impose a true religion but not a false one. He reiterates the standard argument that the imposition of Mohammed's new law by force of arms is proof of its wholly human origin and contrasts with the "divine original of Christianity, that it prevailed against all the force and powers of the world by the mere dint of its own truth, after having stood the assaults of all manner of persecutions, as well as other oppositions, for three hundred years together, and at length made the Roman emperors themselves submit thereto." Yet he then goes on to say that subsequently "this proof seems to fail, Christianity being then established and paganism abolished by public authority, which has had great influence in the propagation of the one and destruction of the other ever since."

While both Mohammed and the Qur'ān provoke Sale's admiration, he sees in this story the hand of man, not God: "That Mohammed was really the author and chief contriver of the Koran, is beyond dispute," despite the affirmations of his pious followers (64). He nonetheless relates, without reserve or polemic, the standard Muslim account of the revelation of the Qur'ān and its compilation during the reign of ʿUthmān. He insists on its beauty and elegance. He relates (from Qur'ān 2) the story of the Meccan poet Labid, who had one of his finest poems displayed in the Kaʿba; when Muhammad put up one of the Qur'ān's suras next to it, Labid, "struck with admiration, immediately professed the religion taught thereby" (61).

Sale describes in detail the Qur'ānic teachings concerning the end of the world, the destiny of the damned in hell and the blessed in paradise, in passages for the most part free both of the standard invective of the polemicists and of the partisan manipulations of Unitarians and Deists. He presents the Qur'ānic basis of Muslim practice (prayer, ablutions, circumcision, alms, and so on) and prohibitions (wine, pork, etc.). He gives a long, detailed description of the rites of the hajj, noting the geography of Mecca, the different holy sites there, the rituals to be performed at each (114–22). "The pilgrimage to Mecca," he says, "and the ceremonies prescribed to those who perform it, are, perhaps, liable to greater exception than any other of Mohammed's institutions; not only as silly and ridiculous in themselves, but as relics of idolatrous superstition" (121). Yet, he says, one must excuse Mohammed's "yielding some points of less moment, to gain the principal." He was able to abolish idolatry by allowing the Arabs to continue to venerate the Ka'ba and to perpetuate many of their traditional rituals. "And herein he followed the example of the most famous legislators, who instituted not such laws as were absolutely the best in themselves, but the best their people were capable of receiving" (122). Like Boulainvilliers, Sale presents Mohammed as a sage legislator who forges laws appropriate to his people.

The "injunction of warring against infidels," he says "was well calculated for his purpose, and stood him and his successors in great stead: for what dangers and difficulties may not be despised and overcome by the courage and constancy which these sentiments necessarily inspire?" (142). These Qur'ānic passages had, as we have seen, provided grist for the mills of countless Christian polemicists. Sale responds, with irony:

> The Jews, indeed, had a divine commission, extensive and explicit enough, to attack, subdue, and destroy the enemies of their religion: and Mohammed pretended to have received one in favour of himself and his Moslems, in terms equally plain and full; and therefore it is no wonder that they should act consistently with their avowed principles: but that Christians should teach and practise a doctrine so opposite to the temper and whole tenor of the gospel, seems very strange ; and yet the latter have carried matters farther, and shown a more violent spirit of intolerance than either of the former. (143)

For Sale, as for many of the eighteenth-century authors he cited (Boulainvilliers, Gagnier, Reland), Mohammed was above all a reformer and a destroyer of idols—the pagan idols of Mecca, but also the new idols erected by false Christians. A hero who smashed priestcraft: "They take their priests and their monks for their lords, besides God, and Christ the son of Mary; although they are commanded to worship one God only: there is no God but he; far be that from him, which they associate with him! They seek to extinguish the light of God with their mouths; but God willeth no other than to perfect his light, although the infidels be adverse thereto."[18] Sale's translation had considerable impact on how Western intellectuals perceived Muhammad and Islam. Thomas Jefferson bought a copy from a Williamsburg, Virginia, bookseller in 1765; Goethe had read a German translation of Sale's version by 1771.[19] One of the readers most marked by his reading of Sale was a certain François-Marie Arouet, better known as Voltaire.

Voltaire's Mahomet

It is well known that in 1741 Voltaire cast Mahomet at the archetype of fanaticism in his drama *Le fanatisme, ou Mahomet le prophete: Tragédie*. What is much less known is that the *philosophe* subsequently revised his view of the Muslim prophet, in part due to his reading of Sale's Qur'ān, to the point where toward the end of his life Voltaire came to see Muhammad as a sort of role model, a great man who through texts and persuasion was able to reshape history and reform religion.[20] In the first case, he casts Mahomet as a crass impostor, incarnation of fanaticism, the better to attack the fanaticism of the Catholic Church; in the latter case, he finds Mahomet more useful as a figure of renewal, a foil against fanaticism.

In 1741, he makes a cynical fraud the centerpiece of his *Le fanatisme, ou Mahomet le prophete*. The drama takes place at Mecca, still in the hands of Mahomet's opponents, the "Senate" whose "shérif," Zopire, denounces Mahomet as an impostor and tyrant lording over Medina: "a lowly camel driver, insolent imposter to his first wife."[21] Mahomet himself later brags: "The sword and Qur'ān in my blood-stained hands bring silence down on everyone else."[22] Yet Mahomet confesses his one weakness to Omar:

> I've banished this nefarious drink that causes such relentless weakness; I won't have it near me. Together with you amidst the desolate rocks and burning sands, I weather the all-changing winds. My only consolation and reward is love, my worshipped idol, and the purpose of my work: Mahomet's god. This desire is matched by furious ambition.[23]

A lustful, ambitious impostor with a penchant for violence—this Mahomet seems much like Prideaux's. Yet Voltaire's drama is based on a plot of his own invention that has nothing to do with earlier polemics against the prophet. Mahomet sends Omar in embassy to Zopire, asking him to surrender Mecca; the false prophet later arrives to pursue the negotiation. Zopire refuses, and we learn that the "Senate" has condemned Mahomet to death. Mahomet and Omar decide there is only one way out: to have Zopire assassinated. But the prophet cannot have Zopire's blood on his hands; they order their young charge Seïde to kill him. This also provides Mahomet with a chance to get Seïde out of his way, since the youth is in love with beautiful Palmire, whom Mahomet lusts after. Seïde stabs Zopire, who reveals that he is the father of both Seïde and Palmire (which Mahomet knew all along). Mahomet has Seïde poisoned; Seïde denounces him as a fraud and impostor and leads a revolt against him. Yet at the key moment of confrontation, Seïde falls dead from the poison, and Mahomet announces that this is the fate of those who oppose God's will. The rebellious Meccans, cowed, accept Mahomet as God's prophet; Palmire, disconsolate, throws herself on Seïde's dagger. None of the fabrications of the medieval polemicists were as groundless as this pure invention; none of their stories were more zealous in denigrating Mahomet as a cynical, power-hungry leader driven, by lust and raw ambition, to feign prophecy.

When Mahomet arrived in Mecca to negotiate with Zopire, he presented his program:

> Find out more about who I am. We're alone, so listen: I'm ambitious, just as all men are, but no king, chief, pontiff or citizen ever conceived of a project as great as mine. All people enjoy brilliance in their turn: through the arts, through law, and, most of all, through war. Arabia's time has come at last. These noble people, unknown for so long, have kept their glories buried in the sand, but these new days are marked for victory. From north to south the world is in distress. Persia is drenched in blood, its empire felled. India has become a timid slave, and Egypt's dignity has been debased. Constantine's splendid walls are eclipsed, and Rome is falling apart limb by limb, its severed members drained of all honor and life. Let us raise Arabia upon the debris. The blind world is in need of new laws, a new religion and a new god. Osiris in Egypt, Zoroaster in Asia, Minos in Crete, and Numa in Italy, easily dispensed inadequate laws to people with no morals, creeds or kings. I have come a thousand years later to change the crude laws of states with a new, nobler yoke, abolishing the false gods. My purified faith is

the cornerstone of my ever-expanding grandeur. Don't for one minute blame me for betraying my homeland as I destroy its idols and weakness. I'll reunite its people with one god and one king. It won't know glory until it is enslaved.[24]

Mahomet's project is to raise the Arab nation to new heights; the hour of the Arabs has at last come. In order to do this, Mahomet has brought them both a new God and a new law, has united them under one God and one king, himself. To empower them he has to subject them. Voltaire's Mahomet compares himself to the great lawmakers of other peoples, in a passage lifted from George Sale's "Preliminary discourse." Indeed, from his letters we know that by 1738 he had discovered Sale's Qur'ān. He wrote to his friend Nicolas-Claude Thieriot, "there is a devil of an Englishman who has made a very beautiful translation of the holy Alcoran"; two years later, he wrote to Frederick II of Prussia, "Mr. Sale, who has given us an excellent translation of the Alcoran into English, wants us to regard Mahomet as a Numa and a Theseus."[25] That Voltaire read Sale's work with attention is clear from the copious notes he scribbled into the margins of his copy.[26] Here Mahomet vaunts himself a new Numa. Whereas for Sale the comparison was meant to historicize the prophet of Islam by comparing him to the great lawmakers of antiquity, here it is braggadocio, part of the pompous insolence of an impostor. It is indeed hard to imagine a portrait more opposed to Sale's than that of Voltaire. Yet the real target of Voltaire's work is not Islam, but the Catholic Church. As Voltaire said himself in a letter in 1742, "I wanted to show in this work the horrible excesses that fanaticism can inspire when weak souls are seduced by scoundrels. My play represents, under the name of Mahomet, the prior of the Jacobins placing the dagger in the hand of Jacques Clément" (the assassin of King Henry III).[27]

Yet if in 1741 he uses Sale to refute his vision of the prophet, Voltaire's views change considerably over the following years. His close reading of Sale's Qur'ān is apparent in his *Essai sur l'histoire générale et sur les moeurs et l'esprit des nations* (1757), his attempt to write a new universal history in which the place of Europe and Christendom would be reduced. It is perhaps the first European attempt to write world history that was not determined by biblical and Roman history, though in fact after chapters on ancient China, India, Persia, and Arabia, his focus is overwhelmingingly on the history of Europe from the time of Charlemagne to that of Louis XIV.[28] It is in his sixth chapter, "Of Persia, Arabia and Mahomet," that he deals with to the history of Persia from Alexander to Cosroes in five pages and then devotes ten to the history of Mahomet and another nine to the rules of his successors; he then devotes his seventh chapter to "the Alcoran and Muslim law."[29]

He sets the stage in much the same way as Sale in the "Preliminary discourse" (though far more succinctly); at the time of Mahomet's birth, his country "defended its liberties against the Persians and against the princes of Constantinople." He describes the divisions within these empires and the conflicts between them, which make them ripe for conquest. Voltaire briefly relates that Mahomet, from a poor family, was in the service of a Meccan woman named Cadige whom he married and that he "lived an obscure life until he was forty." It is then that he began to display "the talents that rendered him superior to all his countrymen." Voltaire ascribes to him a simple and forceful eloquence, fine features, and "besides the intrepidity of Alexander, his liberality, and that sobriety which Alexander wanted, in order to render his character complete." Mahomet well knew his fellow Meccans, their "ignorance, credulity and disposition for enthusiasm." He thus "pretended to receive revelations."[30]

Voltaire then gives a summary of these revelations: that the Arabs should cease worshiping the stars and worship the God who created them; that the books of the Jews and Christians are corrupted; that the Arabs should pray five times a day, give alms, to acknowledge only one God and Mahomet as the last of his prophets, and "to hazard their lives in defence of that faith." He banned wine, enjoined circumcision, and (in accordance with Eastern custom since time immemorial) allowed polygamy. Voltaire writes that the interpreters of the Qur'ān all affirm that its moral is contained in the following words: "Court him who discards thee; give to him to taketh from thee; forgive those who have offended thee; do good to all; and never dispute with the ignorant."[31] While Voltaire charges that the Qur'ān contains "contradictions, absurdities and anachronisms," other passages he describes as "sublime."

Voltaire narrates Mahomet's Hijra and his success at unifying the Arabs under the banner of Islam and lauching conquests against the Romans and Persians, demanding tribute of those who submit to his power. "Of all the legislators, who founded a new religion, he is the only one that extended his by conquests." Then, at the age of sixty-three, Mahomet fell ill:

> Resolving to behave in his last moments like a hero and a man of integrity, he cried out "Let him to whom I have done violence and injustice appear; I am now ready to make him reparation." On this a man stood up, and desiring the restitution of some money, he ordred to to be given him, and expired a short time after, with the character of a great man even in the opinion of those who knew him to be an impostor, and revered as a prophet by all the rest.[32]

The Mahomet of the *Essai sur les mœurs* is an impostor to those in the know, yet still a great man and a hero. He is the epitome no longer of fanatacism (*fanatisme*) but of enthusiasm (*enthousiasme*).[33] Indeed, this description of the message of the Qur'ān and the life and teachings of Mahomet cast him very much in the role of a biblical figure. Voltaire makes this even more explicit in the following pages. "How came it that Mahomet and his successors, who began their conquests exactly like the Jews," Voltaire asks, "achieved such great things, and that the Jews did so little?" (49). The reason is that the Jews kept to themselves, not wanting to mingle with the conquered, whereas "the courage of the Arabians was more enthusiastic, and their conduct more generous and bold" (49–50).[34]

The Arabs are superior to the Jews, and this explains their success. He returns to a favorite polemical saw (whose expression is tinged with anti-Semitism): those (like Bossuet, one of his favorite targets) who pretend to base "universal" history on the story of a small and insignificant people, should look elsewhere—to the Chinese or the Arabs. Moreover, by presenting Muhammad as a biblical figure who succeeded where Jews had failed, Voltaire further undermines Christian narratives of history. The obvious comparison, made by others before him, would have been Moses, but Voltaire here avoids mentioning his name, instead invoking that of Abraham. This allows him to follow Toland, Sale, and Boulainvilliers in asserting that Mahomet did not found a new religion, but renewed an old one:

> He claimed to restore the simple cult of Abraham or Ibrahim, from whom he claimed to be descended, and to recall men to the dogma of the unity of God, which he claimed had been distorted in all religions. This is in effect what we clearly read in the third Sura or chapter of his Qur'ān: "God knows, and you do not know. Abraham was neither a Christian nor Jew, but he was of the true religion. His heart was resigned to God, and who was not at all among the idolators."[35]

Mahomet is a descendant of Abraham and is a more successful prophet than Moses, whom Voltaire elsewhere portrays as weak and dependant on God's intervention.[36] Mahomet is greater than Alexander. Indeed, he becomes the great man against whom others are to be measured, a touchstone that he returns to time and again in the *Essai sur les mœurs*. "As a conqueror, legislator, monarch and pontiff, he played the greatest role that can be played on earth in the eyes of the common people, but the wise will always prefer Confucius, precisely because he was none of these things, and because he was content to teach the purest morality to a more ancient, more populated, and more polite nation than the Arab nation."[37] Yet if the distant Confucius can surpass the prophet of Islam, heroes closer to home are not quite up to snuff. We have seen that English royalists compared Cromwell with Mahomet; Voltaire compares them as well and concludes, "Mahomet accomplished infinitely greater things."[38] In the preface to his history of the Russian empire, he proclaims that Mahomet far surpasses the great legislators of antiquity such as Romulus or Theseus.[39]

Voltaire's reimagining of Mahomet in the *Essai sur les mœurs* permits him, in his chapters on the Middle Ages, to present Islam no longer as fanaticism but as the foil to the true fanaticism found in the medieval church, which preaches papal infallibility, burns heretics, and excites Christian knights to war against Muslims. Sultans such as Saladin or his nephew "Mélédin" (al-Malik al-Kamil) represent the height of refinement, education, and tolerance; the crusaders who oppose them are fanatical brutes.[40] Voltaire contrasts the trajectories of the two religions:

The legislator of the Muslims, a powerful and terrible man, established his dogmas with his arms and courage; however his religion became indulgent and tolerant. The divine institutor of Christianity, living in peace and humility, preached pardon, and his holy, sweet religion became, through our fury, the most intolerant and barbaric of all.[41]

In 1763 Voltaire published a pamphlet titled *Catéchisme de l'honnête homme, ou dialogue entre un caloyer et un homme de bien*,[42] a fictitious dialogue between a "caloyer," or Greek monk, and an "honest man." The two meet on a street in Aleppo, and the monk asks the honest man what his religion is. The latter responds, "I worship God; I try to be fair, and I seek learning." The monk asks him what he thinks of the sacred books of the Jews, and the *honnête homme* launches into a diatribe against all that he sees as irrational, impossible, or absurd in them: the parting of the Red Sea, the sun stopping in its orbit for Joshua, and so on. The prophets and the kings are immoral and the stories told about them absurd. No wonder, he says to the monk, that you have abandoned the Old Testament in favor of the New. Yet the *honnête homme* doesn't like the New Testament either; Jesus's miracles are petty (changing water into wine, cursing a fig tree); he himself announced none of the doctrines or rites that were to become central to Christianity; God has proved unable to stop the bickering of Christian sects. In Europe Christians persecute and kill each other, affirms the *honnête homme*; the caloyer responds that he hates persecution and thanks heaven that "the Turks, under whose rule I live in peace, persecute no one." "Ah! May all the peoples of Europe follow the example of the Turks!" proclaims the *honnête homme*.

In the original 1763 version of *Catéchisme de l'honnête homme*, there is no mention of Mahomet. But in a revised version published several years later, the prophet makes a brief but important appearance.[43] The interpolated passage is part of the *honnête homme*'s diatribe against the New Testament. He mocks the "fanatic who wrote the Epistles of Paul" for his predictions concerning the end of time. The Caloyer asks how, if the book is absurd as he claims, it managed to convert so many thousands of men? Because he preached to the ignorant and illitererate, charges the honest man: "Is it through reading that one persuades ten million peasants that three equals one, that God is in a piece of dough, that this dough disapears and has suddenly been transformed by a man into God? It is by imposture, through miraculous legends, that one can easily form a little flock" (190). Here the impostor is neither Jesus nor Mahomet, but Paul. Indeed, Voltaire seems to have a very Muslim idea of Paul as one who, having never met Jesus and being ignorant of what he taught, invented a new religion: "Three or four hotheads like Paul were sufficient to attract rogues" (191). Paul is simply one of a series of founders of Christian sects, he says.

> Almost all the sects have been established in this way, except that of Mahomet, the most brilliant of all of them, which, alone among so many human inventions, seems to be born under God's protection, since it owes its existence only to its victories.
>
> The Muslim religion is still, twelve hundred years later, what it was under its founder; nothing has been changed. The laws written by Mahomet himself have survived completely. His Alcoran is as respected in Persia as it is in Turkey; in Africa as in the Indies; everywhere, it is respected to the letter; the only division is over the succession between Ali and Omar. Christianity, on the contrary, is completely different from Jesus' religion. This Jesus, son of a village carpenter, never wrote anything; probably he did not know how to read or write. He was born, lived, and died a Jew, observing all the Jewish rites; circumcized, sacrificing according to the Mosaic Law, eating the paschal lamb with lettuce, avoiding pork, ixion and griffon, as well as hare, since it ruminates and it doesn't have a split hoof, according to the Mosaic Law. You Christians, on the contrary, you dare to believe that the hare has a split hoof and that it doesn't ruminate, you eat it to your full; you roast an ixion or a griffon, when you find one; you are not circumcized; you do not sacrifice; none of your holidays was instituted by your Jesus. What can you have in common with him? (191–92)

Here Voltaire's aim, as always, is to *écrasez l'infâme,* to crush fanaticism, in particular, the violent, repressive, and irrational policies and doctrines of the Catholic Church. In 1741, he made Mahomet and Islam into incarnations of fanaticism, as proxies that he could denounce in order to evade censorship, all the time making clear that his real target was the *infâme* closer to home. Here, on the contrary, Islam and Mahomet are a foil for Christianity and Jesus. Jesus, a circumcised Jew who respected kashrut and died the death of a criminal, bears no resemblance to the adherents of a religion that has renounced the Jewish laws he followed. Mahomet, on the contrary, benefited from divine favor, as his military victories show; he established a law that Muslims throughout the world still follow.

Ziad Elmarsafy goes as far as to suggest that Voltaire came to identify with the prophet of Islam, that he saw parallels in their lives: pride of having amassed a fortune, desire to reform the morals of the surrounding society and to promote social justice, forced exile because of the unpopularity of one's ideas, the use of writing, of persuasive words, to forge fundamental change in society. "Voltaire begins to see Muhammad as a second self, another prophet doing battle with *l'infâme* of seventh-century Arabia. . . . The story of Muhammad and the reading of the Qur'ān allowed Voltaire to establish and advance models not only of demystified history, free of superstition, or of the man who single-handedly changed the entire course of world history, but also, and perhaps most significantly, of the unlimited potential of the power of the text, which can turn Europe of *l'infâme* into 'la France de Voltaire.'"[44] While in principal, Voltaire may have admired Confucius more, he no doubt identified more with Mahomet, pugnacious and polemical. And after all, each great man must adapt himself to the needs of his people. Confucius the sage was well adapted to the "polite nation"of the Chinese (as Voltaire imagined). The French (and more generally the Europeans) were a rougher nation, like the Arabs, querulous and prone to violence. They needed a Mahomet, or a Voltaire.

Gibbon and Mahomet

Edward Gibbon, British parliamentarian, essayist, and historian, gave a detailed portrait of Muhammad and the rise of Islam in the fifth volume of his *History of the Decline and Fall of the Roman Empire*, published in 1788.[45] Gibbon as a student had converted to Catholicism, only to be forcibly brought back into the Anglican fold by his father. He subsequently became an avid reader of Toland,

Voltaire, and other *philosophes*, and adopted many of his Whig predecessors' criticisms of the Anglican Church. The first volume of *Decline and Fall* appeared in 1776 and provoked fierce criticism from conservative ecclesiastical circles (as did subsequent volumes). Critics chided Gibbon for presenting Christianity as one of the causes of the decline of the empire and for his positive portrayal of Roman paganism. In describing the religious policies of the Antonine emperors, for example, he had quipped: "The various modes of worship which prevailed in the Roman world were all considered by the people as equally true; by the philosophers as equally false; and by the magistrate as equally useful."[46] David Womersley has shown how Gibbon strove in the first volume to create a literary persona for himself, a combination of erudition, eloquence, and wit.[47] Gibbon perfected the use of the footnote as a way to display the extent of his reading and skewer those with whom he disagrees: "M de Voltaire, unsupported by either fact or probability, has generously bestowed the Canary Islands on the Roman Empire."[48] In his notes, Gibbon spars with many of his predecessors, but none more than Voltaire. If Voltaire's *Essai sur les mœurs* was a retort to Bossuet, Gibbon's *Decline and Fall* is in many respects a response to Voltaire. He read him with pleasure and admiration; Voltaire "casts a keen and lively glance over the surface of history."[49] The *philosophe* is one of the authors Gibbon cites most often, frequently to agree with, though at times to criticize, in particular his consistent anti-Christian bias. In relating the story of how fifteenth-century sultan Amurath abdicated to join a convent of dervishes, he notes that Voltaire praised this *philosophe turc*: "would he have bestowed the same praise on a Christian prince for retiring to a monastery? In his way, Voltaire was a bigot, an intolerant bigot."[50] Gibbon's ambition is to match Voltaire's wit and eloquence and to marry to it the erudition of scholars like Pococke, Reland, and Gagnier.

In dealing with the story of the early Church in his second volume (published in 1781), Gibbon, after devoting chapter twenty to the establishment of Christianity as state religion of the Roman Empire, uses chapter twenty-one to present his vision of the conflict between Arians and Trinitarians, and the persecution that Constantine and his followers imposed on those who refused to accept their doctrinal formulations. Yet not for Gibbon to make the facile

denunciations of a Stubbe; his portrait of Constantine and Athana-
sius is richer and more ambivalent, and it is Julian the Apostate,
who brutally attempts to reinstate paganism, whom Gibbon denounces as a "fanatic." David Womersley has shown how Gibbon
carefully crafted this and later installments of the *Decline and Fall*
bearing in mind the sharp criticism his Anglican clerics had made
of his earlier installments; he will cede them not an inch but will be
careful to base his judgments on the close analysis of his sources and
to eschew the polemical excesses of a Toland or a Voltaire.[51]

Like Sale, whom he read carefully, Gibbon opens his portrait of
Islam with a "Description of Arabia and Its Inhabitants": a rough
and inhospitable land, a simple and noble people. "The slaves of
domestic tyranny may vainly exult in their national independence:
but the Arab is personally free; and he enjoys, in some degree, the
benefits of society, without forfeiting the prerogatives of nature."[52]
He also follows Sale in his depiction of Mahomet's eloquence, good
looks, and charm, as well as his affability with both the influential
and the poor, qualities that earned him the respect and admiration
of all. "His memory was capacious and retentive; his wit easy and
social; his imagination sublime; his judgment clear, rapid, and decisive. He possessed the courage both of thought and action; and,
although his designs might gradually expand with his success, the
first idea which he entertained of his divine mission bears the stamp
of an original and superior genius."[53] In another page taken from
Sale, he has Mahomet contemplate the degenerate state of Persia
and Rome; he "resolves to unite under one God and one king the
invincible spirit and primitive virtues of the Arabs." While some
have accused him of having cobbled together the Qur'ān from bits
and pieces offered by Christian and Jewish collaborators, for Gibbon
the unity and vision of the Qur'ān are those of a single focused
mind:

> Conversation enriches the understanding, but solitude is the school of
> genius; and the uniformity of a work denotes the hand of a single artist.
> From his earliest youth Mahomet was addicted to religious contempla-
> tion; each year, during the month of Ramadan, he withdrew from the
> world, and from the arms of Cadijah: in the cave of Hera, three miles
> from Mecca, he consulted the spirit of fraud or enthusiasm, whose

abode is not in the heavens, but in the mind of the prophet. The faith which, under the name of Islam, he preached to his family and nation, is compounded of an eternal truth, and a necessary fiction, That there is only one God, and that Mahomet is the apostle of God.[54]

Fraud or enthusiasm: Gibbon leaves a door open, he is careful not yet to choose sides between Sale and Prideaux. Yet in what follows, he echoes the radical Enlightenment view of seventh-century Christianity as a degenerate faith in need of a radical reformer. In one of the more lyrical passages of chapter fifty, he writes:

The Christians of the seventh century had insensibly relapsed into a semblance of Paganism: their public and private vows were addressed to the relics and images that disgraced the temples of the East: the throne of the Almighty was darkened by a cloud of martyrs, and saints, and angels, the objects of popular veneration; and the Collyridian heretics, who flourished in the fruitful soil of Arabia, invested the Virgin Mary with the name and honors of a goddess. The mysteries of the Trinity and Incarnation appear to contradict the principle of the divine unity. In their obvious sense, they introduce three equal deities, and transform the man Jesus into the substance of the Son of God: an orthodox commentary will satisfy only a believing mind: intemperate curiosity and zeal had torn the veil of the sanctuary; and each of the Oriental sects was eager to confess that all, except themselves, deserved the reproach of idolatry and polytheism. The creed of Mahomet is free from suspicion or ambiguity; and the Koran is a glorious testimony to the unity of God. The prophet of Mecca rejected the worship of idols and men, of stars and planets, on the rational principle that whatever rises must set, that whatever is born must die, that whatever is corruptible must decay and perish. In the Author of the universe, his rational enthusiasm confessed and adored an infinite and eternal being, without form or place, without issue or similitude, present to our most secret thoughts, existing by the necessity of his own nature, and deriving from himself all moral and intellectual perfection. These sublime truths, thus announced in the language of the prophet, are firmly held by his disciples, and defined with metaphysical precision by the interpreters of the Koran. A philosophic theist might subscribe the popular creed of the Mahometans; a creed too sublime, perhaps, for our present faculties.[55]

No more than a page or two earlier, Gibbon had hesitated between fraud and enthusiasm to describe Mahomet's mission. Here he comes down firmly on the side of enthusiasm, indeed "rational enthusiasm." Gibbon is careful not to reject outright the doctrine of the Trinity; he does not want his enemies to be able to dismiss him as simply a Unitarian apologist, a new Nye or Bury. Some would do so nonetheless: Samuel Johnson jokingly referred to him as "Mahometan."[56] The Qur'ān is a "glorious testimony to the unity of God" whose "sublime truths" are the essence of Muslim doctrine. This religion he describes as Unitarianism; it is moreover a doctrine that a Deist, or as he says a "philosophic theist," might adopt. Not a creed likely to seduce Gibbon's clerical opponents, though, he seems to suggest, as he fears it is "too sublime for our present faculties." This is the formidable force of Gibbon's prose; he suggests that his clerical opponents are too obtuse to comprehend the sublime, Unitarian truths contained in the Qur'ān. His opponents seem to have neither Mahomet's enthusiasm nor his rationality.

Gibbon goes on to relate the preaching of Mahomet and the oppositions of the Meccans, who asked him for miracles. Some Muslims attribute miracles to him (the celestial voyage, the splitting of the moon), and "the vulgar are amused with these marvelous tales." Yet the more serious theologians reject them, considering that to preach the true religion there was no need to transgress the laws of nature, and that "the sword of Mahomet was not less potent than the rod of Moses." Gibbon then describes the Qur'ānic injunctions to ablutions, prayer, fasting, alms. Mahomet prohibited wine to his followers; this legislator "cannot surely be accused of alluring his proselytes by the indulgence of their sensual appetites," he says, echoing Voltaire.[57]

He narrates the flight to Medina, where "the choice of an independent people had exalted the fugitive of Mecca to the rank of a sovereign." He became a war leader, like Moses and the prophets before him. Indeed, he was milder than they; for the Bible "the seven nations of Canaan were devoted to destruction; and neither repentance nor conversion shield them from the inevitable doom, that no creature within their precincts should be left alive." Mahomet, rather, allowed those he defeated to join the victorious ranks as converts to Islam or to be protected as tributaries. He recounts in detail the battles that opposed the Muslims to the Meccans and to the Medinan Jewish tribes. He relates the Muslims' victory and Mahomet's leniency to his former opponents.

Mahomet was sixty-three, Gibbon writes, when his health declined and he felt death coming on. "As soon as he was conscious of his danger, he edified his brethren by the humility of his virtue or penitence." He proclaimed that if there is anyone who he had unjustly punished, he would let him whip him; if there be anyone to whom he had an unpaid debt, let him say so now. A man spoke up and said that Mahomet owed him three drams of silver. Mahomet paid him and thanked him for calling in the debt in this world, not in the next. He freed his slaves (twenty-eight of them) and gave his blessings to his friends and followers. He died with his head on the lap of his beloved wife, Aisha. Gibbon's Mahomet dies a holy man's death.

This narrative, based principally on Voltaire and Sale, is a simple, graceful reproach to the polemical tales concerning the prophet's death and demise. His epileptic fits? "An absurd calumny of the Greeks," he inveighs and adds an acid footnote in which he says that the legend was "greedily swallowed by the gross bigotry of Hottinger, Prideaux, and Marracci."[58] As for his tomb, he notes that it is at the very spot where he died in Medina. The story of the floating coffin gets no mention in the body of his text, just a dismissive footnote: "The Greeks and Latins have invented and propagated the vulgar and ridiculous story, that Mahomet's iron tomb is suspended in the air at Mecca, by the action of equal and potent loadstones. Without any philosophical inquiries, it may suffice, that, 1. The prophet was not buried at Mecca; and, 2. That his tomb at Medina, which has been visited by millions, is placed on the ground."[59]

Gibbon has read most of the authors we have discussed and more; his copious footnotes bristle with references to Sale (who, he quips, "is half a Mussulman"), Pococke, Marracci, Savary (whose French Qur'ān translation we will examine in chapter seven), Reland, and others. He uses these notes to remark where these writers differ from each other and why he rejects or accepts their various arguments. He notes, "two professed Lives of Mahomet have been composed by Dr. Prideaux and the count de Boulainvilliers, but the adverse wish of finding an impostor or a hero has too often corrupted the learning of the doctor and the ingenuity of the count."[60] He ironizes that Prideaux reveals the secret thoughts of Mahomet's wives while Boulainvilliers was privy to the patriotic views of Cadijah and the first disciples. He berates Voltaire:

> After the conquest of Mecca, the Mahomet of Voltaire imagines and perpetuates the most horrid crimes. The poet confesses, that he is not supported by the truth of history, and can only allege, "que celui qui fait la guerre a sa patrie au nom de Dieu, est capable de tout". The maxim is neither charitable nor philosophic; and some reverence is surely due to the fame of heroes and the religion of nations. I am informed that a Turkish ambassador at Paris was much scandalized at the representation of this tragedy.[61]

As one reads Gibbon's careful assessments of his predecessors and his cautious construction of the narrative of the life of Mahomet and the formation of the Muslim community, it becomes clear that Gibbon is doing something that Stubbe, Toland, Sale, or Voltaire had not: he is doing history. Toland's *Nazarenus*, for all its scholarly apparatus, as we have seen, was fiercely polemical, and much of it was tongue-in-cheek: a skillful and ambiguous mix of scholarship, diatribe, and parody of scholarship. Voltaire's entertaining and brilliant *Essai sur les mœurs*, while based on an impressive range of reading, was not first and foremost the work of a historian. Voltaire seeks to provide an alternative narrative of world history to that of Catholics like Bossuet; he shows no qualms about tweaking his sources to fit his polemical purposes. It is not that Gibbon is not polemical; he indeed can be, as we have seen. Yet his meticulous scholarship and careful exposition of the errors of his predecessors are as important to his intellectual arsenal as is his razor-sharp irony. And clearly he relishes displaying both.

Gibbon closes his portrayal of Mahomet by noting that the reader may be expecting him to offer an assessment of him, "that I should decide whether the title of enthusiast or impostor more properly belongs to that extraordinary man." He protests that such a judgment would be difficult to make if he were a contemporary and intimate of Mahomet—how much more so at a distance of twelve centuries. The "author of a mighty revolution appears to have been endowed with a pious and contemplative disposition." He preached the unity of God, mapped out the path to salvation, brought new laws to his people: "The energy of a mind incessantly bent on the same object, would convert a general obligation into a particular call; the warm suggestions of the understanding or the fancy would be felt as the inspirations of Heaven; the labor of thought would expire in rapture and vision; and the inward sensation, the invisible monitor, would be described with the form and attributes of an angel of God."[62] Imbued with what he saw as a divine mission, Mahomet violently quashed those who opposed him, Meccan pagans and Medinan Jews; this no doubt "stained" his character (he had made a similar observation concerning Constantine: "the most orthodox saints assume the dangerous privilege of defending the cause of truth by the arms of deceit and falsehood").[63] Gibbon again refuses to choose between imposture and enthusiasm, even though he has made his preference fairly clear in all that has preceded. Instead, he wraps up his portrait of Mahomet as follows: "Even in a conqueror or a priest, I can surprise a word or action of unaffected humanity; and the decree of Mahomet, that, in the sale of captives, the mothers should never be separated from their children, may suspend, or moderate, the censure of the historian."[64]

In the Enlightenment, Mahomet and Islam are objects of intense interest and debate not because people like Boulainvilliers or Voltaire are particularly interested in Islam or the lands in which Islam is professed. For these writers, Islam is "good to think with"; it helps them imagine other ways of organizing European societies, in particular different, better ways of regulating the relations between political power and religious authority. Their views on Islam and its prophet are in some cases no more objective than the polemical stereotypes they seek to replace. Yet they play an important role in secularizing or de-Christianizing European intellectual discourse. The Enlightenment Mahomet is useful above all as a foil for the Christian worldview, an alternative truth to brandish in the face of those who argue for the universal truth of Christianity and the power of the Church. This work of Enlightenment secularization will pave the way to two developments in the nineteenth century: the portrayal of Muhammad as a national Arab hero and legislator, and the integration of the study of Islam and the Qur'ān into the emerging field of religious studies.

CHAPTER SEVEN

Lawgiver, Statesman, Hero

THE ROMANTICS' PROPHET

At the Nile I find him again.
Egypt shone with the fire of his dawn;
His imperial star rose in the East.
Conqueror, enthusiast, shining with prestige,
A prodigy who astonished the land of prodigies.
The old Sheiks venerated the young and prudent Emir;
The people feared his unheard-of arms;
Sublime, he appeared to the dazzled tribes
Like a Mahomet of the West.

—VICTOR HUGO, SUR NAPOLÉON BONAPARTE,
LES ORIENTALES (1850)[1]

FOR VICTOR HUGO, Napoleon appears at the banks of the Nile as a new, Western Mahomet. Hugo's Mahomet was above all a brilliant general and a charismatic leader and Napoleon a latter-day Mahomet. Hugo was not the first to compare the two men. When Goethe heard of Napoleon's victory at Ulm in 1806, he hailed the emperor as "Mahomet der Welt."[2] As we saw in the introduction, when Goethe and Bonaparte met in Erfurt, they discussed the prophet Muhammad in glowing terms and criticized Voltaire's unfair treatment of the "great man." Nineteenth-century European debates about the prophet take place against a background of societal upheavals: Napoleonic conquests in Egypt and in Europe in the wake of the French Revolution (and his subsequent defeat); new political and social developments that call into question the traditional Christian-based political and social order; emergence of nationalism and romanticism.

Napoleon himself sees Mahomet above all as a brilliant general who knew how to motivate his people, the Arabs, to accomplish great things—something of a role model for the emperor himself. The prophet's eloquence, his gift of persuasion, allowed him to change the course of history. Goethe was also fascinated by Mahomet's eloquence, but saw him above all as a poet and a prophet, indeed as one who showed how similar were the figures of poet and prophet. A host of romantic authors in Goethe's wake (Thomas Carlyle, Victor Hugo, Alphonse Lamartine, and others) dismissed the traditional Christian polemics against the prophet, whom they presented as a sincere, virtuous visionary, one of the great figures of history. He fascinates in large part because he allows these authors to explore themes important in the romantic movement—genius, heroism, devotion—outside the constraints of Christian history.

Bonaparte's Mahomet: Model Statesman and Conqueror

Napoleon Bonaparte, in a mixture of real admiration and calculated interest, made the prophet into something of a role model, casting himself as a new world conqueror and legislator walking in Muhammad's footsteps. Napoleon was a twenty-year-old soldier in 1789, and he quickly embraced the revolution, subsequently distinguishing himself by squelching a royalist revolt in the battle of 13 Vendémiaire Year 4 (October 5, 1795). He was then made general of the Army of Italy, which he led to decisive victories over the Habsburgs and their allies. When a large force mustered under his command in Toulon in May 1798, its destination was secret. Perhaps Sicily or Sardinia, some speculated. Perhaps Gibraltar, a strategic outpost of the British enemy, and after Gibraltar, maybe England itself?

But the destination was Egypt, to the surprise of many. Why take troops from Europe to the other end of the Mediterranean? In part, to thwart the English and their East India Company by occupying a country that had long been a hub of trade between the Indian

Ocean and the Mediterranean. Egypt would be a French India, an Oriental source of power, prestige, and wealth for the metropole. And who knows, perhaps one day it would serve as the base for a French/Egyptian expedition against the British in India? The idea was not new; it had been aired and debated during the reign of Louis XVI. French Orientalists such as Volney had argued that the Egyptian masses would be grateful to be freed from the oppression of their Ottoman overlords and their Mamluk rulers; they would welcome a French expedition with open arms.[3] By 1798 things had changed; Napoleon, along with the members of the Directorate that authorized the expedition, clearly also sought to export the republican values of the revolution into the Orient. They had learned, from their reading of many of the eighteenth-century works we examined in chapter six, that Muhammad had been a reformer, that he had preached a purified monotheism stripped of arcane rites, devoid of a priestly caste. Where traditional French Catholicism was associated with oppressive monarchy, Islam seemed a more egalitarian, republican religion. Surely the troops of the revolution, come to free the Egyptians from the Ottomans, would be welcomed as brothers? What's more, for Napoleon, "Great reputations are only made in the Orient: Europe is too small."[4] The Islam that Napoleon and his troops encountered in Egypt did not in fact resemble that of Boulainvilliers or Sale; this is one of the factors that made the expedition fail, and one of the explanations for what seems, with two centuries' hindsight, an adventure clearly destined to fail.

In May 1798, then, Napoleon set off to conquer Egypt at the head of a fleet of some 55,000 men; in June he captured Malta after a brief siege and continued toward Egypt. Hoping to gain the allegiance of the Egyptians and to convince them to throw off the yoke of their Ottoman masters, he addressed the following missive to the Egyptian people:

> In the name of God the Beneficent, the Merciful, there is no other God than God, he has neither son nor associate to his rule.
>
> On behalf of the French Republic founded on the basis of liberty and equality, the General Bonaparte, head of the French Army, proclaims to the people of Egypt that for too long the Beys who rule Egypt

insult the French nation and heap abuse on its merchants; the hour of their chastisement has come.

For too long, this rabble of slaves bought up in the Caucasus and in Georgia tyrannizes the finest region of the world; but God, Lord of the worlds, all-powerful, has proclaimed an end to their empire.

Egyptians, some will say that I have come to destroy your religion; this is a lie, do not believe it! Tell them that I have come to restore your rights and to punish the usurpers; that I respect, more than do the Mamluks, God, his prophet Muhammad and the glorious Qur'ān. . . . Qādī, shaykh, shorbagi, tell the people that we are true Muslims. Are we not the one who has destroyed the Pope who preached war against Muslims? Did we not destroy the Knights of Malta, because these fanatics believed that God wanted them to make war against the Muslims?[5]

It would be easy to dismiss such rhetoric as cynical and self-serving. Indeed, the following year (in autumn 1799), as he prepared to leave Egypt, he left instructions to French administrators in Egypt, explaining among other things that "one must take great care to persuade the Muslims that we love the Qur'ān and that we venerate the prophet. One thoughtless word or action can destroy the work of many years."[6]

Self-serving indeed, yet as Juan Cole has remarked, one of Napoleon's chief weaknesses is his readiness to believe his own propaganda. Napoleon was an avid reader. He had read a number of the works we examined in chapter six, including Voltaire. He had read Claude-Etienne Savary's 1783 translation of the Qur'ān, which he took with him to Egypt. Savary had sojourned in Egypt from 1776 to 1779 (his *Lettres sur l'Egypte*, published in 1785–86, were widely read and, along with the works of Volney and others, prepared the ground for Napoleon's expedition).[7] Savary had read de Ryer's translation of the Qur'ān, which he calls flat and boring. Marracci, he judges, was an accomplished scholar and linguist whose partisanship got the better of him: "it is not the thoughts of the Qur'ān that he expressed, but words which he travestied in a barbarous Latin" (xi). Savary chose to write his translation in Egypt, in the midst of the Arabs, alive to their ways of life and the music of their language. Like other eighteenth-century European writers, he is attuned to the poetic power of the Qur'ān and the admiration it inspires among Arabs thanks to the "magic of its style, the care with which Mahomet embellishes his prose with the ornaments of poetry" (ix).

As for the message, it is very much that of purified monotheism or philosophical deism:

> The Qur'ān's dogma is the belief in one God whose prophet is Mahomet. Its fundamental principles are prayer, alms, fasting during the month of Ramadan and the pilgrimage to Mecca. The morals it preaches are founded on natural law and on what is most appropriate to peoples in a hot climate.[8]

Savary prefaces his translation with a 248-page biography of the prophet, in which he relies on Arab sources in translation, via Gagnier, Pococke, Reland, and others. His Mahomet is much like that of Boulainvilliers and Voltaire (both of whom he also has read). For Savary, Mahomet began at the age of twenty-five, shortly after his marriage with "Cadige," to retire for one month a year to the solitary cave of Hira, where he contemplated the state of the world and began to construct the edifice of "islamisme." Through their "wars of religion," the Greeks had driven Jews and Christians out of their empire; they had taken refuge in Arabia where Mahomet met them and learned of their doctrines. He contemplated the corruption of the two mighty empires with clay feet; he saw how Jews and Christians bickered among themselves. He crafted a new doctrine he hoped could rally Jews and Christians and galvanize the Arabs.

> It took fifteen years to cast the foundations of his religious system. He had to bring it to light and above all to hide the hand that attached to heaven the chain of mortals. He pretended that he did not know how to read or write and, relying on his natural eloquence, on a fertile genius that never failed him, he took the imposing title of prophet. Numa took lessons from the nymph Egeria; Mahomet chose as teacher the archangel Gabriel.[9]

Savary never uses the term "impostor" to describe Mahomet, though clearly he thinks he feigned his revelations. A great man and legislator, like Numa or Mahomet, must invent a divine source for his law, create a myth of origin for a new community. Far be it from Savary to criticize him for it. Savary's admiration for the great man, his lionizing of the warrior and hero, is clear on each of the 248 pages of the biography, up to and including his description of the prophet's death, where, like Voltaire (whom he follows), he portrays a man heroic and resigned in the face of death, surrounded by family and followers. He concludes his portrait in unequivocal praise:

> Mahomet was one of those extraordinary men who, born with superior gifts, show up infrequently on the face of the earth to change it and lead mortals behind their chariot. When we consider his point of departure and the summit of grandeur that he reached, we are astonished by what human genius can accomplish under favorable circumstances.[10]

This is Savary's Mahomet; it is also Bonaparte's Mahomet, as he read Savary's Qur'ān on his expedition. Savary gives detailed descriptions of Mahomet's military exploits and the reasons for their success. We can imagine that the general on his way to Egypt read them with particular attention. After describing the Muslim victory at the battle of Badr, Savary says, "by cultivating in the hearts of his soldiers the notion of a God who protected his arms, he made them invicible."[11] At another point he describes how the Muslims, discouraged and fearful, received the news of a huge Meccan army come to besiege Medina. Mahomet had them dig a trench.

> The ground was rock and difficult to dig. The hard rock resisted the attacks of the workers and disheartened them. Mahomet, seeing their discouragement, took some water in his mouth and spit it on the rock. The rock seemed to soften and soon gave way under the blows of the hammers. The Muslims proclaimed that it was a miracle, attributing to the virtues of this miraculous water the fruits of their renewed efforts. Just like Hannibal, who while making his way across the Alps encouraged his soldiers by sprinkling vinegar on the rock he sought to break. Everywhere the great man is the same; everywhere he flattens the obstacles in his path and makes nature cede to his efforts. The invincible charm he uses to produce prodigies guarantees the success which captivates the hearts of mortals.[12]

Mahomet is a new Hannibal, but of course with a difference: Hannibal succeeded in bringing his elephants across the Alps only to suffer defeat against the Romans. Mahomet rallied his troops to victory against all odds in the battle of the trench, followed by triumph after triumph. There is little question that Napoleon identified more with Mahomet than with Hannibal.

From the books of Voltaire, Savary, and others, Napoleon had understood that Islam was pure, simple monotheism. This vision, deployed as we have seen by eighteenth-century European authors who were concerned principally with criticizing the prominence of the Catholic (or Anglican) Church, showed little knowledge of Islam as it was practiced daily by millions of Muslims. We have seen that for Gibbon the prophet was a reformer and visionary, and Islam was essentially the equivalent of philosophical deism. Napoleon seems to have believed this, and this belief shaped his policy in Egypt, indeed may have been one of the factors in the decision to invade Egypt. The French, having crushed *l'infâme*, having dealt a blow to papist superstition, were Deists who expected to find kindred spirits in Egypt's Muslims.

And if the French are true Muslim Deists, Napoleon is their Corsican prophet. One of the ladies of his court, Madame de Rémusat, says that the emperor had told her that on his way to Egypt, "I was creating a religion, I saw myself leaving on an elephant on the way to Asia, with a turban on my head and in my hand a new Alcoran that I had composed to my liking."[13] This of course, is courtly badinage, the emperor after the fact making light of his own ambitions. Yet it reveals a real identification, confirmed by his own writings.

As ruler of Egypt, Napoleon adopted the title of al-Sultan al-Kabīr, the Great Sultan. He strove to convince Egyptians that he and the French, far from being Christian infidels, were friendly to Islam. In August 1798 was the traditional festival of the Mawlid al-Nabī, the birthday of the prophet. Cairo's Muslim leaders were in no mood to celebrate, but Napoleon saw this as a significant public relations opportunity, and he insisted on funding the festivities, in which the twirling of near-naked Sufi dervishes was mixed with the parade of French soldiers in full regalia, the chants of the Muslims with the martial strains of the marching band. As one officer noted ironically, "The French artillery saluted Mahomet."[14] The Sultan al-Kabīr, regaled in oriental costume, led the festivities and proclaimed himself protector of all the religions. He was hailed as "Ali Bonaparte."

Napoleon sought to persuade Cairo's imams that he and his troops were Muslims, and he requested that they say the traditional Friday prayer (*khutba*) in his honor. Sheikh Abdullah al-Sharqawi explained that they would be delighted to do so—as soon as Napoleon and his troops converted to Islam. The general explained that he was ready to convert, but that his soldiers were loath to be circumcised and were very fond of drinking wine—could special dispensation be made for them? Napoleon hoped to have himself and his troops recognized as Muslim and hence legitimate rulers of Egypt; the sheiks prevaricated in order to avoid a diplomatic clash.[15] Again, the general seems to have thought that French republican Deists could be recognized as Muslims, without any real knowledge of Islam. This bookish, Deist vision of Islam perhaps explains some major diplomatic errors, when for example the French razed shrines to Sufi saints when they widened streets into boulevards. Al-Sharqawi later wrote that the French were monotheistic philosophers who based their ideas on reason rather than accepting revelation. He faulted them for believing that Moses, Jesus, and Muhammad were mere sages, rather than divinely ordained prophets. God, the imam affirmed, sent the prophets, and men should follow God's law, not that of human legislators.[16] Ironically, Napoleon in practice largely ceded to this view, making Cairo's religious elite into his indigenous administrative agents, giving them in fact more power than the Ottomans ever had. As Juan Cole quips: "The French Jacobins, who had taken over Notre Dame for the celebration of a cult of Reason and who had invaded and subdued the Vatican, were now creating in Egypt the world's first modern Islamic Republic."[17]

Yet to their chagrin, and despite the alliance of a part of the Egyptian elite, hostility toward the French occupation remained strong, and the frequent revolts were brutally quelled by the French army. In November 1798, after one particularly violent rebellion (and particularly bloody repression), Napoleon suggests his identification not only with the prophet but also the Mahdī, as he proclaims the formation of a new Diwan in the following terms:

Tell your people that since the beginning of time God has decreed the destruction of the enemies of Islam and the breaking of the crosses by my hand. Moreover he decreed from eternity that I shall come from the

West to the Land of Egypt for the purpose of destroying those who have acted tyrannically in it and to carry out the tasks which He set upon me. And no sensible man will doubt that all this is by virtue of God's decree and will. Also tell your people that many verses of the glorious Qur'ān announce the occurrence of events which have occurred and indicate others which are to occur in the future. Indeed there are some who refrain from cursing me and showing me enmity out of fear of my weapons and great power and they do not know that God sees the secret thoughts, He "knoweth the deceitful of eye, and what men's breasts conceal" (Q 40:19). And those who bear such secret thoughts oppose the decisions of God and they are hypocrites, and the curse and affliction of God shall surely befall them for God knoweth the secret things. Know also that it is in my power to expose what is in the heart of every one of you, for I know the nature of man and what is concealed in his heart at the very moment that I look upon him even though I do not state or utter what he is hiding. However, a time and a day will come in which you will see for yourselves that whatever I have executed and decreed is indeed a divine decree and irrefutable. For no human effort, no matter how devoted, will prevent me from carrying out God's will which He has decreed and fulfilled by my hand. Happy are they who hasten in unity and ardour to me with good intentions and purity of heart.[18]

Did Napoleon believe that such proclamations would have any effect on the Egyptian people? Or are they the deluded decrees of an increasingly desperate general? In the following months, the French crushed further revolts in the Nile delta, launched a failed expedition in Syria, and everywhere faced rebellious Egyptians and an alliance of Ottomans and British. Napoleon decided to leave. In the ship that brought him from Alexandria to France, while his companions worried that they might be intercepted by the British navy, Napoleon remained calm. He stayed in his cabin, reading alternately the Bible and the Qur'ān.[19] Napoleon left General Jean-Baptiste Kléber in charge of the French forces in Egypt. Kléber negotiated with the British the convention of El-Arish in January 1800, by which the French gave up all claims to Egypt and returned to France.[20]

Napoleon's proclamations in Egypt identifying himself with the prophet and the Mahdī, and affirming that his coming to Egypt was predicted by the Qur'ān, appear two centuries later to be self-serving, cynical, and downright silly. Yet Napoleon's admiration for the prophet was not merely a product of his Egyptian propaganda, as we see from the memoirs that he and some of his companions wrote years later, in exile on the windswept island of Saint Helena in the South Atlantic. For it was to this remote island, 1,800 kilometers from the African coast, that the British took Napoleon and a few of his men after his surrender in 1815. There the former emperor had ample time to brood on his triumphs and his failures and also, as we will see, to reflect on the destiny of a man who had succeeded where he had failed, Mahomet.

Napoleon's companion Emmanuel de Las Cases, author of the *Mémorial de Sainte-Hélène*, says that the emperor had brought two thousand French books with him, and that in the spring of 1816, evenings were spent reading and discussing various authors, in particular Voltaire and Racine. The emperor had particularly harsh criticism for Voltaire's *Mahomet*: Voltaire

> prostituted the great character of Mahomet through attributing to him the basest intrigues. He had a great man who had changed the face of the world act like the vilest criminal, worthy only of the hangman. The men who have changed the universe never succeed by winning over the leaders, but always in stirring the masses. The first method is the source of intrigue and only produces mediocre results; the second is the march of genius, and it changes the face of the world![21]

Bonaparte's Mahomet is still very much Savary's, the great man able to inspire the masses and change the face of the world. No wonder that he denounced Voltaire's drama. In so doing, he echoed views that he had aired in France. According to Mme de Rémusat, Napoleon told her

> Voltaire's tragedies are passionate, but they do not plumb the depths of the human spirit. For example, his Mahomet is neither a prophet nor even an Arab. He is an impostor who seems to have been educated at the Ecole polytechnique, for he displays all his forces as I could do it in today's world. The son's murder of his father is a useless crime. Great men are never cruel unless it is necessary.[22]

His conclusion: "Voltaire understood neither things, nor men, nor great passions."[23] Mahomet, and Bonaparte after him, had clearly understood all three.

On Saint Helena, Napoleon also wrote his own memoirs, including an account of his Egyptian campaign. It is here he develops his portrait of Mahomet as a model lawmaker and conqueror. Mahomet, he explained, banished idolatry in Arabia and "introduced the cult of the God of Abraham, Ishmael, Moses and Jesus Christ." While Christians were bickering about the composition of the Trinity, "Mahomet declared that there was one unique God who had neither father nor son; that the Trinity implied idolatry. He wrote on the frontispiece of the Qur'ān: 'There is no other god than God.'"

> He addressed savage, poor peoples, who lacked everything and were very ignorant; had he spoken to their spirit, they would not have listened to him. In the midst of abundance in Greece, the spiritual pleasures of contemplation were a necessity; but in the midst of the deserts, where the Arab ceaselessly sighed for a spring of water, for the shade of a palm where he could take refuge from the rays of the burning tropical sun, it was necessary to promise to the chosen, as a reward, inexhaustible rivers of milk, sweet-smelling woods where they could relax in eternal shade, in the arms of divine houris with white skin and black eyes. The Bedouins were impassioned by the promise of such an enchanting abode; they exposed themselves to every danger to reach it; they became heroes.
>
> Mahomet was a prince; he rallied his compatriots around him. In a few years, his Muslims conquered half the world. They plucked more souls from the false gods, knocked down more idols, razed more pagan temples in fifteen years, than the followers of Moses and Jesus Christ had in fifteen centuries. Mahomet was a great man.[24]

Bonaparte's Mahomet is a model statesman and conqueror; he knows how to motivate his troops and as a result was a far more successful conqueror than Napoleon, holed up on a windswept island in the South Atlantic. If he promised sensual delights to his faithful, it is because that is all they understood; this manipulation, far from being cause for scandal, provokes only the admiration of the former emperor. The great man does not worry himself with scruples about tricking the gullible masses; he need only move

them, use his eloquence to make them undertake great projects—
his projects.

Napoleon is ready to excuse, even to praise, parts of Muslim law
that had been objects of countless polemics. Why did Mahomet
allow polygamy? First, explains Napoleon, it had always been a
common practice in the Orient; Mahomet actually reduced it by
allowing each man a maximum of four wives. Moreover, polygamy
is an effective tool to combat racism, promoting racial mixing. If a
man has several wives, white and black, his sons, "the black and the
white, since they are brothers, sit together at the same table and see
each other. Hence in the Orient no color pretends to be superior to
another." And the ex-emperor concludes with a policy recommenda-
tion: "When we will wish, in our colonies, to give liberty to the
blacks and to destroy color prejudice, the legislator will authorize
polygamy."[25] A number of French writers who had been in the Ottoman Empire, Syria, and Egypt had remarked that black slaves
were treated far better in the Orient than in European and American slave societies.[26] For Napoleon, the particularly Western vice of
racism was eradicated in the Orient through the sage legislation of
the Muslim prophet.

Not a cloud darkens the radiant image that the fallen emperor
paints of the prophet of Islam. There is none of the ambivalence that
we see, for example, in Gibbon. Yet in many ways he remains an
impostor. Bonaparte's Mahomet is the sole author of the Qur'ān and
sole legislator. His revelations are cleverly plotted inventions aimed
at stirring his followers and rallying them to a greater cause.
Bonaparte's Mahomet is, well, Bonaparte, but a far more successful
Bonaparte.

Goethe: Where Is the Line between Poet and Prophet?

Johann Wolfgang von Goethe (1749–1828) was an admirer of both
the prophet and the French emperor. Indeed in 1806, in the wake of
Napoleon's victory over the Austrians at Ulm (in October 1805), he
wrote that Bonaparte was the "Mahomet der Welt"; as we have seen,
the two men met in 1808 and discussed Voltaire's *Mahomet*.[27] The
Muslim prophet and the Qur'ān were recurring themes in Goethe's
work. Goethe's Muhammad was reformer and legislator as he had

been for earlier Enlightenment writers, but he was more than that; he was a prophet and a patriarch, indeed in some ways the archetype for both. And the prophet is troublingly, intriguingly similar to the poet. Muhammad was a key figure in Goethe's world, a figure unjustly lambasted by Europeans for centuries, to whom the German poet strove to do justice.

In 1770, Goethe went to Strasbourg to pursue his studies and there met Johann Gottfried Herder (1744–1803), who was to become a mentor and a close friend. Herder had already shown a keen interest in Islam and its prophet, about whom he wrote with great ambivalence. As a Lutheran pastor, he placed Muhammad in the traditional role of impostor and false prophet, though at times presented Islam as closer to true monotheism than Catholic and Eastern Christianity. Yet he elsewhere portrayed the prophet as a "trader, prophet, speaker, poet, hero, and lawmaker."[28] Indeed, as author of the Qur'ān, poetic expression of the Arab Volk, Muhammad provided a powerful force for unity and conquest; would that the Germans had produced their own Qur'ān! His thought on Islam was in part, no doubt, a product of his exchanges with Goethe.

At Strasbourg, Herder got Goethe interested in the Qur'ān, which they studied together, in Theodor Arnold's German translation of Sale's English version.[29] In a letter to Herder in 1772, Goethe wrote: "I would like to pray like Moses in the Qur'ān: Lord open up my breast!"[30] In 1772 David Friedrich Megerlin published a German translation of *Die türkische Bibel, oder der Koran*, which he describes as "Muhammad's book of lies." Goethe wrote a scathing review in the *Frankfurter gelehrten Anzeigen*, calling the translation a "miserable production," saying that he longed for a translator, who would become an Oriental himself, read the Qur'ān "in a tent" under "oriental skies" and who would produce a book full of the sensibilities of poets and prophets.[31] Goethe never learned enough Arabic to do so himself, and he was painfully aware of depending principally on existing translations that he criticized. He did study Arabic: in 1815 he wrote that he hoped to soon know Arabic enough to read and copy short texts, and his notebooks show that in his sixties he was practicing Arabic calligraphy.[32]

Whereas the pastor Herder maintained a Protestant distance from (and at times disdain for) Islam, Goethe, unsatisfied with Protestant Christianity, read the Qur'ān as a source of both poetic and spiritual inspiration; indeed, for him the two were inseparable. "The style of the Qur'ān, in keeping with its content and purpose, is stern, majestic, terrifying, and at times truly sublime."[33] Muhammad, for Goethe, needed no miracles; the Qur'ān was miracle enough, as it expressed the prophet's poetic genius. On a number of occasions, Goethe cites approvingly God's affirmation in the Qur'ān: "We did not send any messenger except speaking in the language of his people to state clearly for them."[34]

In 1799, Karl August, duke of Saxe-Weimar, commissioned Goethe to translate Voltaire's *Mahomet ou le fanatisme* into German.[35] The commission placed him in a quandary: he was indebted to the patronage of the duke and could not refuse his request. He had an unbound admiration for Voltaire's thought and style. Yet he saw the *philosophe's* portrayal of the prophet as ahistorical and unfair, completely at odds with his own. Goethe thus transforms Voltaire's work, softening the harsh portrait of Mahomet, deflecting some of the attention by giving a greater role to the romance between the young lovers Seïde and Palmire. But it is still Voltaire's work, and the prophet is still a rank impostor. The duke was pleased with the production, but Herder and his wife Caroline were not, as she later described in a letter to a friend:

> I would never have thought Goethe capable of such sins against history—he made Mahomet a brutal, banal charlatan, murderer, and libertine. . . . What do these old anti-Jesuitical farces matter to us, to us Protestants? We have no idea of what to make of them! . . . Shakespeare, Shakespeare, whither have you gone?[36]

One reader who shared Caroline Herder's disappointment with Goethe's (and Voltaire's) portrayal of the prophet was Karoline von Günderrode, who in 1804 published her own *Lesedrama* (a play meant to be read and not staged), *Mahomed, der Prophet von Mekka*, whom she portrays sympathetically as a reformer. She adapts Boulainvilliers glowing portrait to the tastes of her largely Lutheran readers, by (for example) comparing Mahomed's destruction of idols in the Kaʿba to Jesus's expulsion of money changers from the Temple of Jerusalem.[37] Yet not all readers saw Goethe's portrayal of Mahomet as negative. Indeed, for some the ambitious, scheming successful young man looked suspiciously like Napoleon; notably for Viennese censor Franz Karl Hägelin, who prohibited the production.[38] Indeed, Duke Karl August himself wrote in 1813 of the Emperor Napoleon: "He's an extraordinary being. He's not a European spirit, but rather an Oriental genie. He seemed to me like one inspired. I imagine Mahomet must have been like this."[39]

Goethe had in 1772 embarked on the composition of a drama on the life of the prophet, a project that he never completed, but which is extant in fragments; his portrait of Mahomet is starkly different from Voltaire's.[40] Goethe's play opens with the young Mahomet alone at night, contemplating the heavens. He proclaims:

> I cannot share with you the feelings of this soul,
> I cannot feel all for you all that I feel,
> Who, oh who turns his ear to our pleas?
> A glance toward the pleading eye?
> Behold, Gad the friendly star is rising,
> Be thou my Lord, thou, my God. Graciously it beckons!
> Stay! Stay' Are you turning your eye away?
> What? Did I love him who hides?
> Blessings on you, o Moon, leader of all the stars,
> Be thou my Lord, thou my God! Thou lightest the way.
> Let, o let me not in the darkness,
> Lose my way with a people so lost.
> O radiant Sun, to thee the glowing heart is true!
> Be thou my Lord, thou my God, Guide me, all-seeing one!
> Glorious one, do you too descend?
> Deeply am I enshrouded in darkness.
> Loving heart, lift thyself to the Creator
> Be thou my Lord, my God! Thou, who gives life to all!
> Who created the sun and the moon and the stars,
> And Earth and Heaven and me.[41]

This is in fact a loose poetic translation of Qur'ān 6:74–79. There it is Abraham who successively hails God as a star, the moon, and the sun; he rejects each in turn as it sets and then turns his face to Him who created the heavens. The conflation of Muhammad and Abraham highlights how Goethe sees Muhammad as the archetypal figure of the prophet and patriarch, with the distinct advantage of not

having all the Jewish and Christian baggage of Abraham, Moses, or
Jesus.

Goethe next has Halima, the prophet's nurse, ask in concern
what he is doing out alone at night. He responds that he was not
alone, that God was near to him. Did you see Him, she asks? Mahomet responds:

> Do not you see him? At every still spring, under every blossoming tree,
> he meets me in the warmth of his love. How I thank him! He opened
> my chest, took away the hard cover of my heart, that I can feel its
> nearness.[42]

There follows a dialogue between Halima and Ali, which Goethe
subsequently published separately as "Mahomets Gesang." He presents the prophet, whose name is not mentioned, through the metaphor of a river that begins as a joyfully sparkling mountain spring,
that flows down the mountain into the valley where flowers spring
from its banks, gathers force and power, has cities and lands named
for him, then bears his brothers on his surging current out to the
ocean, where they will be united with their father. The prophet is a
force of nature: joyous, beneficent, and awesome.[43]

Goethe's deepest engagement with Islam and with Persian culture is his *West-Ostlicher Divan*, a poetic anthology composed between 1815 and 1827.[44] In 1815, he regaled lettered women of Weimar with readings from German translations of Ferdowsi's
Shahnama and the Qur'ān.[45] In 1812–13, Joseph von Hammer-
Purgstall published the first German translation of the *Dīvān* of
fourteenth-century Persian poet Hāfez; Goethe soon read it. He
conceived his *West-Ostlicher Divan* as a response, both playful and
reflective, in which the poet (Dichter) seems to stand for Goethe
himself, is in dialogue with Hafiz, though at times the two seem to
be conflated into one. The title page sports two titles, in German,
West–östlicher Divan (West–Eastern Diwan), and in Arabic, الديوان
الشرقي للمؤلف الغربي (The Eastern Diwan of the Western Author). The
dual title thus plays with the East/West dichotomy and blurs it: his
Diwan is a hybrid (East/West) poetry collection but is also an Eastern poetry collection by a Western author. This overturning of geo-
graphical categories is carried over into the first stanza of the opening poem, "Hegire":

North and South and West are quaking,
Thrones are cracking, empires shaking;
You must flee; the East will right you,
Patriarchs' pure air delight you;
There in loving, drinking, singing
Youth from Chiser's well is springing. [46]

In the wake of the destruction wrought in Europe by the Napoleonic wars (1815, as we have seen, is the year the British shipped Bonaparte off to Saint Helena), the poet seeks to flee East, to be rejuvenated through drinking the water from Chiser's well (the well of the Qur'ān's al-Khidr, the legendary source of Hafiz's inspiration) and through breathing in the air of the patriarchs. Through the choice of title, "Hegire," Goethe identifies with Muhammad; his is to be the exile not of a prophet but of a poet, as his voyage is one of the spirit and not the body. In the *Morgenblatt für gebildete Stände* (February 24, 1816), he explains the poem: "The poet considers himself a traveler. He has already arrived in the Orient. He delights in the customs, habits, objects, religious beliefs, and opinions: indeed, he does not countermand the suspicion that he is a Muslim himself."[47] The poet calls on "Holy Hafiz" for guidance and proclaims the spiritual nature of his "Hegire":

You should learn that poet's diction
I no commonplace of fiction,
Hovering soft by heaven's portal
It seeks life that is immortal.[48]

This conflation of poet and prophet is a recurring theme. In the *Divan*'s book of Suleika, consisting of love poems between Suleika and the poet Hatem, she proclaims, "tell me poet, tell me prophet."[49] Goethe makes this clear in his commentary to the *Divan*:

This extraordinary man [Muhammad] vehemently claimed to be a prophet rather than a poet, so that his Koran should be considered a divine law and not a man-made book destined for study or entertainment. Now, if we were to determine carefully the difference between the poet and the prophet, we would say that whereas both are possessed and enflamed by a God, the poet spends that gift that he has received on joy, and does so in order to produce joy, and to obtain glory or at least an enjoyable life through his production. He neglects all other aims, he aims for variety, showing an unbounded capacity for feeling and representation. The prophet, on the other hand, has a single precise aim, for the attainment of which he uses the simplest possible means. He wants to announce a doctrine, to assemble the masses through and for it, as if around a flag. In order for this to happen, it is enough that the world believe, and that the prophet keep playing the same tune; for we do not believe in the multifarious, we perceive it.[50]

Goethe frames the Book of Hafiz as a dialogue between the poet and Hafiz. Hafiz invokes his fidelity to the Qur'ān, to the words of the prophet. The poet responds, "If we share another's mind, we shall be the other's equal." He evokes his own Christian sacred books, which are impressed in his breast just as the image of the Lord was impressed on a holy cloth (referring to the legend of the Veronica, the cloth that Christ wiped his face with as he walked toward Calvary, and which retained his likeness). In other words, in a mutual striving for spiritual truth, the Persian poet offers the Qur'ān, word of the prophet, and the German poet offers the Bible and the image of Christ.[51]

Not that all of the books of the *Divan* share this earnest spiritual quest. Goethe revels in the profane, notably through the love poems in the *Book of Love* and the *Book of Suleika*. The *Schenkenbuch*, *Book of the Tavern* and the *Tavern Boy*, consists principally of exchanges between the drunken poet and his young waiter. The poet proclaims that he does not know whether or not the Qur'ān is eternal, but that wine was certainly created before the angels: "In the drinker's sight, however it may be, God's countenance is more freshly caught."[52] At one point, the tavern boy refuses to serve the drunken poet, reminding him, "Mahomet forbids it."

The final book is the *Book of Paradise*. The poet celebrates the sensual delights that await the faithful, with playful dialogues in which the poet tries to convince a houri to admit him to heaven. The prophet, aware of our failings, sends us reminders of the pleasures that he has promised, beautiful human lovers that ensnare us and reaffirm our belief in Paradise.[53] Goethe also inserts a poem in which Mahomet gives a rousing speech after the battle of Badr, on a starry night, exhorting the Muslims not to mourn their dead, who have entered into the gates of Paradise, describing the beauties and pleasures of "the faithful heroes' dwelling."[54]

Hammer, whose translation of Hafiz had inspired Goethe's *Divan*, subsequently wrote a bilingual prayer book in German and Arabic. He meant the prayers, redolent of the language of the Qur'ān, to be "suitable for members of all religions." Hammer's funerary monument (1856), with inscriptions in ten languages, reflects the same spirit, the Arabic inscription invoking an ecumenical God in Qur'ānic epithets (calling him the living one, الحي, and the everlasting one, الباقي).[55] Goethe's *Divan* can be read as a similar exercise, in poetry rather than in prayer, to transcend divisions between religions and between East and West. Goethe reads the Qur'ān in admiration, he sees Muhammad as a prophet and poet. His poetry and his autobiographical writings reflect a constant spiritual quest in which religion and poetry, the spirit and the heart, are closely tied. Blending elements from his own Lutheran background, Islam, and other spiritual traditions, he creates his own spirituality in an early example of (and inspiration for) nineteenth-century romanticism. But is his religion Islam? Stupid question, he would say:

> Stupid, that each his own special opinion
> Praises as though his case be odd!
> If Islam means submission to God
> We all live and die in Islam's dominion.[56]

The Romantics' Muhammad: From Carlyle to Lamartine

Bonaparte's Mahomet was a statesman and conqueror; Goethe's a poet and prophet. Numerous nineteenth-century writers of the Romantic movement portray Muhammad in both veins, echoing the assessment of Gibbon that he was a "great man," or, in the words of Thomas Carlyle, a "hero." Carlyle was an avid reader of Goethe and corresponded with him frequently. He lauded Goethe's spiritual quest, which offered relief from the growing atheism and materialism of English culture. It is his reading of Goethe, above all, it seems, that made Carlyle want to write a portrait of Muhammad as part of his own pantheon of heroic men.[57]

In May 1840, Carlyle gave a series of six lectures, On Heroes, Hero-Worship, and the Heroic in History: the hero as divinity (with the example of Odin from Scandinavian mythology), as prophet (Mahomet), as poet (Dante and Shakespeare), as priest (Luther and Knox), as man of letters (Johnson, Rousseau, and Burns), and as king (Cromwell and Napoleon). Carlyle avoids including Moses, Jesus, and other biblical figures in his list. Carlyle is free to explore and elaborate on the prophetic figure through Mahomet without the constraints that he would feel in presenting a biblical prophet to his mostly Protestant listeners.

Carlyle rejects the ridiculous legends of Mahomet the impostor: the trained pigeon and bull. Mahomet, he says, is not a false man, for how could a false man found a religion? A false man cannot even build a brick house (41). A great man cannot help but be sincere. Carlyle has read Sale's Qur'ān and takes his account of Mahomet's life largely from Sale. His Mahomet is a "silent great soul" (50), and as such knows nothing of personal "ambition." His message is simple: that God is all there is; that man must practice Islam as submission to God (he cites approvingly Goethe's lines that under this definition we all live in Islam) (52). This, he says, is the essence of Islam, as it is the essence of true Christianity. "That Mahomet's whole soul, set in flame with the grand Truth vouchsafed him, should feel as if it were important and the only important thing, is quite natural" (53). If he sees Mahomet as a hero and indeed the archetype of prophet, he does not share Goethe's admiration for the Qur'ān, which he describes as ill constructed and uninspiring, though he acknowledges that this may be because he has only read it in Sale's English translation. Islam itself is a "confused form of Christianity" (52), a great improvement over what passed for Christianity in the seventh-century Orient, and of course over pre-Islamic Arab idolatry, but not, it seems, on a level with Anglicanism.

In 1865, Alphonse de Lamartine published his *Les grands hommes de l'Orient: Mahomet, Tamerlan, le sultan Zizim*.[58] He, like Sale, Voltaire, and others, opens with a presentation of the "geography of religions," where a region of rocks and sand has given rise to the "patriarchal race" characterized by "an imagination more active, more fertile and more religious than that of the races of the West." This "race" of desert nomads resides under a warm and mild sky, lives from pastoralism (with no need for agricultural labor), and thus has the leisure to contemplate the heavens and their creator. "Is meditation indeed not the astronomy of the soul?"[59] This idea of a distinction between races is of course common in the nineteenth century, as we will see (chapter eight) in the case of Lamartine's contemporary Ernest Renan. But, insists Lamartine, this does not mean that he looks down on these people of the desert, on the contrary:

> Far from affecting upon this mystical and pious race the superiority, which the men of our time attribute to the exclusively calculating and skeptical peoples of the West, we believe that God has given to the pastoral peoples of Arabia the best part, according to the Gospel. We believe that the noblest use of the faculties of every created being is to discover its Creator, in order to worship and serve Him; that God is the sole purpose of creation; that the race which is truly dominant in the different families of humanity is the one which contains most of that feeling of presence and adoration of God. Among these races the greatest men in the eyes of the supreme ruler of all greatness, are neither the greatest possessors of land, nor the greatest killers of men, nor the greatest founders of empires, but the greatest men are the most holy. (45)

Lamartine tells how the young Mahomet, accompanying the caravans of his uncle Aboutaleb, meets the Christian monk Bahira in the desert. This encounter, he says, was "the starting point of the thoughts and of the future mission of the prophet of Arabia. The Coran was clearly, in his spirit, the slow growth of this seed of the Gospel tossed in passing by the wind of the desert in his soul" (73). Lamartine affirms that Mahomet visited the monk frequently on his visits in later years, when he was employed by Kadidjé. Mahomet was disgusted with the pagan rites and superstitions of his native Mecca, as were many of his compatriots: "a man destined to succeed is never more than the living synthesis of a common inspiration of

the spirit of his times. He is ahead of it, which is why he is persecuted; but he expresses it, which is why people follow him" (74). It
is in this context that Mahomet receives his first revelations. Unsure,
he confides in his wife Kadidjé, who tells him that she hopes he will
be "the prophet of our nation." His first revelations are to a limited
circle of his family and close friends; he hopes that this modest following will be pleasing to God. Yet the zeal of his disciples and his
own inner voice pushed him to preach against the idolatrous cult of
Mecca, provoking the hostility of the Quraysh.

The Muslims face hostility, persecution. Muhammad sends some
of them to Abyssinia, whose Christian king welcomes them and asks
them about their "new religion." They respond by explaining, "A famous, virtuous man of our race arrived; he taught us the unity of
God, the contempt of idols." He taught them to eschew vice, to respect one's word, to show honor to widows and orphans. He ordered
them to practice prayer, abstinence, fasting, and almsgiving (110).
The king responds that this is just like Christianity. He and his bishops ask more: the Muslims recite a sura on John the Baptist, they
explain what they believe about Jesus and his birth from the Virgin
Mary. The king responds that the difference between this religion
and Christianity is no wider than a blade of grass; he tells them they
are welcome in his kingdom. Why, then, did Mahomet and his followers not simply declare themselves Christian? Because of his prophetic spirit, says Lamartine:

> Mahomet did not possess his spirit; it possessed him. His constant pen-
> chant of his imagination towards invisible things or his almost contin-
> ual ecstatic hallucination had manifested itself in him since his child-
> hood, but especially since his nocturnal trances in the cave of Safa. It
> was perhaps epilepsy or intermittent catalepsy, which seems to have
> affected him as it did Caesar and other great men who had deformed
> their organs by dint of thinking. It seems evident that Mahomet was
> visited by visions and especially by dreams. These dreams and visions
> naturally related to the enthusiasm of the awakened enthusiast; he took
> them for revelations from Allah to his soul. He picked them up when he
> woke up, dressed them in the figurative style of his nation, the biblical
> and evangelical imitations of which his mind was enlightened by his
> studies and his contacts with the Jews and Christians in his travels. He

then professed them to his disciples as the direct laws of heaven transmitted to men by the faithful echo of his lips. One can see only a trace
of pious artifice in the evidently careful, literary, eloquent, poetic writing of these pages of the Koran or of these sermons written on palm
leaves and distributed to the Arabs as the very expression of the reveal-
ing spirits that inspired them. This thoughtful drafting of his religious,
moral and civil code was evidently a work of his will, of his politics, of
his meditation. The writer helped the prophet. But this very work of
the writer at rest, after the moment of vision or after the awakening of
the dream, does not prove that the poet was knowingly an impostor.
This only proves that during the access he had believed he had seen,
he had thought he heard, he had believed in the divinity of dreams,
and then employed all his genius as a legislator and a preacher to present his revelations to men in the form and in the style best suited to
inspire their souls. Historians should give no credence to those who
accuse him of imposture, which the spirit of sect and ignorance pour
from afar upon men who have renewed the face of the human mind in
all ages. Hypocrisy is not a force in man, it is a weakness. The mask
always explodes one way or another. The great hypocrites are great
actors, but are not great men. Good faith enthusiasm is the only lever
strong enough to lift the earth; but, in order that this lever may have
all its power, it must first have as its point of support the faith of an
enthusiastic, intrepid and convinced spirit. The prophet of the Arabs
appears more and more to us in the vicissitudes of his religious preaching: a convinced ecstatic, a visionary of good faith, a political enthusiast, but one whose enthusiasm did not cloud the lucidity of his genius.
(112–13)

Lamartine refuses to see in Mahomet an impostor or hypocrite; as
for Napoleon, and as for other Romantic authors, for Lamartine a
great man is necessarily sincere. Nor does he accept the Muslim
point of view of the divine origins of his revelations. He returns to
the legend of his epilepsy, which, far from being negative, is something that he shares with other great men, such as Julius Caesar, and
is an effect of the power of his thought. His visions and dreams, in
part the result of these epileptic fits, he sincerely took to be revelations from God, which he then expressed eloquently in his Coran,
showing his skill as preacher and legislator.

For Lamartine, the Hijra marks a rupture in the life of Mahomet: the warrior replaces the prophet. He describes Mahomet's skill as a general, a statesman, a diplomat, and a legislator. His one vice is his sensuality, which "was the dominant weakness of his character and became the vice and the ruin of his legislation." By not respecting the equality of the sexes, Mahomet violated justice; here Christian marriage is superior and more just. This is the only cloud, it would seem, that troubles Lamartine's otherwise laudatory portrait of the prophet, who eats frugally, sleeps on a thin straw mat, performs his own menial work (including milking his own ewes). His house and the surrounding area were a haven for the poor, the ill, widows and orphans; he gave them protection and each evening went out among them to speak with them and to give them from his own hands the same simple food he ate, dates and barley. His death was that of a holy man loved by his people.

In conclusion, Lamartine affirms that never had a man undertaken a more sublime mission: "render God to man and man to God, restore the rational and holy idea of the Divinity in the midst of a chaos of material gods disfigured by idolatry" (208). Never had a man accomplished so much with so little: starting with himself and "a handful of barbarians in a corner of the desert," he established an empire that was to reign from the Himalayas to the Pyrenees. No modern hero can compare to Mahomet; no conqueror has established an empire which did not crumble quickly. Mahomet was no impostor; he was rather the greatest of men.

One could cite many other examples of the Romantics' Mahomet, but we will as a final example return to Victor Hugo, who in 1858 published "L'an 9 de l'hégire," a poem narrating the prophet's death. He presents Mahomet as a figure of modesty and asceticism, who milks his own ewes and sews his own clothing, a pillar of sagacity and justice revered by all his followers. Hugo has Mahomet deliver a final sermon to the Muslims, stressing how he, like all of them, is a mere mortal made of dust. The day of his death, he uttered his final prayers, reciting with Abu Bakr verses from the Qur'ān. Then he returned to Aisha's bed and waited.

> And the Angel of Death appeared at his door in the evening
> Asking that he be allowed to enter

"Let him enter"
One saw then his countenance brighten
With the same brilliance as on the day of his birth
And the Angel said "God desires your presence"
"Very well", he replied. A shiver ran across his forehead.
A breath opened his lips, and Mahomet died.[60]

The list is long of Romantic writers who painted Muhammad as inspired poet, legislator, genius of the Arab nation. This is an age of nationalism and expansive imperialism: if the writings of the Romantics cannot be facilely dismissed as the programmatic production of apologists for empire, nor can the broader political and social context be ignored.[61] If Mahomet is no longer a trickster and impostor, he also no longer poses the challenge to European religious and political ideals as he had for writers from Stubbe to Voltaire. A genius and a reformer, yes, but to his nation, the Arabs.

This vision of Mahomet as sage lawgiver to the Arabs lives on in the twentieth-century United States, as we see in two striking examples. In 1905, Mexican-born sculptor Charles Albert Lopez produced a large freestanding marble statue of Muhammad for the New York Appellate Courthouse in Manhattan, where it joined the figures of other great world lawgivers. Lopez portrays Muhammad standing, wearing a turban and long robes, with a long beard. With his left hand he holds in front of him an open book, while over it, in his right hand, he holds a sword.[62] Here is a dignified, strong figure, corresponding to the canons of nineteenth- and early twentieth-century romanticism and orientalism. Muhammad is one of a series of ten "national" lawgivers. His dignified presence among these great legislators both elevates and constrains his mission, implicitly denying any universal message to the book he is clutching. Adolf A. Weinman, a German-born American sculptor, gave visual expression to the image of Muhammad as lawgiver in his 1935 frieze in the main chamber of the US Supreme Court, where Muhammad takes his place among eighteen lawgivers.[63] Weinman renders the different legislators in period costumes that could have been concocted in 1930s Hollywood. His Muhammad (like Lopez's) concurs with Romantic Orientalist models: from the flowing robes and head coverings to the open Qur'ān and sword in his hand. The legitimacy of

Muhammad and the Qur'ān as sources of law are confirmed at the same time as they are subsumed into an overarching scheme of divinely inspired justice that finds its fullest and finest manifestation in the Supreme Court of the United States.

The Muslim prophet was a figure to emulate for Bonaparte and Goethe; one to be admired from a distance for most of the Romantics. Islam and Muhammad looked different to one group of Europeans who had reason to fear the drumbeats of nationalism, Europe's Jews, as we will see in the following chapter.

CHAPTER EIGHT

A Jewish Muhammad?

THE VIEW FROM JEWISH COMMUNITIES OF NINETEENTH-CENTURY CENTRAL EUROPE

MANY OF THE MOST prominent nineteenth-century scholars on Islam were central European Jews. What these scholars write about Islam and Muhammad is inevitably linked to social and intellectual upheavals in Europe around them, notably in their own Jewish communities.[1] Enlightenment thinkers argued that the state should no longer be associated with one religion and that adherents of all faiths should enjoy the same legal freedoms and be subject to the same obligations. John Toland published in 1714 a pamphlet addressed to the British Parliament titled *Reasons for naturalizing the Jews in Great Britain and Ireland: on the same foot with all other nations : containing also a defense of the Jews against all vulgar prejudices in all countries*.[2] Others, including Jewish Enlightenment figures such as Moses Mendelssohn, similarly argued that Jews should be full citizens with equal rights. Various European rulers abolished key aspects of traditional European Jewry law: in 1781, Holy Roman Emperor Joseph II eliminated the Jewish badge and taxes on Jewish travelers; he subsequently abolished other regulations concerning Jews, in particular concerning where they could live. The American and French revolutions were to bring these ideals into practice: the US Constitution granted equal rights to Jews in 1789, and the new French republic proclaimed the emancipation of French Jews in 1791. In the parliamentary debate leading to the emancipation decree, Stanislas de Clermont-Tonnerre proclaimed, "we must grant everything to the Jews as individuals and nothing to them as a nation." In other words, a French Jew was a Frenchman with the equal rights of any other Frenchman, to whom the same laws applied; there was to be no recognition of group rights of Jews, or of the authority of rabbis in any area other than those defined as strictly religious. *Écrasez l'infâme* implied restricting the power of the rabbis as well as that of Catholic priests. Napoleon's armies brought emancipation to many of Europe's Jews. While these laws were in many cases reversed after Napoleon's defeat, the principle of emancipation was subsequently adopted in many parts of Europe, including in the German Reich by 1871. Yet putting these principles into practice was often another matter, as there was considerable resistance from both Jews and non-Jews.[3]

Indeed, European Jews reacted in diverse ways to their own "emancipation." Some welcomed it with open arms, seeing it as a path to social equality and full access to European society; others saw it as a threat to their traditional ways of life. This led to a profound split between Orthodox traditionalists and proponents of integration and assimilation; the latter often called for a reform of Judaism to make its practice and doctrines more compatible with modern European life and scientific truth. To this disagreement (and often strife) within European Jewry, were to be added, as the century progressed, debates about the emerging movements of communism and Zionism. For a handful of Jewish scholars, studying the early history of Islam became a way of thinking through the history of Judaism and its relations with both Christianity and Islam.

Abraham Geiger: The Prophet as Monotheistic Reformer

Abraham Geiger (1810–1874) was a leader, in many ways one of the founders, of the reform movement in Judaism, which sought to bring innovations to the practice of Judaism. This included the use of the vernacular and the revision of traditional rabbinic regulations in an attempt to make life as a Jew more appealing and compatible to those who wished to integrate into an increasingly secular

European society. A reformed, modernized Judaism, Geiger and others hoped, would also diminish anti-Semitism by presenting a more attractive face to Gentile society. Geiger's scholarship on the history of Judaism, Christianity, and Islam was closely related to his reform project, as it was for the other scholars embarked in the *Wissenschaft des Judentums* movement.[4] Geiger was inspired in part by the work of German Protestant biblical scholars who had submitted the Bible to critical study, seeing it not as the product of divine revelation but of human composition. Careful textual critique could place scripture in its historical context and reveal the formation and development of religious communities.[5]

Part of Geiger's project was to show the priority and superiority of Judaism to Christianity and Islam, which he saw as derivative versions of Judaism. In 1833, as student in Bonn, he wrote a prize essay, *Was hat Mohammed aus dem Judentume aufgenommen?* (*What Has Muhammad Taken from Judaism?*, published in English under the rather innocuous title *Judaism and Islam*).[6] As the title indicates, Geiger, like Jewish and Christian polemicists before him, saw Mohammed as the author of the Qur'ān who exploited Jewish and Christian sources. But whereas earlier authors had used this idea to discredit both prophet and book, for Geiger Mohammed's dependence on, and relative faithfulness to, many of the fundamental texts and doctrines of Judaism is for the most part positive. Far from being an impostor, Mohammed was convinced of his mission as a reformer who, inspired by Jewish teachers, transmitted to the Arabs versions (sometimes modified) of biblical narratives and laws.

Geiger sought to show that the Qur'ān is largely derived from Rabbinical Judaism, that it reflects what Mohammed had learned from his Jewish teachers faithful to Torah, Mishna, and Talmud. Christian polemicists as early as the eighth century had situated the rise of Islam in the context of Christian heresy: Mahomet had been taught by heretics and it is their doctrine that he infused into his Alcoran. Some of them, for good measure, added bad Jews to the bad Christians who had taught Mahomet. Toland, as we have seen, turned this accusation on its head; the Nazarene Christians in seventh-century Arabia were the last followers of Jesus's true monotheism, which Mahomet renewed and reinvigorated. For a number of Enlightenment writers, Mahomet was essentially a Deist, proffering a pure monotheism stripped of needless laws and rituals, purified of pagan accretions, Trinity, saints.

Geiger has something else in mind. Through a rich and well-documented comparative study of Talmud and Qur'ān, he sought to show that Islam is essentially derivative of Judaism; indeed, that it is a form of Judaism, truer to the spirit and law of Moses than was Christianity. Yet it was an inferior form of Judaism, as the Qur'ān imperfectly transmitted biblical teachings. Why? In part because the Jews that Mohammed frequented were ignorant, as the compilers of the Talmud attest.[7] Mohammed "desired no peculiarity, no new religion which should oppose all that had gone before; he sought rather to establish one founded on the ancient creeds purified from later changes and additions."[8] Mohammed was not an impostor. He "seems rather to have been a genuine enthusiast [*Schwärmer*], who was himself convinced of his divine mission, and to whom the union of all religions appeared necessary to the welfare of mankind. He so fully worked himself into this idea in thought, in feeling and in action, that every event seemed to him a divine inspiration."[9]

Geiger's essay won acclaim from other specialists of Islam; indeed, it heralded new directions in the study of the Qur'ān, and more generally in comparative religion. He was twenty-three when he published his essay, and he would then leave aside scholarship on Islam, concentrating his academic efforts on the relations between Judaism and Christianity. Geiger followed with interest the recent developments in Protestant biblical exegesis, particularly the work of the Tübingen school, which critically analyzed biblical texts as entirely human creations and sources for understanding the history of the emergence and development of Christianity. David Strauss, in his *Das Leben Jesu, kritisch bearbeitet* (*The Life of Jesus, Critically Examined*, 1835), interpreted Jesus's miracles and resurrection as mythical elements created by the New Testament authors to lend a divine aura to Jesus's teaching. Geiger hailed Strauss's work as "epoch-making"[10] and sought to carry his methodology further by submitting rabbinical sources to the same critical methods and using them to complement and significantly modify Strauss's and the Tübingen school's vision of the emergence of Christianity from biblical Judaism. As early as 1836, Geiger wrote excitedly to Joseph Derenbourg that Talmud and Bible should no longer be seen as divinely authored texts, but as human creations.[11]

Geiger's scholarship, and his command of a wide range of texts in Hebrew, Aramaic, Greek, and Arabic, are impressive. His academic work was inseparable from his engagement for reform within German Judaism. In 1840, he was elected chief rabbi at Breslau, despite fierce opposition from more conservative members of the community, who subsequently attempted to have the Prussian authorities invalidate his election. In 1841, Geiger expressed his frustration in a letter to Leopold Zunz, confiding that efforts for compromise were unlikely to succeed and that the result would be a schism between Orthodox and Liberal factions. Tellingly, he likened the Orthodox Jews to the Catholics, clinging superstitiously to arcane rites, whereas the reformers were Jewish Protestants, attempting to purify their religion of superstition and return to a spiritual life consistent with rational science. Orthodox Jewry and the Catholic Church will both eventually wither and die.[12] Among Geiger's prescriptions for the reform of Jewish practice were the abolishment of phylacteries and the easing of dietary restrictions.

In 1863, Geiger published his *Das Judentum und seine Geschichte* (*Judaism and Its History*); his analysis of rabbinical texts alongside New Testament texts allowed him to present Jewish Palestine in Jesus's time as sharply divided between the priestly class, the Sadducees, who clung to ritual and were obsessed by purity, and the reforming Pharisees, whose interpretation of Judaism was more spiritual. Geiger's innovation is above all to make Jesus a Pharisee, engaged alongside the most dynamic and reforming tendencies of Judaism at the time against a sclerotic priestly oligarchy. The negative portrayal of Pharisees in various passages of the New Testament reflects not Jesus's own perspective but that of later (Pauline and post-Pauline) authors. Paul is truly the first Christian; he modifies Jesus's teachings, creating a new religion by mixing in elements of Greek philosophy, in order to attract Gentile converts.

Geiger's Jesus is a reforming Jew. Geiger bases his vision of the Pharisee/Sadducee split on a deep familiarity with the biblical and postbiblical sources and a projection onto the first centuries of the current era of the nineteenth-century conflicts within German Jewry. Orthodox Jews reacted negatively, some accusing him of hostility to Judaism; Gershom Scholem subsequently called him "diabolical."[13] Many Protestant scholars also were hostile to his portrayal of Jesus as a Pharisee; Pharisaic Judaism had been classically a foil for Jesus, the sclerotic traditional Judaism against which he was rebelling. Geiger's Jesus was a Jewish reformer, and it is hence Jewish reformers like Geiger himself who are closest to following the real teachings of Jesus; they better understand and more faithfully live out what Jesus had preached.

This vision was anathema to many traditional Jews and Christians. His arguments were all the more galling to them in that few could match his scholarly acumen and his impressive command of a huge arsenal of sources. Susannah Heschel has noted how both Paul and Mohammed represent paradoxical figures for Geiger, what she calls "strong misreaders"; inspired by Jewish tradition, they produced their own (mis)readings of it, tapping into the rich legal and spiritual fount of Judaism to produce new faiths more or less faithful to Judaism—less, in the case of Paul's Christianity, more, in the case of Mohammed's Islam. Yet Geiger himself produced new "strong misreadings" of the very texts produced by Paul, Mohammed, and their followers, in order to promote an agenda of religious renewal in which Judaism is recognized as the fount of Abrahamic spirituality rather than its despised offshoot. His Judaism is not hide-bound Orthodox/Sadducee ritual, but the spiritual renewal taught by Jesus and Mohammed. Geiger became increasingly anti-Christian as he saw persistent anti-Semitism around him and was frustrated that his Protestant fellow scholars did not seriously engage with his work on the early history of Christianity. Christianity, cursed by a "lust for destruction" (*Zerstöringswuth*), "smashed and destroyed everything humane, beautiful and noble that earlier times had produced." This is in stark contrast to Islam. Judaism, he says, "developed its own fullest potential in closest union with Arab civilization."[14] If for Toland Mahomet was a better Christian than eighteenth-century European Christians, Geiger's Mohammed is a better Jew than hide-bound Orthodox European Jews.

Gustav Weil's Reforming Enthusiast

Gustav Weil was a fellow student with Geiger at Heidelberg. Weil's grandfather was a rabbi at Metz, engaged in the movement of reform, and his family envisaged for him a career as a rabbi and theologian. Yet unlike Geiger, Weil decided he did not wish to become a rabbi and to join the intellectual and political struggle for reformed Judaism. He instead preferred to follow his love for Arabic. From Heidelberg, he went to Paris, to study under Silvestre de Sacy; he then went to Algeria with the French forces in 1830 (as a correspondent for a German newspaper), and, over the next five years went on to Cairo and Istanbul—writing for German newspapers, teaching French, studying Arabic, Persian, and Turkish.[15] One of the publications he wrote for was the *Morgenblatt für gebildete Stände*, whose contributors included Goethe, Heine and Humboldt. It is to this audience, and with the situation of German Jews in mind, that he wrote his observations of Egyptian Muslims, whose religious beliefs and practices he often compares to those of European Jews, frequently to criticize both. He derides the rituals of Jewish kosher and Muslim hallal butchers; mocks Jews' and Muslims' superstitious use of amulets and fear of the evil eye. Yet there is hope for both, and here Weil presents reform Judaism as a model for Muslim reform:[16]

> The Muslim religion is also capable of improvement and spiritualization and one does not understand why Islam cannot be friendly with Christianity like enlightened Judaism. Like the civilized part of European Israelites who become enemies of orthodox 'rabbinism' the more they take part in universal culture, so also will Muslims soon, once they have rejected their crass ignorance, differentiate the elements of their Koran which come from specific circumstances from those that are eternally true and are not subject to change.[17]

Weil returned to Germany in 1837; the following year he became librarian at Heidelberg, where he was finally appointed professor in 1861. He published works on Arabic poetry and German translations of Arabic texts, in particular the *1001 Nights*. He also embarked on a series of studies of the early history of Islam: a biography of Muhammad (1843), a *Historisch-kritische Einleitung in den Koran* (*Historical-Critical Introduction to the Koran*, 1844), a *Biblische Legenden der Muselmänner: Aus arabischen Quellen zusammengetragen und mit jüdischen Sagen verglichen* (1845, published in English the following year as *The Bible, the Koran, and the Tal-*

mud), and a history of the caliphate (in several volumes between 1846 and 1862).

Weil shared Geiger's methods of applying the tools of biblical criticism to the text of the Qur'ān, and he shared his concerns for the renewal of Judaism, though unlike Geiger he never became a rabbi. But while Geiger moved on to focus on Jewish-Christian relations after publishing *Was hat Mohammed aus dem Judentume aufgenommen* at the age of twenty-three, Weil devoted his life and career to the study of Arabic literature and history and to Islam. His approach to these texts showed more sympathy and more maturity than that of the twenty-three-year-old Geiger to the Qur'ān. Geiger used the Muslim holy text to show that Muhammad derived his teachings from Jewish sources, whereas Weil, without ignoring the context of rabbinic Judaism, placed the Qur'ān in a broader context of Jewish, Christian, and pre-Islamic Arab textual history. Like Geiger, Weil sees Mohammed as a reformer; unlike him, he does not portray Islam as an inferior form of Jewish monotheism. Geiger never left Europe, his knowledge of Arabic and of Islam was acquired through books; whereas Weil had spent five years studying in the Near East. The result was a profound knowledge of the language and foundational texts of Islam and a detachment from the earlier European polemics about the prophet.

Let us take the example of Mohammed's alleged epilepsy, which Weil tackles in a short article published in 1842.[18] He notes that Hottinger and Marracci affirmed that "Mahomet" was indeed epileptic and that they cited Byzantine historians and several ambiguous passages in the Qur'ān. Others (Ockley, Gagnier, and Sale) rejected these accusations, judging that little trust could be put in the testimony of hostile Christian authors. In other words, those seeking to denigrate Islam and its prophet were ready to believe anything nasty they read, whereas those who defended him rejected anything negative. Weil is the first non-Muslim author to take a close look at Muslim traditions to see what they say on this issue. He cites passages from two sixteenth-century texts: al-Halabi's biography of the prophet, *Insān al-ʿuyūn* and Husayn ibn Muhammad Diyar Bakari's *Tarikh al Khamis*, both of which refer to a passage in Ibn Ishaq's *Sira* and to various hadiths. These texts describe how, when the prophet received a revelation, his body shook, he fell to the ground, he foamed from the mouth, his eyes closed, he moaned like a camel, his forehead was soaked in perspiration. Aisha is reported to have said that each time he was in the throes of a revelation, all feared that his soul would leave him. Weil presents each of these texts in Arabic with a French translation and a brief analysis. In conclusion, he says that he no longer has the slightest doubt that Mahomet indeed suffered from epilepsy. However, he rejects the view of Marracci and others that he pretended to be a prophet in order to hide his illness.

> I believe, on the contrary, that Mahomet himself attributed his fits to the visits of an angel. Nothing is more natural than to suppose that Mahomet, always occupied with his ideas of reform (for he at first thought of destroying idolatry and purging Judaism and Christianity of their errors), and probably provoking his fits by excessively strong spiritual struggles, believed indeed in the visionary state in which the epileptics find themselves at the moment of coming to their senses, that he had learned from an angel what his reason dictated to him, which was his subject of preoccupation before his fit. و الله اعلم [And God knows best]. (112)

This example is illustrative of Weil's approach to texts, which he will develop over the following years. His access to the earliest sources is often indirect. He carefully sifts through them and bases his conclusions, always reasonable and well argued, on the evidence they present. Yet there is little trace here of the healthy skepticism toward his sources that we find in the biblical scholarship of the Tübingen school or in Geiger's deconstruction of postbiblical Jewish sources. Weil presents these hadiths, which he gleaned from sixteenth-century compilations on the biography of the prophet, as unproblematically reporting the words of Aisha, of various of Mahomet's companions, of the prophet himself. Like his predecessors, he seeks to explain religious phenomena through wholly human causes, and the prophet's supposed epilepsy allows him to do so while respecting Mahomet's integrity and zeal for reform. This is of course a vision that could displease pious Muslims, and as if to soften this he adds the standard Arabic "God knows best."

This same lack of critical approach to his sources appears in his biography of the prophet published the following year. He states his purpose in very positivistic, Rankean terms:

> I have studied the active life of Mohammad without prejudice in any form and followed the sources, exploring and scrutinizing them step by step, and most assiduously aspired after the historical truth, free from the aura in which it is wrapped.[19]

His life of the prophet is indeed free of the bias that is so apparent in many of the texts we have examined in this book. Weil does not make the prophet into a caricature or the symbol of a cause. Yet his approach to the (often rather late) Muslim sources that he uses in his biography of Mohammed consists largely in stripping them of their obviously legendary or miraculous elements, rather than studying the history of their composition.

Weil's Mohammed is no impostor, but a sincere reformer. In accordance with Geiger and with many of the eighteenth-century authors we examined in chapter six, Weil's Mohammed seeks to renew the pure, primitive monotheism of Abraham.[20] Weil prides himself in relying on Muslim Arabic sources and not on the polemical texts of Christianity, and by and large he does so. Yet his portrait of the prophet remains framed by many of the texts we have examined here. We see this particularly clearly in the central role he assigns to Waraqa, Khadīja's cousin who, for most Muslim commentators of the Qur'ān, was Christian—and one of the first to recognize in Muhammad God's prophet. Whereas some Christian polemicists had made him (along with Bahīra) as a heretical Christian and one of the authors of the "heretical" text of the Qur'ān, Weil paints a very different portrait of him:

> Mohamed was probably indebted for his religious education to a man who, abandoning the religion of Arabia, his native country, had sought refuge first in Judaism, and then in Christianity, though even in the latter he does not seem to have found perfect satisfaction. This man . . . urged forward by an irresistible desire after the knowledge of truth but, as his repeated apostasies would serve to show, being of a skeptical nature, may have discovered the errors that had crept into all the religious

systems of his time; and having extracted from that which is purely Divine, and freed it from the inventions of men, may have propounded it to his disciple.[21]

Waraqa is a searcher for truth who, in dissatisfaction, goes from one religion to another, and who inculcates into his young disciple a desire for a purified religion in the service of Truth. This depiction of Waraqa is an implicit condemnation of both Judaism and Christianity, and Weil's nineteenth-century preoccupations show through his (largely speculative) portrait of Waraqa as a seventh-century reformer. In later work Weil more explicitly lambasted Christianity for its abstruse doctrines whose interpretations have given rise to conflicts and divisions, for its elaborate sacraments; to this he contrasts the simplicity of Islam and its lack of priesthood.[22]

Many of the previous authors we have dealt with contrast the prophet and visionary of the Meccan period with the warrior, lawgiver, and statesman of the Medinan period. Weil stresses and sharpens this divide, portraying favorably Mohammed's life and message in Mecca but largely negatively the developments in Medina. As Ruchama Johnston-Bloom has suggested, this corresponds with Weil's vision for Jewish reform, which should concentrate on spiritual and moral purity (as Mohammed in Mecca) and not on hair-splitting legal distinctions (which he sees in Medina).

> He appears to us as a prophet only so long as he was a persecuted man in Mecca. Then seized by religious enthusiasm he might have felt the call to proclaim a new faith, and, in consequence of his bodily infirmity, may have believed God revealed himself to him by means of angels, visions and dreams. But upon his arrival at Medina self-deception ceased, and at best he could have only justified himself in deceiving others by the maxim "The end justifies the means."[23]

At Mecca, the faithful disciple of Waraqa seeks a purified reformed monotheism very close to Weil's own vision for reformed Judaism; in Medina, he becomes someone else, no longer a pure searcher for Truth, but nevertheless one who inspires esteem:

> We would pronounce him a crafty statesman who accomplished great things, partly from love for his people, partly from ambition. We can give him our approval as reformer of Judaism and Christianity, as a

civilizer [*Sittenverbesserer*], and as the preacher of pure monotheism and of the doctrines of immortality and the judgment, and, considering his many misfortunes at first, we cannot withhold our admiration.[24]

It is above all in the study of the Qur'ān that Weil made a lasting impact on scholarship. He sought to refine Geiger's method and carry his work further. It was Weil, in the 1840s, who first took up the traditional Muslim division of the Qur'ān into Meccan and Medina suras; he reassessed the dating of some of them and further tried to order them into four different chronological groups (three for the Meccan suras and one for Medinan). This careful attention to the language of the suras, their formulaic elements and their structure, is a first in European scholarship and in many ways represents the foundation of modern European Qur'ānic studies. Theodor Nöldeke followed up on Weil's methods and insights in his own *Geschichte des Qorāns* (1860), which has been indispensable to Qur'ānic scholars ever since.[25]

In Weil's account, Islam was a purified version of both Judaism and Christianity. He describes it in *The Bible, the Koran, and the Talmud* as, "A Judaism without the many ritual and ceremonial laws, which, according to Mohamed's declaration, even Christ had been called to abolish, or a Christianity without the Trinity, crucifixion and salvation connected therewith."[26] Weil's Islam, like Sale's or Voltaire's, is Enlightenment Deism: Judaism without law, Christianity without dogma.

Heinrich Graetz's Brilliant Pupil of an Arabian Rabbi

Heinrich Graetz (1817–1891) was critical of the work of Geiger and many of the reformers; he set out to defend his vision of Orthodox Judaism through exegesis and through the study of Jewish history.[27] His massive eleven-volume *History of the Jews* (1863–70), sweeping from biblical times to the nineteenth century, celebrates the Jews' special place in history. Graetz deals with Jesus by making him an Essene, a good, spiritual Jew perhaps, but one who was on the margins of institutional Judaism—a very different character from Geiger's reforming Pharisee. Indeed, Geiger and his ilk were anathema to Graetz; their reform was nothing less than the surreptitious

Christianization of Judaism, and he vowed to fight them to his "last breath."[28] In his *History*, Graetz chronicles Christian persecution of Jews and rails against its perpetrators, including medieval popes such as Innocent III. Islam serves as a foil to his Christianity, both closer to Judaism as a faith and more tolerant of Jews in society. Oriental Jews had welcomed the Muslim conquerors of the seventh century as "liberators from the yoke of Christianity"; the "Mahometans" treated Jews with respect and friendship.[29]

In the third volume of his *History of the Jews*, he describes the Jewish communities of the Arabian Peninsula in the sixth and seventh centuries and in this context evokes the life of Muhammad.

> Mahomet, the prophet of Mecca and Yathrib, was, it is true, no loyal son of Judaism, but approached to its highest aims, and was induced by it to give to the world a new faith, founded on a lofty basis and known as Islam. This religion has exercised a wonderful influence on the aspect of Jewish history and on the evolution of Judaism. In the peaceful meetings in Mecca, his birthplace, Abdallah's son heard much spoken in the temples and on his travels of the religion which acknowledges the belief in one God who rules the world. He heard much of Abraham, who devoted himself to the service of God, and of religion and morality, which gave the disciples of Judaism the advantage over infidels. Mahomet's mind, at once original and receptive, was powerfully impressed by all this. Waraka Ibn-Naufal, a celebrated Meccan, and a descendant of the noble Khoraish race, was a cousin of Chadija, Mahomet's wife, and he had embraced Judaism and knew Hebrew well. He certainly imbued Mahomet with a love for the religion of Abraham.[30]

Graetz's Mahomet is singularly well disposed toward Judaism. While Muslim tradition in general presented Khadīja's cousin Waraqa as a Christian, Weil, as we have seen, made him first a Jew, then a Christian, but satisfied with neither; for Graetz he is an Arab convert to Judaism. Thus Graetz portrays Qur'ānic doctrine as the result of the teaching that a sage Arabian Jew dispensed on a smart and dutiful pupil. One of the things Mahomet learned from Waraka was to insist on God's unity and thus to reject the Christian doctrine of the Trinity. When he went to Yathrib, that city's Jews welcomed him as a learned and pious man and saw him as a potential proselyte to Judaism. Yet his haughtiness and love of women, Graetz affirms, turned them against him. This leads Mahomet to hate the Medinan Jews and plot their destruction.

Geiger wrote scathing reviews of Graetz's work, saying that Graetz "lacks totally that historical perspective, that insight, which would make constructive use of the subject matter"; he writes "stories" (*Geschichten*), but not "history" (*Geschichte*).[31] Graetz had none of Geiger's deep familiarity with the Arabic texts, and his naive, positivistic view of history was starkly different from Geiger's critical approach to his sources. Yet their portraits of Mahomet are in many ways similar. The prophet's mission is on the whole positive, and it is positive precisely because he takes inspiration from Judaism, taps into its texts and traditions, and offers a society for the most part tolerant of Jews. "The best teachings of the Koran are borrowed from the bible or the Talmud," says Graetz;[32] Geiger had concluded largely the same. Mahomet errs where he departs from his Jewish sources and his Jewish teachers. Neither of them explicitly compares Mahomet to Jesus; Graetz compares him to Paul, suggesting that both started out preaching "the ancient religion of Abraham" but subsequently were led astray by their own ambitions.[33] Geiger and Graetz both compare Islam to Christianity, the better to criticize the latter as irrational and intolerant. Graetz follows Weil in giving a central importance to Waraqa, but with a key distinction: Weil's Waraqa was a restless reformer who went from traditional Arabic paganism to Judaism to Christianity—ever unsatisfied, he inspired Mohammed's new teachings, which resemble nothing more than Weil's (or Geiger's) own notions of Jewish reform. Graetz's Waraqa is a good Jew who clearly is uninterested in reform, who on the contrary teaches pure Jewish tradition to his bright (but alas finally wayward) pupil.

Ashkenaz Dreams of a Lost Sefardi Paradise

Islam and Muhammad were important to many nineteenth-century European Jews among other things because they served as a foil to Christian Europe. They provided arguments against anti-Semites, who accused Jews of being unable to assimilate into European culture. By underlining the tolerance shown toward Jews (and Christians) by Islam, and by highlighting how Jews flourished under

Islam and contributed to the development of Islamic culture, these Jewish thinkers argued (sometimes explicitly, often implicitly), that the problem was with Christianity, an intolerant and irrational faith. Writing about Islam was both a way of arguing about Jews' proper place in European society (hence the lessons to be drawn were of course not the same for assimilationists as for traditionalists) and of indulging in a fantasy world, far from the persecution and pogroms of nineteenth-century Europe, a land where Jews could live in harmony with their non-Jewish neighbors.

Al-Andalus, Muslim Spain, became a particular focus of interest. This is a time when European Romantics, travelers, artists, and writers rediscovered Muslim Spain, and when historians of science and philosophy documented the crucial role that it had played in European intellectual history. Heinrich Heine's play *Almansor* (1823), set in sixteenth-century Alhambra, dramatizes the contrast between tolerant Islam and bigoted Christianity. The protagonists are Muslims subjected to increasing persecution at the hands of their new Christian overlords. One character laments, "On the tower where the muezzin called to prayer there is now the melancholy tolling of church bells. On the steps where the faithful sang the words of the Prophet, tonsured monks are acting out their lugubrious charades."[34] The protagonist Almansor reports to his friend Hassan that "Ximenes the Terrible" has burned the Qur'ān at Granada. Hassan responds, "That was only a prelude; where they burn books they will, in the end, burn human beings too."[35]

Nothing speaks more eloquently of this image of Andalus as a lost paradise of flourishing Judaism within Islamic culture than the string of Moorish-style synagogues built throughout central Europe in the nineteenth century. The legal emancipation of Jews meant, among other things, that they could buy land and build synagogues to serve not only as houses of worship for growing communities but also as prominent symbols of their new place in European society. While many synagogues were built in "Christian" styles (neo-Gothic, neo-Classical), with only decorative elements distinguishing them from churches, a number of reformed Jewish communities chose the Moorish Revival style. In Leipzig (1855), Vienna (1858), Budapest (1859), Berlin (1866), and elsewhere, sumptuous synagogues rose up, graced with domes, horseshoe arches, elaborate stucco tracery, and towers that looked like minarets.[36] Yet Ludwig Förster, designer of the Vienna and Budapest synagogues (and one of the chief architects of Vienna's Ringstraße), explained that the twin towers on either side of the entrance to the Vienna synagogue were based on those that graced the temple of Solomon—an ancient "Oriental" model that was adapted by Muslims.[37]

Ignác Goldziher

Ignác Goldziher (1850–1921) revolutionized the study of Islam by Europeans.[38] Born in the central Hungarian town of Székesfehérvár, Goldziher met Geiger and was inspired by his vision of a reform of Judaism. Schooled in Hebrew and Arabic, he studied in Pest, Berlin, Leipzig, Leiden, and Vienna. In two essays written in Hungarian in 1872–73, he portrays Mohammed as the bearer of a universal message of pure monotheism, who struggled to overcome tribal divisions among Arabs.[39] In 1873–74, at the age of twenty-three, he traveled to Istanbul, Beirut, Damascus, Jerusalem, and Cairo, where he became the first European enrolled in al-Azhar. He sought out Muslim thinkers, particularly those interested in reform. This sets him apart from many of his contemporary European Orientalists who were interested above all in texts: "I wanted to observe the people, their ideas and institutions, not chase after yellowed papers."[40] In Damascus he met Tāhir al-Jazā'irī, a twenty-two-year-old partisan of Islamic reform and Arab cultural renewal. Goldziher enthusiastically joined the group of young reformers around al-Jazā'irī; the deep friendship and mutual admiration is seen in the writings of both.[41] In Cairo he similarly developed a close friendship with Jamāl al-Dīn al-Afghānī, whose attempts to reform Islamic doctrine and practice, unite Muslims, and resist British and French imperialism provoked Goldziher's enthusiasm. Muslim reform could serve as a model for Jewish reform.

> In those weeks, I truly entered into the spirit of Islam to such an extent that ultimately I became inwardly convinced that I myself was a Muslim, and judiciously discovered that this was the only religion which, even in its doctrinal and official formulation, can satisfy philosophic minds. My ideal was to elevate Judaism to a similar rational level.

Islam, as my experience taught me, is the only religion, in which superstitious and heathen ingredients are not frowned upon by rationalism, but by orthodox doctrine.[42]

Goldziher, in his own words, becomes a Muslim without ever ceasing to be a Jew. His experience of Islam inspires him to try to reform Judaism, to bring it up to the level of Islam. As he describes his studies at al-Azhar, he says,

My formal way of thinking was through and through oriented toward Islam; subjectively, my emotional empathy also drew me hither. I called my monotheism Islam, and I did not lie when I said that I believed in the prophecies of Muhammad. My copy of the Qur'ān can bear witness to how I was inwardly inclined to Islam. My teachers earnestly awaited the moment of my open profession of faith.[43]

Yet that moment did not come. Goldziher preferred the ambiguous liminal position, neither inside nor outside, still a Jew and almost a Muslim, or perhaps both Jew and Muslim. Because he had not professed Islam, he was not allowed to participate in Friday services. He describes how a Syrian friend helped him, how he visited the tomb of Shāfi'ī and then rode, clad in turban and kaftan, to the mosque where, amid thousands of the faithful, he prayed and rubbed his forehead against the floor of the mosque. "Never in my life was I more devout, more truly devout, than on that exalted Friday."[44]

Not that he was uncritical of what he saw; many Muslims, like Jews, clung to silly rites for which he showed contempt: the whirling of Istanbul dervishes or the scraping and bowing of Damascenes performing *salat*.[45] Yet he holds up Islam, in the reformed vision of Jazā'irī, Afghānī, and others, and contrasts it with the conservatism of traditional rabbinic Judaism, whose partisans are frequent targets of Goldziher's contempt: "sniffing some mishnayot" they practice arcane rites tainted with "the most cunning power of idol worship."[46] "I cannot think of rabbinism without adding an *écrasez l'infâme*," he says, taking up Voltaire's rallying cry, denouncing the "cynical raw stuff which is called Synagogue or Church."[47] We are far from Geiger's vision of Islam as a respectable but inferior form of Judaism. As for Christianity, it is an "abominable religion, which invented the Christian blood libel"; it engenders "the worst degree of fanaticism."[48] When he visits the Church of the Holy Sepulchre in Jerusalem, he laments that, far from being a site of monotheism, it has become a place of idolatry, where the superstitious genuflect and kiss stones.[49]

Goldziher returns home from his glorious "Mohammedan year" to disappointment. The chair he had been hoping for had been given to someone else. It was not to be his until 1905. In the intervening years, he toiled as secretary of the Neolog, the Reformed Jewish community of Budapest, going to work every day at the community's Moorish synagogue. He describes the work as drudgery, and his position there was no doubt at times made more difficult for him by the frosty reception given to his ideas on Jewish reform not only among the Orthodox but also in his own community. Yet he stayed on, refusing prestigious positions at Cambridge, Heidelberg, Königsberg, Prague, and Strasbourg as well as at the new universities in Cairo and Jerusalem. He was a Hungarian who remained committed to nationalism and integration—and hostile to Zionism. In his early work, published in the 1870s, he dealt with both Islam and Judaism.[50] He was interested in the scientific study of the fundamental texts of Judaism as a key both to pushing reform within European Judaism and to countering the arguments of anti-Semites. In 1876 he published his *Der Mythos bei den Hebräern und seine geschichtliche Entwickelung* (*Mythology among the Hebrews and Its Historical Development*), a learned rebuttal to French Orientalist Ernest Renan. Renan had drawn a sharp distinction between the mindset of the Aryans, inclined to polytheism, mythology, the perception of multiple truths and possibilities (and hence also to science), and that of monotheistic Semites (Jews and Muslims), who had no mythology and no propensity for philosophical or scientific thinking. "I am the first person to recognize that the Semitic race, compared to the Indoeuropean race, really represents an inferior mix of human nature," affirmed Renan in his *Histoire générale et système comparé des langues sémitiques* (*General History and Comparative System of the Semitic Langauges*).[51] Goldziher's work methodically, coldly, and completely destroyed Renan's arguments, which hence (*pace* Edward Said) would have little impact on future Orientalism.[52] Goldziher had no problem showing that both the

Hebrew bible and the Qur'ān were full of myth, and that Jews and Muslims had shown themselves fully capable of science and philosophy. He sent his work to Renan, who responded with a graceful thank you note, showed him exquisite hospitality on a visit to Paris, and completely ignored his criticisms in his subsequent writings. Renan died in 1892, and the following year Goldziher published an essay on "Renan as Orientalist," which was both an homage to him as a scholar and at the same time a scathing rebuttal of his pet theories on the Semitic mind.[53]

At the same time as he struggled against Renan's anti-Semitic theories, he continued to promote his vision of Enlightenment reform of Judaism in Hungary. In 1877 he received a diploma from the Israelite Teaching Association, according him the status of honorary member. The diploma itself illustrates the ambitions of the Neolog community to education, emancipation, and Magyarization of the Jewish community. At the top center is Moses descending from Mount Sinai bearing the tablets of the law, with at each side educational materials: Hebrew books on the right; other books, along with scientific instruments, on the left. Moses is flanked by scenes of modern European Jewish teaching. Immediately underneath are portraits of Moses Maimonides and Moses Mendelssohn, emphasizing the twin bases of rational philosophical theology and of Haskala, or Jewish Enlightenment. Below them are two non-Jews: Johann Heinrich Pestalozzi, representing reform in modern education, and István Széchenyi, Hungarian nationalist. The Dohány Synagogue is pictured. The texts, in Hebrew, German, and Hungarian, emphasize the three languages central to the culture and identity of Hungarian Jews. This vision corresponds well with Goldziher's own ideas on the place of education and reform in the reshaping of Hungarian Jewry, and he is no doubt in agreement with the members of the Neolog community that employed him at their synagogue. Yet over the coming decade, their visions would diverge and Goldziher would be increasingly marginalized within his own community.

Goldziher delivered a series of six lectures in Budapest in 1887–88 on "The Essence and Evolution of Judaism." He cast Judaism as a prophetic religion corrupted by rabbinic superstition; he grounded the need for reform and purification on the thought of Judaism's outstanding historical figures. Purified Judaism, moreover, is consistent with modern civilization and scientific truth. His Islam, and his vision of Muhammad as reformer and purifier of Abrahamic religion, clearly played a role in his conception of the reform needed for Judaism, just as it had for Geiger. These lectures were badly received by the Budapest Jewish community, who increasingly saw Goldziher as a threat to Judaism. Deeply disappointed, Goldziher abandoned his study of Judaism and henceforth devoted his scholarship almost exclusively to Islam. He wrote prolifically in Hungarian and offered carefully crafted summae of his research in German, notably in his *Muhammedanische Studien* (1889–90).[54]

Goldziher did not write a biography of Muhammad. He no doubt felt that there was no need for him to do so. What he tries to do is to use the fundamental texts of Islam, Qur'ān and hadiths, to trace the emergence of the Muslim community and of Muslim religious and legal doctrine over the course of the first Muslim centuries. The Qur'ān, for Goldziher, offers a glimpse at two key moments in the emergence of the Muslim community. In the Meccan period, before the Hijra, Muhammad, a "warner and messenger," preached asceticism and moral reform before the imminent apocalypse; he "saw himself as the last of the ancient prophets" and had not intended to found a new religion.[55] The Medinese suras show a quite different picture of the prophet and his growing community; here the prophet is "further inspired by the holy spirit" but is concerned foremost with governing his fledgling Muslim community. From a warner, he became a warrior, conqueror, statesman, and organizer. It is in Medina that Islam was born as a faith community. The hadiths, for Goldziher, represent a third phase in the development of the Muslim community; they reflect the debates and struggles within the new Muslim empire, debates that were projected back on to the now mythic figure of the prophet, arguments about Islam in eighth-century Syria or ninth-century Iraq presented as sayings in the mouth of the prophet.

The result is a religion and a civilization that is both hybrid and eclectic, based on elements gleaned from Judaism, from Christianity, from Neoplatonic philosophy, from Persian, Greek, and Indian cultures. For Christian polemicists, this hybrid and derivative nature of Islam had been proof that Mahomet was an impostor. For others, it had shown that, despite its merits, the faith of Mahomet was an imperfect form of true Christianity or Judaism. Yet for Goldziher this eclectic, inclusive, integrative nature is the great strength of Islam:

> Its dogmatic development betrays Hellenistic thought; its legal form shows the unmistakable influence of Roman Law; its civic organization, as it is unfolded in the Abbasid caliphate, shows the moulding of Persian civic ideas, while its mysticism illustrates the appropriation of Neoplatonic and Indian ways of thought. But in each one of these fields Islam proves its capability to assimilate and work over foreign elements, so that its foreign character is evident only through the sharp analysis of critical investigation. This receptive character stamps Islam from its very birth. Its founder, Mohammed, proclaims no new ideas. He brought no new contribution to the thoughts concerning the relation of man to the supernatural and infinite. This fact, however, does not in the least lessen the relative worth of his religious conception. When the historian of morals wishes to decide on the effect of an historical event, the question of its originality is not uppermost in his consideration. In an historical estimate of the ethical system of Mohammed the question is not whether the content of his proclamation was original in every way, the absolute pioneer conception of his soul. The proclamation of the Arabian Prophet is an eclectic composition of religious views to which he was aroused through his contact with Jewish, Christian and other elements, by which he himself was strongly moved and which he regarded as suitable for the awakening of an earnest religious disposition among his people. His ordinances, although taken from foreign sources, he recognized as necessary for the moulding of life in accordance with the divine will. His inmost soul was so aroused that those influences which had thus awakened him became inspirations that were confirmed by outward impressions and by divine revelations, of which he sincerely felt himself to be the instrument.[56]

Goldziher approaches his Muslim sources with no preconceived notions of the superiority of Jewish or Christian sources; he carefully studies the development of these sources over time in an attempt to trace the parallel development of the Muslim community and doctrine. His work was fundamental to European studies of Islam. According to twentieth-century scholar Carl Heinrich Becker in homage to Goldziher following his death in 1921, he "gave us the tools with which we work; he created the categories in which we think."[57]

The Tübingen school had demoted Bible to the production of human authors and had analyzed it as source material for the history of Judaism and Christianity. Geiger had applied the same techniques to postbiblical Jewish sources and to the Qur'ān. Goldziher's innovation was to apply these same techniques to hadiths, showing how they reflected the concerns not of the prophet himself but of Muslims who lived in a very different world from Muhammad's, the sprawling, religiously diverse, culturally heterogeneous Umayyad and Abbasid caliphates. Many hadiths are little more than pious fabrications, for Goldziher, who quotes Basra traditionist 'Asim al-Nabil, who affirmed, "I have come to the conclusion that a pious man is never so ready to lie as in matters of the hadith."[58] Abbasid scholars created hadiths and Quranic exegesis that bolstered the legitimacy of their dynastic line; at the same time, they invalidated traditions that might be seen to legitimate Shi'i dynastic claims.[59]

Goldziher devotes a long chapter of his *Muhammedanische Studien* to the "Veneration of Saints in Islam."[60] He begins by noting, "In ancient Islam an insurmountable barrier divides an infinite and unapproachable Godhead from weak and finite humanity."[61] The Qur'ān makes clear that Mohammed, like the prophets who came before him, is fully human. When asked to perform miracles, he retorts that he is only a man. Early Islamic doctrine, reflected in the earliest hadiths, emphasizes Mohammed's humanity and fallibility. The one thing that separates him from earlier prophets is that while they were sent each to a nation, Mohammed alone had a universal mission. God's choice of Mohammed as prophet is an arbitrary act of divine will; it can in no way be the result of the prophet's own merits. The Qur'ān unequivocally condemns as *shirk* (heresy) the veneration of humans, however pious they be, and specifically warns Muslims against attributing anything more than human status to Mohammed.

Yet quite early, Goldziher shows, no doubt even during the prophet's lifetime, some of his followers were convinced that he was graced with supernatural gifts, omniscience, and had performed various miracles. Within a century after his death, a thousand miracles had been attributed to him. Relics of the prophet, hairs, shoes, or footprints, became objects of veneration. Whereas earlier writers had used stories of Muhammad's miracles or of his celestial voyage to discredit the prophet, Goldziher draws a clear distinction between the prophet whose message is faithfully transmitted in the Qur'ān and the later legendary accounts that go against the simple and pure message that Mohammed had preached.

For the authors whose work we have examined in this chapter, thinking and writing about Muhammad and Islam is inseparable from thinking and writing about Judaism and Christianity. Geiger, Weil, and Goldziher were scholars who sought to understand the origins of Islam, but their concerns about European Jews, about the tensions between tradition and reform, assimilation and anti-Semitism, were never far from their minds. Just as contemporary European Christians looked to Muhammad as a spiritual hero whose piety could serve as a model for disenchanted European romantics, for some nineteenth-century Jews the Muslim prophet could serve as a heuristic model for reforming Judaism. And increasingly some European Christians, in the late nineteenth and twentieth centuries, would argue that Muhammad should be recognized as a prophet, as we shall see in the next chapter.

CHAPTER NINE

Prophet of an Abrahamic Faith

IN 1931, JUST FOUR YEARS before Adolf Weinman sculpted his vision of Muhammad as part of a pantheon of lawgivers, French painter Louis Bouquet presented a very different portrait of the prophet as part of a mural for the Musée des colonies in Paris (fig. 17). Muhammad sits on cushions on a stone seat, behind him a horseshoe arch perhaps meant to represent a mihrab. A winged angel sporting a fez, no doubt meant to be Gabriel, descends from heaven: the angel's left hand makes a sign of blessing over the prophet's head; the right hand is cupped over the prophet's ear, suggesting that a revelation is being made. Muhammad sits upright, arms open, facing the viewer. A pastiche of minarets and other fragments of North African architecture rises to create a cityscape running along the top of the scene. The other panels of the mural depict Arab philosophers and mathematicians as well as musicians, artisans, and everyday figures. Whereas other nineteenth- and twentieth-century artists and writers avoided the religious nature of Muhammad's role, portraying him as a political genius, military hero, sage lawmaker, and moral model, Bouquet on the contrary recognizes, and seems to celebrate, Muhammad as a prophet receiving revelation from Gabriel and transmitting it to his followers.

Bouquet's Muhammad is part of a fresco in the salon Reynaud or salon d'Afrique, celebrating Africa's contribution to world civili-

FIGURE 17. Muhammad, detail from the mural by Louis Bouquet, Salon du Ministre Paul Reynaud in the Musée des Colonies, Paris, 1931. © RMN-Grand Palais / Jean-Gilles Berizzi. © ADAGP, Paris, 2018

zation. It may seem curious to make Muhammad into an African, but from Paris in 1931, in the context of France's colonial empire, Islam was perhaps seen first and foremost as the principal religion of many of France's African colonies. Indeed, Bouquet's work was part of a major program of painting and sculpture for the 1931 museum, which was part of the L'Exposition coloniale, a showcase for French colonialism.[1] The exposition stretched over a vast expanse from the Porte Dorée through much of the Bois de Vincennes, with pavilions meant to represent the indigenous architectural styles of French colonies, while the "métropole" was represented by modern architecture, highlighting the developmental gap between France and its colonies. The purpose of this costly and elaborate endeavor was to promote and celebrate France's colonial empire. As Marcel Olivier, commissionner of the exposition, affirmed, "Colonization, born of the spirit of domination, appears finally as an instrument of peace."[2] The exposition provoked hostility and protests notably from "indigènes" living in Paris. Paris between the wars was a colonial metropolis—not only the capital of empire but also a place where the colonial elites from Africa, Lebanon, Southeast Asia, and elsewhere met, compared their experiences, and increasingly denounced the contradictions between republican ideals and colonial realities.[3] Members of the French left also protested the exhibition: the communist party as well as Parisian surrealists, including André Breton, Paul Éluard, and Louis Aragon. Opponents published pamphlets denouncing the violence and oppression of French colonialism and organized a counterexposition cataloging massacres, forced labor, and exploitation.[4] The main exposition's organizers, Olivier and Marshal Louis Hubert Gonzalve Lyautey, were careful to keep such dissent away from the exposition, which on the contrary offered Parisians and other visitors a chance to visit a sanitized, pacified miniature version of France's colonial empire, without conflict or contestation, without dirt or blood, populated by smiling subservient natives in traditional garb.

In this context, Bouquet's African salon celebrated a peaceful, exoticized African culture, of which Islam was an integral part. Other painters and sculptors illustrated the benefits that France brought to its colonies. In larger-than-life art deco murals, Pierre-Henri Ducos de la Haille depicts pères blancs freeing half-naked

Africans from their chains, French doctors healing Asian patients, French archaeologists and scientists conducting their research. Everywhere, natives are engaged in peaceful and productive agriculture, crafts, and commerce. A background of billowing sails and white doves of peace sets the tone. The facade of the building sports a huge monumental frieze by Alfred-Auguste Janniot, depicting natives of France's colonial empire similarly engaged in farming, fishing, and trade, working together for French grandeur. Inscribed on the side of the building, in huge letters, is an homage of the nation to "its sons who through their genius extended the empire and made the nation's name loved beyond the seas," followed by a list of names from Godfrey of Bouillon (hero of the First Crusade and king of crusader Jerusalem) to Saint Louis and a long list of national heroes of French colonialism down to 1926. In this monument to French colonialism, "colonized and colonizer danced in a fascinating, ambivalent embrace."[5] This is a "sommet de l'art colonial,"[6] both a jewel of art deco and a work of unabating (and not particularly subtle) propaganda. As such, it has been something of an embarrassment to French historians of art, who have been reticent to address it.

Bouquet's Muhammad is thus an enigmatic figure. On the one hand, a rare acknowledgment of the spiritual nature of the prophet's mission, in clear and positive terms: Muhammad is the prophet of Islam, he receives revelations from God via the Archangel Gabriel and transmits them to his followers, who include the various scholars and mystics represented around him. Yet he is in some ways a colonized prophet; this African Mahomet is part of a regional culture that is subsumed into a larger and greater whole. Islam is regional; France is universal. It is the French empire, not Islam, that represents modernity and progress. Mahomet has his assigned role in the drama of French colonial glory; it is a respectable, important role—but a subservient one.

Other European authors and artists acknowledge the spiritual nature of Muhammad's mission and recognized him as a prophet. Reginald Smith in 1874 affirms that Christians would one day uphold the prophethood of Muhammad.[7] Various British Protestant writers of the second half of the nineteenth century recognize Muhammad as a prophet and stress the similarity of his message to that of the Old Testament prophets. For Edward Freeman in 1856, Christians should acknowledge him as a "faithful though imperfect servant of God"; pastor George Smith, in a 1908 sermon, reflects on Muhammad's accomplishments and affirms, "this is a phenomenon, which, as religious men, we are bound to confess as one of the direct acts of God."[8] In the twentieth century, in the context of interreligious dialogue, a number of Christians have called for recognition of the prophet's positive role in the divine plan.[9]

In this chapter, we will look at how various Christian writers of the twentieth century tried to reconcile their Christian faith with the recognition of the positive, spiritual nature of Muhammad's mission. We will first look at French Orientalist Louis Massignon and some of his followers, then at Catholic theologians working in the aftermath of Vatican II, and finally will concentrate on Montgomery Watt, distinguished scholar of Islam and priest of the Scottish Episcopal Church.

Louis Massignon and Giulio Basetti-Sani

Louis Massignon (1883–1962) is a prominent and original figure among twentieth-century Orientalists. Massignon's career is brilliant and unique. In 1905, the budding twenty-two-year-old Orientalist met Ignác Goldziher at a conference in Algiers. This encounter marked Massignon, who was particularly inspired by Goldziher's advocacy of *Verinnerlichung* (internalization), which combined scholarly rigor and a deep empathy with the object of study.[10] A fervent Catholic, Massignon owed his profound faith to Muslim friends in Baghdad who helped him out of a difficult situation in 1908. He had arrived in Ottoman Mesopotamia the previous year to engage in archaeological prospection. The young scholar of Arabic avoided Europeans, lived in a working-class neighborhood of Baghdad, and dressed in Arab clothing. During one of his archaeological expeditions in the desert, Ottoman authorities suspected him of being a French spy. Arrested on a boat on the Tigris during his return trip to Baghdad, he was chained to a bed and threatened with death. Once in Baghdad, he was assigned to a hospital bed and waited in fear. At this point, his Muslim friends in Baghdad intervened, bore witness to his innocence, had him released from prison, and took him into their homes. This generosity and this profound hospitality, coming from friends whom he knew only slightly, a hospitality anchored in their Muslim faith, shook the young man. Massignon became a fervent Catholic at the same time as he developed a deep admiration for Islam and for his Muslim friends. For the rest of his life, he tried to use his considerable erudition to reconcile these two elements: his Catholic faith and his admiration for the faith of his Muslim hosts.

Massignon devoted his 1922 dissertation to Mansūr al-Hallāj, a Sufi who was executed for heresy in Baghdad in 922. Hallāj had declared that his burning love for God filled him with the desire for martyrdom. For Massignon, Hallāj is a Christ figure within Islam, who suffers death to testify to Muslims that God is love and that Christ died for all men. In a prayer published in 1921, Massignon expresses his hope that Hallāj might one day be canonized by the Catholic Church.[11] God speaks through the Qur'ān, Massignon affirms, not only to bring the Arabs to monotheism but also to make Islam into a "flaming sword" for monotheism, a reproach to self-satisfied Jews and Christians and a provocation for them to affirm their faith.[12] Massignon views Islam as a positive spiritual challenge to Christianity, yet an imperfect religion since it does not accept Christ's divinity and his sacrifice for mankind. One of the objects of his peculiar erudition was the *mubāhala* (theological disputation) of Najran. Various hadiths relate that Muhammad proposed to the Christians of Najrân, who refused to recognize in him a prophet, a trial by fire.[13] The Christians were frightened and refused, accepting Muhammad as a prophet. Centuries later, Francis of Assisi went to Egypt and (according to his hagiographer Bonaventure), proposed to enter into the flames to prove the superiority of Christianity; it was now the sultan who refused this confrontation in which Francis, burning with love for Muslims, sought to testify to them the truth of Christianity.[14]

Massignon stands alone among European orientalists: a former French colonial officer and professor at the Collège de France who became both a proud nationalist and fiercely anticolonial; protector of Palestinian rights and staunchly anti-Zionist; forger of a unique ecumenism and at the same time patronizing toward Islam and often hostile to Judaism. He favored anti-Jewish policies in the 1930s while at the same time keeping close working friendships with Jewish colleagues. One of his students, a young English Jew by the name of Bernard Lewis, said that he never knew if Massignon mistrusted him because he was of the perfidious race that crucified Jesus or because he was of the treacherous race that burned Joan of Arc. Little wonder that one historian has dubbed him a "holy madman."[15]

In the fall of 1936, Massignon met Giulio Basetti-Sani (1912–2001), a twenty-four-year-old Franciscan who was in Paris studying theology and Arabic, planning on going to Egypt to engage in mission. Basetti-Sani describes how the encounter made a profound impression on him.[16] Basetti-Sani went to Egypt in 1939, teaching in the Franciscan seminary of Giza. He was subsequently arrested as a spy; Britain was at war with Italy, and his travels to Paris, London, Rome, and Cairo made him suspicious to the Egyptian and British authorities. British intelligence declared that the friar was "very dangerous for the British Empire."[17] During his incarceration, he had long friendly theological discussions with one of his jailers, a Muslim Egyptian, in which they discussed among other things the prophet Muhammad. The Franciscan's ideas on the "false prophet" of Islam came principally from his close reading of Marracci's seventeenth-century Qur'ān translation and biography of Muhammad. Years later, he realized how offensive his ideas must have been to his Muslim friend and expressed admiration for the patience and gentleness with which he had answered and given his own view of Muhammad. Torn between Marracci's portrayal of a false prophet and impostor and the Muslim view of Muhammad as the seal of the prophets, Basetti-Sani tried to find a compromise solution. In a lecture he delivered while in captivity, he explained that "Muhammad, though in good faith, was the unwitting instrument of Satan"; Satan "succeeded in founding through Muhammad a religion which is the antithesis of Christianity, an anti-Christianity."[18]

At the end of the war, Basetti-Sani regained his freedom; Massignon returned to Egypt in 1946, and the two men met once again. Basetti-Sani gave Massignon a text he had written about Muhammad, and reading it, Massignon grew angry. He then softened and told the friar that there was nothing new in what he had written, that for centuries Christians had been insulting Muhammad. What he needed to do is follow the teaching of Augustine, "love gives new eyes"; reread the Qur'ān in love, Massignon told him, with the knowledge that God has passed there. A retreat in the desert of upper Egypt, where he studied the Qur'ān and observed with admiration the piety of local Muslims, created what Basetti-Sani later described as a conversion experience.[19] Yet his new approach to Islam, along with his interest in dialogue with Eastern Christians, garnered him severe rebuke from fellow Franciscans; he was suspended from teaching at the Giza seminary and asked to leave Egypt. He went to Montreal, to McGill (even though his Franciscan superiors would not let him accept a stipend from a Protestant university). There he wrote his *Mohammed et Saint François*, published in 1959, taking up Massignon's scheme of the trial by fire proposed by Francis as a response to the abortive *mubāhala* of Najran.[20] This book was fiercely attacked by traditionalist Catholics who looked askance at this gesture of accommodation toward Islam. The author relates how a fellow friar branded the book a historical and doctrinal fraud.[21]

Massignon died in 1962, and over the following decades, Basetti-Sani developed a positive theology of Islam, which he sees as a development of that of his master and friend, to whom he devoted a monograph in 1971.[22] Basetti-Sani concluded that Muhammad was divinely inspired and that Islam plays a positive role in the history of redemption. This role, for Basetti-Sani as for Massignon, is one that would have scarcely pleased Muhammad or his followers, a sort of phase of preparation for their ultimate integration into the Catholic Church. If Islam is positive, it is never more than an imperfect expression of the ultimate truth, Christianity. In his *Koran in the Light of Christ*, Basetti-Sani gives a Christian reading of the Qur'ān that, while devoid of polemics, passes over in silence the Qur'ān's rejection of Christian doctrines and practice and places the accent on the elements in the Muslim holy book that are in harmony with Christian doctrine, in particular concerning Jesus.[23] The goal, as expressed in the title of another of his books, is to find "Jesus Christ hidden in the Qur'ān."[24]

Basetti-Sani makes every effort to approach the Qur'ān and the prophet Muhammad with respect and veneration. But his is still of course a very Christian reading of the Qur'ān, of Islam, and of Muhammad's role in the divine plan. The real meaning of the Qur'ān is "hidden," unknown to its readers and commentators for centuries, until Massignon and Basetti-Sani. Hardly a posture apt to endear him to Muslims. To find Christ "hidden" in the Qur'ān, Basetti-Sani reinterprets various Qur'ānic passages traditionally understood as applying to Muhammad as in fact referring to Jesus. For example, when (Q 2:129) Abraham prays that God send a messenger to the Arabs, Basetti-Sani affirms that this in fact refers to Jesus.[25] He skirts around the seemingly unambiguous condemnations of Christian doctrines such as the Incarnation and the Trinity by affirming that the Qur'ānic passages condemn not the orthodox beliefs of true Christians but the variant doctrines of heretic and schismatic Christians.[26] Muhammad is a true prophet, inspired by God, who revealed the Qur'ān to him. Islam remains a "catechumenate" toward the full mystery of Christ.

His work continued to spark sharp criticism in many Catholic circles, not least in his own order. At times when he arrived in his refectory while residing in Italy fellow friars mocked him by calling him Khomeini, Qaddafi, or Muhammad.[27] He had been condemned by the Holy See and, after he published *Mohammed et Saint François*, was expelled from the Franciscan order (in 1959, to be readmitted in 1974). He often had difficulty finding publishers in Italy. Yet he had better luck obtaining teaching positions and publishers in Canada and the United States, and his ecumenical vision gradually became more widely accepted in the Church. Indeed, there was a renewed interest in Franciscan circles for dialogue with Islam, and the elderly Friar Giulio found himself increasingly hailed as a precursor and trailblazer. In 1985, he had an audience with Pope John Paul II; the following year, the pope called the first world day of prayer for peace, bringing together representatives of the Catholic Church, of Protestant and Eastern churches, and of Muslim, Buddhist, Jewish, and other religious leaders.[28]

Vatican II and Hans Küng

Basetti-Sani's rehabilitation was of course linked to the Church's evolution on these issues between 1959 and 1974, principally seen in various declarations of Vatican II on non-Christian religions. On November 21, 1964, Pope Paul VI proclaimed the Dogmatic Constitution on the Church, *Lumen gentium*, which affirms "the plan of salvation also includes those who acknowledge the Creator. In the first place amongst these there are the Muslims, who, professing to hold the faith of Abraham, along with us adore the one and merciful God, who on the last day will judge mankind."[29] While the traditional doctrine of the Church had been *extra ecclesiam nulla salus*, no salvation for those outside of the Catholic Church, *Lumen gentium* affirms that non-Christians could indeed obtain salvation. Muslims are singled out as closest to Christianity since they, along with Christians, adore the God of Abraham and await the Day of Judgment. The council subsequently elaborated on the Church's relation to non-Christians in *Nostra aetate*, which was passed by a vote of 2,221 to 88 of the assembled bishops and promulgated on October 28, 1965, by Pope Paul VI.[30] The declaration begins by affirming the need for the Church to promote love and understanding among men at a time when ties across cultures and religions are becoming stronger. The starting point is the common belief in the supernatural and the common yearning for answers to questions about the purpose of our life. *Nostra aetate* then looks at how different religions, in different cultural contexts, have attempted to address these questions. It begins with an appreciation of the positive models provided by Hinduism and Buddhism and affirms, "The Catholic Church rejects nothing that is true and holy in these religions." On the contrary, the Church "regards with sincere reverence" these traditions. The document then addresses Islam:

> The Church regards with esteem also the Muslims. They adore the one God, living and subsisting in Himself; merciful and all-powerful, the Creator of heaven and earth, who has spoken to men; they take pains to submit wholeheartedly to even His inscrutable decrees, just as Abraham, with whom the faith of Islam takes pleasure in linking itself, submitted to God. Though they do not acknowledge Jesus as God, they revere Him as a prophet. They also honor Mary, His virgin Mother; at times they even call on her with devotion. In addition, they await the day of judgment when God will render their deserts to all those who have been raised up from the dead. Finally, they value the moral life and worship God especially through prayer, almsgiving and fasting. Since in the course of centuries not a few quarrels and hostilities have arisen between Christians and Moslems, this sacred synod urges all to forget the past and to work sincerely for mutual understanding and to pre-

serve as well as to promote together for the benefit of all mankind social justice and moral welfare, as well as peace and freedom.

The declaration's subsequent (and longest) section concerns the Jews. It rejects the notion that Jews collectively are responsible for the death of Christ and decries hatred and anti-Semitism in any form. In his memoirs, Swiss Catholic theologian Hans Küng describes the fierce opposition of a relatively small but virulent minority of bishops to Vatican II's declaration concerning the declaration concerning the Jews.[31] Küng was present and active at Vatican II and pushed for the ecumenical opening up of the Church represented in *Lumen gentium* and *Nostra aetate*. As we will see, he subsequently criticized *Nostra aetate* for not going far enough in its recognition of Islam.

In 1982, at Tübingen, Küng organized a series of exchanges concerning Christianity in its relations with three other "world religions": Islam, Hinduism, and Buddhism; these were published in book form in 1984.[32] The dialogue was not with adherents of those religions, but with German scholars, Küng's colleagues, specialized in each of the three religions. The goal is to make this a first step for Christians' rethinking their relations with other religions, for Küng a necessary prelude to real dialogue with Muslims, Hindus, and Buddhists. Küng sought to provide both a self-critique of Christianity in light of what could be learned through these other religions and a frank Christian critique of certain elements of the other religions. Above all, he affirms, we need to avoid the twin dangers of absolutism and relativism: absolutism leads to the sterile affirmation of the superiority of one's own religion, while relativism gives equal legitimacy to everything and makes critique (including self-critique) impossible. Critical dialogue implies give and take, Küng affirms; one must avoid defending and justifying reflexively every element of one's own religion, but rather seek to express what is best and most profound in one's religion. We are all on the path to a greater truth.

In the section concerning Islam, Küng laments that it has been an object of fear for Christian European writers since the Middle Ages. He salutes the work of those who sought to understand Islam in its own terms, from the pioneering Scotsman Alexander Ross (in his *Pansebeia* of 1650, which is in fact a quite bit more negative than

Küng allows), through various Enlightenment authors. He also praises the efforts of European Orientalists in elucidating the history of Islam; he gives a long list of scholars, and the final name on his list is that of Montgomery Watt. In the light of this new knowledge in Europe and of the new situation in the world, Vatican II, through *Nostra aetate*, came to a positive understanding of the role of Islam in the divine plan. There shall be no return to outdated Christian polemics, he affirms; no more immunization through defamation.

Küng addresses the issue of whether Christians can consider Islam to be a path to salvation. He recalls that the traditional Catholic position, confirmed by the Council of Florence in 1442, is *extra ecclesiam nulla salus*: there is no salvation outside the Church. But the Vatican II constitution *Lumen gentium*, as we have seen, recognized that those outside the Catholic Church, including Muslims, could gain salvation. This means, Küng emphasizes, that Christians should recognize Islam as a viable path to salvation.

This, for Küng, raises the question of Muhammad's status as prophet and the status of the Qur'ān. Küng compares Muhammad to the biblical prophets of Israel. Like them, he affirms, Muhammad spoke not with an authority vested in him by any human community, but through a special relationship with God; like them, he had a strong personality and was convinced that he was invested with a divine mission; like them, he spoke in the context of a profound social-religious crisis and provoked a hostile reaction on the part of the political elites; like them, Muhammad asserted that he proclaimed not his own word, but that of God; like them, Muhammad incessantly preached one God who does not accept other gods beside him; like them, he links obedience to God with a strong commitment to social justice. Moreover, Küng continues, Muhammad is a model and an inspiration for over 800 million Muslims worldwide. He concludes that the inhabitants of seventh-century Arabia were right to listen to Muhammad, that by so doing they created a great world religion.

> In truth, Muhammad was and is for persons in the Arabian world, and for many others, *the* religious reformer, lawgiver, and leader; the prophet *per se*. Basically Muhammad, who never claimed to be anything

more than a human being, is more to those who follow him than a prophet is to us: he is a model for the mode of life that Islam strives to be. If the Catholic Church, according to the Vatican II "Declaration on Non-Christian Religions," "regards with esteem the Muslims," then the same church must also respect the one whose name is embarrassingly absent from the same declaration, although he and he alone led the Muslims to pray to this one God, for through him this God "has spoken to humanity": Muhammad the prophet.[33]

Acknowledging Muhammad as a prophet entails recognizing the divinely inspired nature of the Qur'ānic revelation but does not, for Küng, imply accepting that the whole Qur'ān is literally the word of God. He calls for the same critical approach that has been applied to the texts of the Bible to be used to better understand the Qur'ān. Just as the historical criticism of the Bible has been useful to Jews and Christians seeking to adapt their faiths to the world around them, so a historical critique of the Qur'ān is necessary to help Muslims adapt their faith. Küng concludes his book on Christian dialogue with three other world religions with a call for renewed dialogue. Not for colonial-style mission, where Christians (or Muslims) convinced of their religious and cultural superiority try to win others to their religion. But an exchange in which each testifies to the truth and beauty contained in his own faith and recognizes that contained in other faiths. There will be no world peace without religious peace, he concludes.

In Chicago in September 1993, Küng participated in the Parliament of the World's Religions, which brought together representatives of strands of Judaism, Christianity, Islam, and Buddhism as well as of Hindus, Sikhs, Zoroastrians, Native American cults, Rastafarians, Anthroposophists, and others. The parliament agreed on the text of a manifesto for a new planetary ethos, based on the axiom that every human being must be treated humanely. The manifesto upheld four principals: nonviolence and respect for life, solidarity and economic justice, tolerance, and equality of men and women. The manifesto was published in ten languages, and Küng wrote a preface and a commentary in which he explained the history, importance, and method of the adoption of the manifesto.[34] He affirms in his preface that the new planetary ethic is not meant as a substitute for the ethical requirements of the various religions, on the contrary, the Torah for the Jews, the Sermon on the Mount for the Christians, the Muslims' Qur'ān, the Hindus' Bhagavad Gita, the sayings of Buddha or Confucius all maintain their fundamental role as the basis of law and faith for millions of people, and as sources of inspiration for them. The goal is not the erasure of difference but rather the affirmation of common ethical ground. The manifesto declares that in their diverse doctrines the world's religions share a common core of essential values that constitute the basis of a new planetary ethic.

In the 1990s, Küng undertook a trilogy of books on the three Abrahamic religions: Judaism (1991), Christianity (1999), and Islam (2004).[35] In each the object is to carry further Küng's project of critical dialogue between religions, to give an introduction to the history of the religion, looking critically at its historic strengths and weaknesses, and to look at the principal challenges that the adherents of that religion face at the turn of the twenty-first century. He opens his volume on Islam with a discussion of Samuel Huntington's schema of a clash of civilizations, in which Islam now plays the role formerly given to Soviet Communism as the principal rival and threat to Western democracy and civilization. Such simplistic schemas not only blind us to understanding the variety and richness of Islamic cultures, affirms Küng, they also serve as a convenient scapegoat that helps us avoid looking critically at our own (European and American) responsibilities for the injustice, inequality, and violence in the world. Huntington's stereotype is based on a well-established archetype of fear of the Saracen or the Turk. Küng traces the history of this European hostility toward Islam and then chronicles the work of those Orientalists who struggled to understand Islam on its own terms (again, Montgomery Watt is the final name on his list). He also notes the salutary effect of Edward Said's *Orientalism* (1978), which (although polemical to an excess) forced Western scholars to question their own objectivity and the uses to which their scholarship could (wittingly or not) be put. He then traces, in considerable detail (the book runs 741 pages in the English translation) the history of Islam. He elaborates on many of the themes already evoked in his 1984 book, in some cases taking up his earlier arguments verbatim (on Islam as a path to salvation or on

Muhammad as a prophet in the biblical mode). He offers an extensive argument in favor of the critical study of the Qur'ān along the lines of twentieth-century historical biblical criticism and cites approvingly the names of various Muslim intellectuals engaged in this process.

In his various writings on ecumenical dialogue, Küng affirms that there is the possibility of salvation outside the Church and that scripture is divinely inspired but may contain errors (he applies this to the Bible and asks Muslims to apply the same sort of criticism to the Qur'ān); this allows him to brand scriptural passages that proffer exclusivist claims as contrary to the spirit of bona fide revelation. He affirms that there can be revelation outside the Church (and that Muhammad is the principal example of this). Yet Küng criticizes early Catholic doctrines of what he calls "inclusivism": the idea that Islam or other faiths are good and true but are imperfect, that they are so many preparations for the true religion of Christianity. This of course is the approach of Massignon and Basetti-Sani (though he does not mention them): "what looks like tolerance proves in practice to be a sort of conquest by hugging, an integration by relativization and loss of identity."[36] Yet Küng's is a delicate balancing act, because at the same time he affirms that a Christian theology of ecumenism must remain Christian and that Jesus Christ is the "normative" revelation of God. In order to practice ecumenism while retaining his Christian perspective, Küng offers three criteria for judging religions: a "general ethical" criterion (whether the religion promotes human flourishing and human dignity), a "general religious" criterion (a religion judged "true and good" remains faithful to its own canon and principals), and a "specifically Christian" criterion, which is faithful to the "Spirit of Christ" in dogma and practice. Yet as Paul Sands has noted, this is hardly satisfying, since the first two criteria are not standards of truth and the third allows truth only to Christianity.[37]

Another Catholic who struggled with the same issues of ecumenical theology is Jacques Dupuis, professor of theology at the Gregorian University in Rome. In his *Toward a Christian Theology of Religious Pluralism* (1997), this Jesuit theologian tries to understand, from a Catholic point of view, the positive role that non-Christian religions play in God's plan.[38] He concludes that these religions can lead to salvation and criticizes those who argue for Christian exclusivism. The charismatic gift of prophecy, Dupuis asserts, is not a monopoly of the Hebrews, as the case of Muhammad shows. Muhammad's message of monotheism is a divine revelation transmitted by a true prophet. This is why, Dupuis asserts, numerous twentieth-century theologians have recognized Muhammad as a prophet, even if many of them (Dupuis included) do not accept the entire Qur'ān as the word of God.

Dupuis's ecumenism is an exercise in squaring a circle; as a Catholic and Jesuit, he must affirm the unique salvific role of the Church and of Jesus Christ. But he also wants to recognize the positive role of other religions without reducing them to the status of imperfect expressions of Christianity. He says that those outside the Church can find grace through the path of "baptism of desire." The ultimate goal of ecumenical dialogue is not conversion from one religion to another, but the ultimate convergence of all religions, at the end of time, in the recognition of the Unique Truth. He affirms that revelation after Jesus Christ is possible, and that Muhammad is the principal example, though no subsequent revelation can equal that made to Christ.

This book by a Jesuit, professor of theology in one of the principal universities of the Catholic Church, did not please the Vatican hierarchy. The Congregation for the Doctrine of the Faith, under the direction of Cardinal Joseph Ratzinger (future Pope Benedict XVI), opened an inquiry into the orthodoxy of the book in 1998. The Gregorian University announced that professor Dupuis would be relieved of his teaching duties in order to have time to prepare his response. In 2001, after these investigations, the congregation published a "Notification," which saluted the book's erudition and spirit of ecumenical dialogue, but which warned the faithful against its "ambiguous formulation and insufficient explanations," susceptible, it was feared to "provoke confusion and misunderstanding." The congregation recalled the unique role of Christ in the Church and for salvation. This decision was seen as a warning against those inside the Church who promoted religious "relativism."

We have seen how various Catholic intellectuals engaged in dialogue with Islam struggled to find ways in which to affirm truth in non-Christian religions, to allow salvation to non-Christians, and in particular affirm that Muhammad, the Qur'ān, and Islam more generally played positive roles in God's scheme for humanity. Yet in so doing, they had to navigate between the Scylla of inclusivism (Islam is a preparation for or an inferior version of Christian truth) and the Charybdis of relativism (all faiths are equal). Their compromises often displeased their Muslim counterparts and infuriated their Catholic hierarchy.

Montgomery Watt

Let us turn now to Montgomery Watt, Scottish orientalist and Anglican minister, and look at how he struggled with these issues over a half a century (1953–2002). In Watt's scholarship we see traces both of a tension and of its resolution; his scholarly rigor makes him much more detached from his subject than is Massignon, but he applies that rigor to (among other things) questions concerning the relations between Christianity and Islam. This is apparent in the two volumes that constitute his magnum opus, *Muhammad at Mecca* (1953) and *Muhammad at Medina* (1956).[39] He explains that he writes simultaneously for three audiences: historians, Christians, and Muslims. He affirms that the historian's objective critique of religious history is in no way a threat to religious belief and can be pursued in a way that shows respect to believers. Thus, for example, in order to avoid sterile disputes about the authorship of the Qur'ān, when he cites the Qur'ān he says neither "God says" (as Muslims might) or "Muhammad says" (for Christian polemicists who attribute the Muslim holy book to the prophet), but simply "the Qur'ān says."[40]

His project can only be understood by keeping three audiences in mind. To the historian he seeks to provide a thorough and balanced account of the life of Muhammad and the beginnings of Islam. To the Christian, he seeks to rehabilitate the prophet of Islam, since, he says, "none of the great figures in history is so poorly appreciated in the West as Muhammad."[41] For the Muslim reader Watt places the message of the Qur'ān in historical perspective, in particular those passages that have been interpreted as establishing the exclusive nature of Muslim truth and the rejection of Christian doctrine. In *Muhammad at Mecca*, Watt refutes those European polemicists who affirmed that Muhammad fabricated the Qur'ān from scraps of biblical legends. "Western studies in the Qur'ān," affirms Watt, "have made a fetish of literary dependence."[42] The form of the Qur'ān, its unity of message and Muhammad's force of conviction, make it a revelation different and distinct from earlier ones, recurring themes and stories notwithstanding.

The conclusion to *Muhammad at Medina* is a chapter titled "The Man and His Greatness." "Of all the world's great men none has been so much maligned as Muhammad,"[43] he says, lamenting the lingering effects of "medieval war propaganda." Those who cast Muhammad as an impostor accuse him of being insincere, sensual, and treacherous. Watt takes up each of these accusations in turn. The idea that Muhammad deliberately fabricated revelation in order to hoodwink his followers Watt rejects as preposterous, as it fails to explain his steadfastness in adversity and hardship and the immense respect in which he was held by his followers. Indeed, the prophet's sincerity and integrity is a golden thread running through the two volumes; as he said in *Muhammad at Mecca*, "To suppose Muhammad an impostor raises more problems than it solves."[44] When (in *Muhammad at Medina*) Watt discusses the treaty of Hudaybiya, he emphasizes the material sacrifices made by Muhammad in this treaty (in particular, renouncing the lucrative raids on Meccan caravans), which for him show that the prophet was guided by a long-term strategy of winning over Meccans to Islam, not by material considerations. To refute the accusation that he was "an old lecher," Watt emphasizes his long monogamous marriage with Khadīja during the Meccan period and explains that his multiple marriages in Medina were consistent with the traditions of the time, and often consolidated alliances with important allies. The question remains open, however, as to whether Muhammad can serve as a model only for Muslims or for all of humanity; for the latter to happen, Muslims need to refine their image of the prophet and explain and justify his singular virtue.

Watt addresses the questions of the relationship between emerging Islam and the two rival monotheistic faiths. The Qur'ānic notion of tahrif is based on Qur'ān 4:46, "Among those who are Jewish, some distort the words beyond the truth." Watt shows how this revelation is a reaction to specific groups of Medinan Jews who mocked what they saw as Muhammad's pretension of being a prophet. "In the Qur'ān this need mean nothing more than deliberately interpreting passages to suit oneself, and neglecting the plain and straightforward meaning; but later Muslim apologetic took this to mean that the Jewish and Christian scriptures were textually corrupt."[45]

Watt notes that neither Muhammad nor his companions show awareness of some of the fundamental doctrines of Christianity, in particular about the teachings of Jesus as recorded in the Gospels, his role as savior in Christian theology, and the place of the Holy Spirit as the third person of the Trinity. "The blame for this state of affairs probably rests on those Christians with whom Muhammad and his Companions were in contact, who may themselves have had little appreciation of the doctrines mentioned."[46] In other words, the Qur'ānic perception of Christianity is in error because Muhammad had only had contact with Christians who failed to understand their own religion. This is an idea that Watt will return to, and at times struggle with, in his later work on ecumenism.

In 1954, Watt met Massignon in Cambridge at the International Congress of Orientalists; they then regularly met each time Watt passed through Paris. Beyond their common scholarly interests, the two were devoted to interreligious dialogue. In a volume dedicated to Massignon's legacy, Watt wrote in 1984, "As I come towards the end of my own life I become more concerned with the reconciliation of Islam and Christianity, and I believe in the probability of this happening. By reconciliation I mean not some syncretistic amalgam of doctrines, but a mutual recognition of their common goals by those seeking to serve God more fully; and I regard Louis Massignon's contribution to this reconciliation as one of the greatest."[47] Watt and Massignon shared an admiration for martyred French Cistercian Charles de Foucauld and for the confraternities he founded, the Petits Frères de Jésus and the Petites Sœurs de Jésus. Watt was well aware of Massignon's work though his approach was quite different.

In 1963, Watt published *Truth in the Religions: A Sociological and Psychological Approach.* His goal is to look at the challenges posed by sociology and psychology to religion, to examine the assertions, "religion is the opiate of the people" and "God is a projection." "I have attempted to defend religion in general and not Christianity specifically, since I think that in the present world situation the

great religions, whether they realize it or not, are allies against opposing forces."[48] Watt laments that "Eur-America" (a term he prefers to "the West") has a negative vision of Islam based on medieval
"war propaganda," which painted Islam as violent, sexually lax, and
intellectually inferior to Christianity; this legacy explains that until
today Islam does not have as much appeal to Europeans and Americans as does, for example, Buddhism.[49] One of the principal charges
levied against Islam is that it is derivative and unoriginal because
it incorporates narrative, ritual, and doctrinal elements from Judaism and Christianity. Here as in other works, Watt affirms that on
the contrary all world religions borrow creatively from other, earlier
traditions: Christianity from Judaism, from Oriental savior cults,
from the various mother goddess cults which informed the Christian veneration of the Virgin Mary, and so on. Originality, for Christianity as well as for Islam, involves creating a new and compelling
synthesis of these elements.[50] He argues against the Marxist ma-
terialist view of religion, while acknowledging the important role
that political and economic factors play in the specific forms that
religions take; he cites examples from early Christianity and early
Islam.

For Watt to affirm the fundamental compatibility and common
interest of the world religions, he has to deftly negotiate a few major
stumbling blocks. Religious communities generally consider themselves superior to other communities; we find this in the Old Testament concept of the Jews as God's chosen people, and it is prominent in both Christianity and Islam. Some Muslim theologians
affirmed that only Muslims could attain salvation, while the medieval Catholic doctrine taught "*extra ecclesiam nulla salus.*" For Watt,
such notions of superiority are "distortions," born not of strength but
of defensiveness, "contrary to the deepest insights of both communities."[51] He in particular discusses the medieval Christian polemical view of Muhammad and the Muslim notion that Jews and Christians have falsified their scriptures (both themes, as we have seen,
that he addressed in his volumes on Muhammad). Both of these, for
Watt, are defensive tactics by those who fear the rival claims of other
religions; they are signs of weakness, not confidence. Christians
should look again at Muhammad and appreciate his positive role in

the creation of the Muslim community; Muslims should abandon the idea of *tahrif*.[52]

For Watt in 1963, at the height of the Cold War, religious peace and unity was essential to world peace—and no doubt (though he does not say so explicitly) a bulwark against Godless communism. Soviet Orientalists had attacked the prophet of Islam: Liutsian Klimovich had even claimed that Muhammad never existed, that he was an invention of later Islamic scholars; Watt defends the prophet and gives him a key role in sacred history. The concluding chapter of his book is titled "Towards One Religion," echoing the hopes of medieval authors such as Nicholas of Cusa who hoped that reasoned dialogue could bring religious sages to agree on common doctrine (though for these medieval Christian authors that one religion would of course be Christianity). Cusa sought "fides una, ritus diversus": unity of faith and diversity of ritual. Watt's "one religion" does not involve eradicating doctrinal or institutional differences between religions but recognizing common bases and shared interests. He begins by giving four maxims around which all Christians should be able to unite: the acceptance as brothers of all who acknowledge Jesus as Lord, the acceptance by each of his place in his own specific religious community (or church), the acceptance that others may best serve the Lord in their own churches, and finally that differences between the individual and his Christian brothers are understood by God alone, and that each believer must be ready humbly to learn from all his brothers. Watt then takes these same four principles and applies them to "the religion of Abraham," Jews, Christians, and Muslims, by simply changing Jesus to God. This means that Jews, Christians, and Muslims should recognize one another as "brothers," and should not affirm the superiority of their individual religions over those of their brothers, and should be ready humbly to learn from one another. While other traditions (such as Buddhism or Hinduism) are further from the Abrahamic religions, the same general principles should, mutatis mutandis, be able to create fruitful and peaceful dialogue among religions.

What does this mean for mission? Watt asserts that mission remains important, that is the sign of a healthy religious community that its members wish to spread the good news of their religion. Yet true mission is, for Watt, performed with humility and modesty; it does not involve, as many Christian missions of the colonial era did, a complex of superiority and a will to add others to one's own sectarian community. On the contrary, the true missionary should be ready to speak well of his own community and to listen to others tell of their community in willingness to learn about it. Over time, this will allow new forms of religiosity to emerge that mix the best elements of different religious traditions and perhaps to move toward one religion. "The climax of the argument of this book is that there can be no genuine world-unity without religion."[53]

In 1969, Watt published *Islamic Revelation in the Modern World*.[54] He explores the reasons for Islam's success as a world religion, and in particular over and against Christianity in the regions of the former Christian Roman Empire that it incorporated into the Dar al-Islam. He also looks at why Christianity failed, in these regions, to remain the dominant religion. Much of it has to do with divisions within Christianity, as the Orthodox church marginalized Oriental Christians who did not accept the doctrines laid out by the Church and who were branded as heretical by Constantinople.

> The Christian will only fully understand what happened if he is prepared to admit that here Christianity may have been inferior, perhaps even spiritually inferior. It is at least a plausible theory that the orientals became estranged somewhat from Christianity when the latter became overidentified with the Greek dualistic conception of man. By this is meant the view that a man consists of body and soul, and that the soul is the essential man, and the body only a garment or instrument of the soul, or even (as some extremists held) its tomb. On the other hand, among the oriental Christians and other peoples of the Middle East it would seem that some form of monistic conception of man was dominant. A distinction might be made between body and soul, but the body was just as much the man as the soul, or more so. . . . It seems plausible to hold that among the oriental Christian peoples many became Muslims because they found in Islam an expression of monotheism more suited to their distinctive mentality than any provided by Christianity.[55]

The question of Muhammad's status as prophet is key for Watt in tackling the issue of the legitimacy and reality of prophetic calling to a modern scientific-minded audience. He proposes a "modern account of revelation," which he bases on the Jungian notion of the collective unconscious: "according to the Jungian scheme . . . the revelations on which Judaism, Christianity and Islam are based are 'contents' which have emerged from the collective unconscious."[56] For Watt, this provides a rational, scientific explanation for the source of revelation and places different revelations from different religions on an equal footing. He is aware of course that this explanation may offend pious Jews, Christians, or Muslims, who believe that God is the source of these revelations. Yet the collective unconscious, he explains, is the vehicle for these revelations, and not necessarily the ultimate source. The pious thank God for giving them their food; this does not mean that there are not intermediaries—farmers, bakers, butchers, and brewers—between God and their dinner table. In the same way, understanding the dynamics of the collective unconscious need not take anything away from God's agency.

In the concluding chapter, Watt raises the issues of the relations between world religions and between those religions and the scientific outlook of secular modernity. Here again, he insists that mission in the traditional sense, as understood by nineteenth-century European and American Christian missionaries, is no longer possible. What needs to replace it is dialogue. Dialogue involves not only an ability to speak but also a capacity to listen, a willingness to learn from the other. He insists that for real dialogue, each religion must abandon what he calls its defense mechanisms; here as elsewhere, he cites principally the Muslim notion of *tahrif* and the medieval Christian caricature of Muhammad.[57] To abandon these defenses is not tantamount to abandoning one's religion; rather, it enables one to affirm the kerygma, the positive message of one's religion, in clearer terms. We learn from psychology that assertions of superiority are in fact signs of insecurity and weakness; the same rule holds true in religious dialogue.

"In the long term, of course, it is to be expected that there will be one religion for the whole world, though it may contain within itself permitted variations, comparable to the four permitted legal rites (*madhāhib*) in Sunni Islam."[58] Most Christians, he says, assume that Christianity is best placed to be the eventual world religion, but

Watt expresses doubts, in particular since Christian societies have been incapable of adequately responding to racism within their own midst (thinking, no doubt, in 1969, of South Africa, the United States, and what was left of the European colonial empires). Islam, with its emphasis on brotherhood and its "depth of conviction," is "certainly a strong contender for the supplying of the basic framework of the one religion of the future."[59] "It is unnecessary, however, at the present date to try to forecast the future more clearly. What precisely happens will not be the result of human planning but will be the work of forces emerging from the unconscious, or, if one likes, will be the divine overriding of all human plans."[60]

Watt further develops his reflections on the role of religion in general, and Christianity and Islam in particular, in today's world in his *Islam and Christianity Today: A Contribution to Dialogue* (1983).[61] The goal is to defend religion from what Watt calls "scientism": the belief that rational scientific thinking has made religion an irrational, atavistic survival tactic in modern society. The faithful of different religions need to unite to defend spiritual values against scientism. The foundation of this unified effort is interreligious dialogue. He cites Thomas Merton, who said that "the good Christian is not one who can refute other religions, but who can affirm the truth in them and then go further."[62] This is the method he proposes to both Christians and Muslims for a mutual dialogue.

He returns again to what he considers the two fundamental stumbling blocks in Christian-Muslim rapprochement. First, the black legend concerning the prophet. "Muhammad," he says, "claimed to receive messages from God and conveyed these to his contemporaries. On the basis of these messages a religious community developed, claiming to serve God, numbering some thousands in Muhammad's lifetime, and now having several hundred million members. The quality of life in this community has been on the whole satisfactory for the members. Many men and women in this community have attained to saintliness of life, and countless ordinary people have been enabled to live decent and moderately happy lives in difficult circumstances. These points lead to the conclusion that the view of reality presented in the Qur'ān is true and from God, and that therefore Muhammad is a genuine prophet."[63] Watt insists that in order to further dialogue, Christians should accept that Muhammad is a genuine prophet. Muslims, for their part, should rethink the notion of *tahrif* or corruption of the scriptures. He further argues that in order for Muslims to understand and appreciate the Christian notion of salvation, they should recognize the historical fact of Jesus's crucifixion.[64]

In 2002, Watt published *A Christian Faith for Today*, which he offers as "an attempt to present the truth incorporated in the Christian religion in a form which is not incompatible with the dominant intellectual outlook at the present day."[65] The goal is to show that Christian faith and practice can be coherent with scientific truth and modern secular values. While the book is concerned with Christianity and directed principally at a believing Christian audience, the final section is "a word to Muslims."[66] He emphasizes the common elements in Christianity and Islam and affirms that "Muhammad truly received revelations from God," concluding again that Christians should recognize Muhammad as prophet and the Qur'ān as divine revelation. Yet, he says revelation is "far from simple." Some of the revelations in the Old Testament were appropriate to the time and culture in which they were revealed, but are no longer applicable; for example, God's command to Joshua to destroy certain towns and kill their inhabitants. The same is true of the Qur'ān, and Muslims should be ready to treat its text critically. Cutting off a hand in punishment of theft, for example, "would no longer seem to be appropriate." Watt also addresses the Qur'ān's rejection of certain key elements of Christianity:

> The question must be asked, however: Does the Qur'ān give the full and final truth about God, or is Qur'ānic truth open to something additional? Christians take the latter view, namely, that it needs to be supplemented, and also occasionally corrected. There is, of course, already some knowledge of Judaism and Christianity in the Qur'ān, but it reflects the views of the Jews and Christians whom Muhammad and the earliest Muslims had met; and these people do not seem to have had a full and proper knowledge of their own religions.[67]

European polemicists from the thirteenth century to the nineteenth had attributed the errors of the Qur'ān to the influence of Jews and heretical Christians; for them, it discredited the false prophet and his false revelation. For Watt, this influence excuses the Qur'ān and does not affect its essence, though it calls for "correction."

Watt's conundrum is that in order to explain away, in the spirit of ecumenism, the anti-Christian passages of the Qur'ān, he needs to scapegoat oriental Christians. While he does not denounce them as "heretics," he claims that they were Christians who did not properly understand their own religion. This is a clear departure from his *Islamic Revelation in the Modern World* of 1969, where, as we have seen, he was more sympathetic to oriental Christian's rejecting of the Greek dualism represented in Chalcedonian orthodoxy.

Watt, like Massignon, Basetti-Sani, and Küng, was committed to ecumenical dialogue and struggled to find ways to eliminate (or at least reduce) doctrinal barriers to that dialogue. For all of them, Christian recognition of the prophetic role of Muhammad was central. For Massignon and Basetti-Sani, Islam was positive and could lead to salvation, but it was imperfect because it did not recognize Christ as God and savior. Their vision, as we have seen, is what Küng classified as inclusive, "conquest by hugging." Küng and Watt try to go further, though each reaches his own limits. Küng remains grounded in the Catholic Church and, though he confers more legitimacy than Massignon and Basetti-Sani on non-Christian religions, in the end the recognition of Jesus Christ as God and savior remains the highest truth. Watt seems ready to go further still, at times imagining that one new world religion will emerge from a sort of fusion by emulation of the best elements of current religions, and that Islam has as good a claim, or better, than Christianity for providing the basis for that new world religion. Such ecumenical visions, however, were marginal among European Catholics and Protestants; Massignon, Basetti-Sani, and Küng were all looked on with deep ambivalence by the Catholic hierarchy. Watt in 1963 thought he perceived on the horizon a future in which there would be one unified world religion, a basis for world peace. In his later writings, that prospect seems to have faded from his view. Few today claim to see such a prospect on our horizon.

Conclusion

OVER THE COURSE of the nine preceding chapters, we have seen the shifting perceptions of the prophet of Islam in European discourse and culture. While we have moved forward chronologically, from the twelfth century to the twentieth, I have concentrated each chapter on emerging trends in the portrayal of Muhammad. Yet in each century, of course, a great variety of conflicting images coexists. If I have concentrated in chapter nine on Christian theologians struggling to assign a positive role to Muhammad in God's plan, that does not of course imply that various other ways of portraying him (as a national lawgiver, or as an impostor) have not been common in the twentieth and twenty-first centuries. It would be impossible to attempt to read, much less analyze, the plethora of books written about Muhammad in the last two centuries in English, not to mention other languages. These books range from the pious to the scholarly to the polemical. Moreover, as Kecia Ali has shown, the distinction between "Muslim" and "Western" perceptions of the prophet has become blurred as many works are written by American Muslims, Tunisians educated in France, and so forth.[1]

This globalized context, provoked by colonization, decolonization, and immigration, has brought negative European perceptions of Islam and its prophet to the attention of Muslims and has provoked resentment, reproach, and violence, as attested by the furor around the caricatures of Muhammad published by *Jyllands-Posten* and *Charlie Hebdo*. Even positive portrayals of the prophet can provoke resentment and disagreement. In 1997, the Council on American-Islamic Relations petitioned Chief Justice William Rehnquist, asking him to remove or cover the depiction of Muhammad from Adolf Weinman's frieze in the courthouse. Rehnquist denied this request. Iraqi American jurist Taha Jaber al-Alwani subsequently issued a fatwa on the issue and concluded, "What I have seen in the Supreme Courtroom deserves nothing but appreciation and gratitude from American Muslims."[2]

Readers may be surprised, even at times confused, by the sheer multiplicity and diversity of European perceptions of the prophet of Islam that we have encountered in this book. I have distinguished between different strategies for portraying the prophet: as idol, heresiarch, reformer, statesman, mystic, or poet. But in fact, as we have amply seen, the lines between these portrayals are blurred, and various authors and artists have crossed them frequently and often deliberately.

Polemical portraits have taken up a significant part of this book: Mahomet is cast as a golden idol to be toppled by righteous crusaders; a scheming heresiarch; a lustful, power-hungry impostor. These images live on in European and American cultures, to be sure. We have already noted how Geert Wilders vilifies Muhammad as part of his anti-Muslim, anti-immigrant rhetoric. The denigration of Muhammad is a key element in several apocalyptic evangelical movements in the United States and Europe. Jack Chick's 1988 comic book *The Prophet* makes Islam into a creation of the Vatican. Roman Catholicism, for Chick, is an invention of the Devil to turn people away from true Christianity, and the Vatican decided to create Islam in order the better to persecute true Christians. Khadīja's cousin Waraqa is a "Roman Catholic" agent of the Vatican; he composed the Qur'ān with Muhammad. The popes then plotted with Muslims and permitted them to conquer North Africa. Ever since, Muslims and Catholics have colluded to divide the world between them "to block and destroy their common enemy, Bible believing Christian missionaries."[3] Islam itself, for Chick, is derived from paganism: its God, Allah, is an Arabic moon God who was married to a sun goddess who bore him three daughters; the rites of pilgrimage perpetuate this idolatry. "Allah," affirms Chick, "is only an idol."[4] Chick thus blends the centuries-old notion of Islam as pagan idolatry (which we examined in chapter one) with Protestant polemics associating Islam and Catholicism. Chick's work is one example of the polemical visions of Muhammad that thrive in the blogosphere, fueling conspiracy theories about the imminent Islamization of Europe or America.[5] The strategy of attacking Muhammad in order to promote anti-Muslim and anti-immigrant policies in Europe and the United States no doubt will be with us for some time to come.

While polemical portraits of the prophet have been frequent in these pages, we have also seen much that is either ambiguous or downright laudatory. Indeed, a number of the writers we have studied identified with Muhammad. Even Voltaire, who in his early work cast Mahomet as a fanatic, came to identify with him later in life, as a reformer and visionary who used his eloquence to move his people. Bonaparte, too, saw himself as a new Mahomet, which for him meant charismatic leader, wise lawgiver, and brilliant general. For his part, Goethe identified with the prophet, as poet and visionary. Some nineteenth-century Jewish scholars (such as Abraham Geiger, Gustav Weil, and Ignác Goldziher), while not directly comparing themselves to Muhammad, saw him as a quasi-Jewish reformer who offered lessons in how to strip Judaism of what they saw as its irrational accretions of pointless ritual. Muhammad, for these various Europeans, is a model and an inspiration. He is of course not the only model for them; Bonaparte compared himself to Alexander, Caesar, and other military giants as well. Goethe identified with other poets, and perhaps identified more with Hafiz than with Muhammad.

What emerges from this survey, if nothing else, is that Muhammad and Islam are integral elements of European culture. Whether used as a foil to define what is not Christian or not European or Western, or whether brought into European debates about the Trinity and Immaculate Conception, religious tolerance, spirituality, or law, Muhammad has loomed large from the Middle Ages until today. For those who might think that Islam and Muhammad are somehow marginal to Western culture, think again: Europeans have been talking about him, and arguing about him, for centuries.

Muslim readers of this book, European or not, may also be disconcerted by much of what they have read in these pages. If they thought that European perceptions of the Muslim prophet were invariably hostile, inspired by Orientalist disdain, they have, I hope, come to realize the richness, variety, and ambiguity of European perceptions of the prophet. Some of the more positive portrayals by George Sale, Henri Boulainvilliers, Gustav Weil, or others may also be disconcerting, as they do not correspond to any of the many and various Muslim images of the prophet.

Here, comparison with Jesus may be useful. We have seen that many Christian polemicists contrast the two men, generally in order to denigrate Muhammad. I compared them from a different perspective in the introduction, exploring the difficulty for the historian of understanding these two key historical figures, of reading as a historian the scriptural and other sources describing their lives. Here I would like to explore another comparison between Jesus and Muhammad: the variegated facets of the living memories of the two men. Jesus is for Christians God and Son of God, though there have been significant differences among Christians over the centuries as to how to understand Jesus's relationship to the Godhead. These issues created sharp divergences among Christians and led to the establishment of rival churches. Even among adherents to one tradition, such as Catholicism, the ways of understanding Jesus have varied immensely: as almighty King of heaven, as suffering man-God who takes on the sins of the world, as a teacher of a higher moral order, as a model for mystical practice.[6] To these multiple Christian images of Jesus, we can add the Muslim Jesus, whom the Qur'ān portrays as a prophet preaching pure monotheism and who according to Muslim tradition will return at the end of time to judge the living and the dead. We have seen that some Muslims (such as the anonymous author of the *Gospel of Barnabas*) minimize Jesus's role, reducing it essentially to announcing the coming of Muhammad. Then there is the Jewish Jesus. Some medieval Jews portrayed him as a heretic, a false Jew who led his followers astray, denigrating him much as Christian polemicists did Muhammad, attributing to him bogus miracles and clever lies.[7] Others, Jews and non-Jews, have tried to understand Jesus as first and foremost a Jew, to place him in the context of his practice of Judaism and of the spiritual and political turmoil of Roman Palestine. Various Jewish intellectuals, since Moses Mendelssohn, have seen Jesus as a Jew who was faithful to Mosaic law and suffered persecution at the hands of Gentiles—

hence closer to modern European Jews than to their Christian persecutors. While historians may legitimately search for the "real" Jesus behind these various Jewish, Christian, and Muslim visions of him, clearly these visions are important historical phenomena in their own right. Various Christian fundamentalists might insist that they have the monopoly of truth, that their particular visions of Jesus are the only accurate ones, but the historian cannot take such claims seriously.

The same principles apply to the myriad images of Muhammad. Jews, Christians, Muslims, and others have, for almost fourteen centuries, portrayed the prophet in a great variety of ways. The historian may struggle to perceive the historical man of seventh-century Arabia behind the many thousands of texts and images that portray him. But no one, Muslim or not, may plausibly claim to have a monopoly of truth about the prophet of Islam. The sheer variety and diversity of portraits of Muhammad have become both major fields of research and important elements in the dialogue of religions and cultures. Much has been written about the innumerable Muslim portraits of the prophet, who appears in differing lights in different historical and cultural circumstances. One could write a book about the Iranian Muhammad, the Ottoman Muhammad, the Maghrebi Muhammad, the Wahhabi Muhammad, and so on, each of which would be made up of multiple and diverse portraits, each telling us more about the cultures and individuals that produced those portraits than about the man of seventh-century Arabia. The same holds true for what we have examined in these pages, where the prophet of Islam appears as a mirror for European writers, expressing their fears, hopes, and ambitions. He is an integral part of "Western" culture, an object of fascination and speculation for writers and artists for centuries: a European Muhammad.

Introduction

1. Gustav Seibt, *Goethe und Napoleon: Eine historische Begegnung* (Munich: C. H. Beck, 2008); Jeffrey Einboden, *Islam and Romanticism: Muslim Currents from Goethe to Emerson* (London: Oneworld, 2014), 20–21.

2. Geert Wilders, *Geert Wilders Weblog*, March 30, 2011, http://www.geertwilders .nl/index.php/component/content/article/80-geertwildersnl/1741-time-to-unmask -muhammad-by-geert-wilders.

3. On Moses, see Jean-Christophe Attias, *Moïse fragile* (Paris: CNRS Éditions, 2016). On David, see Joel Baden, *The Historical David: The Real Life of an Invented Hero* (New York: Harper One, 2013).

4. For a recent overview, see Dale Allison, *Constructing Jesus: Memory, Imagination, and History* (Grand Rapids, MI: Baker Academic, 2013).

5. Maxime Rodinson, *Mohammed* (New York: Random House, 1971), x.

6. See *The Cambridge Companion to the Qur'an* (Cambridge: Cambridge University Press, 2014).

7. See Hela Ouardi, *Les derniers jours de Muhammad* (Paris: Albin Michel, 2016); Stephen Shoemaker, *The Death of a Prophet: The End of Muhammad's Life and the Beginnings of Islam* (Philadelphia: University of Pennsylvania Press, 2015).

8. See Fred Donner, *Muhammad and the Believers: At the origins of Islam* (Cambridge, MA: Harvard University Press, 2012).

9. Christiane Gruber, *The Praiseworthy One: The Prophet Muhammad in Islamic Texts and Images* (Bloomington: Indiana University Press, 2019), intro.

10. Tarif Khalidi, *Images of Muhammad: Narratives of the Prophet in Islam across the Centuries* (New York: Doubleday, 2009); Annemarie Schimmel, *And Muhammad Is His Messenger: The Veneration of the Prophet in Islamic Piety* (Chapel Hill: University of North Carolina Press, 1985); *Cambridge Companion to Muhammad* (Cambridge: Cambridge University Press, 2010); Gruber, *Praiseworthy One.*

11. W. Montgomery Watt, *Truth in the Religions: A Sociological and Psychological Approach* (Edinburgh: Edinburgh University Press, 1963), vii.

12. Tomoko Masuzawa, *The Invention of World Religions; or, How European Universalism Was Preserved in the Language of Pluralism* (Chicago: University of Chicago Press, 2005), 121.

13. Kecia Ali, *The Lives of Muhammad* (Cambridge, MA: Harvard University Press, 2014).

14. The best attempt at synthesis of this vast subject of the history of Christian-Muslim relations is the continuing multivolume collaborative work directed by David Thomas, *Christian-Muslim Relations: A Bibliographical History* (Leiden: Brill, 2009–) (hereafter *CMR*).

15. Edward W. Said, *Orientalism* (New York: Vintage Books, 1978); for asessment's of Said's book and of his influence on subsequent scholarship, see in particular Daniel Martin Varisco, *Reading Orientalism: Said and the Unsaid* (Seattle: University of Washington Press, 2007); Robert Irwin, *Dangerous Knowledge: Orientalism and Its Discontents* (Woodstock, NY: Overlook Press, 2006).

16. Humberto Garcia, *Islam and the English Enlightenment, 1670–1840* (Baltimore: Johns Hopkins University Press, 2011), 13–17.

Chapter One. Mahomet the Idol

1. Matthew Dimmock, *Mythologies of the Prophet Muhammad in Early Modern English Culture* (Cambridge: Cambridge University Press, 2013), 113.

2. Richard Johnson, *Seven Champions of Christendom, 1596–97* (Aldershot, England: Ashgate, 2003), 16–17.

3. Johnson, *Seven Champions of Christendom*, 17.

4. Johnson, *Seven Champions of Christendom*, 18; Dimmock, *Mythologies of the Prophet Muhammad*, 113.

5. Johnson, *Seven Champions of Christendom*, 21.

6. Johnson, *Seven Champions of Christendom*, 92; Dimmock, *Mythologies of the Prophet Muhammad*, 114.

7. *Liber contra secta, sive haeresim Saracenorum* §14, in Peter of Cluny, *Schriften zum Islam* (Altenberge, Germany: CIS-Verlag, 1985), 50.

8. On the image of Saracen idolatry, see Suzanne Conklin Akbari, *Idols in the East: European Representations of Islam and the Orient, 1100–1450* (Ithaca, NY: Cornell University Press, 2009); Tolan, *Saracens: Islam in the Medieval European Imagination* (New York: Columbia University Press, 2002), chap. 5; Sharon Kinoshita and Siobhain Bly Calkin, "Saracens as Idolators in Medieval Vernacular Literatures," in *CMR* 4:29–44.

9. Jerome, *Saint Jerome's Hebrew Questions on Genesis*, trans. Robert Hayward (Oxford: Clarendon Press, 1995), 49. For a more detailed treatment of the analysis that follows, see John Tolan, "'A Wild Man, Whose Hand Will Be against All': Saracens and Ishmaelites in Latin Ethnographical Traditions, from Jerome to Bede," in *Visions of Community in the Post-Roman World*, ed. Pohl Walter, Gantner Clemens, and Payne Richard (Farnham, England: Ashgate, 2012), 513–30. See also Walter D. Ward, *The Mirage of the Saracen: Christians and Nomads in the Sinai Peninsula in Late Antiquity* (Oakland: University of California Press, 2014).

10. Jerome, *Commentarii in Ezechielem*, Corpus Christianorum Series Latina (Turnhout, Belgium: Brepols Publishers, 2010), 25.

11. Bede, *On Genesis*, trans. Calvin B. Kendall (Liverpool: Liverpool University Press, 2008), 278–79.

12. Tolan, "'A Wild Man, Whose Hand Will Be against All'"; Tolan, *Saracens*, chap. 4.

13. Raoul de Caen, *The Gesta Tancredi of Ralph of Caen: A History of the Normans on the First Crusade*, trans. Bernard S. Bachrach and David S. Bachrach (Farnham, England: Ashgate, 2007), 19.

14. Raoul de Caen, *Gesta Tancredi of Ralph of Caen*, 144–45. On this passage see Michelina Di Cesare, "The Prophet in the Book: Images of Muhammad in Western Medieval Book Culture," in *Constructing the Image of Muhammad in Europe*, ed. Avinoam Shalem (Berlin: De Gruyter, 2013), 9–32 (esp. 27–29); Michael Camille, *The Gothic Idol: Ideology and Image-Making in Medieval Art* (Cambridge: Cambridge University Press, 1989), 142–45.

15. Fulcher of Chartres, *Historia Iherosolymitana* c. 26 (RHC occ. 3:357), (c. 28, pp. 359–60). See Tolan, *Saracens*, chap. 5. The chronicle known as *Tudebodus imitatus et continuatus* tells us that Tancred entered the temple, where he saw a huge silver statue of Mahomet enthroned. Comparing the statue to a crucifix, he proclaimed that this was not Christ but Antichrist and ordered his men to destroy it and put the silver to good use. *Tudebodus imitatus et continuatus* c. 124 (RHC oc. 3:222–23).

16. *La Chanson d'Antioche* (Paris: P. Geuthner, 1977), vv. 205–11 (pp. 27–28); *The Chanson d'Antioche, an Old-French Account of the First Crusade*, trans. Susan Edgington and Carol Sweetenham (Farnham, England: Ashgate, 2011), 107. On the *Chanson d'Antioche*, see Carol Sweetenham, "The Old French Crusade Cycle," in *CMR* 3:422–33.

17. *Chanson d'Antioche*, vv. 4891ff.; *The Chanson d'Antioche, an Old-French Account of the First Crusade*, 219–20. This passage is discussed by Alexandre Eckhardt, "Le Cercueil flottant de Mahomet," in *Mélanges de philologie romane et de littérature médiévale offerts à Ernest Hoepffner, membre de l'Académie des inscriptions et belles-lettres: Doyen honoraire de la Faculté des lettres de Strasbourg par ses élèves et ses amis* (Paris: Les Belles Lettres, 1949), 77–88. On this legend, see Tolan, *Sons of Ishmael: Muslims through European Eyes in the Middle Ages* (Gainesville: University Press of Florida, 2008), chap. 2.

18. For the parallel practice of rubbing or scratching images of Christ's tormentors in passion scenes, see Debra Higgs Strickland, *Saracens, Demons and Jews: Making Monsters in Medieval Art* (Princeton, NJ: Princeton University Press, 2003), 114.

19. *La Chanson d'Antioche*, vv. 4968–70, *The Chanson d'Antioche, an Old-French Account of the First Crusade*, 221. Earlier in the epic, the poet had expressed the same prophecy in a slightly different form (vv. 3447–50).

20. *La Chanson d'Antioche*, vv. 9242–48; *The Chanson d'Antioche, an Old-French Account of the First Crusade*, 317. In the *Chanson de Jérusalem*, Godfrey of Bouillon swears that he will conquer Mecca and take the golden candelabra that stand before the idol of Mahon (Nigel Thorpe, ed., *The Old French Crusade Cycle*, vol. 6. (Tuscaloosa: University of Alabama Press, 1992), vv. 7276–87).

21. *La Chanson d'Antioche*, vv. 5310–12; *The Chanson d'Antioche, an Old-French Account of the First Crusade*, 229 (here I have modified the translation slightly).

22. *La Chanson d'Antioche*, vv. 5323–47; *The Chanson d'Antioche, an Old-French Account of the First Crusade*, 230.

23. *La Chanson d'Antioche*, vv. 6620–21; *The Chanson d'Antioche, an Old-French Account of the First Crusade*, 258.

24. *La Chanson d'Antioche*, vv. 9111–16, p. 448; *The Chanson d'Antioche, an Old-French Account of the First Crusade*, 314.

25. *The Chanson d'Antioche, an Old-French Account of the First Crusade*, 57n48.

26. For the text of the *Chanson de Roland* and translation (which I have at times slightly modified), I have used *The Song of Roland*, trans. Gerard Brault, 2 vols. (University Park: Pennsylvania State University Press, 1978). For an introduction to the immense bibliography on the *Chanson de Roland*: Sharon Kinoshita, "La Chanson de Roland," in *CMR* 3:648–52; Tolan, *Saracens*, chap. 5; Sharon Kinoshita, *Medieval Boundaries: Rethinking Difference in Old French Literature* (Philadelphia: University of Pennsylvania Press, 2006), 15–45.

27. See Akbari, *Idols in the East*, 209–10.

28. On this practice, see Patrick Geary, "L'humiliation des saints," *Annales: Histoire, Sciences Sociales* 34 (1979): 27–42.

29. On the role of Queen Bramimonde in the *Chanson de Roland*, see Sharon Kinoshita, " 'Pagans Are Wrong and Christians Are Right': Alterity, Gender, and Nation in the *Chanson de Rolan*," *Journal of Medieval and Early Modern Studies* 31, no. 1 (2001): 79–111; Kinoshita, *Medieval Boundaries*, 35–45.

30. Jean Bodel, *Le jeu de Saint Nicolas* (Geneva: Droz, 1981). See Camille, *Gothic Idol*, 129–35; Akbari, *Idols in the East*, 210–13; Kinoshita and Calkin, "Saracens as Idolators in Medieval Vernacular Literatures," 33–35.

31. Michael R. Paull, "The Figure of Mahomet in Middle English Literature" (PhD diss., University of North Carolina, 1970), 207.

32. Paull, "Figure of Mahomet in Middle English Literature," 209–10.

33. Paull, "Figure of Mahomet in Middle English Literature," 218. On the iconography of this common theme of the fall of the idols during the flight into Egypt, see Camille, *Gothic Idol*, 1–9.

34. Quoted from Paull, "Figure of Mahomet in Middle English Literature," 207.

35. Paull, "Figure of Mahomet in Middle English Literature," 220–27.

36. Citation from Akbari, *Idols in the East*, 124.

37. Michael Paull, "The Figure of Mahomet in the Towneley Cycle," *Comparative Drama* 6 (1972): 187–204.

38. The term "mahommet" appears six times in the play (ll. 458, 465, 513, 585, 779).

39. *Dictionnaire du Moyen Français*, s.v. "Mahomet; Oxford English Dictionary, "Mahomet, n." (Oxford University Press); *Middle English dictionary*, s.v. "Makomet."

40. Dorothee Metlitzki, *The Matter of Araby in Medieval England* (New Haven, CT: Yale University Press, 1977), 119, 208.

41. On this window, see Michelina di Cesare, "Reading the Bible through Glass: The Image of Muhammad in the Sainte Chapelle," in *The Image of the Prophet between Ideal and Ideology a Scholarly Investigation*, ed. Christiane Gruber and Avinoam Shalem (Berlin: De Gruyter, 2014), 187–99.

42. This image is discussed by Debra Strickland, "Meanings of Muhammad in Later Medieval Art," in Gruber and Shalem, *Image of the Prophet*, 147–63. See also Strickland, *Saracens, Demons and Jews*, 166–68.

43. Camille, *Gothic Idol*, 1–9.

44. "Machometus utroque parente orbatus, sub patrui sui custodia annos pueritie transegit aliquantoque tempore cum gente sua Arabica idolorum cultui deservivit,

potissime tamen Veneris venerationi deditus fuit." Ranulphus Higden, *Polychronicon Ranulphi Higden, Monachi Cestrensis; Together with the English Translations of John Trevisa and of an Unknown Writer of the Fifteenth Century*, trans. John Trevisa, 9 vols. (London: Longman, 1865), 6:20–21.

45. Higden, *Polychronicon Ranulphi Higden*, 24–25. See Metlitzki, *Matter of Araby in Medieval England*, 205–7.

46. On Robert Greene's *Alphonsus of Aragon*, see Dimmock, *Mythologies of the Prophet Muhammad*; Matthew Dimmock, "Materialising Islam on the Early Modern English Stage," in *Early Modern Encounters with the Islamic East* (Farnham, England: Ashgate, 2012), 115–32; Matthew Dimmock, "Robert Greene," in *CMR* 6:833–40. The text of the play is available online at http://www.elizabethanauthors.org/alphonsus101.htm.

47. Dimmock, "Materialising Islam on the Early Modern English Stage," 130.

48. Antoine Caillot, *Tableau des croisades pour la conquete de la terre-sainte* (Paris, 1843).

49. Marlène Albert-Llorca and Jean-Pierre Albert, "Mahomet, la Vierge et la frontière," *Annales: Histoire, Sciences Sociales* 50, no. 4 (1995): 855–86; Max Harris, *Aztecs, Moors, and Christians: Festivals of Reconquest in Mexico and Spain* (Austin: University of Texas Press, 2000), 221–26.

Chapter Two. Trickster and Heresiarch

1. On the two versions of his translation, see Anne Hedeman, *Translating the Past: Laurent de Premierfait and Boccaccio's De casibus* (Los Angeles: J. Paul Getty Museum, 2008); Guyda Armstrong, *The English Boccaccio: A History in Books* (Toronto: University of Toronto Press, 2013), 42–65.

2. "seductor ille nequam Mahumeth veniebat, cuius artes quam libentissime audissem novit Deus, et qualiter post prophete nomen assumptum legesque letiferas datas in suam luxuriam, deperisset." Giovanni Boccaccio, *De casibus virorum illustrium* (Milan: A. Mondadori, 1983), ix:1, p. 748. On Boccaccio's knowledge of Muhammad and Islam, see Roberta Morosini, "Giovanni Boccaccio," in *CMR* 5:76–87.

3. See for example Paris, BNF MS Français 132, f. 160, online at http://gallica.bnf.fr/ark:/12148/btv1b9009617f. There are eleven extant manuscripts of the 1400 translation and fifty-seven of the 1409 translation, according to Laurent Brun et al., "Laurent de Premierfait," http://www.arlima.net/no/1494.

4. I have used the text of Paris, BNF MS Français 226, f. 243v–245r, online at http://gallica.bnf.fr/ark:/12148/btv1b9009520k.

5. For example, Geneva, Bibliothèque publique et universitaire, MS fr. 190, f. 147; Paris, Bibliothèque de l'Arsenal MS 5193, f. 317v; see Hedeman, *Translating the Past*, 230–31.

6. John Lydgate, *Lydgate's Fall of Princes* (Washington, DC: Carnegie Institution of Washington, 1923). On Lydgate and his translation, see James Simpson, "John Lydgate," in *The Cambridge Companion to Medieval English Literature, 1000–1500*, ed. Larry Scanlon (Cambridge: Cambridge University Press, 2009); Armstrong, *English*

Boccaccio; Nigel Mortimer, *John Lydgate's Fall of Princes: Narrative Tragedy in Its Literary and Political Contexts* (Oxford: Oxford University Press, 2005).

7. Tolan, *Sons of Ishmael*, chap. 1. For an anthology of fifty-three brief medieval texts, in Latin, concerning Muhammad, with commentary and bibliography, see Michelina Di Cesare, *The Pseudo-Historical Image of the Prophet Muhammad in Medieval Latin Literature: A Repertory* (Berlin: De Gruyter, 2012).

8. On this meaning of "Frank," see John Tolan, "Constructing Christendom," in *The Making of Europe: Essays in Honour of Robert Bartlett*, ed. John Hudson (Oxford: Oxford University Press, 2016), 277–98.

9. Guibert de Nogent, *Dei gesta per Francos et cinq autres textes* (Turnhout, Belgium: Brepols, 1996), 89–93; Guibert de Nogent, *The Deeds of God through the Franks: A Translation of Guibert de Nogent's Gesta Dei per Francos*, trans. Robert Levine (Rochester, NY: Boydell Press, 1997), 30–32. On Guibert, see Jay Rubenstein, *Guibert of Nogent: Portrait of a Medieval Mind* (New York: Routledge, 2002); Tolan, "Guibert de Nogent," in *CMR* 3:329–34; Fernando González Muñoz, *Mahometrica: Ficciones poéticas latinas del siglo XII sobre Mahoma* (Madrid: Consejo Superior de Investigaciones Científicas, 2015), 75–78, 243–57.

10. Guibert de Nogent, *Dei gesta per Francos et cinq autres textes*, 94; trans., *The Deeds of God through the Franks: A Translation of Guibert de Nogent's Gesta Dei per Francos*, 32.

11. Guibert de Nogent, *Dei gesta per Francos et cinq autres textes*, 100; trans., *The Deeds of God through the Franks: A Translation of Guibert de Nogent's Gesta Dei per Francos*, 36.

12. Theophanes, *The Chronicle of Theophanes Confessor: Byzantine and Near Eastern History, AD 284–813*, trans. Cyril A. Mango and Roger Scott (Oxford: Clarendon Press, 1997), 464–65; Tolan, *Saracens*, chap. 3; Di Cesare, *The Pseudo-Historical Image of the Prophet Muhammad*, 52–54.

13. For a comparison of Guibert's text with those of three other early twelfth-century Latin authors, see Tolan, *Saracens*, chap. 6.

14. Guibert de Nogent, *Dei gesta per Francos et cinq autres textes*, 95; Guibert de Nogent, *The Deeds of God through the Franks: A translation of Guibert de Nogent's Gesta Dei per Francos*, 36. On the Bahira legend and its Christian deformations, see Barbara Roggema, *The Legend of Sergius Bahira Eastern Christian Apologetics and Apocalyptic in Response to Islam* (Leiden: Brill, 2009).

15. On the Muslim sources on Muhammad's marriage to Khadīja and the various opinions expressed on the marriage by both Christian and Muslim writers, see Kecia Ali, *The Lives of Muhammad* (Cambridge, MA: Harvard University Press, 2014).

16. Theophanes, *Chronicle of Theophanes Confessor*, 464.

17. On the prophet's supposed epilepsy, see Andrea Celli, " 'Maometto cascava del male caduco': Epilessia e profetismo islamico nella trattatistica storico-religiosa e medica in lingua italiana (Cinque-Seicento)," in *Eroi dell'estasi: Lo sciamanismo come artefatto culturale e sinopia letteraria*, ed. A. Barbieri (Verona: Fiorini, 2017), 240–62.

18. Tolan, *Saracens*, chap. 5.

19. Guibert de Nogent, *Deeds of God through the Franks: A Translation of Guibert de Nogent's Gesta Dei per Francos*, 34.

20. Tolan, *Saracens*, chap. 5.

21. For Guibert's description of Cathar orgies, followed by their burning their babies and eating the ashes, see Guibert de Nogent, *Monodies and On the Relics of Saints: The Autobiography and a Manifesto of a French Monk from the Time of the Crusades*, trans. Jay Rubenstein (New York: Penguin Books, 2011), c. xvii.

22. Guibert de Nogent, *Dei gesta per Francos et cinq autres textes*, 99; Guibert, *Deeds of God through the Franks: A Translation of Guibert de Nogent's Gesta Dei per Francos*, 33. On this passage, see Robert Levine, "Satiric Vulgarity in Guibert de Nogent's *Gesta Dei per Francos*," *Rhetorica: A Journal of the History of Rhetoric* 7, no. 3 (1989): 261–73.

23. Rubenstein, *Guibert of Nogent: Portrait of a Medieval Mind*, 124–30.

24. Guibert, *Dei gesta per Francos et cinq autres textes*, 100; Guibert, *Deeds of God through the Franks: Aa Translation of Guibert de Nogent's Gesta Dei per Francos*, 36.

25. Gautier de Compiègne, *Otia de Machomete*, vv. 1059–74, Latin text with Spanish translation in González Muñoz, *Mahometrica*, 238–39.

26. See Tolan, *Sons of Ishmael*, chap. 2.

27. Petrus Alfonsi, *Dialogue against the Jews*, trans. Irven Resnick (Washington, DC: Catholic University of America Press, 2006). On Petrus Alfonsi see Tolan, *Petrus Alfonsi and His Medieval Readers* (Gainesville: University Press of Florida, 1993); Tolan, "Petrus Alfonsi," in *CMR* 3:356–62.

28. Laura Bottini, "al-Kindī, ʿAbd al-Masīḥ ibn Isḥāq (pseudonym)," in *CMR* 1; Tolan, *Saracens*, chap. 3.

29. I have used the French translation of the *Risālat al-Kindī: Dialogue islamo-chrétien sous le calife Al-Ma'mûn (813–834): Les épitres d'Al-Hashimî et d'Al-Kindî*, trans. Georges Tartar (Paris: Nouvelles Ed. Latines, 1985), 86–87, 120–21.

30. *Risālat al-Kindī: Dialogue islamo-chrétien*, 133–34. Qur'ān 4:169–71.

31. *Risālat al-Kindī: Dialogue islamo-chrétien*, 129–33.

32. *Risālat al-Kindī: Dialogue islamo-chrétien*, 125–27.

33. *Risālat al-Kindī: Dialogue islamo-chrétien*, 137–53.

34. *Risālat al-Kindī: Dialogue islamo-chrétien*, 148–53. On the stories of Muhammad's wives in both Muslim and Christian texts, see Ali, *Lives of Muhammad*. On the story of Zayd and Zaynab, see David Powers, *Muhammad Is Not the Father of Any of Your Men: The Making of the Last Prophet* (Philadelphia: University of Pennsylvania Press, 2009).

35. *Risālat al-Kindī: Dialogue islamo-chrétien*, 152–53.

36. *Risālat al-Kindī: Dialogue islamo-chrétien*, 166. On the Muslim and Christian versions of Muhammad's death and burial, see Krisztina Szilagyi, "After the Prophet's Death: Christian-Muslim Polemic and the Literary Images of Muhammad" (PhD diss., Princeton University, 2014).

37. Alfonsi, *Dialogue against the Jews*, 146.

38. Alfonsi, *Dialogue against the Jews*, 154.

39. Alfonsi, *Dialogue against the Jews*, 157.

40. Alfonsi, *Dialogue against the Jews*, 159.

41. Alfonsi, *Dialogue against the Jews*, 162–63.

42. See Szilagyi, "After the Prophet's Death."

43. Tolan, *Petrus Alfonsi and His Medieval Readers*, 108–10.

44. Fernando González Muñoz, *Exposición y refutación del Islam: La versión latina de las epistolas de al-Hasimi y al-Kindi* (A Coruña, Spain: Universidade da Coruña, Servizo de Publicacións, 2005); Fernando González Muñoz, "Peter of Toledo," in *CMR* 3:478–82.

45. John Tolan and Dominique Iogna-Prat, "Peter of Cluny," in *CMR* 3:604–10; Tolan, *Saracens*, chap. 6.

46. See Walter Cahn, "The 'Portrait' of Muhammad in the Toledan Collection," in *Reading Medieval Images*, ed. Elizabeth Sears and Thelma Thomas (Ann Arbor: University of Michigan Press, 2002), 50; Strickland, *Saracens, Demons, and Jews*.

47. See Rita George Tvrtković, *A Christian Pilgrim in Medieval Iraq: Riccoldo da Montecroce's Encounter with Islam* (Turnhout, Belgium: Brepols, 2012); Thomas E. Burman, "Riccoldo da Monte di Croce," in *CMR* 4:678–91; Ricoldus de Monte Crucis, *Tractatus seu disputatio contra Saracenos et Alchoranum: Edition, Übersetzung, Kommentar*, ed. Daniel Pachurka (Wiesbaden: Harrassowitz Verlag, 2016).

48. George Tvrtković, *Christian Pilgrim in Medieval Iraq*, 163.

49. Riccoldo da Montecroce, "Contra Sectam Sarracenorum," ed. Jean-Marie Mérigoux and Emilio Panella (2011). http://www.e-theca.net/emiliopanella/riccoldo2/cls001.htm, accessed March 31, 2016.

50. Riccoldo da Montecroce, "Contra Sectam Sarracenorum," chap. 4.

51. Riccoldo da Montecroce, "Contra Sectam Sarracenorum," chap. 14. On the *mi'rāj*, see *Encyclopaedia of Islam*, 2nd ed. (Leiden: Brill, 2012), s.v. "mi'rādj."

52. Riccoldo da Montecroce, "Contra Sectam Sarracenorum," chap. 14. On the idea that Saracen philosophers rejected the Qur'ān, see Tolan, *Sons of Ishmael*, chap. 8.

53. On Dante's treatment of Islam, and in particular of Muhammad in *Inferno* 28, see Andrea Celli, "'Cor per medium fidit': Il canto XXVIII dell'Inferno alla luce di alcune fonti arabo-spagnole," *Lettere italiane* 2 (2013): 171–92; Jan M. Ziolkowski, ed., *Dante and Islam* (New York: Fordham University Press, 2015); Paolo de Ventura, "Dante Alighieri," in *CMR* 4:784–93.

54. See Karla Malette, "Muhammad in Hell," in Ziolkowski, *Dante and Islam*, 178–90; Heather Coffey, "Encountering the Body of Muhammad: Intersections between *Mi'raj* Narratives, the *Shaqq al-Sadr*, and the *Divina Commedia* before print (c. 1300–1500)," in *Constructing the Image of Muhammad in Europe*, ed. Avinoam Shalem (Berlin: De Gruyter, 2013), 33–86.

55. Lydgate, IX:49–161 (vol. 3, pp. 920–23).

56. London, British Library Harley MS 1766, f. 223; see http://www.bl.uk/catalogues/illuminatedmanuscripts/record.asp?MSID=8737&CollID=8&NStart=1766.

57. See Tolan, *Sons of Ishmael*, chap. 2; Folker Reichert, "Der eiserne Sarg des Propheten: Doppelte Grenzen im Islambild des Mittelalters," in *Grenze und Grenzüberschreitung im Mittelalter*, ed. Ulrich Knefelkamp and Kristian Bosselmann-

Cyran (Berlin: De Gruyter, 2007); Sandra Sáenz-Lápez Pérez, "La peregrinación a la Meca en la edad media a tra vés de la cartografía occidental," *Revista de poética medieval* 19 (2007): 177–218.

58. Felix Fabri, *The Wanderings of Felix Fabri* (New York: AMS Press, 1971), 2:251.

59. Fabri, *Wanderings of Felix Fabri*, 668.

60. See http://expositions.bnf.fr/marine/arret/03-2-2.htm.

61. See chapter five herein.

62. Mary Wollstonecraft, *A Vindication of the Rights of Woman* (London: Walter Scott, 1891), 44.

63. "Un dicton hongrois, 'Il flotte entre ciel et terre comme le cercueil de Mahomet' (Lebeg mint Mohammed koporsója ég és föld között) traduit plaisamment la situation de quelqu'un qui mal assuré de son avenir redoute l'état d'incertitude où il se trouve." Eckhardt, "Le Cercueil flottant de Mahomet," 77. He also tells (pp. 87–88) of a nineteenth-century Sicilian peasant who recounted the story of Muhammad's coffin (apparently believing it was true) and said that the way to make the coffin fall down was to rub garlic on it, since garlic is supposed to counter magnetism.

Chapter Three. Pseudoprophet of the Moors

1. Juan de Mata Carriazo, *Hechos del condestable Don Miguel Lucas de Iranzo: Crónica del siglo XV* (Granada: Universidad de Granada; Madrid: Marcial Pons, 2009), 98–99; Thomas Devaney, *Enemies in the Plaza: Urban Spectacle and the End of Spanish Frontier Culture, 1460–1492* (Philadelphia: University of Pennsylvania Press, 2015), 93–96; Harris, *Aztecs, Moors, and Christians*, 57–58.

2. Matthias Maser, "Rodrigo Jiménez de Rada," in *CMR* 4:343–55; Maser, *Die Historia Arabum des Rodrigo Jimenez de Rada: Arabische Traditionen und die Identität der Hispania im 13. Jahrhundert* (Berlin: Lit, 2006); Lucy Pick, *Conflict and Coexistence : Archbishop Rodrigo and the Muslims and Jews in Medieval Spain* (Ann Arbor: University of Michigan Press, 2004).

3. Nàdia Petrus Pons, ed., *Alchoranus latinus, quem transtulit Marcus canonicus Toletanu* (Madrid: Consejo Superior de Investigaciones Científicas, 2016).

4. Rodrigo Jiménez de Rada, *Historia Arabum* (Turnhout: Brepols, 2010); Ana Echevarria, "La reescritura del Libro de la escala de Mahoma como polémica religiosa," *Cahiers d'études hispaniques médiévales* 29 (2006): 173–99.

5. Rodrigo Jiménez de Rada, *Roderici Ximenii de Rada Historia de rebus Hispanie siue Historia Gothica* (Turnhout: Brepols, 1987), 297–99.

6. On this passage, see Tolan, *Saracens*, chap. 7.

7. Alfonso X, *Las Siete Partidas Underworlds—The Dead, The Criminal, and the Marginalized*, trans. Samuel Parsons Scott (Philadelphia: University of Pennsylvania Press, 2000), 1438.

8. José Muñoz Sendino, *La escala de Mahoma: Traducción del árabe al castellano, latín y francés, ordenada por Alfonso x el Sabio* (Madrid: Ministerio de Asuntos Exteriores, Dirección General de Relaciones Culturales, 1978); Echevarria, "La reescritura del Libro de la escala de Mahoma como polémica religiosa"; Ana Echevarria,

"Liber scalae Machometi," in *CMR* 4:425–28; Steven J. McMichael, "The Night Journey (al-isrā') and Ascent (al-miʿrāj) of Muhammad in Medieval Muslim and Christian Perspectives," *Islam and Christian-Muslim Relations* 22, no. 3 (2011): 293–309. For an English translation, see *The Prophet of Islam in Old French: The Romance of Muhammad (1258) and the Book of Muhammad's Ladder (1264)*, trans. Reginald Hyatte (Leiden: Brill, 1997).

9. See Christiane Gruber and Frederick Colby, eds., *The Prophet's Ascension: Cross-Cultural Encounters with the Islamic miʿraj Tales* (Bloomington: Indiana University Press, 2010).

10. Echevarria, "La reescritura del Libro de la escala," 188.

11. Alfonso X, *Primera crónica general de España que mandó componer Alfonso el Sabio y se continuaba bajo Sancho IV en 1289* (Madrid: Gredos, 1955), 4.

12. Alfonso X, *Primera crónica general de España*, 264–66.

13. Szilagyi, "After the Prophet's Death."

14. *Istoria de Mahomet*, cited here from the translation by Kenneth Baxter Wolf, "The Earliest Latin Lives of Muhammad," in *Conversion and Continuity: Indigenous Christian Communities in Islamic Lands, Eighth to Eighteenth Centuries*, ed. Michael Gervers and Ramzi Jibran Bikhazi (Toronto: Pontifical Institute of Mediaeval Studies, 1990), 89–101, 97–99. On this text, see Tolan, "Istoria de Mahomet," *CMR* 2:721–22.

15. Martín de Ximena Jurado, *Catalogo de los obispos de las iglesias catedrales de la diocesi [sic] de Jaen y Annales Eclesiasticos deste obispado* (Madrid: Domingo Garcia y Morras, 1654), 320; see Simon Barton, *Conquerors, Brides, and Concubines: Interfaith Relations and Social Power in Medieval Iberia* (Philadelphia: University of Pennsylvania Press, 2015), 106.

16. See Fernando González Muñoz's introduction to Pedro Pascual, *Sobre la seta mahometana* (Valencia: Universidad de Valencia, 2011).

17. What follows is based in large part on Tolan, "Pedro Pascual," *CMR* 4; Tolan, *Sons of Ishmael*, chap. 9. On his use of the *Liber Scalae*, see Echevarria, "La reescritura del Libro de la escala," 191–95.

18. Pedro Pascual, *Sobre la seta mahometana*, 84.

19. Pedro Pascual, *Sobre la seta mahometana*, 199.

20. Pedro Pascual, *Sobre la seta mahometana*, 86.

21. Pedro Pascual, *Sobre la seta mahometana*, 88.

22. Pedro Pascual, *Sobre la seta mahometana*, 97.

23. Pedro Pascual, *Sobre la seta mahometana*, 102–3.

24. Pedro Pascual, *Sobre la seta mahometana*, 104–11.

25. Pedro Pascual, *Sobre la seta mahometana*, 98–99.

26. Pedro Pascual, *Sobre la seta mahometana*, 116–19.

27. Pedro Pascual, *Sobre la seta mahometana*, 34.

28. Pedro Pascual, *Sobre la seta mahometana*, 126–29.

29. Pedro Pascual, *Sobre la seta mahometana*, 157–59.

30. Pedro Pascual, *Sobre la seta mahometana*, 159.

31. Pedro Pascual, *Sobre la seta mahometana*, 267.

32. Pedro Pascual, *Sobre la seta mahometana*, 84.

33. Tristan Vigliano, *Parler aux musulmans: Quatre intellectuels face à l'Islam à l'orée de la Renaissance* (Geneva: Droz, 2016); Ana Echevarria, *The Fortress of Faith: The Attitude towards Muslims in Fifteenth Century Spain* (Leiden: Brill, 1999); David Wrisley, "Jean Germain's Debat du Crestien et du Sarrasin (Paris, BnF fr. 948): Illumination between Multi-Confessional Debate and Anti-Conciliarism," in *The Social Life of Illumination*, ed. Kathryn Smith et al. (Turnhout: Brepols, 2013), 177–205.

34. Nicholas of Cusa, *Nicholas of Cusa's De pace fidei and Cribratio Alkorani: Translation and Analysis*, trans. Jasper Hopkins (Minneapolis: A. J. Banning Press, 1990); *Nicholas of Cusa and Islam Polemic and Dialogue in the Late Middle Ages* (Leiden: Brill, 2014); Tolan, "Nicholas of Cusa"; Vigliano, *Parler aux musulmans*, 139–207.

35. Anne Marie Wolf, *Juan de Segovia and the Fight for Peace: Christians and Muslims in the Fifteenth Century* (Notre Dame, IN: University of Notre Dame Press, 2014), 129–74; Vigliano, *Parler aux musulmans*, 209–303.

36. Wolf, *Juan de Segovia and the Fight for Peace*, 138–39.

37. Thomas E. Burman, *Reading the Qur'an in Latin Christendom, 1140–1560* (Philadelphia: University of Pennsylvania Press, 2007), 178–88; Wolf, *Juan de Segovia and the Fight for Peace*, 188–92; Gerard Wiegers, "Içe de Gebir," in *CMR* 5:462–68; José Martínez Gázquez, "El Prólogo de Juan de Segobia al Corán (Qur'ān) trilingüe (1456)," *Mittellateinisches Jahrbuch* 38 (2003): 389–410; Davide Scotto, "'De pe a pa': Il Corano trilingue di Juan de Segovia (1456) e la conversione pacifica dei musulmani," *Rivista di Storia e Letteratura Religiosa* 48 (2012): 515–78; Echevarria, *Fortress of faith*.

38. Juan de Segovia, *De gladio divini spiritus in corda mittendo Sarracenorum: Edition und deutsche Übersetzung*, ed. and trans. Ulli Roth, 2 vols., Corpus Islamo-Christianum (Wiesbaden: Harrassowitz Verlag, 2012), 2:516–37.

39. "De his vero tribus ex libro Alchoran vix ulla habetur versisimilitudo," Juan de Segovia, *De gladio divini spiritus in corda mittendo Sarracenorum*, 520.

40. Cited by Wolf, *Juan de Segovia and the Fight for Peace*, 149.

41. Juan de Torquemada, *Contra principales errores perfidi Machometi* (Rome: Gulielmi Facciotti, 1606). See Ana Echevarria, "Juan de Torquemada," in *CMR* 5.

42. Nancy Bisaha, "Pius II," *CMR* 5:456–61.

43. Nicholas of Cusa, *Opera omnia*, vol. 8 (Hamburg: Meiner, 1986), 92–96; Nicholas of Cusa, *Nicholas of Cusa's De pace fidei and Cribratio Alkorani: Translation and Analysis*, 1027–29. See *Nicholas of Cusa and Islam Polemic and Dialogue in the Late Middle Ages*; Tolan, "Nicholas of Cusa," *CMR* 5:421–28.

44. See Jasper Hopkins's introduction to *Nicholas of Cusa's De pace fidei and Cribratio Alkorani*, 22–23.

45. Nicholas of Cusa, *Nicholas of Cusa's De pace fidei*, 968–69.

46. Juan Andrés, *Confusión o confutación de la secta Mahomética y del Alcorán* (Mérida, Mexico: Regional de Extremadura, 2003); Juan Andrés, *The Confusion of Muhamed's Sect: Or a Confutation of the Turkish Alcoran*, trans. Joshua Notstock (London: H. Blunden, 1652). The citations that follow are to the Spanish edition and the translations are my own. See Hartmut Bobzin, "Observaciones sobre Juan Andrés

y su Libro confusion dela secta mahomatica (Valencia, 1515)," in *Vitae Mahometi: Reescritura e invención en la literatura cristiana de controversia*, ed. Cándida Ferrero Hernández and Óscar de la Cruz Palma (Madrid: Consejo Superior de Investigaciones Científicas, 2014), 209–22.

47. See Isabelle Poutrin, *Convertir les musulmans: Espagne, 1491–1609* (Paris: Presses Universitaires de France, 2012).

48. Andrés, *Confusión*, 90.

49. Andrés, *Confusión*, 91. To my knowledge, there is no extant manuscript of this work.

50. Ryan Szpiech, "Preaching Paul to the Moriscos: The Confusión o confutación de la secta Mahomética y del Alcorán (1515) of 'Juan Andrés,'" *Corónica: A Journal of Medieval Hispanic Languages, Literatures, and Cultures* 41, no. 1 (2012): 317–43.

51. Andrés, *Confusión*, 91.

52. Szpiech, "Preaching Paul to the Moriscos."

53. As Szpiech observes, this "points to the link between his written polemical arguments and an oral delivery through preaching and sermonizing," Szpiech, "Preaching Paul to the Moriscos," 322.

54. "digo a ti, moro, que no has que fazer otro sino callar," Andrés, *Confusión*, 188.

55. Andrés, *Confusión*, 194.

56. "en las quales palabras porás saber tú, moro, cómo declare que Jesuchristo es Dios y hombre," Andrés, *Confusión*, 217.

57. For the Dutch translation, see Juan Andrés, *De zeer wonderlijcke ende warachtighe historie van Mahomet: Inde welcke beschreven ende verhaelt wordt zijn gheboorte, afcomste, leven ende valsche leeringhe, mette confutatie oft wederlegginge van den Alcoran ende quade secte des selfs Mahomet* (Gheprint t'Antwerpen: By Guillaem van Parijs, 1580). The editions of the other translations are listed by Elisa Ruíz García in her introduction to Andrés, *Confusión o confutación de la secta Mahomética y del Alcorán*, 54–56.

58. Mercedes García-Arenal, *The Orient in Spain: Converted Muslims, the Forged Lead Books of Granada, and the Rise of Orientalism*, trans. Fernando Rodríguez Mediano (Leiden: Brill, 2013), 58–60; Stefania Pastore, *Un'eresia spagnola: Spiritualità conversa, alumbradismo e inquisizione (1449–1559)* (Florence: L. S. Olschki, 2004).

59. Gerard A. Wiegers, "The Persistence of Mudejar Islam? Alonso de Luna (Muhammad Abū 'l- Āsī), the Lead Books, and the Gospel of Barnabas," *Medieval Encounters* 12, no. 3 (2006): 498–518; García-Arenal, *Orient in Spain*.

60. Leonard Harvey, *Muslims in Spain, 1500 to 1614* (Chicago: University of Chicago Press, 2005), 271.

61. *Encyclopaedia of Islam, THREE* (Leiden: Brill, 2010), s.v. "Gospel of Barnabas"; Gerard Wiegers, "Muhammad as the Messiah: A Comparison of the Polemical Works of Juan Alonso with the Gospel of Barnabas (English)," *Bibliotheca Orientalis* 52, no. 3–4 (1995): 245–91. For an edition of the Italian manuscript with an English translation, see *The Gospel of Barnabas*, trans. Lonsdale Ragg and Laura Ragg (Oxford: Clarendon Press, 1907). On the preeminence of the Italian version, see Jan Joosten,

"The 'Gospel of Barnabas' and the Diatessaron," *Harvard Theological Review* 95, no. 1 (2002): 73–96.

62. *Gospel of Barnabas*, 32–33.

63. *Gospel of Barnabas*, 105, 380.

64. *Gospel of Barnabas*, 88–91.

65. *Gospel of Barnabas*, 96–97.

66. *Gospel of Barnabas*, 256–59. Cf. *Gospel of Barnabas*, 487.

67. On the role the Gospel gives to Muhammad at the last judgment, see *Gospel of Barnabas*, 126–29.

68. *Gospel of Barnabas*, 224–27.

69. This work has been frequently confused with a play with a similar title written by Francisco de Rojas Zorrilla, though Cándida Ferrero Hernández argues that the author is probably Mira de Amescua. "Vida y muerte del falso profeta Mahoma," *Parte treinta y tres de doze comedias famosas de varios autores* (Valencia: por Claudio Macé acosta de Iuan Sonzoni, 1642); Cándida Ferrero Hernández, "Mahoma como personaje teatral de una comedia prohibida del siglo de oro, *Vida y muerte del falso profeta Mahoma*," in *Vitae Mahometi*, 237–54; "El poeta morisco: De Rojas Zorrilla al autor secreto de una comedia sobre Mahoma [Vida y muerte del falso]," *Ehumanista* (Santa Barbara, CA) 19 (2011): 595–98; Joseph M. Sola-Sole and Montserrat D. Sola-Sole, "Los Mahomas de Rojas Zorrilla," *Revista de Estudios Hispánicos* 6, no. 1 (1972): 3; Francisco de Rojas Zorrilla, *El profeta falso Mahoma* ([Valencia]: [Imprenta de la viuda de J. de Orga], 1761).

70. "Vida y muerte del falso profeta Mahoma," 46–47.

71. "Vida y muerte del falso profeta Mahoma," 46–47.

Chapter Four. Prophet of the Turks

1. Michele Luposignoli, *Disputa* (1727), copy of an original by Nikola Bralič (1518), Santa Maria de Poljud (Split). http://www.accademiamariana.org/Islam/page3.html.

2. Cited by Réjane Gay-Canton, "Lorsque Muḥammad orne les autels: Sur l'utilisation de la théologie islamique dans la controverse autour de l'Immaculée Conception de la fin du XIVe au début du XVIIIe siècle," *Revue des Sciences Philosophiques et Théologiques* 94, no. 2 (2010): 201–48, here at 243–44.

3. Johannes Schiltberger, *Hans Schiltbergers Reisebuch* (Tübingen: Litterarischer Verein in Stuttgart, 1885), 84–86; Johannes Schiltberger, *The Bondage and Travels of Johann Schiltberger, a Native of Bavaria, in Europe, Asia, and Africa, 1396–1427* (London: Hakluyt Society, 1879), 65–70.

4. Martin Luther, *Explanations of the Ninety-Five Theses*, in *Luther's Works*, 55 vols. (Saint Louis, MO: Concordia Publishing House, 1955–75), 31:83–252 (citation p. 92). For the German text, see Martin Luther, *D. Martin Luthers Werke: Kritische Gesamtausgabe*, 121 vols. (Weimar: H. Böhlau, 1883–2009, hereafter *Werke*), 1:525–628. On Luther's perception of Islam, see Adam Francisco, "Martin Luther," in *CMR* 6:225–34; Adam Francisco, *Martin Luther and Islam: A Study in Sixteenth-Century*

Polemics and Apologetics (Leiden: Brill, 2007); Johannes Ehmann, *Luther, Türken und Islam: Eine Untersuchung zum Türken- und Islambild Martin Luthers (1515–1546)* (Gütersloh: Gütersloher Verlagshaus, 2008).

5. *Luther's Works* 46:161–205 (citation p. 170). *Vom Kriege wider den Türcken, Werke*, 30 III:107–48.

6. *Luther's Works* 43:219–41 (citation p. 224). *Vermahnung zum Gebet wider den Türkcen, Werke*, 51:585–625.

7. *Werke*, 30/2:206. Translation (modified) from Sarah Henrich and James Boyce, "Translations of Two Prefaces on Islam: Preface to the Libellus de ritu et moribus Turcorum (1530) and Preface to Bibliander's Edition of the Qur'ân (1543)," *Word and World* 16 (1996): 250–59.

8. Luther, *Luther's Works*, 43:227.

9. *On War against the Turk*, Luther, *Luther's Works*, 43:175.

10. *Werke*, 207; Henrich and Boyce, "Translations of Two Prefaces on Islam," 260.

11. *On War against the Turk*, *Luther's Works*, 46:181. Cited by Francisco, *Martin Luther and Islam*, 114.

12. Heinrich Knaust, *Von geringem herkomen, schentlichem leben, schmehlichem ende des Tuerckischen Abgots Machomets, vnd seiner verdamlichen vnd Gotßlesterischen Ler, allen fromen Christen disen geferlichen zeiten zur sterckung vnnd trost im glauben an Jesum Christum* (Berlin: Hans Weissen, 1542). On this text, see Francisco, *Martin Luther and Islam*, 55–56.

13. "Wo nu die Türcken oder Sarracenen solchem Buch des Mahmets, dem Alcoran, mit Ernst gleuben, So sind sie niche werd, das sie Menschen heissen, als die gemeiner Menschlichen vernunft beraubt, lauter ummenschen, Stein und Klotz worden sind." Preface to Riccoldo da Montecroce's *Verlegung des Alcoran, Werke*, 53:388–89. Citation and translation from Francisco, *Martin Luther and Islam*, 200.

14. *Verlegung des Alcoran, Werke*, 53:334. Citation and translation in Francisco, *Martin Luther and Islam*, 115.

15. *Verlegung des Alcoran, Werke*, 53:334. Citation and translation in Francisco, *Martin Luther and Islam*, 193.

16. Harry Loewen, *Ink against the Devil: Luther and His Opponents* (Waterloo, ON: Wilfrid Laurier University Press, 2015).

17. Loewen, *Ink against the Devil*, 195.

18. *Verlegung des Alcoran, Luther, Werke*, 53:396. Citation and translation in Francisco, *Martin Luther and Islam*, 208–9.

19. *Werke*, 30:2, 195. Cited by Robert O. Smith, "Luther, the Turks, and Islam," *Currents in Theology and Mission* 34, no. 5 (2007): 351.

20. Dimmock, *Mythologies*, 88.

21. Jean Calvin, sermon 10, preached January 24, 1558, in Bibliothèque de Genève Ms. Fr. 19, f. 80; thanks for this reference to Ruth Stawarz-Luginbuehl, who is preparing a critical edition of these sermons.

22. Dimmock, *Mythologies*, 154.

23. Dimmock, *Mythologies*, 77–79.

24. Thomas More, *The Complete Works of St. Thomas More: A Dialogue concerning*

Heresies (1981), 374–75, 407. Spelling standardized, punctuation modernized, and glosses added by Mary Gottschalk, https://www.thomasmorestudies.org/docs /DialogueConcerningHeresies2015-etext.pdf. Cf. Dimmock, *Mythologies*, 82.

25. Johannes Sleidanus, *De statu religionis et reipublicae Carolo V caesare commentarii* (Strasbourg: Wendelin Rihel, 1555), 60. See Dimmock, *Mythologies*, 92.

26. Christine Isom-Verhaaren, "Guillaume Postel," in *CMR* 6:712–25; Brannon Wheeler, "Guillaume Postel and the Primordial Origins of the Middle East," *Method and Theory in the Study of Religion* 25, no. 3 (2013): 244–63; Oscar de la Cruz Palma, "Sobre el Coran latino de Guillaume Postel," *Rivista di storia e letteratura religiosa* 51 (2015): 515–39; Linda Bisello, "L'idea di concordia universale in Guillaume Postel (1510–1581) tra unità religiosa e linguistica," *Rivista di storia e letteratura religiosa* 48 (2012): 579–602.

27. Guillaume Postel, *Alcorani seu legis Mahometi et Evangelistarum concordiae Liber: Additus est libellus de universalis conversionis* (Paris: Petrus Gromorsus, 1543).

28. William Rainolds, *Calvino-Tvrcismvs: Id est, Calvinisticae perfidiae, cum Mahumetana collatio, et dilucida utriusque sectae confutatio* (Antwerp: In aedibus Petri Belleri, 1597). See Clinton Bennet, "William Rainolds," in *CMR* 6:862–65.

29. Theodor Bibliander, *Ad nominis christiani socios consultatio* (Basel, 1542); Theodorus Bibliander, *A Godly Consultation vnto the Brethren and Companyons of the Christen Religyon* (Basel, Radulphe Bonifante [i.e., M. Crom], 1542). On this passage, see Dimmock, *Mythologies*, 86–88 and 90–92. On Bibliander's views of Islam and Muhammad, see Gregory J. Miller, "Theodor Bibliander's *Machumetis saracenorum principis eiusque successorum vitae, doctrina ac ipse alcoran* (1543) as the Sixteenth-Century 'Encyclopedia' of Islam," *Islam and Christian-Muslim Relations* 24, no. 2 (2013): 241–54; Katya Vehlow, "The Swiss Reformers Zwingli, Bullinger, and Bibliander and Their Attitude to Islam (1520–1560)," *Islam and Christian-Muslim Relations* 6 (1995): 229–54; Oscar de la Cruz, "La llegenda de Mahoma a l'Edat Mitjana i al Renaixement La compilació de Bibliander," *Estudi General Revista de la Facultat de Lletres de la Universitat de Girona* 23–24 (2004); Bruce Gordon, "Theodor Bibliander," *CMR* 6:675–85.

30. Dimmock, *Mythologies*, 88.

31. Michael Servetus, *The Two Treatises of Servetus on the Trinity: On the Errors of the Trinity, 7 books, A.D. 1531; Dialogues on the Trinity, 2 books; On the Righteousness of Christ's Kingdom, 4 chapters, A.D. 1532*, trans. Earl Morse Wilbur (Cambridge, MA: Harvard University Press, 1932); Michael Servetus, *Christianismi restitutio* (Vienne en Dauphine: Balthazar Arnollett, 1553). Peter Hughes, "Servetus and the Quran," *Journal of Unitarian Universalist History* 30 (2005): 55–70; Karel Steenbrink, "Michael Servetus," *CMR* 6:645–53; *Michel Servet (1511-1553): Hérésie et pluralisme du XVIᵉ au XXIᵉ siècle* (Paris: Honoré Champion, 2007).

32. Michael Servetus, *Sept livres sur les erreurs de la Trinité* (Paris: Honoré Champion, 2008), 297–99; Servetus, *The Two Treatises of Servetus on the Trinity: On the Errors of the Trinity, 7 books, A.D. 1531; Dialogues on the Trinity, 2 books; On the Righteousness of Christ's Kingdom, 4 chapters, A.D. 1532*, 66–67.

33. Servetus, *Christianismi restitutio*, 35–36; Michael Servetus, *The Restoration*

of Christianity: An English Translation of Christianismi restitutio, 1553, trans. Christopher A. Hoffman and Marian Hillar (Lewiston, NY: Edwin Mellen Press, 2007), 48–51; Miguel Servet, *Restitution du christianisme* (Paris: Honoré Champion, 2011).

34. Servet, *Restitution du christianisme,* 77; *Restoration of Christianity,* 51.

35. Servet, *Restitution du christianisme,* 193; *Restoration of Christianity,* 62.

36. Servetus, *Restoration of Christianity,* 66.

37. Bruce Gordon, *Calvin* (New Haven, CT: Yale University Press, 2011), 217–28.

38. *De Falsa et vera unius Dei Patris, Filii et Spiritus Sancti cognitione libri duo: (Albae Iuliae) 1568* (Budapest: Akadémiai Kiadó, 1988). See Martin Mulsow, "Socinianism, Islam, and the Radical Uses of Arabic Scholarship," *Al-Qanṭara* 31 (2010): 549–86 (esp. 565–66); Peter Hughes, "In the Footsteps of Servetus: Biandrata, Dávid, and the Quran," *Journal of Unitarian Universalist History* 31 (2006): 57–63.

39. *De Falsa et vera unius Dei,* 37–38. For a translation and discussion of this key passage, see Hughes, "In the Footsteps of Servetus," 58–60.

40. Cited by Mulsow, "Socinianism, Islam, and the Radical Uses of Arabic Scholarship," 560–61. See Jan Loop, *Johann Heinrich Hottinger: Arabic and Islamic Studies in the Seventeenth Century* (Oxford: Oxford University Press, 2013).

41. Johann Heinrich Hottinger, *Historia orientalis,* translation in Loop, *Johann Heinrich Hottinger,* 210.

42. Hottinger, *Historia orientalis,* translation in Loop, *Johann Heinrich Hottinger,* 215–16.

43. Cited by Mulsow, "Socinianism, Islam, and the Radical Uses of Arabic Scholarship," 563.

44. Mulsow, "Socinianism, Islam, and the Radical Uses of Arabic Scholarship," 563–5.

45. Georg B. Michels, "The 1672 Kuruc Uprising: A National or Religious Revolt?" *Hungarian Studies Review* 39 (2012): 1–20.

46. Marcell Sebők, "The Galley-Slave Trial of 1674: Conviction and Expulsion of Hungarian Protestants," in *Expulsion and Diaspora Formation: Religious and Ethnic Identities in Flux from Antiquity to the Seventeenth Century,* ed. J. Tolan (Turnhout: Brepols, 2015).

47. *L'Alcorano di Macometto* (Venice, 1547). On this translation, see Pier Mattia Tommasino, *L'Alcorano di Macometto: Storia di un libro del Cinquecento europeo* (2013); Maria Teresa Chicote Pompanin, "L'Alcorano of Andrea Arrivabene: An Iconographical Framework," *Church History and Religious Culture* 96 (2016): 130–54; Pier Mattia Tommasino, "Giovanni Battista Castrodardo" *CMR* 6:506–11.

48. *L'Alcorano di Macometto,* preface, "La vera vita di Macometto, tratta dall'historie di christiani," f. iii.

49. Johann Israel de Bry and Johann Theodor de Bry, *I. Acta Mechmeti I. Saracenorum principis: Natales, vitam, victorias, imperium & mortem ejus ominosam completentia; Genealogia successorum ejusdem ad modernum usque Mechmetem III. II. Vaticinia . . . interitum regni Turcici praedicentia* (Frankfurt: De Bry, 1597). On this text and its illustrations, see Ulrike Ilg, "Religious Polemics and Visual Realism in a Late 16th-Century Biography of the Prophet Muhammad," in *The Image of the Prophet,*

241–59; Saviello, *Imaginationen des Islam*, 81–112. The De Brys published a series of books with travel narratives, particularly concerning the Americas and the Middle East, with similar images; see Maureen Quilligan, "Theodor De Bry's Voyages to the New and Old Worlds," *Journal of Medieval and Early Modern Studies* 41, no. 1 (2011): 1–12.

50. The images discussed may be consulted online: http://reader.digitale -sammlungen.de/de/fs1/object/display/bsb11208631_00025.html.

51. See Tolan, *Sons of Ishmael*, chap. 2.

52. Alastair Hamilton, *The Forbidden Fruit: The Koran in Early Modern Europe* (London: London Middle East Institute, 2008).

53. *Mahomets Alkoran* (Amsterdam: Timotheus ten Hoorn, 1696). See Hamilton, *Forbidden Fruit*; Isabella Henriette van Eeghen and Jean Louis de Lorme, *De Amsterdamse boekhandel, 1680–1725*, 5 vols. (Amsterdam: Scheltema and Holkema, 1960), 3:165.

54. See https://www.forumrarebooks.com/item/_quran__de_arabische_alkoran _door_de_zarazijnsche_en_de_turcksche_prophete.html?c=94684889A2BD.

55. Thomas M. Izbicki, "The Immaculate Conception and Ecclesiastical Politics from the Council of Basel to the Council of Trent: The Dominicans and Their Foes," *Archiv für Reformationsgeschichte* 96 (2005).

56. Much of what follows is based on Gay-Canton, "Lorsque Muḥammad orne les autels"; I explore this issue in greater detail in Tolan, "Un Mahomet d'Occident? La valorisation du prophète de l'islam dans l'Europe chrétienne (xive–xviie siècles)," in *À la rencontre de l'autre au Moyen Âge*, ed. Philippe Josserand and Jerzy Pysiak (Rennes: Presses Universitaires de Rennes, 2017), 173–95.

57. *Sahih Muslim*, Book 43, hadith 193.

58. Stephen Mossman, "The Western Understanding of Islamic Theology in the Later Middle Ages: Mendicant Responses to Islam from Riccoldo da Monte di Croce to Marquard von Lindau," *Recherches de théologie et philosophie médiévales* 74, no. 1 (2007): 169–224; Gay-Canton, "Lorsque Muḥammad orne les autels."

59. Citation and translation from Mossman, "Western Understanding," 218.

60. Bartomeu Xiberta, "Fra Francesc Martí, carmelita de Barcelona I el dogma de la inmaculada," *Paraula cristiana* no. 59 (1929): 420–28; Gay-Canton, "Lorsque Muḥammad orne les autels," 227–28.

61. Andrés, *Confusión o confutación de la secta Mahomética y del Alcorán*, chap. 11.

Chapter Five. Republican Revolutionary in Renaissance England

1. Nabil Matar, *Islam in Britain, 1558–1685* (Cambridge: Cambridge University Press, 1998), 7. The following paragraphs are based principally on Matar's book.

2. Matar, *Islam in Britain*, 123–24.

3. Matar, *Islam in Britain*, 124. Matar cites Francis Bacon, *The Works* (London: Longmans, 1889), 8:204.

4. Matar, *Islam in Britain*, 50–58.

5. For this quote, and a discussion of the debates about coffee in mid-seventeenth-century England, see Matar, *Islam in Britain*, 110–19.

6. *The Alcoran of Mahomet, translated out of Arabick into French, by the Sieur Du Ryer, Lord of Malezair, and resident for the French king, at Alexandria. And newly Englished, for the satisfaction of all that desire to look into the Turkish vanities. To which is prefixed, the life of Mahomet, the prophet of the Turks, and author of the Alcoran. With A needful caveat, or admonition, for them who desire to know what use may be made of, or if there be danger in reading the Alcoran* (London, 1649). See Mordechai Feingold, " 'The Turkish Alcoran': New Light on the 1649 English Translation of the Koran," *Huntington Library Quarterly* 75, no. 4 (2012): 475–501; Noel Malcolm, "The 1649 English Translation of the Koran: Its Origins and Significance," *Journal of the Warburg and Courtauld Institutes* 75 (2012): 261–95. I follow Feingold in the attribution of the translation to Thomas Ross, on whom, see Philip Lewin, "Ross, Thomas (bap. 1620, d. 1675)," in *Oxford Dictionary of National Biography: In Association with the British Academy; From the Earliest Times to the Year 2000* (Oxford: Oxford University Press, 2004). On Ryer's French translation, see Sylvette Larzul, "Les premières traductions françaises du Coran (XVIIe–XIXe siècles)," *Archives de sciences sociales des religions* 54, no. 147 (2009): 147–65.

7. Dimmock, *Mythologies*, 168. See also Matthew Birchwood, *Staging Islam in England: Drama and Culture, 1640-1685* (Cambridge: D. S . Brewer, 2007), 64–7.

8. *The Alcoran of Mahomet*, (preface, unnumbered page).

9. *Alcoran of Mahomet* (preface, unnumbered page).

10. *Alcoran of Mahomet* (preface, unnumbered page).

11. I am following here the excellent analysis of Matar, *Islam in Britain*, 78.

12. *Alcoran of Mahomet*, iv–v.

13. *Alcoran of Mahomet*, v–vi.

14. *Alcoran of Mahomet*, vii.

15. *Alcoran of Mahomet*, vii–viii; Dimmock, *Mythologies*, 166; Matar, *Islam in Britain*, 73–83.

16. Lewin, "Ross, Thomas (bap. 1620, d. 1675)"; Feingold, "Turkish Alcoran," 476–79.

17. *The Famous Tragedie of King Charles I. Basely Butchered* ([London?], 1649); Birchwood, *Staging Islam in England*, 52–64.

18. Dimmock, *Mythologies*, 166–74.

19. Lancelot Addison, *The First State of Mahumedism; or, An Account of the Author and Doctrines of That Imposture* (London: Printed by J. C. for W. Crooke . . . 1679), 115–19; Dimmock, *Mythologies*, 187–88; William Bulman, *Anglican Enlightenment: Orientalism, Religio,n and Politics in England and Its Empire, 1648-1715* (Cambridge: Cambridge University Press, 2015).

20. Feingold, "Turkish Alcoran," 491–500.

21. John Milton, *The life and reigne of King Charls, or, The pseudo-martyr discovered: With a late reply to an invective remonstrance against the Parliament and pres-*

ent government (London: Printed for W. Reybold, 1651), 184–85; Dimmock, *Mythologies*, 175.

22. Matar, *Islam in Britain*, 104.

23. Henry Stubbe and N. I. Matar, *Henry Stubbe and the Beginnings of Islam: The Originall & Progress of Mahometanism* (New York: Columbia University Press, 2014). See also Humberto Garcia, "A Hungarian Revolution in Restoration England: Henry Stubbe, Radical Islam, and the Rye House Plot," *Eighteenth Century* 51 (2010): 1–25; James R. Jacob, *Henry Stubbe, Radical Protestantism, and the Early Enlightenment* (Cambridge: Cambridge University Press, 1983); Garcia, "Hungarian Revolution in Restoration England."

24. Stubbe and Matar, *Henry Stubbe and the Beginnings of Islam*, 1.

25. Loop, *Johann Heinrich Hottinger*, 214–15.

26. Stubbe and Matar, *Henry Stubbe and the Beginnings of Islam*, 69–70.

27. Stubbe and Matar, *Henry Stubbe and the Beginnings of Islam*, 85.

28. Stubbe and Matar, *Henry Stubbe and the Beginnings of Islam*, 89.

29. Stubbe and Matar, *Henry Stubbe and the Beginnings of Islam*, 91.

30. Stubbe and Matar, *Henry Stubbe and the Beginnings of Islam*, 187–88, 99–100.

31. Stubbe and Matar, *Henry Stubbe and the Beginnings of Islam*, 100.

32. Stubbe and Matar, *Henry Stubbe and the Beginnings of Islam*, 102.

33. Stubbe and Matar, *Henry Stubbe and the Beginnings of Islam*, 122.

34. Stubbe and Matar, *Henry Stubbe and the Beginnings of Islam*, 122–23. On the legends around Muhammad and Isidore, see Patrick Henriet, "Mahomet expulsé d'Espagne par Isidore de Séville: Sur la postérité moderne d'un épisode hagiographique rejeté par les Bollandistes," in *Vitae Mahometi*, 255–75.

35. Stubbe and Matar, *Henry Stubbe and the Beginnings of Islam*, 125.

36. Stubbe and Matar, *Henry Stubbe and the Beginnings of Islam*, 127.

37. Stubbe and Matar, *Henry Stubbe and the Beginnings of Islam*, 131.

38. Stubbe and Matar, *Henry Stubbe and the Beginnings of Islam*, 133.

39. Stubbe and Matar, *Henry Stubbe and the Beginnings of Islam*, 134.

40. Stubbe and Matar, *Henry Stubbe and the Beginnings of Islam*, 166.

41. Jacob, *Henry Stubbe, Radical Protestantism, and the Early Enlightenment*, 8–24.

42. Thomas Hobbes, *Leviathan*, chap. 31.

43. Stubbe and Matar, *Henry Stubbe and the Beginnings of Islam*, 152–53.

44. Stubbe and Matar, *Henry Stubbe and the Beginnings of Islam*, 189–93. That these legends were still given currency in seventeenth-century England is seen in the *Leviathan* (I:12) by Stubbe's friend Thomas Hobbes, who asserts that "Mahomet, to set up his new Religion, pretended to have conferences with the Holy Ghost, in the forme of a Dove."

45. Stubbe and Matar, *Henry Stubbe and the Beginnings of Islam*, 174. Cf. p. 194–95, where he cites Pococke's refutation of the legend.

46. Stubbe and Matar, *Henry Stubbe and the Beginnings of Islam*, 200.

47. Stubbe and Matar, *Henry Stubbe and the Beginnings of Islam*, 177.

48. Stubbe and Matar, *Henry Stubbe and the Beginnings of Islam*, 179.

49. Stubbe and Matar, *Henry Stubbe and the Beginnings of Islam*, 185.

50. Stubbe and Matar, *Henry Stubbe and the Beginnings of Islam*, 209.

51. *Nova Solyma, the Ideal City; or, Jerusalem Regained* (London: J. Murray, 1902), 163. Cited by Matar, *Islam in Britain*, 109.

52. Matar, *Islam in Britain*, 109.

53. Garcia, "Hungarian Revolution in Restoration England," 42–51.

54. Bulman, *Anglican Enlightenment*, 249–51.

55. John Locke, *A Letter concerning Toleration* (New York: Bobs and Merrill, 1955), 25. Cited by Nabil Matar, "John Locke and the 'Turbanned Nations,'" *Journal of Islamic Studies* 2 (1991): 67–77.

56. Arthur Bury, *The naked gospel discovering I. What was the gospel which our Lord and his apostles preached, II. What additions and alterations latter ages have made in it, III. What advantages and damages have thereupon ensued : Part I. Of Faith, and therein, of the Holy Trinity, the incarnation of our Blessed Saviour, and the resurrection of the body* (London: Printed for Nathanael Ranew, 1691), 2. See Garcia, "Hungarian Revolution in Restoration England," 162–64; Jim Benedict, "Bury, Arthur (1623/4–1713)," in *Oxford Dictionary of National Biography*.

57. Stephen Nye, *A Letter of Resolution concerning the Doctrines of the Trinity and the Incarnation* (London, 1691), 18; Matar, *Islam in Britain*, 108. On Nye, see H. McLachlan, "Nye, Stephen (1647/8–1719)," in *Oxford Dictionary of National Biography*.

58. Humphrey Prideaux, *The True Nature of Imposture Fully Display'd in the Life of Mahomet: With a discourse annex'd for the vindication of Christianity from this charge. Offered to the Consideration of the Deists of the Present Age.* (London: Printed for E. Curll against Catharine-Street in the Strand, J. Hooke against St. Dunstan's Church in Fleetstreet, W. Mears and F. Clay without Temple-Bar, 1723).

59. Stubbe and Matar, *Henry Stubbe and the Beginnings of Islam*, 1.

60. Humphrey Prideaux, *Den regten aard en eigenschap der bedriegerye, naakt ten toon gesteld in het leven van Mahomet. Waar by gevoegd is, een verdediging voor de Christelyke Godsdienst, tegens de lasteraars der zelve, tot overtuiginge van de hedendaagse deïsten*, trans. B. Jaques (Tot Delft: By Adriaan Beman, 1698); Humphrey Prideaux, *La vie de Mahomet: Où l'on découvre amplement la vérité de l'imposture* (Amsterdam: Gallet, 1698).

61. John Toland, *Nazarenus* (Oxford: Voltaire Foundation, 1999).

62. Toland, *Nazarenu*, 118.

63. Toland, *Nazarenu*, 135.

64. Toland, *Nazarenu*, 135.

65. Toland, *Nazarenu*, 135.

66. Toland, *Nazarenu*, 176.

67. Justin Champion, introduction to Toland, *Nazarenu*; Justin Champion, *Republican Learning: John Toland and the Crisis of Christian Culture, 1696–1722* (Manchester: Manchester University Press 2003); Justin Champion, *The Pillars of Priest-*

craft Shaken: The Church of England and Its Enemies, 1660–1730 (Cambridge: Cambridge University Press, 1992); Garcia, "Hungarian Revolution in Restoration England," 51–58.

68. Champion, *Pillars of Priestcraft Shaken*, 179.

69. Toland, *Nazarenu*, 182.

70. Toland, *Nazarenu*, 187.

71. Toland, *Nazarenu*, 192.

72. García-Arenal, *Orient in Spain*, 423–24.

73. Champion, *Pillars of Priestcraft Shaken*, 24.

Chapter Six. The Enlightenment Prophet

1. The first edition was published in a book titled *La vie et l'esprit de Mr. Benoit de Spinosa* (Amsterdam: Charles le Vier, 1719); it was subsequently printed under the title *Le traité des trois imposteurs* in 1721 and republished numerous times in the eighteenth century; some of the material in the treatise may have circulated in manuscript during the sixteenth century. For an English translation, based on the 1777 edition, see Abraham Anderson, *The Treatise of the Three Impostors and the Problem of Enlightenment: A New Translation of the Traité des trois imposteurs (1777 edition) with Three Essays in Commentary*, trans. Abraham Anderson (Lanham, MD: Rowman and Littlefield, 1997); the page number references are to this translation. On this text, see Ahmad Gunny, *The Prophet Muhammad in French and English Literature, 1650 to the Present* (Markfield, England: Islamic Foundation, 2010), 78–84; Mario Biagioni, "Christian Francken e le origini cinquecentesche del trattato De tribus impostoribus," *Bruniana and Campanelliana* 16, no. 1 (2010); Miguel Benitez, "La diffusion du 'Traité des trois imposteurs' au XVIIIe siècle," *Revue d'histoire moderne et contemporaine* 40 (1993): 137–51; Silvia Berti, Françoise Charles-Daubert, and Richard H. Popkin, *Heterodoxy, Spinozism, and Free Thought in Early Eighteenth-Century Europe: Studies on the Traité des trois imposteurs* (Boston: Kluwer Academic, 1996).

2. Anderson, *Treatise of the Three Impostors*, 31–33.

3. Henri de Boulainvilliers, *La vie de Mahomed* (Amsterdam: Humbert, 1730); Henri Boulainvilliers, *The Life of Mahomet Translated from the French Original, Written by the Count of Boulainvilliers* (London: Printed for T. Longman, and C. Hitch and L. Hawes, and J. and J. Rivington, 1752). The work, published posthumously, was left incomplete at the author's death; part three, by another author, is of a quite different spirit: Muhammad is described as an "impostor" and "false prophet" who "feigned a journey from Mecca to Jerusalem" (350). On this text, see *Histoire de l'Islam et des musulmans en France du Moyen Âge à nos jours* (Paris: Albin Michel, 2006), 466–68. On Boulainvilliers, see Harold A. Ellis, *Boulainvilliers and the French Monarchy: Aristocratic Politics in Early Eighteenth-Century France* (Ithaca, NY: Cornell University Press, 1988); Jonathan I. Israel, *Radical Enlightenment Philosophy and the Making of Modernity, 1650–1750* (Oxford: Oxford University Press, 2001); Israel, *Enlightenment Contested: Philosophy, Modernity, and the Emancipation of Man, 1670–1752* (Oxford: Oxford University Press, 2006).

4. Boulainvilliers, *Life of Mahomet Translated from the French*, 179.

5. Boulainvilliers, *Life of Mahomet Translated from the French*, 206–7.

6. George Sale, *The Koran, commonly called the Alcoran of Mohammed: Translated into English immediately from the original Arabic; With explanatory notes, taken from the most approved commentators; To which is prefixed a preliminary discourse* (London: J. Wilcox, 1734); Gunny, *Prophet Muhammad in French and English Literature*, 60–63; Arnoud Vrolijk, "Sale, George (b. in or after 1696?, d. 1736)," in *Oxford Dictionary of National Biography*; Ziad Elmarsafy, *The Enlightenment Qur'an: The Politics of Translation and the Construction of Islam* (Oxford: Oneworld, 2009), chaps. 1–3; Alexander Bevilacqua, "The Qur'an Translations of Marracci and Sale," *Journal of the Warburg and Courtauld Institutes* 76 (2013): 93–130.

7. John Swinton et al., *An Universal History, from the Earliest Account of Time*, 65 vols. (London: Printed for T. Osborne [etc.], 1747–66); Garth Fowden, "Gibbon on Islam," *English Historical Review* 131 (2016), 261–92.

8. *Alcorani textus universus ex correctioribus arabum exemplaribus summa side, atque pulcherrimis characteribus descriptus eademque side, ac para diligentia ex arabico idiomate in latinum translatus*, trans. Ludovico Marracci (Patavi: Ex Typographia Seminarii, 1698).

9. *Alcorani textus universus*, 37. Translation by Bevilacqua, "The Qur'an Translations of Marracci and Sale," 107.

10. Adrian Reland, *Four Treatises concerning the Doctrine, Discipline, and Worship of the Mahometans* (London: Printed by J. Darby for B. Lintott and E. Sanger, 1712); Adrian Reland, *Adriani Relandi De religione Mohammedica libri duo* (Trajecti ad Rhenum: Broedelet, 1705).

11. Antonio Possevino, *Bibliotheca selecta, qua agitur de ratione studiorvm* (Rome, 1593), 443. See Tommasino, *L'Alcorano di Macometto: Storia di un libro del Cinquecento europeo*, 241; Chicote Pompanin, "L'Alcorano of Andrea Arrivabene: An Iconographical Framework," 145.

12. Jean Gagnier, *Ismael Aboulfeda de Vita et rebus gestis Mohammedis, . . . Textum arabicum primus editit latine vertit, praefatione et notis illustravit Joannes Gagnier* (Oxford: e theatro Sheldoniano, 1723), 58–60; Gunny, *Prophet Muhammad in French and English Literature*.

13. Jean Gagnier, *La vie de Mahomet* (Amsterdam: Chez les Wetsteins and Smith, 1732).

14. Sale, *Koran, commonly called the Alcoran of Mohammed*, vii–viii.

15. Sale, *Koran, commonly called the Alcoran of Mohammed*, 37–38.

16. Sale, *Koran, commonly called the Alcoran of Mohammed*, 39.

17. Sale, *Koran, commonly called the Alcoran of Mohammed*, 37–38. Machiavelli, *The Prince*, chap. 6.

18. Qur'ān 9:31–32, translation Sale, *Koran, commonly called the Alcoran of Mohammed*, 153.

19. On Jefferson, see Denise Spellberg, *Thomas Jefferson's Qur'an: Islam and the Founders* (New York: Knopf, 2013), 81–82. On Goethe, chapter 7 herein, and Elmarsafy, *Enlightenment Qur'an*, 158.

20. Djavâd Hadidi, *Voltaire et l'Islam* (Paris: Association Langues et civilisations, 1974); Gunny, *Prophet Muhammad in French and English Literature*, 96–106; Elmarsafy, *Enlightenment Qur'an*, chap. 4.

21. Voltaire, *Le fanatisme; ou, Mahomet le prophète; De l'Alcoran et de Mahomet*, Les Œuvres complètes de Voltaire, vol. 20B (Oxford: Voltaire Foundation, 2002), 185.

22. Voltaire, *Le fanatisme*, 207–8; Voltaire, *Voltaire's Fanaticism, or Mahomet the Prophet a New Translation*, trans. Hanna Burton (Sacramento: Litwin Books, 2013), 57.

23. Voltaire, *Voltaire's Fanaticism*, 55–56.

24. Voltaire, *Voltaire's Fanaticism*, 57–58.

25. Quotations with translations from Elmarsafy, *Enlightenment Qur'an*, 84.

26. Elmarsafy, *Enlightenment Qur'an*, 84–86.

27. Voltaire, *Lettres inédites de Voltaire* (Paris: Didier, 1856), 1:453.

28. Voltaire, *Essai sur les mœurs et l'esprit des nations (II): Avant-propos; chapitres 1–37*, Les Œuvres complètes de Voltaire (Oxford: Voltaire Foundation, 2009); Voltaire, *An Essay on Universal History, the Manners, and Spirit of Nations, from the Reign of Charlemaign to the Age of Lewis XIV* (London: Printed for J. Nourse, 1759).

29. Voltaire, *Essay on Universal History*, 1:41–50.

30. Voltaire, *Essay on Universal History*, 1:43.

31. This is a loose translation of Qur'ān 7:199; Voltaire, *Essay on Universal History*, 1:44.

32. Voltaire, *Essay on Universal History*, 1:48–49.

33. Elmarsafy, *Enlightenment Qur'an*, 92–94.

34. Voltaire, *Essay on Universal History*, 1:41–50.

35. Elmarsafy, *Enlightenment Qur'an*, 106–7.

36. On Voltaire's Moses, and the implicit contrast with Mahumet, see Elmarsafy, *Enlightenment Qur'an*, 113–16.

37. Quotation and translation from Elmarsafy, *Enlightenment Qur'an*, 116–17.

38. Voltaire, *Supplément à l'essai sur les mœurs*, cited by Elmarsafy, *Enlightenment Qur'an*, 94–95.

39. Henry Laurens, *Les origines intellectuelles de l'expédition d'Egypte: L'orientalisme islamisant en France, 1698–1798* (Istanbul: Ed. I.S.I.S., 1987), 29.

40. See John Tolan, *Saint Francis and the Sultan: The Curious History of a Christian-Muslim Encounter* (Oxford: Oxford University Press, 2009), 242–45.

41. Voltaire, *Essai sur les mœurs et l'esprit des nations (II): Avant-propos; Chapitres 1–37*, 159–60. Translation from Elmarsafy, *Enlightenment Qur'an*, 112.

42. Voltaire, *Writings of 1763–1764* (2014), 83–196; Gunny, *Prophet Muhammad in French and English Literature*, 136–37.

43. The text is published as an appendix in Voltaire, *Writings of 1763–1764*, 189–96. This was added in versions published perhaps as early as 1768, see Graham Gargett's description of the editions in Voltaire, *Writings of 1763–1764*, 135–38, 189, 359–65.

44. Elmarsafy, *Enlightenment Qur'an*, 99, 120.

45. On Gibbon's views on Muhammad and Islam, see Gunny, *Prophet Muhammad*

in French and English Literature, 161–66; David Womersley, *Gibbon and the "'Watchmen of the Holy City": The Historian and His Reputation, 1776-1815* (Oxford: Oxford University Press, 2002), 147–72; Fowden, "Gibbon on Islam."

46. Edward Gibbon, *The History of the Decline and Fall of the Roman Empire,* 3 vols. (London: Penguin, 1994), 1:56.

47. Womersley, *Gibbon and the "'Watchmen of the Holy City,"* 1–9.

48. Gibbon, *History of the Decline and Fall of the Roman Empire,* 1:54n87; Womersley, 2.

49. Gibbon, *History of the Decline and Fall of the Roman Empire,* 3:252n55.

50. Gibbon, *History of the Decline and Fall of the Roman Empire,* 3:916n13. On Gibbon and Voltaire, see Pierre Force, "The 'Exasperating Predecessor': Pocock on Gibbon and Voltaire," *Journal of the History of Ideas* 77 (2016): 129–45; Arnaldo Momigliano, "Gibbon's Contribution to Historical Method," *Historia: Zeitschrift für alte Geschichte* 2 (1954): 450–63.

51. See Womersley, *Gibbon and the "'Watchmen of the Holy City,"* 100–146.

52. Gibbon, *History of the Decline and Fall of the Roman Empire,* 3:160.

53. Gibbon, *History of the Decline and Fall of the Roman Empire,* 3:174.

54. Gibbon, *History of the Decline and Fall of the Roman Empire,* 3:176.

55. Gibbon, *History of the Decline and Fall of the Roman Empire,* 3:177.

56. James Boswell, *Life of Johnson* (Oxford: Oxford University Press, 1980), 695; Garth Fowden, *Before and after Muhammad: The First Millennium Refocused* (Princeton, NJ: Princeton University Press, 2014), 22; Womersley, *Gibbon and the "'Watchmen of the Holy City,"* 148–49.

57. Gibbon, *History of the Decline and Fall of the Roman Empire,* 3:186.

58. Gibbon, *History of the Decline and Fall of the Roman Empire,* 3:210n149.

59. Gibbon, *History of the Decline and Fall of the Roman Empire,* 3:211–12n151.

60. Gibbon, *History of the Decline and Fall of the Roman Empire,* 3:190n111.

61. Gibbon, *History of the Decline and Fall of the Roman Empire,* 3:204–5n139.

62. Gibbon, *History of the Decline and Fall of the Roman Empire,* 3:212–13.

63. Gibbon, *History of the Decline and Fall of the Roman Empire,* chap. 20; Fowden, "Gibbon on Islam," 22.

64. Gibbon, *History of the Decline and Fall of the Roman Empire,* 3:177.

Chapter Seven. Lawgiver, Statesman, Hero

1. Victor Hugo, *Les orientales,* Grands écrivains ed. (Paris: Grands écrivains, 1992).

2. Gustav Seibt, Goethe und Napoleon: Eine historische Begegnung (Munich: C. H. Beck, 2008); Einboden, Islam and Romanticism, 20–21.

3. Laurens, *Les origines intellectuelles de l'expédition d'Egypte.*

4. Elie Krettly, *Souvenirs historiques du capitaine Krettly, ancien trompette major des guides d'Italie* (Paris: Biard, 1838), 72; translated by Juan Ricardo Cole, *Napoleon's Egypt: Invading the Middle East* (New York: Palgrave Macmillan, 2007), 17.

5. Quoted in Henry Laurens, *L'expédition d'Egypte: 1798–1801* (Paris: Armand Colin, 1989), 108.

6. Napoleon, *Campagnes d'Egypte et de Syrie* (Paris: Imprimerie nationale, 1998), 275.

7. Claude Savary, trans., *Le Coran, traduit de l'arabe, accompagné de notes, et précédé d'un abrégé de la vie de Mahomet, tiré des écrivains orientaux les plus estimés* (Paris: Knapen et Onfroy, 1783); Claude Savary, *Lettres sur l'Egypte* (Paris: Onfroi, 1785); Larzul, "Les premières traductions françaises du Coran (XVIIe–XIXe siècles)."

8. Savary, *Le Coran*, v.

9. Savary, *Le Coran*, 21.

10. Savary, *Le Coran*, 239. Translation from Elmarsafy, *Enlightenment Qur'an*, 147.

11. Savary, *Le Coran*, 78.

12. Savary, *Le Coran*, 101.

13. Citation and translation from Elmarsafy, *Enlightenment Qur'an*, 148.

14. Cole, *Napoleon's Egypt*, 125–26.

15. Cole, *Napoleon's Egypt*, 127–29.

16. Cole, *Napoleon's Egypt*, 159.

17. Cole, *Napoleon's Egypt*, 130.

18. Citation of French original and English translation of Arabic decree from Elmarsafy, *Enlightenment Qur'an*, 155. On this passage, see Cole, *Napoleon's Egypt*, 216–18.

19. Emmanuel Auguste Dieudonné Marius Joseph de Las Cases, *Le mémorial de Sainte-Hélène*, 2 vols. (Paris: Gallimard, 1956–57), 1:1109.

20. Cole, *Napoleon's Egypt*, 243–4.

21. Las Cases, *Mémorial de Sainte-Hélène*, 1:501.

22. Claire Elisabeth Jeanne de Rémusat, "Mémoires Inédits de Mme De Rémusat.—1802–1808.—Le voyage en Belgique, conversations du premier consul à Boulogne, arrestation du Général Moreau," 34 (1880): 304–21.

23. Las Cases, *Mémorial de Sainte-Hélènes*, 736.

24. Napoleon, *Campagnes d'Egypte et de Syrie*, 275.

25. Napoleon, *Campagnes d'Egypte et de Syrie*, 153. On the widespread condemnation of polygamy by European writers of the nineteenth century, see Philip C. Almond, *Heretic and Hero: Muhammad and the Victorians* (Wiesbaden: O. Harrassowitz, 1989), 59–63.

26. Laurens, *Les origines intellectuelles de l'expédition d'Egypte*, 122.

27. Seibt, *Goethe und Napoleon: Eine historische Begegnung* ("Mahomet der Welt," see p. 42).

28. On Herder's largely positive if ambiguous and shifting views of Islam, see Ian Almond, "Terrible Turks, Bedouin Poets, and Prussian Prophets: The Shifting Place of Islam in Herder's Thought," *PMLA* 123, no. 1 (2008): 57–75 (citation p. 74). See also Suzanne Marchand, *German Orientalism in the Age of Empire: Religion, Race, and Scholarship* (Cambridge: Cambridge University Press, 2009), 43–52; Einboden, *Islam and Romanticism*, 23–34.

29. *Der koran, oder insgemein so genannt Alcoran des Mohammeds, unmittelbahr*

aus dem arabischen Original in das englische Ubersetzt, und mit beygefügten aus den bewährtesten commentatoribus genommenen Erklärungs-Noten, wie auch einer vor-läuffigen Einleitung versehen von George Sale. Aufs treulichste wieder ins Teutsche verdollmetschet von Theodor Arnold (Lemgo, 1746); Elmarsafy, *Enlightenment Qur'an*, 158.

30. Goethe, *Goethes Briefe und Briefe an Goethe*, 6 vols. (Munich: Beck, 1988), 1:132. Translation Elmarsafy, *Enlightenment Qur'an*, 158.

31. See Katharina Mommsen, *Goethe und die arabische Welt* (Frankfurt am Main: Insel, 1988), 176–77; Jan Loop, "Divine Poetry? Early Modern European Orientalists on the Beauty of the Koran," *Church History and Religious Culture* 89 (2009): 455–88 (esp. 480); Elmarsafy, *Enlightenment Qur'an*, 159.

32. Mommsen, *Goethe und die arabische Welt*, 44–45; Einboden, *Islam and Romanticism*, 59–67.

33. Goethe, *Noten und Abhandlungen zum West-östlichen Divan*, citation Mommsen, *Goethe und die arabische Welt*, 171. Translation in Katharina Mommsen, *Goethe and the Poets of Arabia*, trans. Michael Metzger (Rochester, NY: Camden House, 2014).

34. Mommsen, *Goethe and the Poets of Arabia*, 83.

35. Mommsen, *Goethe and the Poets of Arabia*, 100–110.

36. Mommsen, *Goethe und die arabische Welt*, 233; Mommsen, *Goethe and the Poets of Arabia*, 107.

37. Stephanie M. Hilger, *Women Write Back: Strategies of Response and the Dynamics of European Literary Culture, 1790–1805* (Amsterdam: Rodopi, 2009), 91–117.

38. Einboden, *Islam and Romanticism*, 19.

39. Letter to Saint-Aignan, no. 146 (April 30, 1813), August Carl, *Politischer Briefwechsel des Herzogs und Grossherzogs Carl August von Weimar*, vol. 3 (Stuttgart: Deutsche Verlags-Anstalt, 1973), 179; Seibt, *Goethe und Napoleon*, 200.

40. Mommsen, *Goethe und die arabische Welt*, 194–203; Mommsen, *Goethe and the Poets of Arabia*, 87–93; Elmarsafy, *Enlightenment Qur'an*, 165–68.

41. Translation from Mommsen, *Goethe and the Poets of Arabia*, 91–92. As Elmarsafy notes, Goethe here is producing not Megerlin's translation, but his own poetic rendition of Marracci's Latin (Elmarsafy, *Enlightenment Qur'an*, 166.).

42. Johann Wolfgang von Goethe, *Sämtliche Werke*, vol. 2 (Stuttgart, 1909), 82.

43. Goethe is not the first European author to come across the river as a metaphor for the prophet; Henry Stubbe says, "The Arabians compare him to the purest streams of some river gently gliding along, which arrest and delight the eyes of every approaching passenger." Stubbe and Matar, *Henry Stubbe and the Beginnings of Islam*, 70.

44. Yomb May, "Goethe, Islam, and the Orient: The Impetus for and Mode of Intercultural Encounter in the West-östlicher Divan," in *Encounters with Islam in German Literature and Culture*, ed. James Hodkinson and Jeffrey Morrison (Rochester, NY: Camden House, 2009), 89–107; Massimo Leone, "The Sacred, (in)Visibility, and Communication: An Inter-religious Dialogue between Goethe and Hāfez," *Islam and Christian-Muslim Relations* 21 (2010); Leone, "The Sacred, (in)Visibility, and Communication; Walter Veit, "Goethe's Fantasies about the Orient," *Eighteenth-Century*

Life 26 (2002); Johann Wolfgang von Goethe, *West-östlicher Divan* (Munich: Carl Hanser Verlag, 1998); *Poems of the West and the east: West-Eastern Divan = West-östlicher Divan: Bi-lingual Edition of the Complete Poems*, trans. John Whaley (Bern: P. Lang, 1998); Mommsen, *Goethe und die arabische Welt; Goethe and the Poets of Arabia*; Einboden, *Islam and Romanticism*, 69–79.

45. Einboden, *Islam and Romanticism*, 76–79.

46. Johann Wolfgang von Goethe, *Poems of the West and the East: West-Eastern Divan = West-östlicher Divan: Bi-lingual Edition of the Complete Poems*, trans. John Whaley (Bern: P. Lang, 1998), 4–5.

47. Citation and translation from Walter Veit, "Goethe's Fantasies about the Orient," *Eighteenth-Century Life* 26 (2002): 164–66.

48. Goethe, *Poems of the West and the East: West-Eastern Divan = West-östlicher Divan: Bi-lingual Edition of the Complete Poems*, 6–7.

49. Goethe, *Poems of the West and the East: West-Eastern Divan = West-östlicher Divan: Bi-lingual Edition of the Complete Poems*, 254.

50. Goethe, *Sämtliche Werke nach Epochen seines Schaffens: Münchner Ausgabe 1 2 1 2* (Munich: Hanser, 1987), 147–48. Translation from Elmarsafy, *Enlightenment Qur'an*, 160–61.

51. Goethe, *Poems of the West and the East*, 52–53; Leone, "The Sacred, (in)visibility, and Communication".

52. Goethe, *Poems of the West and the East*, 352–53.

53. Goethe, *Poems of the West and the East*, 428–29.

54. Goethe, *Poems of the West and the East*, 430–35.

55. Einboden, *Islam and Romanticism*, 54, 205–14.

56. Goethe, *Poems of the West and the East*, 220–21.

57. Thomas Carlyle, *On Heroes, Hero-Worship, and the Heroic in History* (London: Chapman and Hall, 1840); Elmarsafy, *Enlightenment Qur'an*, 177–79.

58. Alphonse de Lamartine, *Les grands hommes de l'Orient: Mahomet, Tamerlan, le sultan Zizim* (Paris: A. Lacroix, Verboeckhoven, 1865); Alphonse de Lamartine, *La vie de Mahomet* (Paris: L'Harmattan, 2005); Gunny, *Prophet Muhammad in French and English Literature*, 188–93.

59. Lamartine, *La vie de Mahomet*, 44–45.

60. Victor Hugo, *La Legende des siècles* (Brussels: Hetzel, 1859), 65.

61. See Masuzawa, *Invention of World Religions*, 179–206.

62. See David Bjelajac, "Masonic Fraternalism and Muhammad among the Lawgivers in Adolph A. Weinman's Sculpture Frieze for the United States Supreme Court (1931–1935)," in *Image of the Prophet*, 360–61.

63. Bjelajac, "Masonic Fraternalism and Muhammad."

Chapter Eight. A Jewish Muhammad?

1. What follows is based in part on John Tolan, "The Prophet Muhammad: A Model of Monotheistic Reform for Nineteenth-Century Ashkenaz," *Common Knowledge* 24 (2018), 256–79.

2. John Toland, *Reasons for naturalizing the Jews in Great Britain and Ireland: On the same foot with all other nations; Containing also a defence of the Jews against all vulgar prejudices in all countries* (London: J. Roberts, 1714).

3. See Rita Hermon-Belot, *L'Emancipation des juifs en France* (Paris: Presses Universitaires de France, 1999); Pierre Birnbaum and Ira Katznelson, *Paths of Emancipation: Jews, States, and Citizenship* (Princeton, NJ: Princeton University Press, 2014).

4. Susannah Heschel, *Abraham Geiger and the Jewish Jesus* (Chicago: University of Chicago Press, 1998). Susannah Heschel, "German Jewish Scholarship on Islam as a Tool for De-Orientalizing Judaism," *New German Critique*, no. 117 (2012): 91–107; Jacob Lassner, "Abraham Geiger: A Nineteenth-Century Jewish Reformer on the Origins of Islam," in *The Jewish Discovery of Islam: Studies in Honor of Bernard Lewis*, ed. Martin Kramer (Tel Aviv: Moshe Dayan Center for Middle Eastern and African Studies, Tel Aviv University, 1999), 103–35; Dirk Hartwig, "Die 'Wissenschaft des Judentums' und die Anfänge der kritischen Koranforschung: Perspektiven einer modernen Koranhermeneutik," *Zeitschrift für Religions- und Geistesgeschichte* 61 (2009): 234–56.

5. L. I. Conrad, "Ignaz Goldziher on Ernest Renan: From Orientalist Philology to the Study of Islam," in *The Jewish Discovery of Islam: Studies in Honor of Bernard Lewis*, ed. Bernard Lewis and Martin Kramer (Tel Aviv: Moshe Dayan Center for Middle Eastern and African Studies, Tel Aviv University, 1999), 137–80 (here at 143).

6. Abraham Geiger, *Was hat Mohammed aus dem Judenthume aufgenommen?* (Bonn: Gedruckt auf Kosten des Verfassers bei F. Baaden, 1833); Abraham Geiger, *Judaism and Islam* (Edinburgh: Williams and Norgate, 1896); Susannah Heschel, "Abraham Geiger and the Emergence of Jewish Philoislamism," in *"Im vollen Licht der Geschichte": Die Wissenschaft des Judentums und die Anfänge der kritischen Koranforschung*, ed. Dirk Hartwig et al. (Würzburg: Ergon, 2008), 65–86; Heschel, *Abraham Geiger and the Jewish Jesus*, https://archive.org/details/cu31924029170236. The English translation was commissioned by the Cambridge Mission in Dehli, in the hopes of showing Muslims the Jewish roots of Islam in order to make them more favorable to Christianity: this aim (very far indeed from those of Geiger) explains the innocuous title; see Lassner, 107–8.

7. Geiger, *Judaism and Islam*, 18.

8. Geiger, *Judaism and Islam*, 21.

9. Geiger, *Judaism and Islam*, 25.

10. Heschel, *Abraham Geiger and the Jewish Jesus*, 108; Marchand, *German Orientalism*, 109–10.

11. Marchand, *German Orientalism*, 33.

12. Marchand, *German Orientalism*, 35–36.

13. Marchand, *German Orientalism*, 24.

14. Abraham Geiger, *Das Judenthum und seine Geschichte* (Breslau: Schletter, 1865), 1:142; Abraham Geiger, *Abraham Geiger's Nachgelassene schriften* (Berlin: L. Gerschel, 1875), 2:40. Citations and translations from John M. Efron, *German Jewry and the Allure of the Sephardic* (Princeton, NJ: Princeton University Press, 2016), 198–99.

15. Ruchama Johnston-Bloom, "Jews, Muslims, and *Bildung*: The German-Jewish Orientalist Gustav Weil in Egypt," *Religion Compass* 8 (2014): 49–59; Johnston-Bloom, "Oriental Studies and Jewish Questions: German-Jewish Encounters with Muhammad, the Qur'an, and Islamic Modernities" (PhD diss., University of Chicago, 2013).

16. Johnston-Bloom, "Jews, Muslims, and *Bildung*," 49–59, 54–55.

17. Cited by Johnston-Bloom, "Jews, Muslims, and *Bildung*," 55.

18. Gustav Weil, "Sur un fait relatif à Mahomet," *Journal Asiatique* 14 (1842): 108–12. Weil revisits the epilepsy question in his biography of the prophet; see Johnston-Bloom, "Oriental Studies and Jewish Questions," 106–9; Almond, *Heretic and Hero*, 24–25.

19. Gustav Weil, *Mohammed der Prophet, sein Leben und seine Lehre: Aus handschriftlichen Quellen und dem Koran geschöpft und dargestellt* (Stuttgart, 1843), xvi. Translation Johnston-Bloom, "Oriental Studies and Jewish Questions," 90.

20. Weil, *Mohammed der Prophet*, 41–42. Translation Johnston-Bloom, "Oriental Studies and Jewish Questions," 109–10.

21. Gustav Weil, *The Bible, the Koran, and the Talmud* (London, 1846), vii–ix. See Johnston-Bloom, "Oriental Studies and Jewish Questions," 115–17.

22. See, for example, Gustav Weil, *Historisch-kritische Einleitung in den Koran* (Bielefeld, 1844), 87–88. See Johnston-Bloom, "Oriental Studies and Jewish Questions," 119–20.

23. Weil, *Historisch-kritische Einleitung in den Koran*, 2nd ed. (Bielefeld: Velhagen and Klasing, 1878), 50. Citation and translation from Johnston-Bloom, "Oriental Studies and Jewish Questions," 118.

24. Weil, *Historisch-kritische Einleitung in den Koran*. Translation Johnston-Bloom, "Oriental Studies and Jewish Questions," 117.

25. Marco Schöller, "Post-Enlightenment Academic Study of the Qurʾān," in *Encyclopaedia of the Qurʾān*, ed. Jane Dammen McAuliffe (Leiden: Brill, 2004); Marchand, *German Orientalism*, 174–78.

26. Gustav Weil, *Biblische Legenden der Muselmänner: Aus arabischen Quellen zusammengetragen und mit jüdischen Sagen verglichen* (Frankfurt a. M: Literarische Anst., 1845); Weil, *The Bible, the Koran, and the Talmud*, ix; Heschel, "German Jewish Scholarship on Islam as a Tool for De-Orientalizing Judaism," 96–97.

27. Shmuel Ettinger and Marcus Pyka, "Graetz, Heinrich," in *Encyclopaedia Judaica*, ed. Michael Berenbaum and Fred Skolnik (Detroit: Macmillan Reference USA, 2007), 26–29.

28. Heschel, *Abraham Geiger and the Jewish Jesus*, 136–37.

29. Heinrich Graetz, *History of the Jews*, vol. 3 (London: Myers, 1904), 89.

30. Graetz, *History of the Jews*, 72–73. See Ned Curthoys, "Diasporic Visions, Taboo Memories: Al-Andalus in the German Jewish Imaginary," *Arena Journal* 33 (2010): 110–38.

31. Cited by Heschel, *Abraham Geiger and the Jewish Jesus*, 79, 220.

32. Graetz, *History of the Jews*, 73.

33. Graetz, *History of the Jews*.

34. Translation in Martin Kramer, introduction to *The Jewish Discovery of Islam: Studies in Honor of Bernard Lewis*, ed. Bernard Lewis and Martin Kramer (Tel Aviv: Moshe Dayan Center for Middle Eastern and African Studies, Tel Aviv University, 1999), 1–48, 5.

35. Translation in Kramer, introduction.

36. Efron, *German Jewry and the Allure of the Sephardic*; Rudolf Klein, "Ludwig Förster's Dohány Tempel in Pest: Moorish Cathedral for the 'Asiates of Europe' / Ludwig Forsterov Dohany Tempel u Pesti: Maurska katedrala za 'Azijate Europe,'" *Prostor* 17, no. 2 (2009).

37. Efron, *German Jewry and the Allure of the Sephardic*, 148.

38. On Goldziher, see Ottfried Fraisse, *Ignác Goldzihers monotheistische Wissenschaft: Zur Historisierung des Islam* (2014); Róbert Simon, *Ignác Goldziher: His Life and Scholarship as Reflected in His Works and Correspondence* (Budapest: Library of the Hungarian Academy of Sciences, 1986); *Goldziher Memorial Conference* (Budapest: Hungarian Academy of Sciences, 2005); Dietrich Jung, "Islamic Studies and Religious Reform: Ignaz Goldziher—A Crossroads of Judaism, Christianity, and Islam," *Der Islam* 90 (2013): 106–26; Ignác Goldziher, *Ignaz Goldziher and His Oriental Diary: A Translation and Psychological Portrait*, trans. Raphael Patai (Detroit: Wayne State University Press, 1987). Patai's rather prejudiced view of Goldziher's personality and some of the errors in his translation are noted by Lawrence I. Conrad, "The Dervish's Disciple: On the Personality and Intellectual Milieu of the Young Ignaz Goldziher," *Journal of the Royal Asiatic Society* 122 (1990): 225–66; Lawrence I. Conrad, "The Near East Study Tour Diary of Ignaz Goldziher," *Journal of the Royal Asiatic Society* 122 (1990): 105–26. See also Jonathan Skolnik, "Heine and Haggadah: History, Narration, and Tradition in the Age of Wissenschaft des Judentums," in *Renewing the Past, Reconfiguring Jewish Culture: From al-Andalus to the Haskalah*, ed. Ross Brann and Adam Sutcliffe (Philadelphia: University of Pennsylvania Press, 2004), 213–25; Marchand, *German Orientalism*, 323–32.

39. L. I. Conrad, "The Pilgrim from Pest: Godziher's Study Tour to the Near East (1873–1874)," in *Golden Roads: Migration, Pilgrimage, and Travel in Mediaeval and Modern Islam*, ed. Ian Richard Netton (Richmond, England: Curzon Press, 1993), 110–59 (here at 125).

40. Ignác Goldziher, *Tagebuch* (Leiden: Brill, 1978), 57; Jung, "Islamic Studies and Religious Reform," 118.

41. Conrad, "Dervish's Disciple," 240–41.

42. Goldziher, *Tagebuch*, 59. Translation Heschel, "Abraham Geiger and the Emergence of Jewish Philoislamism," 81–82.

43. Goldziher, *Tagebuch*, 71. Translation by Conrad, "Pilgrim from Pest," 117.

44. Goldziher, *Tagebuch*, 72. Translation by Conrad, "Pilgrim from Pest," 117.

45. Conrad, "Dervish's Disciple," 239–40; Goldziher, *Oriental Diary*, 98, 123.

46. Goldziher, *Oriental Diary*, 92. See Heschel, "Abraham Geiger and the Emergence of Jewish Philoislamism," 81–82; Conrad, "Dervish's Disciple," 236–37.

47. Goldziher, *Oriental Diary*, 99.

48. Goldziher, *Oriental Diary*, 148. See Heschel, "Abraham Geiger and the Emergence of Jewish Philoislamism," 81–82; Conrad, "Dervish's Disciple," 236–37.

49. Conrad, "Pilgrim from Pest," 131.

50. Bernard Heller, *Bibliographie des oeuvres de Ignace Goldziher* (Paris: Imprimerie nationale, 1927).

51. Ernest Renan, *OEuvres complètes de Ernest Renan*, vol. 8 (Paris: Calmann-Lévy, 1958). Cited in Sabine Mangold, "Ignác Goldziher et Ernest Renan," in *Ignác Goldziher: Un autre orientalisme?*, ed. Céline Trautmann-Waller (Paris: Geuthner, 2011), 73–88 (citation p. 80).

52. On Said's failure to engage with Goldziher and his overestimation of Renan's importance, see Conrad, "Pilgrim from Pest," 143–44; Conrad, "Near East Study Tour Diary of Ignaz Goldziher," 105n1. More broadly on Said's neglect of both German orientalism and the position of Jews (as potentially both "orientals" and "orientalists"), see Heschel, *Abraham Geiger and the Jewish Jesus*, 19–21.

53. Conrad, "Dervish's Disciple"; Mangold, "Ignác Goldziher et Ernest Renan."

54. Ignác Goldziher, *Muhammedanische Studien*, 2 vols. (Hildesheim: Olms, 1889–90); Ignác Goldziher, *Muslim Studies*, trans. S. M. Stern (New Brunswick, NJ: Aldine Transaction, 2006). On the differences between his Hungarian and German writings, see Conrad, "Pilgrim from Pest."

55. Ignác Goldziher, *Mohammed and Islam*, trans. Kate Seelye (New Haven, CT: Yale University Press, 1917), 6.

56. Goldziher, *Mohammed and Islam*, 2–3.

57. Cited by Marchand, *German Orientalism*, 330.

58. Goldziher, *Muslim Studies*, 2:55.

59. Goldziher, *Muslim Studies*, 2:98–104.

60. Goldziher, *Muslim Studies*, 2:255–341.

61. Goldziher, *Muslim Studies*, 2:255.

Chapter Nine. Prophet of an Abrahamic Faith

1. See Patricia Morton, *Hybrid Modernities: Architecture and Representation at the 1931 Colonial Exposition, Paris* (Cambridge, MA: MIT Press, 2000); Dominique Jarasse, "Le décor du palais des colonies: Un sommet de l'art colonial," in *Le palais des colonies: Histoire du musée des arts d'Afrique et d'Océanie*, ed. Germain Viatte (Paris: Edition des la Réunion des musées nationaux, 2002), 83–126; Robert Aldrich, *Vestiges of the Colonial Empire in France: Monuments, Museums, and Colonial Memories* (New York: Palgrave Macmillan, 2005); Catherine Bouché, "Le décor peint du musée national des Arts d'Afrique de l'Océanie," *Revue du Louvre* 35 (1985): 402–7; Patricia Morton, "National and Colonial: The Musée des Colonies at the Colonial Exposition, Paris, 1931," *Art Bulletin* 80 (1998): 357–77; Philippe Dufeux, "Louis Bouquet, 1885–1952, ou le bonheur classique: Un peintre-décorateur de l'entre-deux guerres," *Bulletin de la Société de l'histoire de l'art français* (2000): 283–304. Many thanks to Ashley Miller and Christian Gruber for bringing this fresco to my attention.

2. Quoted by Jarasse, "Le décor du palais des colonies," 88.

3. Michael Goebel, "'The Capital of the Men without a Country': Migrants and Anticolonialism in Interwar Paris," *American Historical Review* 121, no. 5 (2016): 1444–67.

4. Morton, *Hybrid Modernities*, 96–129.

5. Morton, *Hybrid Modernities*, 321.

6. Jarasse, "Le décor du palais des colonies."

7. Reginald Bosworth Smith, *Mohammed and Mohammedanism: Lectures Delivered at the Royal Institution of Great Britain in February and Mmarch 1874* (London: Smith, Elder, 1874), 291; Jabal Muhammad Buaben, *Image of the Prophet Muhammad in the West: A Study of Muir, Margoliouth, and Watt* (Leicester: Islamic Foundation, 1995), 33; Almond, *Heretic and Hero*, 87–88.

8. Edward A. Freeman, *The History and Conquests of the Saracens* (Oxford: John Henry and James Parker, 1856), 59–60; George Adam Smith, *Mohammedanism and Christianity: A Sermon* (London: Arthur H. Stockwell, 1908), 13; Almond, *Heretic and Hero*, 32.

9. David Marshall, "Muhammad in Contemporary Christian Theological Reflection," *Islam and Christian-Muslim Relations* 24, no. 2 (2013): 161–72.

10. Irwin, *Dangerous Knowledge*, 221.

11. *Louis Massignon et le dialogue des cultures* (Paris: Cerf, 1996) (see in particular the contributions of Jacques Berque and François Angelier); Massignon, "Mystique musulmane et mystique chrétienne au Moyen Âge," *Opera minora* 2 (Beirut, 1963 and 1972), 470–84.

12. Pierre Rocalve, *Louis Massignon et l'islam* (Damas: Institut français de Damas, 1993), chap. 6.

13. Massignon, "La Mubâhala de Médine et l'hyperdulie de Fatima," in *Opera minora* 1:550–72.

14. Tolan, *Saint Francis and the Sultan: The Curious History of a Christian-Muslim Encounter* (Oxford: Oxford University Press, 2009), 294–303.

15. Irwin, *Dangerous Knowledge*, 220–29.

16. Barbara Sturnega, *Padre Giulio Basetti Sani (1912–2001): Una vita per il dialogo cristiano-musulmano* (Florence: Galluzzo, 2011), 24.

17. Sturnega, *Padre Giulio Basetti Sani*, 42.

18. Sturnega, *Padre Giulio Basetti Sani*, 42–44.

19. Sturnega, *Padre Giulio Basetti Sani*, 45–49.

20. Giulio Basetti-Sani, *Mohammed et Saint François* (Ottawa: Commissariat de Terre-Sainte, 1959).

21. Basetti-Sani, *The Koran in the Light of Christ: A Christian Interpretation of the Sacred Book of Islam* (Chicago: Franciscan Herald Press, 1977), 32–34.

22. Giulio Basetti-Sani, *Louis Massignon orientalista cristiano* (Milan: Vita e pensiero, 1971); English translation, *Louis Massignon (1883–1962), Christian Ecumenist, Prophet of Inter-religious Reconciliation* (Chicago: Franciscan Herald Press, 1974).

23. Basetti-Sani, *Il Corano nella luce di Cristo: Saggio per una reinterpretazione cristiana del libro sacro dell'Islam* (Bologna: EMI, 1972); English translation *The Koran in the Light of Christ*.

24. Basetti-Sani, *Gesù Cristo nascosto nel Corano* (San Pietro in Cariano: Il segno, 1994).

25. Sturnega, *Padre Giulio Basetti Sani*, 145.

26. Sturnega, *Padre Giulio Basetti Sani*, 148–53.

27. Sturnega, *Padre Giulio Basetti Sani*, 78.

28. Tolan, *Saint Francis and the Sultan*, 314.

29. *Lumen gentium* 16, http://www.vatican.va/archive/hist_councils/ii_vatican _council/documents/vat-ii_const_19641121_lumen-gentium_en.html.

30. For the text, see http://www.vatican.va/archive/hist_councils/ii_vatican _council/documents/vat-ii_decl_19651028_nostra-aetate_en.html.

31. Hans Küng, *Mon combat pour la liberté: Mémoires I* (Ottawa: Novalis, 2006), 502–6.

32. Hans Küng, *Christentum und Weltreligionen: Hinführung zum Dialog mit Islam, Hinduismus und Buddhismus* (Munich: Piper, 1984). English translation: *Christianity and the World Religions: Paths of Dialogue with Islam, Hinduism, and Buddhism* (Garden City, NY: Doubleday, 1986).

33. Hans Küng, "Christianity and World Religions: Dialogue with Islam," in *Muslims in Dialogue: The Evolution of A Dialogue*, vol. 3, ed. Leonard Swidler (Lewiston, NY: Edwin Mellen Press, 1992), 161–75. See also Küng, *Islam: Past, Present, and Future* (Oxford: Oneworld, 2007). Christain W. Troll, "Changing Catholic Views of Islam," in *Islam and Christianity: Mutual Perceptions since the Mid-20th Century*, ed. Jacques Waardenburg (Leuven: Peeters Press, 1998), 56–61; David A. Kerr, "He Walked in the Path of the Prophets," in *Christian-Muslim Encounters*, ed. Yvonne Yazbeck Haddad and Wadi Z. Haddad (Gainesville: University Press of Florida, 1995).

34. Hans Küng, *Erklärung zum Weltethos: Die Deklaration des Parlamentes der Weltreligionen* (Munich: Piper, 1993); Hans Küng and Karl-Josef Kuschel, *A Global Ethic: The Declaration of the Parliament of the World's Religions* (New York: Continuum, 1993).

35. Hans Küng, *Der islam: Geschichte, Gegenwart, Zukunft* (Munich: Piper, 2004); English translation, *Islam: Past, Present, and Future* (Oxford: Oneworld, 2007).

36. Hans Küng, "Dialogability and Steadfastness: On Two Complementary Virtues," in *Radical Pluralism and Truth: David Tracy and the Hermeneutics of Religion*, ed. Werner G. Jeanrond and Jennifer L. Rike (New York: Crossroad, 1991), 237–49, 243. Cited in Paul F. Sands, "The Wider Ecumenism of Hans Küng," *Perspectives in Religious Studies* 33 (2006): 94.

37. Sands, "The Wider Ecumenism of Hans Küng," 103–4.

38. Jacques Dupuis, *Toward a Christian Theology of Religious Pluralism* (Maryknoll, NY: Orbis Books, 1997).

39. W. Montgomery Watt, *Muhammad at Mecca* (Oxford: Clarendon Press, 1953); W. Montgomery Watt, *Muhammad at Medina* (Oxford: Clarendon Press, 1956).

40. Watt, *Muhammad at Mecca*, x.

41. Watt, *Muhammad at Mecca*, 52.

42. Watt, *Muhammad at Mecca*, 26.

43. Watt, *Muhammad at Medina*, 324.

44. Watt, *Muhammad at Mecca*, 52.

45. Watt, *Muhammad at Medina*, 206.

46. Watt, *Muhammad at Mecca*, 320.

47. Thanks to Ann Watt for sending me the text of her father's unpublished talk.

48. Watt, *Truth in the Religions*, vii.

49. Watt, *Truth in the Religions*, vii, 1.

50. Watt, *Truth in the Religions*, 5–6, 61–62.

51. Watt, *Truth in the Religions*, 58.

52. Watt, *Truth in the Religions*, 59–64, 98–99.

53. Watt, *Truth in the Religions*, 175.

54. W. Montgomery Watt, *Islamic Revelation in the Modern World* (Edinburgh: Edinburgh University Press, 1969).

55. Watt, *Islamic Revelation*, 97–98.

56. Watt, *Islamic Revelation*, 109–10.

57. Watt, *Islamic Revelation*, 120–24. Cf. Watt, *Islamic Revelation*, 100: "The ordinary Muslim was protected by the doctrine of 'corruption' (*tahrif*) which meant in practice that, if a Christian wanted to argue with a Muslim, he had to do so on the Muslim's ground, since the doctrine asserted that the Bible was in some way corrupt, and so ruled it out of court as evidence."

58. Watt, *Islamic Revelation*, 127.

59. Watt, *Islamic Revelation*, 128.

60. Watt, *Islamic Revelation*, 128–29.

61. Watt, *Islam and Christianity Today: A Contribution to Dialogue* (London: Routledge, 1983).

62. Watt, *Islam and Christianity Today*, 6.

63. Watt, *Islam and Christianity Today*, 60–61.

64. Watt, *Islam and Christianity Today*, 144–45.

65. Watt, *A Christian Faith for Today* (London: Routledge, 2002), 1.

66. Watt, *A Christian Faith for Today*, 101–4.

67. Watt, *A Christian Faith for Today*.

Conclusion

1. Kecia Ali, *The Lives of Muhammad* (Cambridge, MA: Harvard University Press, 2014).

2. See Christiane Gruber, "Between Logos (*kalima*) and Light (*nur*): Representations of the Prophet Muhammad in Islamic Painting," *Muqarnas* 26 (2009): 1–34; Taha Jaber al-Alwani, "'Fatwa' concerning the United States Supreme Courtroom Frieze," *Journal of Law and Religion* 15 (2000): 1–28.

3. Jack Chick, *The Prophet: Alberto Part Six* (Ontario, CA: Chick Publications, 1988), 24.

4. Chick, *The Prophet*, 17.

5. There are, among many other groups, associations called "Stop Islamisation of

Europe" and "Stop Islamization of America"; see Raphaël Liogier, *Le mythe de l'islamisation: Essai sur une obsession collective* (Paris: Seuil, 2012).

6. See Jaroslav Pelikan, *Jesus through the Centuries: His Place in the History of Culture* (New Haven, CT: Yale University Press, 1985).

7. *Toledot Yeshu ("The Life Story of Jesus") Revisited: A Princeton Conference* (Tübingen: Mohr Siebeck, 2011).

INDEX

Page numbers for figures are in *italic*.

A NOTE ON THE TYPE

{⬅⬇⬆⬇➡}

THIS BOOK has been composed in Miller, a Scotch Roman typeface designed by Matthew Carter and first released by Font Bureau in 1997. It resembles Monticello, the typeface developed for The Papers of Thomas Jefferson in the 1940s by C. H. Griffith and P. J. Conkwright and reinterpreted in digital form by Carter in 2003.

Pleasant Jefferson ("P. J.") Conkwright (1905–1986) was Typographer at Princeton University Press from 1939 to 1970. He was an acclaimed book designer and AIGA Medalist.

The ornament used throughout this book was designed by Pierre Simon Fournier (1712–1768) and was a favorite of Conkwright's, used in his design of the *Princeton University Library Chronicle.*